FUGITIVE TIME

FUGITIVE TIME
GLOBAL AESTHETICS AND THE BLACK BEYOND
MATTHEW OMELSKY

DUKE UNIVERSITY PRESS   DURHAM AND LONDON   2023

© 2023 DUKE UNIVERSITY PRESS
All rights reserved
Printed in the United States of America on acid-free paper ∞
Project Editor: Michael Trudeau
Designed by Matthew Tauch
Typeset in Alegreya and Fivo Sans
by Westchester Publishing Services

Library of Congress Cataloging-in-Publication Data
Names: Omelsky, Matthew, author.
Title: Fugitive time : global aesthetics and the black beyond / Matthew Omelsky.
Description: Durham : Duke University Press, 2023. | Includes bibliographical references and index.
Identifiers: LCCN 2023008298 (print)
LCCN 2023008299 (ebook)
ISBN 9781478025382 (paperback)
ISBN 9781478020615 (hardcover)
ISBN 9781478027508 (ebook)
Subjects: LCSH: Aesthetics, Black. | Time in literature. | Time and art. | Aesthetics in literature. | Literature—Black authors. | Artists, Black. | Authors, Black. | Utopias in literature. | BISAC: SOCIAL SCIENCE / Black Studies (Global) | LITERARY CRITICISM / Semiotics & Theory
Classification: LCC BH301.B53 O445 2023 (print) | LCC BH301.B53 (ebook) | DDC 111/.85—DC23/ENG/20230720
LC record available at https://lccn.loc.gov/2023008298
LC ebook record available at https://lccn.loc.gov/2023008299

Cover art: Leasho Johnson, *Reading beyond the Tragic*, 2022. Mixed media on paper. © Leasho Johnson. Courtesy of the artist.

FOR MY FATHER,
PAUL OMELSKY

CONTENTS

ACKNOWLEDGMENTS ix

INTRODUCTION. BLACK BEYONDNESS 1

1 TONI MORRISON'S ANACHRONIC EASE 33

2 AIMÉ CÉSAIRE, WIFREDO LAM, AND THE AESTHETICS OF SURGING LIFE 62

3 BLACK AUDIO'S ARCHIVAL FLIGHT 99

4 SUN RA, ISSA SAMB, AND THE DRAPETOMANIACAL AVANT-GARDE 132

5 YVONNE VERA, NOVIOLET BULAWAYO, AND THE IMMINENCE OF DREAMING AIR 172

CODA. FUGITIVE ETHER 205

NOTES 209
BIBLIOGRAPHY 239
INDEX 259

ACKNOWL-
EDGMENTS

An amalgamation of experiences and influences have brought me to this point. First hearing the sound of Wes Montgomery's guitar in a friend's living room. Studying Ewe music with Kobla Ladzekpo. Intro to Pan-Africanism with Michael Dash. Studying photography with Lyle Ashton Harris and working in his New York studio. Teaching primary school in Guadeloupe. Studying Wolof and learning to play the *xalam* in Dakar. Almost a decade of graduate school got me to channel these disparate threads into focused work, without sacrificing my love of it all and my commitment to the fields to which I'm privileged and humbled to offer this book as a contribution.

A real debt of gratitude goes to those who helped bring together the early formations of this book during my time at Duke. My deepest thanks to Tsitsi Jaji, my adviser, whose brilliance, thoughtfulness, and care have made this book far stronger than it would've been otherwise. I'm so grateful to Ranjana Khanna, Ian Baucom, and Fredric Jameson for all the time and pressing questions they gave this project in its first life. For conversations, time spent, and mentorship, I thank Fred Moten, Achille Mbembe, V. Y. Mudimbe, Aarthi Vadde, J. Kameron Carter, Sarah Nuttall, Nathaniel Mackey, Negar Mottahedeh, Nancy Armstrong, Kathy Psomiades, Priscilla Wald, Leonard Tennenhouse, and Louise Meintjes. Much love and appreciation to my Duke friends and collaborators: Ainehi Edoro, I. Augustus Durham, Sasha Panaram, Samuel Shearer, Damien-Adia Marassa, Jonathan Howard, Jessica Stark, Nikolas Sparks, Davide Carozza, Zoe Eckman, Patrick Morgan, Phillip Stillman, Christina Chia, Marina Magloire, Christopher Ramos, Stefan Waldschmidt, Jon Stapnes, Lindsay Larre, Ellen Song, Ben Richardson, Morgan Slade, Kathleen Burns, Mary Caton Lingold, Rebecca Evans, Jack Bell, Justin Mitchell, Brian Smithson, and Jacqueline Kellish.

Without a doubt, foundations and influences for this book were laid during my two years at Cornell. I'm grateful to Grant Farred, Petrus Liu, Salah Hassan, Riché Richardson, Carole Boyce Davies, Judith Byfield, Robert Harris, the late and incredibly generous James Turner, Locksley Edmondson, Natalie Melas, Susan Buck-Morss, Eric Acree, and Elizabeth Anker. Much appreciation to Elizabeth Tshele (a.k.a. NoViolet Bulawayo) for introducing me to the work of Yvonne Vera and, it turns out, planting the seed for chapter 5 of this book. After Cornell, I turned to intensive language training and was fortunate to study at the University of Florida's Summer Cooperative African Language Institute and at the Baobab Language Center in Dakar with a series of fantastic Wolof instructors: Fabienne Ngone Diouf, Ismaila Massaly, Abdou Sarr, and Oumoul Sow. At her beautiful home in Dakar, Aby Diallo was the most gracious and generous host. *Jërëjëf samay xarit*. Thanks to the UC Berkeley Center for African Studies for awarding the Foreign Language and Area Studies Fellowship that made this training possible.

Much of the work of transforming this project into a book took place during my postdoctoral fellowship with the Mellon Sawyer Seminar on "Racial Disposability and Cultures of Resistance" based in Penn State's Department of African American Studies. It was a great privilege to have the year to focus on my research, attend fantastic talks, and work closely with Cynthia Young. I'm thankful for the friendships and intellectual community during my time in State College: Courtney Morris, Zachary Morgan, Ebony Coletu, Amira Davis, Timeka Tounsel, Abraham Khan, Maha Marouan, Sam Tenorio, J. Marlena Edwards, Dara Walker, Magalí Armillas-Tiseyra, Alexander Fyfe, Richard Mbe, Sophia Balakian, Morgan Johnson, and Darryl Thomas.

After PSU, I was very lucky to join a group of wonderful colleagues in the Department of English, the Frederick Douglass Institute, and throughout the College of Arts and Sciences at the University of Rochester. I've felt welcomed from the beginning and privileged to be able to research and teach the work that means the most to me. I'm appreciative of the two department chairs, John Michael and Katherine Mannheimer, who have served during my time at UR and been incredibly supportive. Thanks to Rosemary Kegl, who was chair when I was hired, for making me feel part of the fold well before I moved to Rochester. Upon his arrival, Jeffrey McCune transformed the Black studies landscape at UR with his presence and vision, and I'm grateful to be part of the work ahead. I've benefited so much from the friendship and intellectual companionship of many at UR: Brianna Theobald, Joel Burges, Jeffrey Tucker, Pablo Sierra Silva, Kathryn Mariner, Molly Ball, William Miller, Rachel Haidu, Steven Rozenski, Cilas Kemedjio, James

Rosenow, Jennifer Kyker, Ezra Tawil, Sharon Willis, Anna Rosensweig, Cona Marshall, Jason Middleton, Kenneth Gross, William Bridges, Bette London, Thomas Hahn, Joan Saab, Jennifer Grotz, Morris Eaves, Kristin Doughty, Cory Hunter, Joshua Dubler, Ruben Flores, Joan Rubin, Julie Papaioannou, Supritha Rajan, Joanna Scott, and the late and much-missed James Longenbach. My sincere thanks to Dean Gloria Culver for the generous subvention that helped offset the book's production costs and make color images possible. Thanks to the UR Humanities Center for the semester fellowship that helped me finish off the very final stages of the book. I've also had fantastic students in Rochester. Thanks to Catalina Segú Jensen for her deft research assistance as the book moved toward production. Thanks to Ouma Amadou and Peter Murphy for the intellectual collaborations that felt, to me, very much adjacent to this book. And special thanks to the wonderful group in my Spring 2022 Black Fugitive Aesthetics graduate seminar, who always seemed to leave me with fresh perspective on things I've been thinking about for years.

Much appreciation to the institutions that have supported and hosted me during the period of working on this project: the American Council of Learned Societies, the Andrew W. Mellon Foundation, the Johannesburg Workshop in Theory and Criticism, the Robbins Library at the National Museum of African Art in Washington, DC, the Stuart Hall Library at the Institute for International Visual Arts in London, the British Film Institute National Archive in London, the Latin American and Caribbean Collection at the University of Florida's Smathers Libraries, and the Cuban Heritage Collection at the University of Miami Libraries. I appreciate the opportunities I received to present parts of this book at Penn State University, University of Toronto, Universität Bayreuth, Yale University, Harvard University, as well as various African Literature Association, Modern Language Association, and American Comparative Literature Association annual conferences. An abbreviated version of chapter 5 was published in the February 2020 issue of the *Black Scholar*.

While I was working on this book, two dear mentors passed on: Tejumola Olaniyan and J. Michael Dash. At different stages of my career, both gave me what often feels like the most precious thing: their time. For that I'm grateful, and I can only hope the contents of this book do some justice to what they imparted over the years.

Thanks to Cynthia Young, Lindsey Green-Simms, Jeffrey Tucker, Joel Burges, and Alexander Fyfe for reading chapters and providing indispensable feedback. Thanks, too, to Laura Murphy, Ato Quayson, Jeffrey McCune,

Magalí Armillas-Tiseyra, Ebony Coletu, and Rose Casey for conversations that were instrumental at different stages of this project. Everyone at Duke University Press has been fantastic. Elizabeth Ault's keen eye saw something in this project, and I'm grateful. Thanks to Ben Kossak for his thorough guidance throughout the review and production process. And special thanks to my two anonymous readers. Not only did they read it multiple times—during a pandemic, no less—but they did so generously and meticulously. The book is much improved for it.

Many people have impacted this project, directly or indirectly. Thanks to John Nimis, Moradewun Adejunmobi, Matthew H. Brown, Esther de Bruijn, Abioseh Porter, Stéphane Robolin, MaryEllen Higgins, Carmela Garritano, Kenneth Harrow, Kirk Sides, Duncan Yoon, Stephanie Bosch Santana, Bhakti Shringarpure, James McCorkle, Anne Gulick, Erin Fehskens, Nihad Farooq, Carli Coetzee, Cajetan Iheka, Andrés Felipe Torres, Tjawangwa Dema, Sarah Stefanos, George Blake, Robert Hinton, Lyle Ashton Harris, Esi Sutherland-Addy, Manthia Diawara, Michael Gomez, Akin Adesokan, Juliana Nfah-Abbenyi, Brent Edwards, Jennifer Bajorek, Michelle Stephens, Rian Thum, Jennifer Gordon, Amiel Bize, Mark Drury, Sandra Brewster, Huey Copeland, Rio Hartwell, Madhu Krishnan, Taiwo Adetunji Osinubi, Evan Mwangi, Yogita Goyal, Anthony Reed, Krista Thompson, Nasrin Qader, Marquis Bey, Alexie Tcheuyap, Uzo Esonwanne, Kwame Otu, Neil ten Kortenaar, A. James Arnold, Clémentine Deliss, Stanka Radović, Delali Kumavie, Bernard Oniwe, Eskil Lam, Shikeith, Jean Michel Bruyère, Janet Stanley, Kerry Manzo, Ama Bemma Adwetewa-Badu, Juan Villanueva, and Caleb Del Rio.

To my parents, Connie and Paul Omelsky, and to my uncle, Bruce Ackerman, thank you for believing in me and what I do. To those who call me tio, Eve, Elijah, Ezekiel, and Esther, and to those whom I'm lucky enough to be an honorary uncle, let this book be an example of one of the many, many kinds of things you can do when you grow up. Finally, my partner in life, Amanda Richardson. The one who has lived and felt the highs and lows of this decade-long project as much as I have. The one who grounds me, sustains me. Without you this book would not be.

INTRODUCTION
BLACK BEYONDNESS

THREE SCENES AND AN OPENING

I

Against an entirely white background, holding a black balloon with his outstretched hand, a young man rises. His nude body, turned to the side, is silhouetted in black. Toes pointing, chest leaning, he's tilted in flight. He gazes down as he moves up and outward, surveying what he's leaving behind. Another young man, standing below, gazes up at the rising one, reaching out to touch the flying figure's other hand, like he's sending him off. This image from *The Moment You Doubt Whether You Can Fly, You Cease Forever to Be Able to Do It* (2014), an installation by American artist Shikeith, features, at least at first sight, two young men. The contours of the silhouetted figures, though, are unmistakably similar. Could it be a sequence, a movement, of just one? Could it be that the figure standing on the ground is the young man only a moment earlier in time, prior to his flight, in advance of the balloon's lift, imagining himself rising away to new life? He has to imagine, the title suggests. He has to believe. What if this is a visual representation of one young man's anticipatory desire, his imagined movement in time, from moment to moment? A map of the trajectory of his longing for the moment when he's at last unburdened of this world?[1]

Eight minutes and forty-six seconds. The amount of time it took for breath to vanish from George Floyd's body. The elapsed time that ignited Minneapolis, setting America on fire. But it wasn't only cities in the United States that burned in the spring and summer of 2020, while COVID-19 raged. Across the world, people protested for black lives outside US embassies, they burned American flags, they blocked traffic and lay down in the streets for those nearly nine minutes. These protests across the world were in solidarity with the Movement for Black Lives, certainly, but most were infused with the local and the immediate, with the refusal of state violence against their own black lives. Anderson Arboleda in Bogota, Collins Khosa in Johannesburg, thirteen-year-old Yassin Moyo in Nairobi: all killed by either the police or the military during pandemic lockdowns, their deaths pouring people into the streets. In Paris the death of Floyd renewed mass demonstrations against Adama Traoré's 2016 death by asphyxiation in police custody, sparking what many at the time referred to as "Ferguson in Paris." And all of this was cut across by calls to decolonize public spaces. The replacement that July of a 125-year-old statue in Bristol, England, of slave trader Edward Colston, which had been toppled and thrown into the River Avon by protesters, with *A Surge of Power*, a black resin statue of protester Jen Reid, poised with her fist raised to the sky, remains a searing symbol of the global moment.

It all called, and continues to call, for something more. As Barnor Hesse and Juliet Hooker suggest, "Globally, black protest movements originating from local concerns are responding in different ways to the inability of liberal democracy to deliver robust racial justice and inviolable equal rights, drawing attention to the unfinished project of decolonization and the unrelenting dehumanization of black lives resulting from the precarity induced by global white supremacy (however much the latter may have morphed)."[2] The resurgence of protests in recent years, at least in part, points to alternative pathways, visions not aimed at reforming institutions or correcting democratic processes but at the necessity of other worlds, of new life. In this resurgence is the suggestion that perhaps that "project" will remain unfinished for too long or will always be unfinished. That global capital may very well require the imperfections of liberal democracy that keep black lives subjected. That democracy requires the disposability of black life as "the ground we walk on."[3] What these protests signal is an alternative capacity to desire that's immanent to global black cultures. A desire to imagine "a world beyond the coercive technologies" of everyday existence.[4] One that "strives in pursuit of the sublime, struggling to repeat the unrepeatable, to present the unpresentable."[5] A desire in excess of the failed promises of justice and equality espoused by post-Enlightenment liberal societies. A black politics that searches for freedom and belonging beyond the law, beyond the state, in some cases even beyond this world.

Fugitive Time charts this utopian impulse as a theory of the experience of time: memories and anticipations, woundings and desires, culturally and historically marked. Through the lens of time as it manifests in the imagination—time as it passes from moment to moment—this study traces the embodied sensations and coursing thoughts that accompany one's anticipated passage from subjection to freedom. It's in the phenomenal outward vision and the subtle desire for transcendence animating Shikeith's *The Moment You Doubt Whether You Can Fly*. It's in the blink of an eye that separates the one figure's dream of flight and the other's seeming enactment of that dream. What I call "fugitive time" names the phenomenon in which one imagines what it might feel like to be free of the violence that has consumed blackness throughout the world for centuries. The *anticipation* of the outside of subjection is paramount, but the recurring *haunting* of violence as it bleeds into present consciousness remains fundamental, constituting the moment from which one flees. To be clear, this is not a theory of futurity or linear progress. Fugitive time's utopia lies in the anticipated moment when pain has at last vanished from the body, whenever and wherever that may come, bringing with it a new form of being and being-in-the-world. As in all utopias, however, that moment of absolute release is elusive. If one does seem to touch on it, it quickly recedes. Instead, fugitive time is about sustaining the idea of the chase as a social gathering, the shared ecstasy of perpetually imagining in advance that moment of unburdening. As in Shikeith's image, keeping an eye and a hand on the black balloon that just might lead, in that next moment, to new life.

In this book, aesthetics is how we see and witness fugitive time, as this introduction's priming "scenes"—each revealing different valences and formations—demonstrate. The book attends to descriptive anticipation and desire in aesthetic works, how fugitive time manifests at the level of deliberately articulated ideas. But I'm also fundamentally concerned with the myriad ways fugitive consciousness is registered in narrative structure, in metaphor, in cinematic editing, in sonic texture, in physical objects and materials. To use the term Caroline Levine borrows from design theory, aesthetic form takes on "affordances": "the potential uses or actions latent in materials and designs." "Glass affords transparency and brittleness," she suggests. "Enclosures afford containment and security," whereas "the sonnet, brief and condensed, best affords a single idea or experience."

Affordance broadens the idea of form so that we might ask "what potentialities lie latent—though not always obvious—in aesthetic and social arrangements" and how such arrangements "organize experience."[6] Rather than just describe time consciousness, the aesthetic works in this book *afford* time consciousness. By this I mean that their materials, designs, and structures provide additional ways of perceiving the subtle movements of memory and anticipation. Fugitive time's indexing in montage editing, in tense and mood, in one musical instrument's sound set against that of another, surrounds and complements those deliberate ideas of anticipated embodied escape expressed in a song or a film, together evincing layers of kinetic movements, sedimentations of fugitive dreaming. Cultural expression archives and maps these simultaneous temporal vectors, providing a multidimensional lens into black cultures and experiences from around the world. Through the confluence of form and description, aesthetic works make fugitive time consciousness perceivable.

These layers are in the simultaneously singular and double figure in Shikeith's image, the way—at the touching of hands—the one form rises and becomes the next, black starkly set against white, as if the young man is picturing his body lifting through an ethereal passageway toward another world. It's also in this wall stencil's placement in the larger installation—in the affordances of the soil scattered on the floor, the sculpture of a prostrate man, the sound of a female voice singing "Over the Rainbow." "I found a symbolic significance," Shikeith said in one interview, "in working with what I refer to as these mutable, underground, and fugitive substances and forms such as dirt, spills, and blue light."[7] This idea of fugitive form and substance is central to Shikeith's larger excavation of the interior lives and spaces of black queer masculinity, and central to the way I attend to fugitive time in this book.

The other fundamental feature of *Fugitive Time* is its geographic scope. This is a resoundingly global black project, not one limited to North America or even the Western Hemisphere. Perhaps the most evident connection among the circum-Atlantic geographies of this book—from Africa to the Caribbean to North America to Europe—is their common structural subjection that extends back centuries to the first Portuguese sea expeditions to the West African coast. What Frank Wilderson calls "blackened life" is a global historical structure that continues to organize the world today.[8] It's a constellation of interconnected, systemic subjections that has mutated across time and space: from seventeenth- and eighteenth-century African captivity, to the slave castles of Elmina and Gorée, to the plantations across the Americas, to the European partition and colonization of the African continent, to the restructured violence of Jim Crow, to economic structural adjustment and postcolonial autocracy, to the transcontinental migrations of West Indians and Africans to the global North, to the New Jim Crow of mass incarceration, to the ongoing quotidian antiblack and xenophobic violence on the streets of Brussels, Johannesburg, and Rochester. These subjugations are varied, to be sure. But they all extend from that "natal alienation."[9] They all pivot back, however indirectly, to that originary designation as an object in the world.

As evident as these interrelations of subjection may be, however, the principal connection among this book's geographies has more to do with the cultural responses to that violence—that which gets generated through the desire to be free. "The bridge between the people of Gwolu and me," Saidiya Hartman proposes in *Lose Your Mother* (2006), "wasn't what we had suffered or what we had endured but the aspirations that fueled flight and the yearning for freedom."[10] Likewise for Achille Mbembe, the African diaspora, inclusive of the African continent, is organized around the recognition of "a life that must at all costs be pulled out of the dungeon and . . . healed."[11] The idea of diaspora that organizes this project centers on the global circulation of cultures, languages, and discourses produced from these aspirations to be free and healed—understanding this circulation as structured by a network of "practices," as Brent Hayes Edwards puts it, which produce not only "new and unforeseen alliances on a global stage" but also "unavoidable misapprehensions and misreadings, persistent blindnesses and solipsisms . . . a failure to translate even a basic grammar of blackness."[12] The diaspora of this project, in other words, is always contingent, in search of intimacies and alliances among people of African descent, but always marked by difference.

Fugitive Time is allied with inspiring work that frames black life and diaspora as globally differentiated, where the African continent is not just a historical source but a diverse, vital, and coeval contributor to diasporic circulations and belongings. I'm thinking of Tsitsi Jaji's notion of "stereomodernism," a method of reading and listening to cultural production from across the global diaspora that accounts for difference but operates within a relational logic of pan-African solidarity.[13] I also have in mind Keguro Macharia's practice of reading "across geohistories, across difference, toward freedom." Macharia conceives of the black diaspora as constituted by a "multiplicity of sense-apprehensions" that he names "frottage," which includes notions of "recognition, disorientation, compassion, pity, disgust, condescension, lust, titillation, arousal, and exhaustion," altogether composing a desire to "create new ways to imagine and be with one another."[14]

Examining works from Martinique, Zimbabwe, Senegal, Britain, and the United States—ranging from fiction and poetry to music, film, and multimedia installation—*Fugitive Time* builds on and forges new lines of inquiry in this field, showing how this distinct experience of time remains, since the late eighteenth-century slave narrative, a dominant and recurring form of utopian time consciousness in global black cultural production.

> The novel ends in midair. With Verlia "weightless," her body having "fallen away," "just a line, an electric current." Leaping from the cliff, toward the sea, "she's in some other place already, less tortuous, less fleshy." Set between Toronto and an unnamed Caribbean island, shuttling between the mid- and late twentieth century, Dionne Brand's *In Another Place, Not Here* (1996) features a figure who's ahead of herself in her flight, occupying in advance that elsewhere in her mind. Feeling the weight fall from her body, electricity surging through her, as if she's already there and then. Taking flight from the history that haunts blackness, from the heteronormative world that demonizes queer desire, from the suffocations of capital. Most of all, from memory, from the body. She's leaping to her death, but also to her ecstasy, to her release. And this isn't just a final moment. Brand's nonlinear plotting constantly cycles around Verlia's leap and the pain she flees, like a vortex that climbs and accumulates until it bursts out over the cliff. Meditations on insomnia, on loneliness, on "lifting a load but you don't know what that load is" accrue. Persistent mentions of "riding out to sea" in her mind, dreams that she "multiplied into pieces and flew away," prefigure her leap beyond this world.[15]

The concept of fugitive time emerges from the intersection of the study of time consciousness in European continental thought and theories of fugitivity in black studies. These latter theories broadly postulate the ways people of African descent have historically responded to their subjugation by evading the very societal structures that have rendered black life unlivable. In my framing, fugitivity is a refusal to acknowledge the interpellation that negates black being. It enacts "a duty to appose the oppressor, to refrain from the performance of the labor of the negative, to avoid the economy of objectification and standing against, to run away from the snares of recognition."[16] It means, in essence, fleeing the iconic scene in Frantz Fanon's *Black Skin, White Masks* a split second before the child can utter the words "Look, a Negro!" Thinking alongside Fred Moten, it means escaping that encounter altogether, leaving the child breathless and the fugitive figure vanished, off to a world all their own. Fugitivity is a movement that runs in and out of the confines, fleeing the forces of surveillance and control as an ecstatic social gathering, collectively refusing what's been refused to it.

Importantly, in the poems, music, images, and films I've collected in this book, fugitivity's active planning and movement are not the form of agency that has become overwrought in studies in the humanities of subaltern groups countering a hegemonic force.[17] As the Senegalese multidisciplinary artist Issa Samb insists of his own politics and practice, "To contest is not to refuse, it's a form of acceptance," a way of assenting to another's terms. Samb, whose sprawling work I examine in chapter 4, instead opts to "detach," refusing "all forms of existing society."[18] In the various artworks studied in this book, however, I want to be clear that fugitivity—this refusal to engage—is not in itself freedom. It is, more precisely, *not yet* freedom. But it's an insistent imminence. Perhaps something more akin to what Rinaldo Walcott calls "proto-freedom," an almost liberation that evinces a rhythm "difficult to capture, often glimpsed," yet is too often "violently interdicted."[19] There's something in this world that blocks black freedom, that tethers it to unfreedom despite that glimpse. Fugitivity's stealth leans toward freedom, but, as Darieck Scott cautions on the question of agency, with indeterminacy and contingency, where power is always "provisional and to some degree slippery and suggestive."[20] Slipperiness and suggestiveness, we might say, facilitate the operations of eyeing for an opening.

With this contingency in mind, fugitivity names a movement of the physical body, but it also suggests a form of consciousness that corresponds to the myriad desires that signal an as yet unrealized freedom. Fugitive consciousness is integral to the way that Jared Sexton, for instance, characterizes black captivity as "open to an outside about which it will not know anything and about which it cannot stop thinking, a nervous system always in pursuit of the fugitive movement it cannot afford to lose and cannot live without."[21] Hartman likewise describes this frame of mind as a collective "dream of an elsewhere," a ceaseless set of imaginative operations.[22] Ultimately, the broad idea of fugitivity that animates this book aligns with

Neal Roberts's notion of marronage as the "liminal and transitional social space" that separates unfreedom and freedom.[23] But in this project, that transitional space is not just social. It's temporal, affective, ontological. It's saturated with desire for the outside of unfreedom. The elusive other side of fugitivity promises transcendence for black life, even if it always remains just that: a promise.

Fugitive Time builds on the work of Hartman, Moten, Roberts, and others by theorizing fugitivity not just as a structure of consciousness, but of *time* consciousness. This book proposes a way of conceiving of time within this strain of black studies thought by drawing on what's often referred to as "phenomenological time," the study of the human perception of time as a constantly ebbing and flowing system of memories and anticipations. Dating to St. Augustine's eleventh-century *Confessions*, it's an approach that attends to the ways the mind registers the passing of time from moment to moment, and how this expansive system of anticipations and memories contributes to one's sense of being and being-in-the-world. This phenomenological analytic is central to Martin Heidegger's construction of *Dasein* in *Being and Time* (1927), as well as Paul Ricoeur's influential work on narrative and fiction in the three volumes of *Time and Narrative* (1984, 1985, 1988). But it was Edmund Husserl's conception of the "ever expanding now," notably in his turn-of-the-century lectures assembled in *On the Phenomenology of the Consciousness of Internal Time* (1928), that renewed interest in this philosophical method. The example Husserl returns to again and again is the human perception of a musical melody: one's recognition not just of the moment of a tone's articulation (the now point) but also of the simultaneous perception of that tone's continual recession into the past (memory) and the coming of a new articulation (anticipation).[24] But *Fugitive Time* escapes this work, as it were, on this question of the human—what Sylvia Wynter would call Husserl and Heidegger's formulation of the colonial "ethnoclass mode of being human, Man," and its overrepresentation as that of the human species *tout court*.[25] Where these thinkers sought to uncover a universal humanness through phenomenology, *Fugitive Time* zooms in on the memories and anticipations stitched into aesthetic works to uncover a culturally and historical distinct conception of time. The project presents not a monolithic temporality, but one of multitudes, examining how disparate African diasporic cultures produce their own versions of this phenomenological fugitive time.

One of the foundational ideas to emerge from these studies in phenomenology—another, no doubt, in need of amendment—is Ernst

Bloch's notion of "anticipatory consciousness." In the first volume of *The Principle of Hope* (1954), he describes the temporal "poles" of time consciousness as the "darkness" of the lived moment and one's openness to the "outside." The immediacy of "the now," he suggests, is a moment of enclosure. The now is the point from which the human least comprehends experience: it "burrows in itself and cannot feel itself." But in the phenomenal flow of time—specifically the moments just after and just before the now moment—the prior or coming "now" becomes legible as experience: "Only what is just coming up or what has just passed has the distance which the beam of growing consciousness needs to illuminate it." Intuition nevertheless rises from the blindness of the now and the points of illumination phenomenologically surrounding it. "What is driving in the Now at the same time continually surges forward," he maintains. The surge is a kind of outward searching, an "urging, wishing, doing."[26]

For Bloch and the writers and artists studied in this book, "wishing" does critical work in the creation of utopian desire in the surge of openness: "For 'wishing' eagerly looks forward to an imagined idea in which the desire causes what is its own to be pictured." The content of this "wish image" is created in advance, extending, "in an anticipatory way, existing material into the future possibilities of being different and better." The known, or "existing material," is transformed through this act of anticipation, becoming an image of the ideal as the object of desire. Bloch goes on to suggest that the drive that pushes this hopeful work of the imagination emerges from the body: "The drive-instinct belongs to the economy of the individual body and is only employed in so far as it belongs to it, in so far as the body does its own business, fleeing from what damages it, searching for what preserves it."[27] The body, for him, is the driving source point of utopian desire.

The structures of fugitive time that I isolate in the work of Sun Ra, NoViolet Bulawayo, and others also begin with the materiality of the body. The surge toward an otherwise existence is initiated in the body's phenomenological flight from trauma, "fleeing from what damages it," as Bloch says, "searching for what preserves it." If, more pointedly, for Daphne Brooks, nineteenth-century black precarious life meant that "there was no (safe) place for black bodies in America," then the desire for some kind of freedom, utopian or not, must necessarily emerge from the materiality of the black body, in the *desire* for a "(safe) place" to care for the black body, and, along with that (safe) place, a desire for a certain *sensation* in the body.[28] And just as Brooks subtly though significantly pluralizes "black bodies," it's a feeling that must be sought in sociality, in a collective sense of belonging among kindred bodies. It's this collective desire for the sensation of release in the body—of painlessness, to be precise—that is the aim and freedom object of fugitive time, however elusive, even impossible, that this may be to achieve. Indeed, at times in the texts I examine, some of the fugitive figures appear to desire something short of absolute painlessness, indicating even a willingness to inhabit a degree of wounding if some kind of temporary relief can be felt alongside others. It's important to read these texts as they are, and I try in each case to do so. But I contend that even in these instances, absolute painlessness remains the ultimate utopian object structuring the horizon of desire. In most instances, as in Toni Morrison's early novels, such a desire for the soothing of pain appears in subtle moments surrounded by a larger and clear impulse to escape wounding altogether. I argue that these must be read alongside and through that deeper impulse. When a willingness to accommodate pain is articulated in the works I examine, perhaps in search of a degree of transient relief, it is, in other words, a signpost of an undercurrent utopian desire for absolution. Read alongside that deeper structure, they tell us that this world is not enough. That the vanishing of embodied pain has to be pursued.

Whatever the degree of desired release in question, however, we need to consider something more specific than the body that Bloch privileges. Indeed, what makes this book's aesthetic forms fugitive, and distinctly black, is the way violence has historically been registered on the flesh as an irreparable, inescapable wound. The wounded flesh, in Hortense Spillers's influential formulation, is the "zero degree of conceptualization" of black trauma, the "seared, divided, ripped-apartness, riveted to the ship's hold, fallen, or 'escaped' overboard."[29] If such "originating metaphors of captivity and mutilation continue to ground the dominant symbolic activity across the *longue durée*," then black life needs to be understood as always already marked by that mutilation insofar as that marking simultaneously *generates* its escapist energy yet *remains* constitutive of blackness.[30] It's this haunting of the wound that generates the anticipatory consciousness of fugitive time, its outward-oriented lunging toward release. From this enfleshed position, fugitive time begins its stealth in the phenomenal flow of time, in the anticipation of the immediate moment when that ultimate ease might at last wash over the flesh.[31]

This confluence structures Verlia's outward lunge in Brand's *In Another Place, Not Here*, and the thoughts, memories, and histories woven into the novel's narrative time that lead up to it. Shaping who she is and impelling her flight out to sea are the accumulations: her persistent inability to sleep, her alienation in Toronto, the heaviness of home in the West Indies: "Call it what we want—colonialism, imperialism—it's a fucking life sentence. . . . You can't catch five fucking minutes of sleep without it, you can't drink a beer, some fucking breeze passes over your lips smelling of molasses, you can't even fuck, some pain shows up and you weep like a fucking ocean."[32] For Verlia to dream of being weightless, an electric current soaring through the air, is to imagine the other side of this encompassing pain. The wish image of what it might be like to feel "less fleshy" drives her into the beyond, over that West Indian cliff, in search of escape from a wound that may never vanish. For decades, the celebrated Trinidadian Canadian writer's poetry and prose have served as a kind of black critical practice that mines these liminal spaces of diaspora, between belonging and nonbelonging, the sayable and the unsayable, history and memory, desire and interdiction. Across the range of her work, Brand gives voice to what it means to inhabit and care for black flesh.

Given the double bind of escapist desire and inescapable wounding—of imagined flight that never fully or permanently escapes the hold—that anchors this theory of time, I see it running in and through contemporary debates on black life and ontology. It speaks to the "optimism" that inflects the work of Fred Moten, Tina Campt, Jayna Brown, Ashon Crawley, and others, which emphasizes the social and visionary potentialities of blackness, even as they excavate historical constructions of nonbeing. Moten insists that "celebration is the essence of black thought, the animation of black operations, which are, in the first instance, our undercommon, underground, submarine sociality."[33] But the project also dialogues with Afropessimist strains of thought—the idea of black life as "impossibly lived death," as "lived in, as, under, and despite Black death."[34] The line separating these pessimist and optimist positions, as I see it, often blurs, and *Fugitive Time* wades in and moves through that blurriness. For example, insofar as blackness, for Frank Wilderson—Afropessimism's foremost thinker—is the product of centuries of "gratuitous violence" that will never be fully escaped, rendering black life "nonrelational" and "fungible," he acknowledges his own "fantasies of flight," and describes what he calls "gratuitous freedom" as a kind of utopian horizon. An ultimately unattainable site beyond the world of black subjection that effectively constitutes the utopian object of fugitive time: "The Slave needs freedom from the Human race, freedom from the world."[35]

However, Afropessimism does put pressure on the possibilities and limits of fugitivity. In his introduction to a special issue of *Critical Sociology*, Sexton contends that the enduring antiblackness of our world means that "there is no such thing as a *fugitive* slave," that *"there is no outside."* This is because, as he aptly frames it, fugitivity—that deferred, not-yet freedom, "spanning the split difference between grievance and grief, remedy and loss, hope and resignation"—relies on "an outside, however improbable or impossible, as the space of possibility, of movement, of life."[36] That "outside," Sexton maintains, drawing on Fanon, is bound up in the problematic of colonialism and its "imaginary topography." Any vision of that outside, in other words, is created by and inextricable from what constitutes black unfreedom. As sound as this reasoning is, the black radical imaginations presented in *Fugitive Time* believe in the possibility of the outside and the otherwise. They create images of it, aesthetic architectures to house it and tend to it. Sexton's position, in a way, intersects with Fredric Jameson's argument about utopian desire—that "all possible images of Utopia . . . will always be ideological and distorted by a point of view which cannot be corrected or even accounted for." The point of a utopian image, then, including each one studied in this book, is not in its predictive value but in its "critical negativity": "Its function lies not in itself, but in its capability radically to negate its alternative."[37] The imaginings studied in these pages do that work of negation. They don't realize that ultimate release. They don't achieve that "outside" of freedom and absolution. Instead, the wishes and longings of their images cut away, again and again, at the sedimentations of antiblackness. They unravel this world, one thread at a time, so that that outside, "however improbable or impossible," might at any moment come into view. In the end this book sits as much with pessimism as optimism. I side with Tavia Nyong'o's refusal of sides, his call for "a black studies that pulls away from the decisionism and false binarism of life *or* death, pessimism *or* optimism," seeking instead what he calls a "disjunctive synthesis."[38] This is a project that moves in, out, and to the side of this larger confluence of thought in search of new strains and vectors.

Joining these larger conversations, *Fugitive Time* presents a distinct way of thinking about time in global black studies. To date, the dominant mode of theorizing time in African and African diaspora studies has been a philosophy of history approach that emphasizes nonlinearity and nonprogressivity. Most of these critiques associate linear temporalities—which continue to structure normative, late capitalist conceptions of time—with Kant, Hegel, and other Enlightenment thinkers who conceived of history as a singular universal development, progressing toward an open future. Linearity, the widely held black studies critique maintains, presumes a hegemonically white and colonial conception of the human, positioning

Europeanness at the forefront, with all others occupying a historically lagging position. Fugitive time as a concept is allied with these frameworks and critiques, including Jayna Brown's salient claim that "the concept of the future is often fettered by notions of progress."[39] Prominent among these is Ian Baucom's framing of the history of Atlantic modernity around the 1781 massacre of 133 enslaved Africans aboard the *Zong*. In *Specters of the Atlantic* (2005), he argues that the deaths of these women and men, and the insurance claims placed on their lives, initiated a historical temporality of "nonsynchronous contemporaneity" in which the hyperspeculative financialization that marked that late eighteenth-century moment is reasserted a century later, intensifying and haunting in the late twentieth and twenty-first centuries.[40] Also influential is Achille Mbembe's nonlinear "time of entanglement" in the wake of formal colonialism, broadly addressing the African continent. "As an age," he writes in *On the Postcolony* (2001), "the postcolony encloses multiple *durées* made up of discontinuities, reversals, inertias, and swings that overlay one another, interpenetrate one another, and envelop one another: *entanglement*."[41] Instead of conceiving of time principally in increments of years, decades, and centuries like these and other studies, the phenomenological approach I undertake in *Fugitive Time* opens up a new kind of telescopic lens into the inconspicuous markings, woundings, and desires of the body, affording a magnified, microscale view into the relationship between embodied violence and desired freedom in global African diasporic cultures. In the vast majority of instances, I see fugitive time not just complementing these expansive historical theorizations but also working from within them, seeking out the minutiae of desire, memory, and sensation that lie below the surface of the encompassing arc of *longues durées*.

Some of these established black studies approaches to time, I should note, do take on phenomenological valences. Certainly there's the almost undulating confluence of *durées* implied in Mbembe's entanglement. There's also a kind of fluid movement between experiential and historical time in David Scott's examination in *Omens of Adversity* (2014), through the lens of the Grenada Revolution, of the aftermaths of postsocialist and postcolonial political catastrophe.[42] Among the more prominent of these fluid temporal frameworks, though, is Michelle Wright's concept of "epiphenomenal time." Drawing from quantum physics, Wright characterizes this temporality as a processual now: "The present and future are not discrete moments but rather are conflated into the one moment that is the now." Rather than the "middle passage epistemology" that's based on a linear progress narrative, she contends, blackness in her view is best apprehended through the idea that "no moment one experiences depends directly on a previous moment in order to come into being." *Fugitive Time*'s divergence from Wright's *Physics of Blackness* (2015) centers on this primary claim that the encompassing temporality emerging from the historical experience of the transatlantic slave trade is necessarily linear and progressive, and that it largely excludes certain black experiences and identities (namely children, women, as well as LGBTQ and non-US black experience). Habiba Ibrahim's *Black Age* (2021) and Kara Keeling's *Queer Times, Black Futures* (2019) are just two of the recent and fresh perspectives on a nonlinear, ruptural philosophy of history fundamentally structured by the violence of the transatlantic trade. Moreover, the phenomenological approach in *Fugitive Time* is oriented around the ebb and flow of time consciousness as it manifests in the human imagination, in contrast to Wright's epiphenomenal now, which she associates with the physics concept of entropy, "the movement of molecules from 'low' entropy (order) to 'high' entropy (disorder)."[43] By focusing on how memory and anticipation unevenly punctuate one's perception of their embodiedness in the world, this book reveals an unpredictable, nonlinear, and indeed inclusive structure of time that was inaugurated not just by the middle passage but by colonial modernity more broadly.

My conception of fugitive time also bears the marks of recent influential black studies investigations into otherwise dreams and worlds. There's a kinship, for instance, between this study and Brown's *Black Utopias*, where she examines practices of "black alter-world-making" and "radical longing" for unknowable worlds in the thought and experience of nineteenth-century black women mystics, in the music of Alice Coltrane and Sun Ra, and in the speculative worlds of Octavia Butler.[44] Just as resonant is Anthony Reed's study of "new thought and new imaginings" of a liberated future in black experimental writing in *Freedom Time* (2016), including what he identifies as Nathaniel Mackey's "utopian musicality," the "insistent 'ecstatic elsewhere'" in the poet's prose and verse.[45] And certainly the influence of Hartman's *Wayward Lives, Beautiful Experiments* (2019) resounds throughout these pages, a text in which she creatively speculates upon the images and stories of black women in early twentieth-century America and their "experiments in living otherwise," in "creating possibility in the space of enclosure."[46] *Fugitive Time* likewise unravels otherwise dreams and otherwise worlds, but in a global black frame, not exclusively in the US context like these remarkable studies. This project also carves out new lines of inquiry in black utopian thought and experience in its focus on that microscale of otherwise desire.[47]

As in many of these studies on time and the otherwise, the question of space in this book's larger conceptualization of time needs to be addressed. As much as possible, I try to draw out the shape of time consciousness distinct to each artwork. In some cases, such as in my final chapter, where I consider Darling's desire to migrate to the United States in NoViolet Bulawayo's *We Need New Names*, we find something akin to Bakhtin's "chronotope," where, in literary-aesthetic works, "spatial and temporal indicators are fused into one carefully thought-out, concrete whole."[48] In Bulawayo's novel, the Black Audio Film Collective's essay films, and other works studied here, we even find allusions to and representations of ships—the chronotopic "cultural and political units" through which Paul Gilroy influentially reframes modernity by way of the history of the black Atlantic.[49] Especially in the works in the coming chapters that foreground migratory movement, fugitive time signals a desire for a kind of space-time—a time and space of release, where that space is to some degree legible and discernible. For most of the works I examine, though, that anticipated object of escape is unmappable: the darkly lit, nondiegetic queer scenes in Reece Auguiste and Black Audio's *Twilight City*; the seemingly directionless, soaring flight of the dove that closes Aimé Césaire's *Notebook of a Return to the Native Land*; the sounds of the mbira that swirl through and around Mazvita in Yvonne Vera's *Without a Name*, bringing her to the threshold of transcendence. Indeed, the desired utopian object toward which the fugitive figure flees in Shikeith's *The Moment You Doubt Whether You Can Fly* seems more ethereal than a concrete space. In these many instances, the freedom object of fugitive time may not be identifiably spatialized, but it's always material insofar as the body, and the coursing of sensation, are material. As Bakhtin suggests, "Time thickens, takes on flesh."[50] This book is grounded in the matter of the flesh, and indeed in the space that the flesh occupies, however placeless that embodied presence may be imagined to be. Regardless of whether the object of utopian desire is mappable, it's my contention that a phenomenological structure of time—some configuration of that ever-fluctuating relation between memory and anticipation—is the primary valence of utopian yearning in the disparate texts assembled in this book. And of these two temporal orientations, anticipation is the single most distinguishing feature of fugitive time: the imagined idea of living in advance of the devastating present, driven by a desire for release that might, at any moment, transform the body, inaugurating some kind of previously unknowable life. After all, fugitive time is a "desire called utopia": before it's a mapping, it's a feeling, a wish, a set of outward imaginative operations.[51]

Ultimately, fugitive time is many things at once. It's an *experience of time* insofar as it attends to that phenomenal coursing from moment to moment. It's a *theory of black embodied experience* to the extent that this micro-lens of time is indexed in and on the body—or, more precisely, that Spillersian valence of the flesh. It's a *theory of anticipation* in that this experience of time is registered in the mind as both a recognition of embodied violation, but also as a proleptic inhabitation of the seemingly imminent moment in time when pain will be lifted from the flesh. Other than in chapter 1, where I detail the operations of prolepsis in narrative fiction, I use the term much as Michelle Stephens and Sandra Stephens conceptually frame the video installation *People Revisited* (2013) by Sandra Stephens: "It's as if this male figure . . . knows where he is going before he gets there, has already moved himself there mentally before his body actually arrives to join him."[52] Prolepsis in this book refers to the sense of imaginatively and affectively leaping out toward another time and another mode of being-in-the-world *before* that moment, that outside, has been properly lived. Proleptic thought is inherently excessive, it's exorbitant. Finally, fugitive time is a *theory of utopia* because the desire for that feeling of release in the body, that freedom object, never altogether arrives. And when it seems to, it quickly vanishes like a mirage. I call fugitive time a "desire" because of its persistent not-yet-ness, because of the way the term captures the sense of longing for a kind of impossible freedom. Ultimately, the function of fugitive time, played out in myriad ways in this study's aesthetic archive, is both to cut away continually at the ideologies of an antiblack world and to sustain that excessive collective dream, to live in advance of this world, to inhabit that anticipatory desire for release as a life force in itself.

Dream Science, we're told, "obliterates distance as well as time." The thought of a single word delivers the mind, and perhaps the body, away to some untraceable beyond. This is how Arta—purchased "for no small sum in the country of the blacks"—reduces "the time beneath [her] master to almost nothing," and how she escapes bondage. Vanishing, apparently, into thin air. Sofia Samatar's speculative story "An Account of the Land of Witches" is written in a kind of opaque, fugitive code, its meticulous language somehow evading the grasp of rational thought at every turn. In the story, Sagal Said, a twenty-first-century scholar, has set out to decipher the baffling, unverifiable account and its accompanying "lexicon," both of which were written on papyrus and found in a ninth-century BCE grave in Sudan. She pores over the lexicon, the key to the map, "each word translatable" into a cryptic dream of otherwise possibility: "Pomegranate: Dusk. The rattling of dry leaves. Winter, black bile, a cloister, a tooth"; "Fog: A walled city. The cry of a miracle vendor. Home." In search of the mythical Land of Witches, Sagal is somewhere in East Africa, and a state of emergency has just been announced: "Nobody gets out now. The borders are closed." Fearing for her life, she dreams of pomegranates: "'Dusk,' I screamed. 'The rattling of dry leaves.... I tasted blood. Lightning. The door opened." She vanishes.[53]

I imagine the three "scenes" in this introduction as something like contrapuntal animations, interstitial reverberations, showing, before stepping into the fullness of the coming chapters, how this idea of fugitive time emerges from aesthetic form. From the texts themselves. I've also meant for them to gesture to the geographies of fugitive time. Moving from North America to the Caribbean to Northeast Africa, these vignettes signal the sprawl of this book, the multitude of life encompassed by this experience of time. Samatar's "Land of Witches" is distinct among the three in its speculative mode, in its account of a racialized slavery that may or may not have a historical analogue, in its rather indeterminate setting across Somalia, Sudan, and ancient Nubia. That it may not have a historical grounding makes it no less illustrative of fugitive time—indeed, the story, it could be argued, perhaps speaks more to its twenty-first-century moment of production than its fictionalized ancient past, conversing more with the (re)imaginative potentialities of speculative history, of conjuring new ways of escaping subjection that might give a moment of pause, or breath, in our own moment when black death has become all too spectacular, all too viral, all too repeatable. All the texts examined in *Fugitive Time* express some desire to vanish like Arta and Sagal do: a wish to will oneself away to some (un)mappable place and time. The Somali American writer simply literalizes this will to create escapist pathways, to disappear magically from the scene of violence, using the opacity of Dream Science to achieve, it seems, what most of the writers and artists in this book can only point to and long for.

BLACK BEYONDNESS 17

But we don't actually know where Arta has vanished. She might, like the other fugitive figures in this study, still be searching for the outside, wandering through the Horn of Africa, along the Nile, and beyond, in search of that true beyond. From her World Fantasy Award–winning novel *A Stranger in Olondria* (2013) to other stories like "Cities of Emerald, Deserts of Gold" (2017), some form of flight, of dreaming, of stealing away to other worlds, pervades Samatar's radically imaginative speculative fictions.[54]

Part of my intention in assembling this introduction's three vignettes is also to signal the way this study cuts across many of the constructions, whether implicit or explicit, that often sever the continent historically and culturally from the diaspora in Europe and the Americas. Built into the book's organizing logic, in other words, are undercurrent historical and political threads that hold together Africa and the broader diaspora in sustained relation, however muted or underacknowledged those threads may be. For instance, while the "New World" plantation might be considered the paradigmatic historical ground from which the analytic of fugitivity emerged, there were plantations across colonial Africa where the line between slave labor and forced labor was at best ambiguous well into the twentieth century, from Portuguese-held São Tomé and Príncipe to British Kenya to French Congo-Brazzaville.[55] And across the continent, colonial ideologies produced their own structures of racialization—notions of white supremacy set against a kind of colonial "blackening" of indigenous peoples—that were very much conversant with (though certainly not equivalent to) many of the racialized schemas in the Americas imposed by those very same European colonial powers. Such colonial formations of racialized subjection on the continent undoubtedly have their vestiges in our own day, as the fourth chapter of this book signals with Issa Samb's response to Nicolas Sarkozy's 2007 speech in Dakar, where the then president of France insisted that "Africa's challenge is to enter to a greater extent into History . . . to realize that the golden age that Africa is always recalling will not return because it never existed."[56] Yet another grounding current in this book is that such common markings in the eyes of the world have produced kindred population movements across the global diaspora: African-descended peoples searching for better lives, fleeing violence and socioeconomic devastation. I take up these latter intersections most notably in migrations from the West Indies to England in the mid-twentieth century, and from Zimbabwe to the United States in the early 2000s. *Fugitive Time*, in short, is built on a constellation of connective nodes—cultural, geographic, historical—some of which rise to the surface of this text, whereas others lie just below. To use the term *connective* is not to suggest sameness or symmetry, but relation, proximity, intersecting flows, and (under)currents. In the aggregate of the book's chapters, these nodes reveal a constant relational dynamic between the continent and the reaches of diaspora, an insistent tending to consonance and dissonance on multiple sides of the Atlantic.

Put another way, as I've suggested, *Fugitive Time* is a structure without a center. Africa is neither the periphery nor solely a historical source point, but a critical node of global circulation and relation, "part of the syncretic, modern diaspora world."[57] And neither is this exclusively an Americanist project. *Fugitive Time* frames fugitivity as a transnational form of black thought and experience, as the desire to flee the confines not just of the nineteenth-century southern plantation or the contemporary American carceral state, but also of colonial and postcolonial regimes that have suppressed black life globally. To think fugitivity in Zimbabwe and Martinique, for instance, beyond the site of fugitivity's theoretical invention in American black studies, reveals diverse vernacularizations of fugitive thought shaped by southern African practices of prophecy and divination, and Caribbean historical practices of marronage. Fugitivity and its attendant time consciousness, I contend, cannot be fully grasped outside this global frame. The questions of autochthony, land, and ancestral belonging found in southern African iterations of fugitive thought need to be read alongside the errantry and rootlessness of North American and West Indian formations. We need to see the queerness in black British fugitivity to gain a sense of queer fugitivity more broadly, including, perhaps unexpectedly, in the work of Aimé Césaire. Only by seeing the varied ways that sexual violence shapes fugitive consciousness across diasporic geographies in the work of Yvonne Vera and Toni Morrison can we fully comprehend fugitivity as a global formation.

GENEALOGIES

This book's framing and construction also raise the question of antecedents—the representations and modes of thought that precede this study's focus. For the former, we could point back to a number of locations, such as the fugitive sensibilities in early African American fiction, be it Pauline Hopkins's *Of One Blood* (1902–1903) or Martin Delany's *Blake* (1859–1862). But fugitive time's earliest recorded representations are in antebellum cultural production, notably slave narratives by Olaudah Equiano,

Harriet Jacobs, Frederick Douglass, and others. In particular, Equiano's 1789 *The Interesting Narrative of the Life of Olaudah Equiano* holds a foundational place among the aesthetic works studied in this book. As a sailor who traveled throughout the eighteenth-century world, Equiano traces several of the principal geographies that ground *Fugitive Time*'s framing of global black life: he was born and captured in West Africa, and he lived and sailed throughout the West Indies, the United States, and Britain, eventually settling in Britain following his manumission. Regardless of whether the initial section of his narrative is fact or fiction, Equiano's first-person account of the middle passage remains a stunning product of the eighteenth-century black imagination.[58] It's one that is filled, however veiled, with a fugitive consciousness that continues to resonate in global black cultural production.

The ship, Equiano evocatively shows, is where his subjection, his nonbeing, is instantiated. Brought down to the hold, he encounters "the galling of the chains," "pestilential conditions," "air unfit for respiration," nearly suffocating. Although on a number of occasions he recalls "wishing" for the "relief" of death, there's a fleeting and arresting moment when he speaks of something more than simply a death wish: permitted above deck because of his poor physical condition, he remembers, "often did I think of the inhabitants of the deep much more happy than myself. I envied them the freedom they enjoyed, and as often wished I could change my condition for theirs."[59] Certainly, there's a literalist reading of this statement, in which the author longs for the closure of death. But beneath this veil is a suggestion of an alternative capacity to desire. A desire for an opening to an unimaginable, impossible afterlife. Equiano's "mind and imagination [are] given to water," Jonathan Howard suggests of this remarkable passage, to "freedom on a blue planet."[60] We might think of it as a utopian social gathering of the "inhabitants of the deep," less of an afterlife than an *alter*life. Although his object of desire is spatialized in the sea, Equiano uses that Blochian "wish" to express a temporal structure of anticipation, an imaginative lunging in excess of the now so that he might experience, in advance, even if momentarily, that feeling of bodily release among those in the water. At the level of form, this anticipation is notably presented in the past tense (he "wished," he "envied")—the retrospective narrative perspective creating a kind of temporal switchback that gains momentum as it cuts into memory's past and turns around to drive that phenomenal pathway toward anticipated release. If, for Spillers, the middle passage represents a kind of "thrown[ness] into the midst of a figurative darkness," a darkness that renders the captive "culturally unmade" as an object of exchange, then we might think of Equiano's desire for the deep as a longing to escape into that nothingness, into that cultural unmaking, a desire to search for what might lie in that uncharted darkness. And just as Spillers identifies the captive's oceanic nothingness and nowhereness as "a wild and unclaimed richness of possibility," so perhaps did Equiano see some kind of potentiality in those waters, in their sociality, in their refuge from a devastating world.[61]

Significantly, Equiano doesn't just proleptically lunge toward an alternative site of freedom but toward another "condition," as he puts it, another order of (aquatic) being. In his desire for another ontological inhabitation we find Equiano inaugurating a kind of *longue durée* of envisaging release and reimagined black life in the sea. Indeed, his "wish" is perhaps not far removed from the speculative theory that accompanies the liner notes of a techno album called *The Quest* released some two centuries later by James Stinson and Gerald Donald of the iconic Detroit-based duo Drexciya:

> During the greatest holocaust the world has ever known, pregnant America-bound African slaves were thrown overboard by the thousands during labor for being sick and disruptive cargo. Is it possible that they could have given birth at sea to babies that never needed air? Recent experiments have shown mice able to breathe liquid oxygen. Even more shocking and conclusive was a recent instance of a premature infant saved from certain death by breathing liquid oxygen through its undeveloped lungs. These facts combined with reported sightings of Gillmen and swamp monsters in the coastal swamps of the South-Eastern United States make the slave trade theory startlingly feasible. Are Drexciyans water breathing, aquatically mutated descendants of those unfortunate victims of human greed?[62]

Perhaps Equiano desired to be a "gillman" *avant la lettre*, an "aquatically mutated" being of a new world, populated by those who had refused, or had been expelled, from this one. Drexciya's myth brings a science fiction conceit to Equiano's fleeting middle passage wish, his desire to adapt and live otherwise.[63] But in a way his desire for the deep isn't that far from science fact, given that "the atoms of those people who were thrown overboard are out there in the ocean even today." As Christina Sharpe puts it, in the sea the "residence time" of sodium, and therefore human blood, is 260 million years: "We, Black people, exist in the residence time of the wake, a time in which 'everything is now.'"[64] There is indeed an enduring black inhabitation of those waters, black life changed, restructured, perpetually becoming something else. Perhaps Equiano saw sociality and endless possibilities in the deep time of those millions of years. Perhaps he saw black life shaping a new world one breath of liquid oxygen at a time.

The other type of antecedent I want to address is the discursive: not just descriptive accounts of historical fugitive escape, but the deliberate work to engender fugitivity as a body of thought, even in cases where it's not named as such. Fred Moten, La Marr Jurelle Bruce, Lindsey Green-Simms, Keguro Macharia, Saidiya Hartman, and others may be at the vanguard of a renewal in global black theory, but important preceding work by theorists such as Sylvia Wynter, Cedric Robinson, and Nathaniel Mackey opened up fugitivity as a discourse, and one with the potential to be deepened and repositioned, shaped and reshaped.[65] In lieu of an archaeology of fugitive thought, which could fill a book in itself, I want to sit with the antecedent text that has had perhaps the most influence on my conception of fugitive time and its component parts. Frantz Fanon's *Black Skin, White Masks* (1952) has been instrumental to my framing of black ontology, nonlinear time, and the desire for a certain kind of excessive freedom. Most fundamental is his conceptualization of alienation and nonbeing. These categories, he suggests, are wrought through an oppositional structure, through the European construction of black abjection and inferiority. This is enacted in the speech act referenced earlier—"Look, a Negro!"—that transforms black life into a thing, a "nonexistence."[66] "I took myself far off from my own presence, very far, constituting myself an object," Fanon explains. "What else could it be for me but a dismemberment, a wrenching, a hemorrhage that spattered my whole body with black blood?"[67] This imposition of "nonbeing" becomes internalized, sutured into the psyche, but it also engenders a kind of physiological change in the body, as if parts have been excised, leaving phantom limbs of a former wholeness. This objecthood is what Equiano is transformed into when he encounters the "pestilential conditions" of the ship's hold. Fanon's nonbeing names that inaugural condition that has echoed and reverberated across geographies and centuries, seeping into the different aesthetic works studied in this book as the ontological position from which to escape. Like Darling in *We Need New Names*, a novel set between Zimbabwe and the United States in the 2000s, some of the fugitive figures in these chapters are indeed quite historically and experientially removed from Fanon's theoretical framing. But I contend that a certain degree of physical and psychic nonbeing is experienced by these figures, even if residually. They live in the wake of slavery and colonialism, the twin centuries-long operations of white supremacy that continue to bleed into everyday life, both spectacularly and insidiously. However nonbeing's guise may appear to have changed, their black lives are haunted by an inheritance of being transformed into objects.

In *Fugitive Time*'s framing, this is just one half of the dialectic of captivity and prolepsis that constitutes Fanon's well-known "zone of nonbeing": that "extraordinarily sterile and arid region," that "essentially bare rail [*rampe*] where an authentic emergence [*surgissement*] can be born." If *Black Skin* is a treatise on alienation, it's just as much one on *disalienation*: the process of moving toward the point at which the "black man can free himself of the arsenal of complexes that has been developed by the colonial situation," "expelling that feeling of inferiority."[68] This expulsion, Fanon insists, emerges from this zone of pathologized blackness, a paradoxical, volatile (non)ontological site within which Roberts aptly identifies an incipient "hope" and potential "flight."[69] I would add, too, a certain capacity to think, feel, and *desire*. Indeed for a *surgissement*—a surging, an emergence—to come into being, there must be outward vision.

Stepping back to a wider scope, the anticolonial philosopher grounds *Black Skin* in both a sense of ontological transformation but also a particular temporality. The two, indeed, are inextricable. Fugitive time, transposed into his terms, corresponds to the temporal and affective movement from alienation to disalienation, from nonbeing to being. More precisely, it's the *anticipation* of disalienation: for Fanon, any movement toward disalienation requires a shift in consciousness, an *idea* of the site toward which one moves. That "bare rail" of "emergence" in the zone of nonbeing is where this thinking-in-advance takes place. But the desired disalienated ontology, as Sylvia Wynter, Zakiyyah Jackson, and others remind us, is decidedly not that of the (European) liberal subject. Fanon's reconceptualization of the category of the human—and indeed one of his most important contributions to the larger idea of fugitive time—lies in his use of a distinct verb: *dépasser* ("to exceed," "to go beyond"): "I am a part of Being, insofar as I go beyond [*dépasse*] it."[70] There's a fugitive excess to this *dépasser*, as I read it, a lunging toward contingency and a new form of ontology, signaling that Fanon's human is not the human of liberal humanism. As in Equiano's narrative, anything short of this beyond point, for Fanon, would remain within the ontology of colonial alienation. I want to suggest that the (im/possible) parahuman ontology of Equiano's oceanic beings, like the utopian visions of the artists studied in this book, lies in this beyond space.

Just as salient is Fanon's use of *dépasser* to signal a departure from linear, historicist conceptions of time. Historicism is that progressivist European framework for understanding the passage of time as a single world-historical development. Nineteenth-century Europe, V. Y. Mudimbe explains, conceived of Africans as frozen in evolutionary time: "They were defined as 'archaic' or 'primitive' human beings, insofar as they were supposed to represent very ancient social and cultural organizations which had been present in Europe thousands of years earlier." And so, too, we find the concomitant developmentalist binary logics imposed by colonialism, like traditional and modern, primitive and civilized.[71] However, Fanon's text works to extricate black life from these subjecting logics: "It is by going beyond [*en dépassant*] the historical and instrumental given that I initiate the cycle of my freedom" ["*que j'introduis le cycle de ma liberté*"].[72] In refusing the past's determination of the present, he pushes against that colonial, progressive conception of time—one that's critical to my framing of fugitive time not as futural but open, multi-vectored, leaning toward the (ever-deferred) moment, wherever and whenever it may be, when (historical and experienced) pain vanishes from the body. Nonlinearity is built into Fanon's use of the noun *cycle*, which *Le Robert* defines not as a unidirectional movement or return but "a sequence of constantly renewing phenomena." What's more, when Fanon argues that "the past can in no way guide me in the present," and when he questions "Am I going to ask the contemporary white man to take responsibility for the slave ships of the 17th century?" he enacts a break in the progressive movement of historicist time, an "escape [from] the normal teleological form of [history's] writing," as David Marriott puts it, from "everything that imprisons the capacity for infinite realization . . . [and] the ceaseless work of invention."[73] Fanon's break, in other words, pushes against the linear, imperialist understanding of time that instantiates and reinforces the nonbeing of blackness, that encloses black life in a determinate future of continued subjection. His break instead signals an escape route from the reactionary feedback loops of centuries of violence. He cuts into that predetermined teleology, searching for an opening to the outside.[74] Fanon's cut in the fabric of historicist time, I contend, is much like Equiano's cut when he longs to join the inhabitants of the deep: to live outside history, to find his own experience of time, his own being and becoming.

The final piece of Fanon's text that resonates throughout this book centers on his conception of liberation. When Fanon claims that this *dépasser* "initiates the cycle of my freedom," it seems clear that this *liberté* is fundamentally different from the normative conception of liberation that, in the wake of legal emancipation and decolonization across the world, has only served to reinforce and redistribute black violation. Hartman and

Sharpe have shown that "slavery was transformed rather than annulled" in the postbellum American South and that in twenty-first-century America, "the means and modes of Black subjection may have changed, but the fact and structure of that subjection remain."[75] Natasha Lightfoot's work similarly lays bare the nonevent of emancipation in Antigua and across the nineteenth-century British Empire, how legal "freedom" for the formerly enslaved was constituted by racialized distrust, exclusion, coercion, poverty—an ongoing "state of siege"—despite individuals' constant maneuverings to eke out the possibilities of self-determination.[76] And from the perspective of the continent, searching for the "quantitative and qualitative difference" between colonialism and independence, Mbembe incisively asks: "Have we really entered another period, or do we find the same theater, the same mimetic acting, with different actors and spectators, but with the same convulsions and the same insult?"[77] These accounts only reinforce the reading of Fanon's *liberté* as a kind of *beyond-freedom*, a structure of release that's lived, or perhaps only dreamed of, outside the "protracted subjection" of nominal freedom and independence.[78]

The temporal movement of Fanon's *dépasser*, that cycle of constantly renewing vectors, as I read it, is fueled by a desire for an elusive, uncharted freedom: a seemingly unattainable object that nonetheless remains vitally necessary to imagine as the moment, felt in the body, toward which one steals away. This is the unreachable, unimaginable, but necessary freedom that distinguishes utopian thought, including the version I call fugitive time. Brown reminds us that "utopia remains always unfinished," "just beyond the horizon," operating as a "continual reaching forward."[79] Fugitive time is a phenomenal anticipation of the unknown, a paradoxical lunging toward decolonization "as the impossible and unanticipatable content that will shatter its expression, rendering that expression suddenly unrecognizable and incomprehensible."[80] I read the implied threshold that opens, or cuts, out toward Fanon's beyond-freedom as a kind of utopian reconfiguration of "the tear in the world" that Brand attributes to the slave's passage through the Door of No Return: "that place where our ancestors departed one world for another." Like that first step into nonbeing, for Fanon the cut into the beyond is "a rupture in history, a rupture in the quality of being . . . , also a physical rupture, a rupture of geography."[81] But for him, and for Equiano and the artists featured in this book, it's a rupture that gives way to a third world—not the originary ancestral world, not the world of black disposability, but the world of black beyondness. The unanticipatable world of relief that, impossibly, must be dreamed in advance.

This genealogy of the black beyond only scratches the surface, of course. It's meant to give some substance to a body of thought that often feels confined to American studies and to recent black studies thought. Implicitly and explicitly, Fanon and Equiano are threaded throughout this project, as are myriad other forerunning thinkers and practitioners of black fugitivity, such as Nehanda, the nineteenth-century Zimbabwean anticolonial prophet and spirit medium with whom I begin the final chapter. Together they assemble a kind of critical ancestral chorus, a collective conjuring that has made the ideas in this book possible. As Macharia reminds us, "To think about the politics of desire beyond the white supremacist order requires the Fanonian leap of invention, a speculative leap that imagines different configurations of desire and pleasure and livability."[82] This study carries forward and extends the beyond-desire articulated by those who came before and those creating new pathways for fugitive thought today. It seeks out that leap of invention in black art forms from across the world, in the subtler, phenomenal currents of time and desire.

CHAPTERS AND ARCHIVES

Fugitive Time, in a way, is an exercise in curation, a practice of assembling and presenting a series of objects and archives so that we might bear witness to something that we perhaps would not see in the absence of that assemblage. It's about seeing "what happens in the space of understanding work together," as Thelma Golden describes her curatorial practice.[83] It's about selecting aesthetic objects that are somehow representative of a larger pulse, each object shedding light on the others, revealing different creases of this dominant and recurring imaginative mode in global black cultural expression. What should also be clear is that the objects in this book are not the only representations of fugitive time. They merely gesture to a constellation that no single study could possibly address comprehensively. And that gesture in this book requires a certain capaciousness, a sprawling gathering of cultural geographies, historical moments, intellectual disciplines, aesthetic forms, languages, and politics. Each of these chapters has its own archive, its own curated collection not just of writing and artwork but of disciplinary material—literary studies, political economy, black feminist theory, history, ethnomusicology, and beyond—that grounds those creative expressions in the cultures, historical moments, and aesthetic genealogies from which they emerged. I see in my method something like what Susan Buck-Morss undertakes in *Dreamworld and Catastrophe* (2000), where she presents "a series of constellations constructed out of historical facts, theoretical speculations, and visual images," "crossing boundaries between discursive terrains usually kept apart" to reveal "new lines of sight" and speak to a larger global construction.[84] *Fugitive Time* likewise presents a set of constellations and meticulous speculations built to expose new ways of seeing and thinking time, aesthetics, and thought in African diasporic cultures from across the world. These are not insular constellations but ones that constantly signal fugitive time's infinite archive, its infinite vernacularizations. This is indeed how I would frame this book's primary field, global black cultural studies. As I assemble it here, it's an open set: a field of traversal, intersectionality, and boundlessness, a field that follows black life to the farthest reaches of the world and beyond.

A number of considerations have gone into the construction of this capaciousness—the selection of artists and objects, but also the arrangement of this book as a whole. In part, my aim has been to put fresh readings of canonical writers such as Toni Morrison and Aimé Césaire in conversation with lesser-known artists, such as Issa Samb, Wifredo Lam, and NoViolet Bulawayo, who, in my view, demand more critical space and attention in black studies. Each chapter also offers a distinct configuration of media and genres. Chapters 2 and 4 put two artists working in different media in direct conversation, allowing for a distinct iteration of fugitive time to emerge from their confluence. By contrast, chapters 1 and 3 dive into two works by a single novelist (Morrison) and film collective (Black Audio) to trace the through-lines of fugitive time across a body of work. The final chapter remixes the curatorial strategy to show how a feminist formation of fugitive time evolves over time, across writers and texts, and ultimately beyond the boundaries of the nation-state. The inclusion of different media and genres, as I've said, is designed to show not just how fugitive time manifests descriptively in aesthetic works but also how this experience of time is sutured into their layered formal architectures, providing an expansive, multidimensional optic. Finally, there are, of course, the geographic considerations. Moving across the Caribbean, North America, Africa, and Europe, most chapters in fact toggle between multiple diasporic sites in these regions—for instance, France, Cuba, Haiti, but primarily Martinique in chapter 2; Senegal and the United States in the fourth chapter; Dominica but mostly Britain in the third chapter. The different cultural geographies of this project serve as signposts, signaling not comprehensiveness but that infinite sprawl, gesturing to where else we might find this dominant and recurring form of time consciousness in global African diasporic cultural production.

In the opening chapter, "Toni Morrison's Anachronic Ease," I begin not with the earliest produced work in this study but with the work that speaks to the earliest historical moment. Starting with Morrison's *Beloved* (1987) and *Sula* (1973), *Fugitive Time* opens during the period of chattel slavery and its aftermath, grounding this book from the start in America's nonevent of emancipation and how that putative threshold shaped the Nobel laureate's distinct vision of desired embodied release. In this chapter I lay out a set of key concepts that inform the rest of the book, focusing on narrative form and how a desire for bodily release subtly moves throughout a system of narrative flashbacks and anticipations. The dozen times Toni Morrison uses the word *easefulness* in her early works, I contend, provides a key to the utopian map of *Sula* and *Beloved*, a set of guidelines for finding the myriad *intimations* of desired (rel)ease in these iconic works. The ecstatic version of this desire in Morrison's fiction, what I call "otherwise ease," corresponds to an ultimate assurance of release, safety, and peace in one's body and being-in-the-world: a state that always lies in that anticipated moment just prior to the now, such as Sethe's desire in *Beloved* to escape with her children "through the veil," "outside this place, where they would be safe." I show how Morrison disperses this desired state throughout a layered network of narrative prolepses and analepses, putting "ease" constantly on the run, revealing itself in the most unexpected corners of memory and anticipation only to move back below the text's surface and reemerge soon after. Stitched into the author's switchbacks of narrative anachronism is a constant pursuance of an easeful, transcendent body that's unable to extricate itself unequivocally from violence. Together, both novels span just over a century of the black American experience, from *Beloved*'s account of plantation life in 1850s Kentucky to the final chapter of *Sula*, set in 1960s Ohio, revealing a historical arc of this Morrisonian search for release.

In chapter 2, "Aimé Césaire, Wifredo Lam, and the Aesthetics of Surging Life," three sketches drawn by the Cuban painter Wifredo Lam usher us into the shape of fugitive time in Aimé Césaire's négritude epic *Notebook of a Return to the Native Land*. Produced for the 1943 Cuban translation of Césaire's original 1939 *Notebook*, these drawings—which to date have only been cursorily examined in relation to the poem—allow us to appraise anew a canonical text written amid the incipient rise of fascism in Europe and increasing anticolonial demonstrations throughout the colonized world. I contend that Lam's surrealist, multispecies figurations, rather than being mere illustrations, expand and deepen the images and drama of the poem while bringing to the fore its inconspicuous temporalities of wounding and desire. In particular, the sketches bring to life the poem's sprawling phenomenological image of the wounded black body: the way this body registers, on the one hand, deepening layers of historical violence through a pervasive discourse of "scarring" and "blistering," and on the other, a fugitive anticipation of a new form of being through ubiquitous language of growth, hunger, and outward movement. Through the interplay of the visual and the poetic, of surrealist image and surrealist metaphor, we gain a visceral sense of how utopian desire emerges from the body in the *Notebook* and how the poem's sense of becoming surges toward a kind of ontological transcendence. I argue that the structure of utopia found through this inter-animation is less about the desire to be entirely rid of wounding than the desire to reimagine the wound, to allow trauma to become generative in the poem's ecstatic projection toward disalienation.

Turning to fugitive time's appearance in cinema, chapter 3, "Black Audio's Archival Flight," examines the experimental essay films of Britain's celebrated Black Audio Film Collective, established in London in 1982 by a group of university students of West African and West Indian descent. Black Audio's early films sought to chronicle how memory, place, and identity marked the fault lines of what it meant to be black in the age of Thatcherism. At first glance, *Handsworth Songs* (1986) and *Twilight City* (1989) present two adjacent moments in the history of black British subjection: the former centering on the 1985 black uprisings in the Handsworth neighborhood of Birmingham and the latter providing an exposition of black precarious life in the "New London" of late-1980s financialization and development. However, both use archival footage from throughout the twentieth century to capture a historical sense of the coalitional blackness that encompassed people of African, Caribbean, and South Asian descent in 1980s Britain. And both capture the insurgent fugitive sensibility and time consciousness of this blackness. This chapter examines the myriad bodies that seek escape from the sprawling history of black subjugation in these two films—including *Handsworth's* repeated footage of a black youth evading riot police—as well as the ways this desire for escape is sutured into their filmic architectures. Using archival newsreel footage, ambient electronic music, voice-over narration, and other features, Black Audio cinematically locates an ephemeral beyond-world of release in *Handsworth*'s dialectical "third space" of montage and in *Twilight*'s nondiegetic reenactments of queer photographs by the Nigerian British photographer Rotimi Fani-Kayode.

Chapter 4, "Sun Ra, Issa Samb, and the Drapetomaniacal Avant-Garde," shifts our attention to the work of two interdisciplinary artists: the American poet and free jazz musician Sun Ra and the Senegalese sculptor, poet, and performance artist Issa Samb. I begin with the speculative mental illness "drapetomania," first proposed in 1851 by the physician Samuel Cartwright as a pseudoscientific explanation for the propensity of enslaved Africans to escape captivity. Samb and Ra, I argue, transformed this cornerstone of nineteenth-century scientific racism into an insurgent fugitive aesthetics: their avant-garde practices served as escape routes from a world in crisis, yet their practices were widely deemed incoherent madness in their time. The chapter studies how their work envisaged an otherworldly embodied refuge in aesthetic and political opacity. For them, seeming indecipherability aided their trenchant critiques of the world around them and their refusal of the mid-twentieth-century forces subjecting people of African descent across the world. Ra's intergalactic verse, sound, and visual aesthetics represented a flight from the turmoil of racism and violence in 1960s and 1970s America, whereas Samb's ephemeral sculptures and anticapitalist poetics marked a flight from the devastating effects of structural adjustment in 1970s and 1980s Senegal as well as Léopold Senghor's politicization of négritude. Assembling an archive that spans poems, sound recordings, cell phone videos, liner notes, films, multimedia installations, and polemic essays, I take up a kind of kaleidoscopic study of these two influential artists, investigating how from disparate locations of the global diaspora they used opacity to imagine in advance new worlds and new forms of being in times of crisis. This chapter, notably, is methodologically distinct from the others. Whereas the book's other chapters are largely concerned with a single cultural geography, contributing to an aggregate sense of global diasporic temporality built across the project as a whole, chapter 4 asks how a more direct and immediate juxtaposition of disparate African diasporic spaces might deepen our understanding of fugitive time. Such a method demands explicit and sustained attention to diasporic relationality: a sense of the convergent and divergent histories, politics, and aesthetic forms that allow for such a global conversation to be generative of something greater than its component parts. The chapter asks what an imagined back-and-forth between Ra and Samb allows us to see that we might not otherwise.

"Yvonne Vera, NoViolet Bulawayo, and the Imminence of Dreaming Air," the book's final chapter, returns to the novel to trace a history of Zimbabwean women conjuring flight. My starting point is the 1898 execution of the prophet and spirit medium Nehanda, who is said to have departed from her body before the British could place the noose around her neck, which in turn galvanized the nation's First Chimurenga against settler colonial rule. The chapter considers the literary and historical afterlives of Nehanda's fugitive time consciousness in Yvonne Vera's *Without a Name* (1994) and NoViolet Bulawayo's *We Need New Names* (2013), novels that feature women longing to shed their bodies and minds of alienation. Vera places her novel in the late 1970s during Zimbabwe's Second Chimurenga, at the precipice of national independence, while Bulawayo sets this desire for transformation in the 2000s, charting a young woman's flight from her collapsing country to the United States. Like the legend of Nehanda, these works establish a national allegorical desire for release from violence and precariousness. In doing so they reimagine a historically prescribed nationalism, showing how women can have a constitutive voice, how nation can be forged in diaspora, how one's sense of ancestral belonging can evolve. Indeed, ancestrality is central to Vera and Bulawayo's articulations of fugitive time: divination, fetish objects, ancestral land, and the transcendent sounds of the mbira propel their protagonists' minds toward release. Like the different formations of fugitive time in this book, what we find in these works is not a sustained utopian release but an inhabitation of the anticipatory consciousness of escape as a vital life force.

In its broadest considerations, *Fugitive Time* shows how film, literature, music, and other art forms archive the ways that time has been imagined and embodied by the colonized, the enslaved, and their descendants. What the archive assembled here tells us is that this desire is sprawlingly global, enduring, and ceaseless. It collectively registers the "anticipatory illumination," as Bloch calls it, characteristic of utopian aesthetics, "standing on the horizon of the real," evading the snares of capture, laying the groundwork for otherwise worlds.[85] In these works we find that anticipatory illumination in the lower frequencies, in the subtler currents of time, in the inconspicuous ways that art forms register the flow from moment to moment in and on the body, turning the body into a coded map of phenomenal surges, breathless threads of possibility. The set of conceptual tools that I call fugitive time is what this book offers the field of global black studies, providing a way of understanding time beyond—or indeed, *inside of*—the history of philosophy approach predominant in black critical thought today. My hope is also that the varied archive I've assembled signals the seemingly endless archive of black aesthetics in which these conceptual tools are similarly legible—in works by Hannah Crafts, Phaswane Mpe, Nalo Hopkinson, Sandra Brewster, the Otolith Group, Abderrahmane Sissako, Mark Bradford,

Fatou Diome, and on: in any work that somehow illuminates the anticipatory machinations of escape, the way such schemings of the mind race toward an impossible release in the body. Also pivotal is the way that this book's archive and conceptual apparatus aims to extend our understanding of how Africa and the reaches of diaspora are not at all separate cultural and historical spheres, but a singular, heavingly heterogeneous relational entanglement comprising infinite coeval nodes since at least the fifteenth century. Across the global sprawl of this project, fugitivity is decidedly not yet freedom. But the sounds, sculptures, and poetics that anchor these pages bespeak an incessant not-yet-ness, a constant search for an undevastated world. Fugitive time names this social life in prolepsis, this ecstasy of the wretched of the Earth dreaming of an imminently afungible world.

1 TONI MORRISON'S ANACHRONIC EASE

You got to love it. This flesh I'm talking about here. Flesh that needs to be loved. Feet that need to rest and to dance; backs that need support; shoulders that need arms, strong arms I'm telling you. And O my people, out yonder, hear me, they do not love your neck unnoosed and straight. So love your neck; put a hand on it, grace it, stroke it and hold it up.

Toni Morrison, *Beloved*

For Baby Suggs, the Clearing is a threshold to another world, beyond the world that for centuries has used, excluded, and discarded the flesh of black life at whim. In this iconic scene in Toni Morrison's *Beloved*, set in that "wide-open place cut deep in the woods," Suggs pleads with her fellow formerly enslaved men and women to taste the outside of subjection: "She told them that the only grace that they could have was the grace they could imagine."[1] From the neck to the eyes to the face to the skin, Suggs implores her intimate group to *imagine* how it might feel to inhabit a renewed body and being-in-the-world, escaping those ever-searing, ever-deepening wounds. Certainly there's a register of the worldly here, a sense that Suggs is enjoining them to "love it" in the immediacy of the here and now. But as I read it, there's also an undercurrent desire in her words. A pleading, for them, as they attend to each part of the body, to search for a lasting release, an enduring grace. This imaginative lunging out toward that moment when peace at last saturates mind and body is not at all uncommon in Morrison's work, particularly in her early novels. The author's intimations of this imagined grace signal her singular iteration of fugitive time—the Morrisonian mode of that phenomenological desire, from moment to moment, breath to breath, to escape the interpellation that imposes nonbeing on blackness.

In *The Bluest Eye* (1970), *Sula* (1973), and *Beloved* (1987), Morrison gives a distinct name to the desired state of being for which so many of her characters yearn: *easefulness*. In the dozen or so times she uses it—mostly as verb or adjective—there's a sense of bodily relief and comfort that corresponds to a similarly relieving and comforting affective state. Take this early use in *The Bluest Eye*, when Pauline recalls the circumstances of Pecola's birth: "I went to the hospital when my time come. So I could be easeful. I didn't want to have it at home like I done with the boy." Given the context of labor, the first-person singular is very much a bodily "I" that seeks ease, although an attendant affective register is evident. Indeed, this passage tells us just as much about the comfort that Pauline had hoped to find in the clinical hospital setting as it does about the apparent dis-ease she experiences at home. Another clarifying use of the term comes just a few pages later in the chapter that details Cholly's backstory, when the narrator describes the arduous lives lived by a group of elderly women: "Squatting in a cane field, stopping in a cotton field, kneeling by a river bank, they had carried the world on their heads. . . . With relief they wrapped their heads in rags, and their breasts in flannel; eased their feet into felt."[2] At last granted release in old age, these women calmly, soothingly, "eased" their feet into soft fabric. The verb implies a slow, purposeful motion and anticipation. "With relief" modifies both the "wrapping" and "easing," making it clear that it's the body that finds relief but that there's an accompanying affective lightness and comfort.

Importantly, without much change in meaning, the term appears fleetingly in the first section of *Beloved*, after the titular character has walked out of the river and into 124 Bluestone Road: "Beloved looked at the sweet bread in Denver's hands and Denver held it out to her. She smiled then and Denver's heart stopped bouncing and sat down—relieved and easeful like a traveler who had made it home."[3] In this case the sweet bread is the object that creates a smile in one person, which in turn establishes ease in another. "Relief" and "ease"—paired again as in the previous *Bluest* example—are associated with the "heart," which carries both bodily and affective connotations. The simile likening "ease" with "home" expands the term to include presumed notions of familiarity, assurance, and safety.

I begin with these readings to demonstrate just how critical, and subtle, this term is in Morrison's early novels, and all the more so because she uses it so sparingly. When "ease" does manifest, there's an immediate calming effect in the narrative tone as each signals the idea of, and often the desire for, some hard-earned, peaceful state of being, however (im)permanent. Depending on the context, the term can connote a range of meanings, including safety, love, relief, and peace, but also personal autonomy and self-knowledge. For male and female characters alike, it can signify a physical sense of release, but it can also approximate the affective force that Audre Lorde attributes to the erotic: "the assertion of the lifeforce of women," the refusal to be "satisfied with suffering and self-negation," "the nurturer of all our deepest knowledge" that "flows through and colors my life with a kind of energy that heightens and sensitizes and strengthens all my experience."[4] To be clear here at the outset, the explicit mention of ease in Morrison's novels typically signifies a temporary relief, not a sustained painlessness. For her characters to achieve some degree of ease is not to achieve the absolution that is the elusive freedom object of fugitive time. What I contend, though, is that the appearance of ease gestures to a deeper utopian current in these works. These flashes of transient relief serve as a kind of promise, an insistence that some kind of otherworldly painlessness might be possible and that it could arrive at any moment, saturating the body in transcendent release.

There are two kinds of desired ease in Morrison's novels, both intimately related and, in a way, inextricable. In the two cases, rather than the few times the author explicitly uses the term, my interest lies primarily in her frequent *allusions* to their corporeal and affective registers. The first is the more common, temporary genre of ease in Morrison's work, which for clarity I'll call *transient ease*. This category, shown in the short passages from *Bluest* and *Beloved* above, connotes a kind of fleeting relief. This type often appears in the text briefly, sometimes imperceptibly, like at the start of *Beloved* when Baby Suggs longs to escape the "intolerable present" by surrounding herself with lavender and other colors. But each instance in which a character desires this temporary ease, I argue, evinces an undercurrent longing for a more permanent release from pain. This is how I read, for example, the scene when Sethe recalls how Suggs implored her to "Lay em down, sword and shield": "Under the pressing fingers and the quiet instructive voice, [Sethe] would. Her heavy knives of defense against misery, regret, gall and hurt, she placed one by one on a bank where clear water rushed on below."[5] Baby Suggs, with her fingers and voice, brings momentary relief to Sethe, but she also draws out the desire for it all to wash away in that water, releasing all the anxiety and hurt she carries in her body and mind. The undercurrent resonance of this momentary respite from pain is connected to the second type of ease in Morrison's novels, what I'll call, alternatively, *utopian ease* or *otherwise ease*. Each case of desired ease in Morrison's early novels implies a deeper longing for the (im)possible permanence of this utopian ease, but this latter genre also very much exists in these works on its own. Transient ease may be more prevalent across these works, but the desire for otherwise ease is far more ecstatic and exhilarating when it unfolds in the imagination of a character, whether it's Plum in *Sula*, Sethe in *Beloved*, or another.

This utopian ease, like Saidiya Hartman's framing of the desires of the black radical women she gives voice to in *Wayward Lives*, is exorbitant, conjuring a notion of freedom that exceeds the given, however impossible it may be to achieve.[6] It also resonates with Fanon's *dépassé* ("to exceed," "to go beyond") that I detail in the introduction: the fugitive excess that the anticolonial thinker attributes to his own desire to lunge out toward a new world and a new form of being. If Morrison herself describes her novels as "chart[ing] a course that suggests where the dangers are and where the safety might be," then *transient ease* corresponds to a kind of short-lived, embodied safety, and *utopian ease* corresponds to a deeper, utopian permanence of safety.[7] I use "otherwise ease" interchangeably with "utopian ease" because this desired state seems as if it's of another dimension, beyond the reaches of what's attainable, even knowable, in this world. Of course, the permanence, let alone realization, of otherwise ease is never achieved in these works, just as utopia, by definition, is never fully and permanently realized. But as I'll show, this seeming impossibility of absolute painlessness in Morrison's fiction does not foreclose the uncontainable desire for and anticipation of it. Otherwise ease, I want to suggest, is the driving utopian force in Morrison's early novels.

In a way, this utopian ease intersects with Hartman's notion of black embodied redress, which she locates, in *Scenes of Subjection*, in quotidian practices of the enslaved, such as work slowdowns and illicit travel, which in turn produce the work songs and the prayer meetings where that desire for release is articulated. Redress comprises the captive's everyday "utopian and transformative impulses," those desires that remain undetectable in, *in excess of*, the ostensible freedoms attained through emancipation and civil rights. It's about "re-membering" the body that for so long has been "dis-membered," reconceiving of it as a site of desire and sociality, a site of familial and cultural history, a site of intimacy between the living and those who came before. Redress aims at "relieving the pained body through alternative configurations of the self and the redemption of the body as human flesh, not beast of burden." For Hartman, as for Morrison, relief is always incomplete. Hartman suggests that "the event of captivity and enslavement engenders the necessity of redress, the inevitability of its failure, and the constancy of repetition yielded by this failure."[8] Redress may not be fully achievable in this world, but, like utopian ease, the idea of it demands steadfast pursuance. The promise of it is too enticing, too transformative to abandon. Similarly, in Morrison's novels, otherwise ease—as well as transient ease—never permanently arrives, although it persistently reappears, fugitively surfacing in pockets, ebbing and flowing, always fading away only to resurface soon after in another guise. And, importantly, both redress and utopian ease are anticipated states of being, lived in advance, states that, as Hartman maintains, are "aimed at" and "directed toward." Both inhabit, in short, the phenomenological projection of fugitive time, that lunging out toward the moment of the body's absolute unburdening. In decisive, resounding moments, particularly in *Sula* and *Beloved*, utopian easefulness, this redressing of the pained body, appears as the promise of transcendence and the erasure of nonbeing.

Central to deciphering desired ease in Morrison's novels, whether transient or utopian, is its shifting narrative placement. If each of the artists featured in this book somehow accounts for fugitive time's animating dialectic of trauma and desire not just descriptively but also formally—that is, uniquely stitching that dialectic into the aesthetic architecture—what distinguishes Morrison's iteration of fugitive time is the way that she threads both genres of ease into what narratologist Gérard Genette calls "narrative anachronism." She sutures ease throughout a layered network of narrative analepses (flashbacks) and prolepses (flash-forwards) that build from, leap off, and blur into one another.[9] So when Sethe "*wished* for Baby Suggs' fingers molding her nape," we are simultaneously reading Sethe's desire for ease in the narrative present *and* her memory of her prior anticipation of ease.[10] Furthermore, Morrison's anachronic ease is always entangled with memories and anticipations of traumatic violence, often rendering ease and trauma indistinguishable. Wherever we find it in her tortuous narratives, however, the Morrisonian notion of embodied ease remains consistent: it's that release, safety, and peace in one's body and being-in-the-world, a state that always lies in that anticipated moment just beyond the now.

The way that Morrison entangles trauma and utopian desire within this anachronic structure, the way she foregrounds the black body in that entanglement, creates a distinctly black formation of narrative time. It's as if the experiences of those "Sixty Million and more" to whom she dedicates *Beloved*—their terrors and desires, woundings and disorientations—have reverberated across the generations and centuries, with the perpetually mutating afterlives of those experiences bubbling to the surface in the author's switchbacks of narrative time. The desire for a sustained easefulness in the body is the driving force of Morrison's narrative time, appearing at times conspicuously and at others inconspicuously, at times embedded in an analeptic memory and at others stitched in the narrative present. The temporal trajectory of ease in these novels is one that winds and contorts, defying progression and linearity. This is Morrison's formation of fugitive time—this surreptitious, stealthy phenomenological movement of corporeal desire, unpredictably shooting back and forth in narrative anachrony, never settling into itself but never ceasing to move toward that ultimate utopian release.

My discussions in these pages focus primarily on the shape of desired ease in *Sula* and *Beloved*. Whereas *The Bluest Eye* is crucial for determining the author's conception of the term itself, in the process providing the key to the utopian map of these novels, these other two works are far more saturated with insinuations of the transient and utopian iterations of this desired state. They reveal it in an array of generations and characters, male and female, in quietly discrete moments as well as loud, defining ones. *Sula* and *Beloved* also exhibit more complex structures of anachrony, winding narrative landscapes of forward and backward leaps within which desired ease repeatedly rises to the surface.[11] And they stand out in the way they bring us into the interior. By this I mean in particular what Elizabeth Alexander refers to as the "black interior," the "inner space in which black artists have found selves that go far, far beyond the limited expectations and definitions of what black is, isn't, and should be."[12] Compared to many of Morrison's later novels, in *Sula* and *Beloved* we find a heightened sense of these inner selves, an intimate optic into the consciousness of particular characters. It's the omniscient and first-person interior voice that enables the body to be phenomenalized in these works, for us as readers to witness how Morrison's characters experience the passing of time, how they feel pain and pleasure in their bodies, how they register the desires, soothings, markings, and woundings engendered by everyday life.[13]

In what follows I show how the body, utopian desire, and anachronic narrative time intersect in these novels to shape Morrison's formation of fugitive time. But first I want to show how these works are circumscribed by a hegemonic temporality akin to what Paul Ricoeur calls "monumental time," marked by the monotony of chronological dates and times and the figures of authority that enforce that monumentality. Underneath this outer layer of hegemonic time is Morrison's utopian temporal labyrinth, a sprawling underground network of narrative prolepses and analepses through which utopian desire reveals itself in the most unexpected corners of memory and anticipation, only to move back into the shadows and reemerge soon after. The desire for ease in *Sula* and *Beloved* runs its own fugitive course in and out of the world as it repeatedly surfaces and disappears into the body of the text. In this nonlinear structure, Sethe, Sula, and other figures seek an otherworldly ease in the body wherever and whenever they find it, in an effort to escape that subjecting monumental time and seize their own experience of time. Their search is marked by the ever-deferred arrival characteristic of fugitive time, that dwelling in pursuit of absolute release.

SUBJECTION TIME

In the second volume of Paul Ricoeur's influential *Time and Narrative*, the philosopher suggests a two-part temporal structure to Virginia Woolf's novel *Mrs. Dalloway*—a structure, it turns out, that *Sula* and *Beloved* broadly share. On the one hand, there's an "official," or "monumental" time, comprising chronological sequences (centuries, years, hours, minutes) and "all that is in complicity with it," meaning those authorities and institutions of power that maintain the dominance of that progression. In *Mrs. Dalloway*, chronological time is principally measured hourly by the ringing of London's Big Ben, signifying the regulatory capacity of British law and imperial power. On the other hand, there is each character's internal consciousness of time, with each living and experiencing that monumental time in distinct ways. For Septimus, the novel's World War I veteran, monumental time—governed by his diagnosing psychiatrist who deems him psychologically "out of proportion"—is a "radical threat" that ultimately leads to his suicide; for Elizabeth, monumental time, epitomized by her religious tutor, must be "escaped" in order to "acquire a time of her own."[14] Only narrative fiction, Ricoeur says, can reveal the immensity of this juxtaposition between internal and external time.

Toni Morrison's novels, I want to suggest, are structured by a related formation of external and internal time. Like Ricoeur's marking of monumental time in *Mrs. Dalloway* through dates, clocks, and wars, Morrison presents a form of monumental time that might be called the *time of black subjection*, with each novel situating itself within a different historical moment in the evolution of that temporality. Together, *Sula* and *Beloved* span just more than a century of the black American historical experience, from *Beloved*'s account of plantation life in 1850s Kentucky to the final chapter of *Sula*, set in 1960s Ohio. At their most visible level, each novel's temporality of subjection is marked by a surface of chronological accountings: dates of historical and personal significance, events separated by a specific number of intervening years, wars that place the story in US and world history. But there is also a lower frequency to this subjection time, what Hartman would call the "quotidian routine of violence," characterized by the monotonous, repeating acts of violation that frame one's day-to-day experience.[15] Add to this the signature Morrisonian element of seasonal temporalities that reinforce and exacerbate the time of black subjection through devastating cold, failed crops, and sweltering heat.

Throughout both novels, black subjection time has its figures of authority that maintain its hegemony, much like the enforcing role of Septimus's psychiatrist. These are the same figures that Hortense Spillers designates as the enforcers of dominant culture, "whose state apparatus, including judges, attorneys, 'owners,' 'souldrivers,' 'overseers,' and 'men of God,' apparently colludes with a protocol of 'search and destroy.'"[16] The monumental time of Morrison's fiction is a kind of "search and destroy time" regulated and abetted by those figures of power with a vested interest in keeping black life captive and conditioned by dates, times, and intervals: the duration of time a slave is forced to work in the fields, the memory of the year of a war that forever changed the conditions of one's life, the amount of time elapsed since a traumatic event. In short, subjection time is the violation of blackness made possible by a certain monotonous, chronological accounting of time, the structure of which is not self-disciplinary but is deliberately maintained by those representatives of the state and white capital who directly benefit from the subjection of black life. To gain a fuller sense of what motivates and propels the desire for easefulness in these novels, I want to unravel the contours of this larger temporal structure of violence.

At the foundation of subjection time is the black body, specifically what Hartman refers to as the "pained body": "Pain is a normative condition that encompasses the legal subjectivity of the enslaved . . . constructed along the lines of injury and punishment." It corresponds to the exercise of power on black bodies, the enforcement of constraint, need, and violence. It can be understood in temporal terms as the "history that hurts—the still-unfolding narrative of captivity, dispossession, and domination that engenders the black subject in the Americas."[17] Pain thus continues to define the materiality of the black body even after formal emancipation as a kind of sustained trauma that seeps across generations. And, of course, black embodied injury is always spatially located through the body's material existence. The temporal mechanisms that mark the black body are inextricable from those that encase, control, and exclude black life spatially in the world. So although Herman Beavers usefully identifies the prominence of "tight space" in Morrison's novels—a term that "signals a character's spiritual and emotional estrangement from community and the way it inhibits their ability to sustain a meaningful relationship to place"—there is also a crucial temporal component to that estrangement.[18] It's these seemingly invisible structures of temporal violence that I want to bring to the fore.

Beloved, to start with, is filled with signposts of the time of black subjection.[19] The novel's present, 1873, is just eight years removed from the end of the Civil War, ten years from the Emancipation Proclamation, and sixteen years from the *Dred Scott v. Sandford* decision, which denied all citizenship and legal standing to people of African descent. War, as Barbara Christian aptly puts it, "brackets" Morrison's novels, focusing not on the "action of war itself so much as . . . the effects of such tumult on the psyches of [her] respective communities."[20] It's principally Paul D who reveals *Beloved*'s traces of the Civil War: "The War had been over four or five years then, but no body white or black seemed to know it. Odd clusters and strays of Negroes wandered back roads and cowpaths from Schenectady to Jackson. . . . Some of them were running from family that could not support them, some to family; some were running from dead crops, dead kin, life threats, and took-over land."[21] The marking in time of "the War" crucially remains a kind of specter here and throughout the novel, one that, far from ushering in a time of freedom and new life, initiates a time of disorientation and refigured violation. Emancipation, which itself is never explicitly acknowledged in the novel, also carries a ghostly presence in this passage, as if it were refused recognition for merely being a threshold into that renewed unfreedom. The Fugitive Slave Act of 1850 is also a critical historical landmark in the novel's monumental time. That Paul D renames it "the Misery" because of Sethe's "rough response" to it is certainly telling: the bill marks that year when escape from captivity became infinitely more precarious, the year when all pained black bodies, free or enslaved, could potentially be deemed fugitive.

Interspersed among these historical signposts is a barrage of intervals that reinforce the time of black subjection. Eighteen marks the number of years separating the narrative present and Sethe's 1855 arrival in southern Ohio. Twenty-eight marks the number of days between that same arrival and schoolteacher's violent attempt to reclaim his "property": "From the pure clear stream of spit that girl dribbled into her face to her oily blood was twenty-eight days." Twenty marks the number of years that Baby Suggs had had her son, Halle, in her life—"a lifetime," she calls it, considering that all her other children were sold off soon after birth. And "eighty-three days in a row" marks the duration that Paul D was "locked up and chained down" in Alfred, Georgia, after the war.[22] These numbers repeat throughout the novel, like the repetition inherent to the experience of trauma, as insistent reminders of the events and intervals that keep them captive in their own memories of violence.

The "authorities" or "enforcers" of this subjection time in the novel are diverse and numerous: Mr. and Mrs. Garner, Sethe and Paul D's putatively benevolent owners at Sweet Home; schoolteacher and his entourage, who ruled Sweet Home with an iron fist after Garner's death and recorded in their notebooks what they considered to be the everyday animality of blackness; the patrolman moving down the Ohio River who just missed seeing a pregnant Sethe escaping to the other side; the Ku Klux Klan that "infected" southern Ohio; the prison guards in Georgia who enchained Paul D; Sawyer, the restaurant owner who demanded punctuality from Sethe.

Although it may be less prominent than in *Sula* or, for that matter, *The Bluest Eye*, nature forms an added layer to this enforcement capacity in the novel. It *reinforces* this temporality through the passing of the seasons, with their seemingly innocuous ever-recurring cycle. Indeed, poverty—imposed on blackness during slavery and engendered after emancipation by the exclusion of blackness (from work, land ownership)—makes it such that black life acutely experiences the extremes of the seasons, with their sweltering heat, numbing cold, and devastating rains. "In Ohio seasons are theatrical," the narrator tells us. And in the novel this theatricality is an infliction. Winter "hurries in at suppertime and [stays] nine months," forcing everyone to gather around the cooking stove to keep warm. Summers linger with "the stench, the heat, the moisture—trust the devil to make his presence known."[23] Seasons and climate serve as the invisible reinforcement of black subjection time, augmenting the already devastating regulatory capacity of the Klan, the slave driver, and the employer. Christina Sharpe has a name for this encompassing structure of the natural and social worlds that bears down on black life: "The weather is the totality of our environments; the weather is the total climate; and that climate is antiblack. . . . The weather trans*forms Black being."[24]

By the time we get to *Sula*'s 1919 setting, the subjections, exclusions, and poverty we find in *Beloved* have evolved. World War I is now "the war" marking the novel's monumental time, having consumed the bodies and minds of two male characters: Shadrack returns with post-traumatic hallucinations; Plum returns addicted to heroin and numb to the world. Although the novel encompasses more than forty years, we always know the year of the narrative present. Each chapter is titled with a year, beginning with 1919, advancing chronologically but frequently leaping over several years between chapters, creating a veneer of neat, compartmentalized periods of time. We thus know the dates of several everyday experiences of violence: 1919 is the year that Helene and her daughter, Nel, are publicly berated by a train conductor for entering a "whites only" car, leaving Nel, for the duration of her life, "on guard"; 1937 is the year that construction of a nearby tunnel began and black men were systematically denied work. But this is a *veneer* of chronology—part of what Morrison calls her "play with Western chronology" in the novel—because of the novel's frequent analepses and prolepses that extend beyond the reach of the narrative present.[25] Consequently, we don't know for sure what year that Eva, Sula's mother, was left by her husband with only "$1.65, five eggs, three beets," and a toddler who "stopped having bowel movements." But we know it was winter when she had to take the young Plum to the outhouse in the "biting cold" to loosen his stools with her finger. The seasons, as in *Beloved*, exacerbate the effects of subjection time in the novel, amplifying what Hartman describes as the body's "brutal constraint, extreme need, and constant violence." This is again evident when in one cold November "black folks suffered heavily in their thin houses and thinner clothes."[26] Also similar to *Beloved*, the time of subjection in *Sula* is partly structured around pivotal gaps in narrative time, the most significant being Eva's eighteen-month absence from the Bottom. She left impoverished but returned "with two crutches, a new black pocketbook, and one leg," and enough money collected from insurance agents (the narrator presumes) for her and her family to live on. References to this mysterious eighteen-month lacuna repeat throughout the novel, an allegory for the poverty and sacrifice forced upon black life in the time of subjection. In all of this, the adjudicators and regulators of subjection time abound: the train conductor who enforces Nel and her mother's segregation, the insurance executives who effectively buy Eva's leg, the hospital nurse who tries to contain Shadrack's postwar madness.

In a way analogous to Ricoeur's account of time in *Mrs. Dalloway*, monumental time suffocates Morrison's characters, keeping them trapped in a world in which whiteness and capital win the day. But Morrison's temporal subjection is clearly distinct from Woolf's in its focus on the everyday practices of subjection that shape black social life in America, its emphasis on the pains endured by the black body over time, and indeed *by means of* time. As John Murillo puts it, black life is "subject to the singularly violent operations of time."[27] Morrison's formation is also distinct from Ricoeur's in the way that she inscribes into her novels—at times implicitly, at others explicitly—a temporality of trauma distinct to the African diasporic experience. On the one hand are the repeated hauntings of the killed child at 124 Bluestone Road in *Beloved*, as well as the repetitions of dates and intervals in both novels—all phenomena that in a way mimic what Cathy Caruth describes as the continual repetition of a "belated experience," what Freud called *Nachträglichkeit*, and the way that repeated symptoms of trauma cannot necessarily be directly linked to a singularly identifiable violent experience. In Caruth's reading of Freud, the traumatic ur-moment "is not fully assimilated as it occurs," not fully recognizable in its original experience, let alone in its belated repetitions, in which it "simultaneously defies and demands our witness."[28] The belated hauntings and traumatic repetitions we find in Morrison's novels are residues, in one way or another, of the excessive and unspeakable violence of captivity and slavery. They pull at the characters in these works, throwing their minds toward different times and places of subjection that perhaps in some cases weren't registered as such to begin with.

There is also a deeper historical valence to this temporality of trauma that runs in and through Morrison's subjection time. After all, she dedicated *Beloved* to "Sixty Million and more," the estimated number of captive Africans who died in the centuries-long middle passage. Stephen Best rightly identifies *Beloved* as the central literary text that inaugurated a certain "melancholic" turn in black studies criticism, a "drive in critical theory to make death an aspect of knowledge, to 'recover' it for knowledge, as a means of articulating how the past structures our present."[29] Very much germane to Morrison's fiction, then, is Édouard Glissant's well-known description of the ways that the "abyss" of the middle passage has reverberated throughout subsequent African diasporic lives:

> Experience of the abyss lies inside and outside the abyss. The torment of those who never escaped it: straight from the belly of the slave ship into the violent belly of the ocean depths they went. But their ordeal did not die; it quickened into this continuous/discontinuous thing: the panic of the new land, the haunting of the former land, finally the alliance with the im-

posed land, suffered and redeemed. The unconscious memory of the abyss served as the alluvium for these metamorphoses. The populations that then formed, despite having forgotten the chasm, despite being unable to imagine the passion of those who foundered there, nonetheless wove this sail.[30]

These reverberations of violence continued on, structuring the everyday lives of people of color throughout the Americas well after emancipation through laws and institutional practices that have continued to exclude, criminalize, and dispossess black life. They constitute a sprawling intergenerational structure in which the residue of trauma is passed down from generation to generation over centuries. For Glissant, the "unconscious memory" of the middle passage links to later historical experiences of violence. But this "alluvium," he says, is also that which "wove this sail," that which generates social life in diaspora.

This is precisely the idea that Morrison herself gestures toward in her insistence on "making value" from and finding the generativity in black historical experiences of imposed nonbeing that have modulated over centuries.[31] Like Ricoeur's gesture to the desire of the characters in *Mrs. Dalloway* to "escape" monumental time and "find a time of their own," there is a clear desire for escape in Morrison's fiction that I want to isolate in the coming pages. It's a desire driven by the sociality of black life cultivated over centuries of subjugation and pathologization, one that has everything to do with "making value" from historical experience. Like Jared Sexton's suggestion that "black life is not social life in the universe formed by the codes of the state or civil society, of citizen and subject, of nation and culture" and that "black life is not lived in the world that the world lives in, but it is lived underground, in outer space," black life in Morrison's novels importantly seeks the outside of that time of the state, that time of the citizen, and that time of normative culture—all the temporal modes that reinforce the subjection of blackness.[32] That outside begins with the threshold of desired ease, the anticipation of the moment when pain and trauma are lifted from the body.

WET LIGHT, DARK WATER

If Paul Ricoeur is instrumental in isolating the temporality of black subjection that saturates Morrison's novels, narratologist Gérard Genette is just as critical in exposing the internal structure of narrative anachrony in which we find this desire for transient and utopian ease. In *Narrative*

Discourse, Genette makes the fundamental distinction between "story time" (*erzählte Zeit*) and "narrative time" (*Erzählzeit*), where the former corresponds to the order of diegesis, the sequence in which events unfold in the story itself, while the latter pertains to how the diegesis is presented in the narrative. To be sure, the story time of a novel is often not identical to narrative time. Take this relationship in *Beloved*. In the narrative time of the novel, we first encounter Sethe and Denver living at 124 Bluestone Road and contending with a "spiteful" ghostly presence. However, this narrative beginning is quite advanced in the novel's story time: the latter begins with Sethe living on the Sweet Home plantation in Kentucky as a teen, continuing on with her marriage to Halle, the birth of her children, her escape to Ohio, the killing of her daughter, and then eighteen years later arriving at the moment in which the novel's narrative time begins: with Sethe and Denver contending with that spiteful ghost. This type of discordance, or "narrative anachrony," is identifiable, Genette suggests, "to the extent that story order is explicitly indicated by the narrative itself or inferable from one or another indirect clue."[33]

Genette goes on to explain two principal forms of anachrony, both of which pervade Morrison's novels: *prolepsis*, he says, constitutes "any narrative maneuver that consists of narrating or evoking in advance an event that will take place later," whereas *analepsis* designates "any evocation after the fact of an event that took place earlier than the point in the story where we are at any given moment."[34] These terms correspond, in other words, to anticipation and retrospection. Genette continues by presenting various types of prolepses and analepses, such as those entirely external or internal to the "first narrative," those that repeat, and those that explicitly reference other narrative moments as opposed to those that subtly allude to other such moments. Although *Beloved*'s discordance between story time and narrative time is the more complex of the two, I want to begin the following readings by moving through the circuits of anachrony in *Sula*, identifying where and how Morrison threads in that desire for ease. Doing so in *Sula* gives us the tools for deciphering the entanglements of desire and narrative in the later novel.

To begin with, *Sula* presents a formation of ease that's almost always inseparable from trauma and pain. In crucial moments, trauma even transforms into a kind of utopian easefulness. It also presents a narrative not of anachronism *tout court*, but of layered anachronism—such as prolepsis within analepsis, analepsis within analepsis. The layers I isolate below are what Christian gestures to when she suggests that in *Sula* "a particular point in time is but the focus of intertwining circles of other times and events."[35] I focus on three generations of the Peace family: Eva (the elder matriarch), Plum and Hannah (Eva's children), and Sula (Hannah's daughter and Eva's granddaughter). My interest here is in the network of anachronism that links these four figures, and the entanglement of trauma and desire within that network. A kind of ecstatic desire for utopian ease, I'll show, centers specifically on Plum and Sula and how these two figures imagine pain and desired release. But their otherwise desires are surrounded and overlaid by the desire of a chorus of characters for transient ease. These fleeting, quotidian moments ought to be read alongside those louder, more ecstatic ones, their amalgamation together revealing a fugitive, narratively labyrinthine system of desire that presses out toward absolution.

The first component of the novel's intergenerational anachronic structure—one that foregrounds Plum's utopian imagination—is the fraught relationship between Eva and Plum. Without knowing it, the reader is exposed to this relationship in an early moment of explicit narrative prolepsis: "After 1910 she [Eva] didn't willingly set foot on the stairs but once and that was to light a fire, the smoke of which was in her hair for years." The omniscient narrator provides just enough information to steep the reader's sense of anticipation for the coming events. Here, trauma is intimated, at the very least. This passage describes a kind of double prolepsis, what Genette would call its double "extent," or reach: it anticipates the more immediate event of fire to come, but it also anticipates that event's afterlife in the residue of the smoke that remains "in her hair for years." And indeed ten pages later we are given this fiery event at the end of the narrator's account of Plum's postwar depression and addiction. On her one leg and two crutches, Eva hoists herself downstairs to Plum's room, where he lies on his bed in that liminal consciousness just before sleep: "There seemed to be some kind of wet light traveling over his legs and stomach with a deeply attractive smell. It wound itself—this wet light—all about him, splashing and running into his skin. He opened his eyes and saw what he imagined was the great wing of an eagle pouring a wet lightness over him. Some kind of baptism, some kind of blessing, he thought. Everything is going to be all right, it said. Knowing that it was so he closed his eyes and sank into the bright hole of sleep." This "wet lightness," of course, is the infamous kerosene Eva pours over Plum just before she lights a match and "the whoosh of the flames engulfed him."[36]

The interior narrative voice grants us access to Plum's affective state: the unfolding event is horrifying from our perspective but utterly sublime from his. After years of postwar ennui, he feels this light as a release, as "some kind of baptism, some kind of blessing." Hearing the reassuring eagle's words, Plum lays back and anticipates that coming easefulness, living the "bright hole of sleep" in advance, that moment and (indeterminate) place of long-awaited relief. Death and rebirth, trauma and utopia, merge in this passage. The fine line between trauma and utopia here is a perspectival difference between the character's interior consciousness and an outsider's observation. For Plum, feeling himself and his own body, having experienced his own life, this moment is transcendent, a kind of a release from alienation.

I read this moment as utopian precisely because we don't have access to the possible realization of this otherwise desire for Plum, given its entanglement with trauma and death, and that it remains a structure of anticipation for him. He doesn't arrive at that bright hole but "sinks" toward it. Here, perhaps, the verb form of *ease* as anticipation is apt: we very much get a sense of Plum slowly, measuredly, "easing" toward his release. What's more, this passage confirms the previous proleptic mention, retrospectively rendering Eva's years-long smoky hair hauntingly prefigurative. Between this smoky hair and Plum's kerosene-soaked legs and stomach, the materiality of the body is a critical connector of anachronic moments. The body, in Eva's hair, is a kind of threshold surface that transports us in narrative time to Plum's body as it seeks its utopian (rel)ease.

Importantly, the burning of Plum reemerges analeptically later on in the text, this time from Eva's perspective. But the event's reemergence is interrupted by an unexpected detour into another analeptic moment. This temporally complex two-page sequence begins with Hannah boldly asking Eva, "What'd you kill Plum for, Mamma?" immediately after which the narrator slips into Eva's wandering consciousness on this hot August day:

> Eva listened to the [ice] wagon coming and thought about what it must be like in the icehouse. She leaned back a little and closed her eyes trying to see the insides of the icehouse. It was a dark, lovely picture in this heat, until it reminded her of that winter night in the outhouse holding her baby in the dark, her fingers searching for his asshole and the last bit of lard scooped from the sides of the can, held deliberately on the tip of her middle finger. . . . The last food staple in the house. . . . Even on the hottest of days in the hot spell, Eva shivered from the biting cold and stench of that outhouse.[37]

The account of Eva's thoughts here begins in the present or, more precisely, in anticipation of the ice wagon soon to come down her street. She anticipates a moment of transient ease, momentary bodily relief in that "dark, lovely picture," briefly escaping her sweltering immediate present. But suddenly a traumatic memory disrupts that anticipation of easefulness, with the "dark" and "biting cold" pivoting the narrator to analepsis: "until it reminded her of that winter night." The body is again a threshold surface that transports Eva (and the reader) to another moment in (story) time, her "shiver" connecting disparate moments in the text. The remembered trauma is of the child who would not stop crying, the freezing, reeking outhouse, the anxiety of poverty.

The narrator abruptly ends this brief analeptic detour, only to return to the analepsis that began this circuitous sequence: "Hannah was waiting. Watching her mother's eyelids." The body, these eyelids, again are the threshold surface that transport us in narrative time. Eva shifts to that other memory, of Plum, now as an adult, when he "whooshed" up in flames. "He was giving me such a time," she says to Hannah, "look like when he came back from the war he wanted to git back in. . . . Godhavemercy, I couldn't birth to him twice. When I closed my eyes I'd see him . . . trying to spread my legs to get back in. . . . [A] big man can't be a baby all wrapped up inside his mamma no more; he suffocate. . . . I held him close first. Real close. Sweet Plum. My baby boy."[38] Importantly, this is Eva speaking directly to Hannah, giving a kind of unveiled immediacy to Eva's perspective. To have access to Eva's impression of Plum's burning, and what led to the event, again transforms an otherwise traumatic event (for the reader, for Hannah) into something that resembles ease, one that runs parallel to Plum's utopian experience of it as a "blessing." But Eva's desired ease in this instance is not utopian but transient, focused on relief. The passage seems to suggest that Eva remembers a kind of mutual desire for ease between Plum and herself, where she didn't want him to "suffocate," but neither did she. That last line—"I held him close first. Real close."—demonstrates an intention of love and care, making bodily ease possible here for both of them. And "Godhavemercy" exudes Eva's own anticipation of bodily and psychological relief, after years of tending to a child who couldn't make his own way through life. In a way, Eva's desire for transient ease makes Plum's otherwise ease possible, however entangled in trauma they may be: in her desire not to let him "back in," Eva enables Plum's pathway toward the brightness of absolute release. Though of a different tenor and set of experiences than Plum's, there is, I argue, a utopian undercurrent to Eva's desire for a brief respite of ease—here in that Godhavemercy, but even in the memory of the cool icehouse. Read with and through Plum's ecstatic desire for that transcendent bright hole, where he believes he'll be washed of it all, Eva's desire for momentary ease feels like a set of signposts that signal the possibility, further (im)possible evidence, of that ultimate release, not just for one person but for the collective that has lived through the traumas and subjections that Morrison presents in *Sula*'s circuits of narrative time. This utopian undercurrent is further reinforced in the third generation, the final component of this intergenerational structure of trauma and ease.

Sula's final dramatic appearance stands as a kind of culmination of the novel's many temporal and affective registers, linking in critical ways to the narrative anachrony centered on Eva and Plum. The scene I want to focus on is her final moments of life, Sula lying alone in Eva's bed, suffering from an unnamed illness. Her pained body lies at the center of the sequence, with its "wires of liquid pain," the "burning" in her stomach, the overwhelming fatigue. In a moment of desired transient ease, not unlike Eva's desire for relief in the icehouse, Sula asks herself "whether she should turn her cheek to the cooler side of the pillow," to ease—slowly, deliberately—the accumulating heat and sweat. But if she turns, the narrator tells us, "she would not be able to see the boarded-up window Eva jumped out of." Analepsis suddenly takes hold: this brief mention signals the dramatic moment earlier in the narrative when Eva had leaped out of this window as Hannah suddenly burst into flames while lighting a fire in the front yard. Trauma irrupts analeptically into the novel's present, structuring Sula's consciousness as she lies on that bed staring at that window. But, as it often curiously does in *Sula*, trauma fuses with desired ease, ecstatically so:

> Looking at those four wooden planks with the steel rod slanting across them was the only peace she had. The sealed window soothed her with its sturdy termination, its unassailable finality. . . . It would be here, only here, held by this blind window high above the elm tree, that she might draw her legs up to her chest, close her eyes, put her thumb in her mouth and float over and down the tunnels, just missing the dark walls, down, down until she met a rain scent and would know the water was near, and she would curl into its heavy softness and it would envelop her, carry her, and wash her tired flesh always. Always.[39]

This is by far the most utopian moment in the novel. In the memory of trauma and the objects that represent it, Sula searches for "peace" and "soothing." In her mind, she lives in advance, floating down those tunnels, moving closer and closer to the water. The image of her return to infancy—curling into the fetal position, sucking her thumb—recalls Eva's fear of

Plum wanting to return to her womb. And just as this passage and Plum's burning signify the simultaneity of trauma and desire, they both also evince a kind of simultaneity of death and birth, of closure and opening. The room's enclosure gives Sula the solitude she had longed for, allowing her to embrace that coming absolution.

The repetition of "always" at the end of this passage is crucial to what sets this moment of desire in Sula's mind apart from the desire for mere relief on the cool side of her pillow. For her "tired flesh" to be "washed always" signals that otherwise ease, that excessive state of release that just might come, impossibly, at any moment. We might think of this flesh as the same that Spillers identifies as the site and surface of wounding, that "zero degree of social conceptualization" of black trauma.[40] It's also very much akin to Hartman's notion of "redress," of seeking "the redemption of the body as human flesh."[41] It's her moment of impending transcendence, of opening outward toward another world free of the body's burdens, a world where she might occupy her own configuration of time. Importantly, utopian desire is spatialized here, but rather indeterminately in that tunnel with its dark walls, the smell of rain, the enveloping softness that leads on to a place just as undefinable. The spatial indefinition brings the temporality of this sequence to the fore, heightening Sula's sense of anticipation as she moves in her mind, reminding us that this iconic character is a figure of endless unfolding, of *"potential being,"* a "self [that] is multiple, fluid, relational, and in a perpetual state of becoming."[42]

In the wake of this ultimate plunge toward release, Morrison closes the novel with a lyrical summation of the Peace family's desire for that otherworldly, utopian ease. Twenty-five years after Sula's death, Nel, her childhood friend, walks into the cemetery where all passed Peaces rest, and thinks: "Together they read like a chant: PEACE 1895–1921, PEACE 1890–1923, PEACE 1910–1940, PEACE 1892–1959. They were not dead people. They were words. Not even words. Wishes, longings."[43] The chanting repetition of Nel's thoughts suggests that these lives have not passed after all but continue on as "wishes, longings," as fugitive threads lunging out—perhaps *easing* out—toward the final release that always lies just beyond the horizon. These two words are exorbitant. They encompass not just the named Peaces but also the larger collective that wishes and longs for an excessive freedom, a liberatory logic that resides beyond the prescriptions of the liberal democratic processes that have constrained and dehumanized black bodies and lives in America for centuries. These two words also manage to contain the entirety of the desired ease in the novel, whether transient or utopian. Certainly they speak to Plum and Sula's ecstatic wishes and longings, but they also confirm the inconspicuous, otherworldly valences of Eva and Sula's transient desires for coolness: Eva in the icehouse, Sula on the other side of the pillow. "Wishes, longings" is the current that runs underneath the surface of *Sula*, guiding each character, however subtly, toward new possibilities, new bodies, new worlds, new configurations of time. In this final scene, even from the grave there's a constant fugitive pursuance of that phenomenal moment of absolute release. There's also an incisive, searing way in which these lines cut against the function of temporal intervals in Morrison's work, against the interval as an invasive structure of containment within the larger structure of subjection time. Each repetition is a kind of rebuttal of that containment, an insistence that those intervals be remembered as times of yearning, not trauma.

GRAVITATIONAL EASE

In the second of these two ease-saturated novels, we find Morrison building further on these manipulations of narrative time. Like *Sula*, *Beloved* presents an intergenerational drive toward release, a blurring of ease and trauma, and a subtle network of moments of desired transient ease that surrounds and buttresses the novel's more conspicuous drive toward utopian ease. Sethe's own interior account of her daughter's death, situated at the end of the novel's second section, is the gravitational center of the work's temporality—everything leading up to this moment in the text propels us toward it, and everything that follows pulls us back. Morrison builds toward this narrative event through what Genette calls "repeating prolepsis," "brief allusions" that refer in advance to an event that will be told in full in its place.[44] The result is a kind of cumulative prolepsis, in which these brief allusions gradually amass to create a fuller understanding of that central traumatic event—until Sethe's version of the event radically shifts that understanding. The following reading begins by paralleling the author's narrative construction: limning the accrual of trauma until that accumulation flips registers, becoming a kind of ecstatic energy that lunges out toward otherwise ease.

If, as bell hooks claims, *Beloved* is "all about the body," then the principal body around which the text revolves is that of Sethe's two-year-old child.[45] At the outset, however, that body is a kind of furiously present absence, about which we gradually learn more and more. As the proleptic revealings of the central event accumulate, so too does the image of this child's body, as well as how, where, by whom, and under what circumstances she was killed. What initially constitutes this nonbody, then, are cryptic phrases, adjectives, and nouns: "124 was spiteful," the first line reads, "full of baby's venom." It harbors "rage," casting a "powerful spell" as it wreaks havoc on 124, spilling jars, shifting the house's foundation. We learn that this ghost "wasn't even two years old when she died," that her fury stems from "having its throat cut," its "red baby blood" spilled. Except for the brief moments when Sethe recalls her love for the young girl, how she wished she could have had the full phrase "Dearly Beloved" chiseled on the headstone, all we get early on is a sense of haunting trauma surrounding this child's death.[46]

Eerie and uncanny events unfold, reaching a critical threshold when "a fully dressed woman walked out of the water." From this point on, this woman occupies the haunting space previously taken up by the ghost. Beloved, as she calls herself—the word inscribed on the dead baby's headstone—now directs our anticipation of the novel's central event. The accruing image of the baby ghost's body begins to merge with the accruing image of Beloved's: she's "greedy" to hear Sethe speak; resembling a child, "her feet were like her hands, soft and new." Eventually Sethe becomes convinced that Beloved is her dead daughter when Beloved's touch feels the same as the ghost's touch, like "touches from the other side."[47] As in *Sula*, the body becomes a critical threshold separating moments in time, separating, or in this case merging, the living and the dead.

A sense of looming horror continues to drive the narrative following Beloved's arrival, intensifying the sense of anticipation of Sethe's account, and the body at the center of it. For one, we learn of the community's ostracism of the family living at 124, their neighbor's implicit "disapproval" of Sethe's very existence. And at the precipice of the three chapters that recount the killing of the child—the first narrated from the perspective of schoolteacher (Sweet Home's slave driver), the second by Stamp Paid (the man who helped Sethe escape across the Ohio River), and the final by Sethe herself—we're given access to Baby Suggs's haunting premonition ahead of the killing. Suggs senses something "dark and coming"; she smells it, feels it. "What could it be?" she asks herself, standing in her garden, "this dark and coming thing."[48] With all these anticipations, the reader knows well enough this "dark and coming thing," a phrase repeated a half dozen times in just a few pages. Suggs's evocation ushers us into the event with the clear expectation of a violent ethical infraction. Through all these proleptic accountings of trauma and violence in the novel, Morrison has yet to reveal her signature utopian desire for otherwise ease.

The first two of the three short chapters devoted to the killing itself confirm and extend this anticipation of trauma. Given the perspective of the first, the interpretation is unsurprising: schoolteacher sees Sethe as the "nigger woman holding a blood-soaked child to her chest," having "gone wild." There's clearly no way this figure can see Sethe's actions outside a confirmation of her nonbeing. Stamp Paid's account, on the other hand, though it doesn't directly condemn Sethe's actions, is clearly tinged with regret: he wishes he had seen coming that "righteous Look every Negro learned to recognize along with his ma'am's tit."[49] He remembers how Sethe "flew, snatching up her children like a hawk," running toward the shed that housed the saw with which she would kill her daughter. Despite Stamp's concern and schoolteacher's malice, the reader's perception of this event radically shifts in the next few pages.

Trauma does exist in Sethe's mind when she kills her daughter, but it's the trauma of captivity she desperately hopes her children will escape. At the precipice of Sethe's account, one question remains: What was she thinking? By now, the novel's proleptic revealings have filled in most gaps: where, how, and ostensibly why she killed her daughter. We know the object with which she killed her, the blood that poured from her throat. That toddler's body has finally become visible, material. The register of all the traumatic accumulations suddenly flips to ecstatic longing:

> The truth was simple. . . . She was squatting in the garden and when she saw them coming and recognized schoolteacher's hat, she heard wings. Little hummingbirds stuck their needle beaks right through her headcloth into her hair and beat their wings. And if she thought anything it was No. No. Nono. Nonono. Simple. She just flew. Collected every bit of life she had made, all the parts of her that were precious and fine and beautiful, and carried, pushed, dragged them through the veil, out, away, over there where no one could hurt them. Over there. Outside this place, where they would be safe.[50]

The shift to Sethe's interior thoughts moves us away from seeing this event as a traumatic, regrettable death and toward a view of it as a yearning for the outside of subjection, indeed recalling those "wishes, longings" with which *Sula* leaves us. Utopia for Sethe is that place of "safety," "where no one could hurt them," that site of ultimate ease. As Mae Henderson incisively puts it, the shift to Sethe's interior account "subvert[s] the master code of the master('s) text," enabling Sethe to "reconstitute her self and herstory."[51] Her interior voice reveals a kind of counternarrative to all the ways we have come to know and anticipate the killing, standing against those voices that had silenced hers. There's also filial collectivity that underwrites Sethe's power here, for she had intended to pass through the veil with all of her children: "My plan was to take us all to the other side where my own ma'am is."[52] As J. Hillis Miller argues, in Sethe's mind, she and her children form a kind of collective body, her children constituting "all the parts of her" that are to be "carried, pushed, dragged . . . out, away, over there." The one child who does pass through the veil represents the possibility of that otherwise easeful life, its promise, its coming release: a "life beyond life."[53] For Sethe, the sight of that hat suddenly spurs her to find her own experience of time unknown in this world, indeed a collective time of *their* own, as a family, living outside that time of black subjection so devastatingly enforced in that moment by schoolteacher and his slave hunters.

Sethe's refusal to resist the slave hunters by imagining her own structure of logic reveals a critical strain in theories of black fugitivity. That site "through the veil," "outside this place, where they would be safe" lies beyond the coordinates of liberal conceptions of time and space. Sethe underscores what Daphne Brooks describes as the "centrality of the opaque as a mode of narrative agency for the fugitive slave," or what Jasmine Cobb calls the fugitive's practice of "illegibility," evading the other's (re)cognition.[54] This illegibility, in turn, is read by schoolteacher and his hunters as a kind of "madness," a term that La Marr Jurelle Bruce takes up as a critical mode of fugitive thought and experience employed historically by people of color, especially black women, to escape the dictates of putative reason that govern the white supremacist world: "Rather than remain captive behind the barbed fences of slavocratic sanity, [the enslaved woman] might find refuge—however tenuous, vexed, and incomplete—in the fugitivity of madness."[55] What makes Sethe's personal memory of the killing so revelatory of fugitive *time*, though, is the language she uses to *lean in toward* that other side, that space read as madness. The conditional mood of the phrase "Where they *would* be safe" implies a structure of yet to be, of anticipation, a lunging out, a vision in her mind of that excessive, otherworldly, and unmappable easeful place where she and her children would be radically free of violation. Indeed, there's a kind of kinship between Sethe's vision of life beyond the veil and Olaudah Equiano's dream of joining the "inhabitants of the deep" that I discuss in the introduction. Both see with a kind of third eye. Both espy an apparently unfathomable vision of life on the outside, beyond the knowable.

Despite my concentration on *Beloved*'s proleptic movement, this drive toward what's easeful is constantly disrupted by analepses that pull us back in story time. In fact, the advance mentions discussed thus far in this chapter—of the ghost's nonbody, Beloved's growing association with the baby, the gossip of murder—are all simultaneously analeptic in story time. If the killing of the child took place eighteen years prior to the narrative's beginning, then each reference to it points backward while ostensibly directing us forward to Sethe's primary account. Even this utopian gravitational center of the novel is a memory, analeptic in story time. And we should add to this the novel's frequent leaps into different characters' memories, often creating circuitous detours from the narrative present. These expansive analepses, typically to some moment in the traumatic past, have the paradoxical effect of "mak[ing] the narrated time advance by delaying it," as Ricoeur suggests of the flashbacks in *Mrs. Dalloway*, saturating the narrative with long interludes that deepen the affective and historical weight of the novel's present and the anticipations of utopian release.[56]

I want to provide a brief window into these traumatic analeptic detours that weave throughout the novel's articulations of desired ease. Crucially, many of them, as in *Sula*, are structured by a part of the body that serves as a threshold surface connecting the present to the past. Take the early moment in the novel when Sethe's sense of sight and touch in the present tunnels her mind into the past: "Her brain was devious. She might be hurrying across a field, running practically, to get to the pump quickly and rinse the chamomile sap from her legs. . . . Sopping away with pump water and rags, her mind fixed on getting every last bit of sap off. . . . Then something. The splash of water, the sight of her shoes and stockings awry on the path . . . and suddenly there was Sweet Home rolling, rolling, rolling out before her eyes."[57] Her legs covered in chamomile sap is the surface that suddenly transports her mind to the plantation that she fled nearly two decades prior. The memory of a familiar stickiness, of a similar splash of water on her body, guides her unconscious mind back to that time and place of subjection, haunting her present, propelling her desire for ease throughout the novel. A similar moment takes place a few pages later after Sethe tells Paul D, "I got a tree on my back": "After I left you, those boys came in there and took my milk. That's what they came in there for. Held me down and took it. I told Mrs. Garner on em. She had that lump and couldn't speak but her eyes rolled out tears. Them boys found out I told on em. Schoolteacher made one open up my back, and when it closed it made a tree. It grows there still."[58] Here Sethe's scarred flesh is the threshold that transports her and Paul D back to the time of her assault at Sweet Home. For Henderson, this scar is a kind of "archeological site" of past violence, "inscribing her as property" and "as the ultimate Other whose absence or (non)being only serves to define the being or presence of the white or male subject."[59] Sethe's much anticipated interior voice yearning for that world "where no one could hurt them" is almost a direct response to this literal inscription of nonbeing. It's a wound that continually deepens over time—"It grows there still," she says, much like the language of perpetual wounding I examine in the next chapter—of scars, blisters, and rotting flesh—that saturates Aimé Césaire's *Notebook of a Return to the Native Land*. These and innumerable other analepses in *Beloved* plunge the novel's characters into their respective traumatic pasts, driving all of them to some form of easefulness, however momentary or impossibly otherwise.

Rounding out this network of anachronism in *Beloved* are the many scattered instances of transient ease. Mostly tucked away in distant memories, these fleeting analeptic moments manifest for nearly every principal character. These are brief, quiet moments of escape, moments that allow one to persist despite the mercilessness of subjection, to keep the promise of that deeper, more sustained otherwise easefulness alive. They include Paul D's memory of sneaking into the fields of Sweet Home to taste fresh corn: "No matter what all your teeth and wet fingers anticipated, there was no accounting for the way that simple joy could shake you." And Sethe's twenty-eight peaceful days that followed her arrival at 124, "days of healing, ease, and real-talk." And those "berries that tasted like church" that Stamp Paid picked in the brambles behind 124.[60] And, of course, the Clearing behind 124 where Suggs brought healing to former slaves. All of these ephemeral moments surround, like a buttressing constellation, Sethe's memory of those hummingbirds in her hair, her memory of "pushing" and "dragging" her children "out, away, over there" to that ultimate place of ease. They are our guideposts pointing to that outer world, that coming moment.

There's one example of desired transient ease that I want to spend a bit more time unpacking, given how distinct it is from these others and that a kindred desire manifests in some of the other works studied in the coming chapters. My interest here is in the erotic, specifically the pursuit of orgasm. The moment early on in *Beloved* when the sexual desire between Sethe and Paul D quickly reaches climax, I want to suggest, is a genre of transient ease with its own historical and political implications, especially considering its embeddedness in narrative anachronism. Except for a few flashes of remembered conversations from decades prior, these few pages are written entirely in an omniscient voice, set exclusively inside both characters' minds. It being her home, and Paul D the visitor, Sethe seems very much in control as she "led him to the top of the stairs" and "took him into" one of the rooms. "Though she could remember desire," we're told, "she had forgotten how it worked . . . how blindness was altered so that what leapt to the eye were places to lie down, all else—doorknobs, straps, hooks, the sadness that crouched in corners, and the passing of time—was interference." There's clearly an exhilarating sense of anticipation in Sethe's mind that somehow resides outside of time's chronological accountings, but the climax itself appears in the text as a nonappearance, a kind of vanished presence: "It was over before they could get their clothes off. Half-dressed and short of breath, they lay side by side resentful of one another and the skylight above them."[61] The quickly built anticipation and release are over before they know it.

What complicates this scene, though, are the memories and anticipations—or lack thereof—that preceded the pair's reunion on this day. For Sethe, "Her deprivation had been not having any dreams of her own at all," whereas Paul D had been filled with them for years: "His dreaming of her had been too long and too long ago." What couldn't escape Paul D's mind, and what compounds his desire for her in this moment at 124, was their life at Sweet Home decades earlier. Fresh in his mind is the thought of Sethe as "the new girl" that he, Halle, and the others on the Kentucky plantation "dreamed of at night and fucked cows for at dawn while waiting for her to choose." For Paul D, encountering Sethe after decades triggers memories of desire, the text swinging us back analeptically to his prior yearning: "Nothing could be as good as the sex with her Paul D had been imagining off and on for twenty-five years."[62] What's fascinating is that the great majority of this short chapter—in which Paul D and Sethe are in the upstairs bedroom in the narrative present—is organized around a series of personal memories (for both of them) of Sweet Home during their time of bondage, making their sexual experience inextricably bound up with that prior life and world. Indeed, this conflation of moments in time makes Farah Jasmine Griffin's thoughts on "sex stolen away from the gaze of the master" under slavery very much pertinent. Griffin calls it a "dangerous pleasure," a "vulnerable zone of safe space." Especially apt is her framing of the orgasm under slavery: "The orgasm is a site of agency in that it is a moment of self-immersion for the slave—a space beyond the control of the master. . . . Significantly, orgasm is the space where the body loses control of itself. In a system in which the master's control of the slave body is so over-determined, where every activity (particularly procreative sex between black men and women) is within his control, the orgasm constitutes a site where the body moves beyond the control of itself and as such eschews control of any kind."[63] With Sethe and Paul D's desire and intercourse embedded in their multilayered traumatic memories of Sweet Home and the very system of control that Griffin describes, their (presumptive) orgasm takes on a valence of refuge, an experience and a sensation that reside beyond the slaveholder's recognition. "A moment of self-immersion," as Griffin puts it, a brief moment of respite from the devastating, encompassing nature of black subjection. Sethe's and Paul D's anticipation in the present, and the space of their orgasm, is not simply the fleeting pleasure of just any orgasm but one constructed by Morrison as an island of ecstasy, of "safe space," of transient ease amid the overwhelming historical force of antiblack violence. Even if Sethe and Paul D are disappointed afterward—how could they not be?—their immediate anticipation of sexual pleasure as they walk up those white stairs, and Paul D's decades-long yearning, evince a utopian undercurrent that seeps through the transiency of their orgasmic ease. There's an underlying wish, as I read it, for that ecstasy, that safe space, that cognitive flight from the immediacy of the body and the world to last forever. And indeed there's an integral connection between this undercurrent utopian desire and Sethe's ecstatic desire to flee to the other side of the veil. There's a direct line linking this pursuit of orgasm and Sethe's wish to cross over with "all the parts of her that were precious and fine and beautiful."

Toward the end of the novel, Morrison provides one final reprise of those utopian hummingbirds, reinforcing the centrality of Sethe's consciousness of that event in its narrative aftermath. The narrator takes us inside Sethe's mind as she sees a man directing his horse cart toward 124: "Guiding the mare, slowing down, his black hat wide-brimmed enough to hide his face but not his purpose. He is coming into her yard and he is coming for her best thing. She hears wings. Little hummingbirds stick their needle beaks right through her headcloth into her hair and beat their wings. And if she thinks anything it is no. Nono. Nonono. She flies."[64] The hat transports Sethe in time to eighteen years before, when schoolteacher stormed her yard, making her hear wings and fly. That Morrison does not just allude to this previous moment, but restates it verbatim, elicits the entirety of that previous scene, with the saw, the blood, and the uncontainable desire for ceaseless intergenerational ease. In narrative time, this is an analepsis of an analepsis, a reprisal of a moment in the narrative that was a memory to begin with. By the end of the novel, Morrison has built a kind of echo chamber of utopian desire. The yearning for definitive ease reverberates throughout her layered anachronic structures, those accumulating prolepses, those scattered transient eases, those traumatic analeptic detours, and this final echo memory of desired flight. It's as if by the time we get to this reprisal in Sethe's mind, the yearning for absolution has bounced among so many surfaces, so many anachronic corners, extending it, stretching it, appearing slightly differently at each turn but always retaining some sense of desired absolution. The novel is the container of these ceaseless reverberations, the vessel where utopian possibility always resounds and is always imminent. *Sula* may prepare us for the kinds of anachrony found in *Beloved*, but the latter without a doubt stands apart in its temporal sedimentations.

....

Perhaps in order for desired ease to be sustained in Morrison's novels, to maintain its ecstatic vitality at each of those resounding, utopian irruptions, it needs to accumulate in the undercurrent of those transient appearances like a kind of sediment. Perhaps, too, it must be buried under layers of anachrony, twisted into a maze, made to appear only in flashes—what Glissant calls the "sudden flash[es] of revelation" in poetics that "open onto unpredictable and unheard of things."[65] Indeed, the movement of both transient and utopian ease in these novels is decidedly fugitive. It constantly blurs and shuttles between story time and narrative time. It fuses with trauma and violence. It switches unpredictably between those quick, momentary eases—Suggs's respite in those colors, Stamp Paid's escape into the taste of those berries—and the exhilarating flashes of another, endlessly easeful world—Sethe's drive "outside this place," Plum's desire for that "wet light." In these works, imagined ease buries itself in memories and memories of memories and proleptic intimations. It's the thing that escapes the "confines of ontological pinning down," a kind of "elusive interstitiality," wandering in and out and to the side of the text's surface.[66] And although desired ease always lies in that phenomenal moment just beyond the now, its fluctuating position in narrative time precludes, and indeed eludes, teleology. Ease doesn't simply lie in the future or in the past. It takes flight from historicist progression, from those more perfect futures, opting instead for any temporal location that allows it to evade the interpellation that inaugurated its nonbeing. It searches for those crevices where it might catch a breath of air above the surface of the text, only to dive back into the undertow of its "undercommon, underground, submarine sociality," gathering diaspora and momentum in its stealth, making and remaking its shape.[67] Desired ease in Morrison's novels is a perpetually evasive longing that resides principally below the surface, emerging in brief moments just to let you know it's still there, it's still on the run, and it always will be.

Ultimately, this labyrinthine quest for easefulness in Morrison's fiction, like the other formations of fugitive time in this book, presses toward a new world, a new social order, a new, unfathomable formation of freedom—one anticipatory breath at a time. For Morrison, as for Sun Ra, Yvonne Vera, and the Black Audio Film Collective, the push toward that new order begins at the microlevel of feeling in the body. This next chapter continues in search of that feeling, moving us from the hills of southern Ohio to Fort-de-France, Havana, Paris, and beyond. In the dynamic collaboration between Aimé Césaire and Wifredo Lam, amid the turbulence of a world in crisis at mid-century, we find, as in Morrison's novels, a blurring of trauma and utopia, wounding and desire. History and memory, too, seep into their works, propelling that fugitive chase. From the hummingbirds that tell Sethe of the promise of another life, we shift to the dove that rises and rises in Césaire's celebrated epic poem, fleeing toward the cosmos, lunging after that as-yet-unknown, unseen world where violence no longer consumes blackness.

2 AIMÉ CÉSAIRE, WIFREDO LAM, AND THE AESTHETICS OF SURGING LIFE

The creature on the cover of the 1943 Cuban translation of Aimé Césaire's *Notebook of a Return to the Native Land* is a curious one. It resembles a kind of iguana figure with two long-snouted, dog-like heads bearing razor-sharp teeth. Its massive tail is noticeably disproportionate to its thin, rib-protruding torso. It's almost as if Wifredo Lam, the Cuban painter and illustrator of this Spanish-language edition of Césaire's 1939 epic, drew this creature as a kind of gatekeeper, standing guard at the threshold to the poem's world. The menacing mien of its two heads signals the pervasive discourse of animality in the poem, the ubiquitous allusions to the historical treatment of enslaved people as beasts. We might also read this creature as a metaphor for Martinique itself, the island that the poet/speaker returns home to after years abroad, the island of "famines" and "vacated agonies" announced in the first stanzas. Its bulging ribs certainly suggest a hunger, at the very least; its small, vacant eyes hint at something long endured. Curiously, flowers and leaves adorn the creature's tail, suggesting a kind of organic relation to the Earth, that this being is of this island like the people in the poem. Perhaps in addition to preparing us for the catalog of devastation in the *Notebook*'s first section, this creature also signals its later celebrations of rootedness and new life. It may be priming us for both wounding and becoming.

The three sketches drawn by Wifredo Lam for Lydia Cabrera's 1943 translation of Césaire's *Notebook*, retitled *Retorno al país natal*, mark the beginning of a series of sustained conversations and collaborations between the two over four decades. Lam and Césaire both had "at last found a companion soul" when they met by chance in 1941 during Lam's stopover in Martinique while fleeing Nazi Europe for his childhood home of Cuba.[1] They would soon discover that they both had returned—or were returning, in Lam's case—to devastated islands after years studying in Europe, that they both sought to rehabilitate the image of blackness and black culture in their homelands, and that they were both deeply influenced by surrealism, the avant-garde movement that sought to remake a world in crisis through artistic expressions of the subconscious. In poetry and painting, Césaire and Lam developed kindred modes of experimentalism through which they exposed the enduring afterlives of colonialism. In the process, I argue, they expressed similar desires to escape the forces that have historically rendered black life disposable. Both, in short, sought out new worlds. Césaire's search came through the poetic image, which allowed him, as he put it, to "immeasurably extend the field of transcendence." When "A is no longer A," you find "strange cities, extraordinary landscapes, worlds that are twisted, crushed, torn apart . . . being turned to becoming."[2] Similarly for Lam, as we gather from his *Retorno* cover image, A can be A—but also B, C, or Z. The painter likewise turns being into becoming through a visual sleight of hand, thinking of his practice as "an act of decolonization" from which "strange worlds" erupt.[3] It's this common approach to the aesthetic image that makes the interplay between Lam's three sketches and Césaire's poem so generative. It's an interplay, I want to suggest, that leads us into the minutiae of Césaire's distinct formation of fugitive time.

To be clear, the principal object of study in this chapter is Césaire's *Notebook*. But my interest is in how Lam's drawings—which to date have only been superficially examined in relation to the poem—allow us to see this canonical epic anew, showing us unexpected ways of reading its poetics of time and the body. Rather than merely illustrating the *Notebook*'s content, Lam's images enact a kind of improvisatory riff on the poem, like the way a jazz soloist might extend, revise, and weave in and out of the melody of "All the Things You Are," creating something at once distinct but very much of that song's sonic world. Certainly, components of Lam's sketches depict particular features in the *Notebook*, but these images ought to read more as complementary of the poem, as part of a mutual effort to build strange cities, to turn being into becoming. Lam's visual images, I contend, expand and deepen the poetic images and drama of the poem while highlighting inconspicuous features that might otherwise go unnoticed. I want to sit with these three sketches in the way that Darby English sits with single artworks for entire chapters in *To Describe a Life* (2019), excavating the surface and undercurrent layers, the micro and the macro, constantly shifting perspective, conjuring nodes of meaning and relation. In the way that Kerry James Marshall's painting *Untitled (policeman)* "stages an ingression of creative imagination" for English, I want to use Lam's images as a hyperfocused ingression into Césaire's world, turning the images over and over in order to trace the poem's phenomenological temporalities of wounding and desire.[4] Through this interplay of the visual and the poetic, we gain a fuller sense of how utopian desire emerges from the body in Césaire's *Notebook*, how the poem's sense of embodied becoming surges toward a kind of ontological transcendence, a proleptic sense of being toward that transfigurative moment when nonbeing has been stripped from blackness.

My attention in these pages is primarily on the original 1939 *Volontés* version of the poem that Césaire published just prior to his return to Martinique after living in France for nearly a decade. It was on this version that Lam based his sketches. But I also draw on Césaire's later published revisions—the final appearing in 1956—to show how Lam's 1943 drawings, and indeed the pair's sustained conversations, may very well have influenced what the poet added to those later editions. In particular, there's a dimension of sexuality that appears in the *Notebook* only after Lam's visual suggestion of a similar dimension in one of his 1943 drawings—a sexual dimension, it turns out, that affords a distinct optic into the poem's fugitive temporality. My contention, in short, is that the full scope of the *Notebook*'s fugitive time emerged in dialogue with Lam's visual aesthetics, that Wifredo Lam was instrumental in its making.

The task of this chapter is to demonstrate, through Lam and Césaire's generative inter-animations, the materiality of the body as the source point of the *Notebook*'s utopian structure of time. Broadly, this time appears in the poem's language of embodiment in two interrelated ways, both of which Lam's drawings bring to life. On the one hand, Césaire registers a pervasive discourse of historical trauma in the flesh, using language such as "scarring" and "blistering," which imply a temporal sedimentation of the wound. On the other, there's a simultaneous discourse of temporal anticipation that emerges from the body in terms such as "hunger" and "thirst," which suggest otherwise desire and outward projection. But this desire, like all utopias, remains unfulfilled. Césaire's structure of utopia is less about the desire to be entirely rid of trauma—this wounding of the flesh—than the desire to *reimagine* the wound, to allow trauma to become generative in the poem's ecstatic projection toward that ever-deferred moment of disalienation. Weaving in and out of the disciplines of literary studies and art history, this chapter presents Césaire's distinct formation of fugitive time: a temporality at once West Indian and global, metaphorical and embodied, irrevocably wounded and ecstatically surging.

SURREAL ENCOUNTERS

In April 1941 nearly 350 refugees aboard the *Capitaine Paul Lemerle* arrived in Vichy-controlled Martinique, where they were detained for weeks before the ship continued on toward New York. Among the influential artists and intellectuals on board was André Breton, perhaps the most influential of the surrealist poets. Breton, the story goes, was looking for a gift for his daughter in Fort-de-France when he came across a shop window displaying the first issue of *Tropiques*, the cultural studies journal published by Aimé Césaire, Suzanne Césaire, and René Ménil that effectively served as the organ of négritude in the 1940s. Captivated by Aimé Césaire's surrealist-inflected poem in the journal, Breton would share it with his fellow passengers and would soon befriend Césaire and arrange for the publication of an expanded bilingual edition in New York.[5]

What often gets lost in brief mentions of Breton and Césaire's meeting is that Wifredo Lam was also on that ship. In their initial conversations, Césaire discovered in Lam "a similar effort to liberate the psychic mechanisms and open the human spirit"—a similarity that revealed the influence of Breton on both artists.[6] Lam had been working with the French poet and other surrealists in Marseille ahead of their Antilles-bound voyage, and Césaire's search for a black poetics had been significantly influenced by the work of Breton, Apollinaire, and others during his decade of study in Paris. Both were drawn to the disruptive potential of the surrealist method of "automatic writing," the process by which one's thoughts are directly expressed as unfiltered images of "truth," revealing hidden and contradictory associations that break the limits of reason and expectation.[7] In short,

Césaire and Lam saw the radical anticolonial potential in surrealism and were compelled to make it their own. In the coming pages I want to touch briefly on the methods, resources, and bodies of work of these two figures, to gather a set of tools with which to make sense of the temporal registers woven into Césaire's poem and Lam's sketches.

Despite their allied aims, Lam and Césaire bent surrealism in different ways. In a 1980 interview, Césaire explained that surrealism "was an instrument that dynamited the French language. . . . It was a factor of liberation . . . an operation of disalienation. . . . I said to myself, if I apply surrealism to my particular situation, I can bring out unconscious forces."[8] Surrealism as method thus enabled him to undermine the sedimented layers of alienation and subjection that colonialism had wrought in the Caribbean over centuries. It was instrumental to his idea of négritude: "this determination to rehabilitate a history, this feeling of solidarity to develop, this feeling of a faithfulness towards our ancestors."[9] In conversation with his *Tropiques* colleagues as well as fellow students in Paris, this "rehabilitation" centered on the discourses on blackness that the poet simultaneously experienced, inherited, and reinvented. He had lived through the pathological historical connotations of the term *nègre*, but he had also been influenced by a positive discourse on blackness from an array of cultural influences. Surrealism, we might say, was the point of departure in his search for that feeling of solidarity, ancestrality, and historical rehabilitation.

For Césaire, surrealism's "unconscious forces" specifically elicited a "call to Africa."[10] The method of crushing, twisting, and juxtaposing images resulted in a mythical idea of the continent that the poet scattered across his oeuvre, with Africa effectively serving as an expansive metonym for vitality, ancestrality, primordial nature, and irretrievable pasts. "From contemplating the Congo," he writes in the final 1956 edition of the *Notebook*, "I have become a Congo resounding with forests and rivers / . . . / where the water goes / likouala-likouala."[11] Here that automatic mode of writing results in the fantastical, though literal, transformation of the poet/speaker into rushing water, into rooted trees, exuding a primordiality and natural vitality through this larger Congo synecdoche. In this passage, and in other works, like his 1966 play *A Season in the Congo*, the various metaphorical registers of Africa allow the speaker to assume a sense of rootedness and belonging. Shaped by the formative influence of another négritude poet, Léopold Sédar Senghor, Césaire's friend since his time in Paris, and the writings of the German anthropologist Leo Frobenius, Africa becomes a kind of ancient, mythical utopia for Césaire: a site, indeterminately located in time, that lies outside of trauma but ultimately beyond the reach of the "contemplative" poet. This idea of Africa, as I'll show in his vision of fugitive time, is not necessarily historical or even nostalgic, despite elements that might be coded as "traditional," but instead is central to that indeterminate temporal outside position of release that is fugitive time's ultimate (inaccessible) object.

The other critical vector of Césaire's surrealist approach is language, surrealism as "an instrument that dynamited the French language." The poet was intimately aware of the historical contaminations of French as a colonial language: "For me French was an instrument that I wanted to bend into a new expression. I wanted to make an Antillean French, that is, a *'français nègre.'*"[12] Bent to fit the shape of blackness in his poetics, the words of this new language were broken of their normative associations and, as Jean-Paul Sartre put it, emphatically "defrancized" [*défrancisé*].[13] Césaire did so through homonyms, archaisms, unusual lexical juxtapositions, and constantly shifting verb tenses. In his *Glossaire des termes rares dans l'oeuvre d'Aimé Césaire* (2004), which is entirely devoted to Césaire's lexical particularity, René Hénane calls Césaire an *"ingénieur du verbe,"* a poet who engineered a language using uncommon words from the discourses of botany, zoology, medicine, and seafaring.[14] A signature example for Hénane is the feminine noun *fougue*, which momentarily appears in "Poem for the Dawn," part of Césaire's 1946 collection *Miraculous Weapons*: "*les fougues* of vivid flesh / with summers spread from the cerebral cortex / have lashed the contours of the earth."[15] The common twentieth-century French meaning of *fougue* is "energy" or "spirit," which would make the line "the energies of vivid flesh." But in this term, Césaire enacts what Anthony Reed calls a "play of outmoded vocabulary," of "historical reconstitution," because the noun *fougue* in seventeenth-century French was understood to be a mast that supported a ship's sail. Césaire's line takes on another valence altogether: "the masts of vivid flesh [*chair*] / . . . / have lashed [*flagellé*] the contours of the earth."[16] And if the "mast" is a metonym for the ship itself, we arrive at an allusion to the slave ship, which in turn leads to an association of "flesh" and "lash" with the violent image of a slave being beaten. As with so many other words and turns of phrase in his poetry, Césaire reshapes a relatively banal term to the contours of black experience.

In Césaire's oeuvre there is perhaps no term more contorted or politicized than *nègre*. "Since there was shame in the word *nègre* we then reclaimed [it]," he explained. "There was in us a will of defiance, a violent affirmation."[17] Indeed, this transformation has a particular history in the

French language. Brent Edwards explains how *nègre* assumed a connotation of alterity, becoming a synonym of *esclave* (slave) around the time that the French began their involvement in the Atlantic slave trade in the seventeenth century. Edwards traces the first positive use of *nègre* to "Le Mot Nègre," an essay written by the Senegalese Marxist Lamine Senghor, published in 1927 in the Paris-based newspaper *La Voix des Nègres*. "You have tried to use this word as a tool to divide," Senghor writes, excoriating the French public. "But we use it as a rallying cry. . . . It is our *race nègre* that we want to guide on the path of total liberation from its suffering under the yoke of enslavement."[18]

Césaire's particular innovation, however, comes in his poetic contortions of the word *nègre*, which produce a kind of indistinguishability between its shameful and liberatory valences. These mutations of the term are featured in the final pages of the *Notebook* as the tone of emancipatory exhilaration approaches its climax. Césaire establishes the term's stereotypically inferior meaning through irony and hyperbole—"The whites say he was a good *nègre*, a really good *nègre*, the good *nègre* to his good master / I say hurrah!"—before he transforms the even more pejorative plural term *négraille*: "The seated *négraille* / unexpectedly standing [*debout*] / . . . / standing in the wind / standing under the sun / standing in the blood / standing / and / free." It's as if the act of this collective figure physically lifting its body *debout*—emphasized through anaphora—switches the code of *négraille*, transforming it into a term of exultation and striving. Césaire then returns to *nègre* in the final three stanzas, galvanizing energy from the reshaped signification as he builds a sense of becoming and anticipation of flight: "Come to me my dances / my bad *nègre* dances / . . . / the it-is-beautiful-and-good-and-legitimate-to-be-a-*nègre* dance."[19] Through his own method of surrealist "bending," employing satire, hyperbole, and repetition, Césaire transfigures the term in a matter of stanzas.

If Sartre once identified Césaire's surrealist-inflected négritude as a kind of "becoming," a "perpetual going-beyond," he very well could have said the same about Lam's approach.[20] In conversation with Gerardo Mosquera in 1980, Lam described how, after fleeing to Paris from fascist Spain in the late 1930s, a "new world began to surface": "I had carried all of this in my subconscious, and by allowing myself to produce automatic painting, especially by means of that unexpected drawing whereby one does not know what one is going to paint, this strange world started to flow out of me."[21] "I could act as a trojan horse," he said elsewhere, "that would spew forth hallucinating figures with the power to surprise, to disturb the dreams of the exploiters."[22] As with Césaire, surrealism was an initial tool to find in himself ideas and images that would undercut the existing order.

But Lam's style was in transition between 1939, the year Césaire's *Notebook* was first published, and 1943, when the Cuban translation of the poem appeared with Lam's illustrations. Prior to the eight months he spent in the South of France awaiting transit back to Cuba in 1940–1941, Lam painted portraits, landscapes, and still lifes heavily influenced by Cézanne, Matisse, and especially the cubist forms of Picasso, his mentor while in Paris. Leaning into automatic painting and drawing, his style transformed in Marseille over the course of his collaborations with Breton, Max Ernst, and other surrealists, a shift that's unmistakable in the six ink and graphite illustrations Lam drew for Breton's *Fata Morgana* (1942). In these images we still find some angular cubist forms, but the departure is in the surrealist hybrid figures: beings at once human, plant, beast, and bird. Nipples, stars, and small reptiles emerge from human heads. Grimacing gazes and jutting spikes and spears seem to register the fear and contingency of the world-historical moment as Lam and his collaborators awaited the Emergency Rescue Committee's West Indies–bound ship. Importantly, the streaming hair, the multi-creatures, and the stars and crescent moons also prefigure the drawings Lam would produce in 1942 and 1943 for Césaire's *Notebook*, all of which are constitutive elements of the fugitive temporality that Lam draws out of the poem. Like the flowing hair in the *Fata Morgana* images that Lowery Stokes Sims reads as simultaneously "water, beard, hair, and the tail or mane of a horse," the lines of streaming hair in Lam's *Notebook* drawings can be read from multiple surrealist perspectives.[23]

In the following years, now in Cuba, Lam moved toward what he called "expressing the negro spirit" of his island, establishing his own genre of surrealism in a series of oil and gouache paintings.[24] In these, plant life and the human female figure merge in a syncretic excavation of Afrocuban culture and history, establishing an aesthetic that subverts the logics of (neo) colonialism and, in Lam's words, locates "black cultural objects in terms of their own landscape and in relation to their own world."[25] In paintings such as *Light of the Forest* (1942) and *The Murmur* (1943), female forms blend with tobacco leaves, their legs doubling as tall stalks of sugarcane; faces resemble African masks, some with jutting double horns; round breasts and buttocks approximate hanging fruit. *The Jungle* (1943), Lam's best-known work, magnifies and pluralizes these elements on a massive scale, with deep greens and yellows making the distinction between plant and human that much more indecipherable. The cane, the breasts, the masks combine to form a sprawling constellation of Cuba's violent history, cultural vitality, and mythical pre-slavery pasts. If, for Kobena Mercer, Lam ushers us into a "realm of becoming" in which "elements can be dislocated and relocated to unfix established codes," then we might say that crucial elements in *The Jungle* become even more dislocated and relocated when they appear almost identically in Lam's *Notebook* drawings, sutured into the codes of Césaire's epic.[26] After all, Lam's work on *The Jungle* effectively coincided with the production of the three drawings for the 1943 *Notebook* translation. The breasts, the masks, the horns, the crescent shapes, the vacant eyes, and the fusions of human and plant travel between *The Jungle* and the *Notebook*, between Antillean worlds, between historical dramas.

As with Césaire, African cultures and mythologies had a formative influence on Lam. James Arnold rightly suggests that Césaire saw in Lam "a vision of négritude close to his own" and that, in the work of both, Africa is a "construction, an ideal built on an abyss."[27] Lam had been introduced to African art and sculpture in Paris, but his return to Cuba brought him back to Afrocuban culture. Ethnologist Lydia Cabrera encouraged Lam to draw on his childhood experiences with his godmother, Montonica Wilson, who had trained him in the ideas and rituals of Santería, the syncretic Afrocuban religion heavily influenced by Yoruba cosmology.[28] As Lam deepens his négritude-surrealist aesthetic in the mid- to late 1940s and 1950s, we find increasing references and allusions in his work to different Afrocuban cosmologies and, following his 1944 trip with Breton to Haiti, to Vodun. His *Altar for Elegua* (1944) and *The Wedding* (1947), for instance, depict altar-like settings with candles, horseshoes, double bull horns, and egg-like forms, suggesting a concatenation of Afro-Caribbean cosmological influence. The horseshoes and bull horns are of particular interest here: the former associated with Ogun (the god of metalwork in the Yoruba cosmology and various Afro-Caribbean religions), the latter with Oya (the Yoruba orisha of death and rebirth). Both appear in Lam's second *Notebook* drawing.

Moving through the 1950s and beyond, Lam's work would expand and evolve—from more oil paintings and drawings to new forms and media such as etching and ceramics—much like Césaire's work would expand to new plays, poetry collections, political writing, and, of course, to electoral politics. For now, though, I want to stay in this period from the late 1930s to the mid-1940s to work through the nuances of their initial collaboration. I want to use Lam's sketches as a kind of multi-vectored, hallucinatory map of the embodied temporality of Césaire's *Notebook*, the first component of which is the temporal structure of the poet's discourse of corporeal wounding. In the development of the poem, Césaire must reckon with this wounded flesh of blackness before he can look outward toward a new, disalienated body. It's from the wound that his utopia begins its phenomenal trajectory to the outside of subjection.

SEDIMENTED WOUNDS

If Lam's *Retorno* cover image gestures to a devastated body, his second drawing is no mere gesture. Citing and extending disparate vectors of the poem, the centerpiece of Lam's three sketches features a multispecies beast with the head of a horned bull and a body that almost looks human, as if stooped over on all fours with exhaustion. The violence in the image centers on the beast's second head, having fallen limp with blood, it appears, pouring from its neck, its eyes stunned just like the bull's eyes, as if this creature has just witnessed or experienced an atrocity. Among other scenes, this devastated being is reminiscent of the moment in the *Notebook* when a group of captive enslaved Africans crowded in the hold of a ship are likened to dying beasts of burden: "the death gasps of the dying," "the baying of a woman in labor."[29] The blood spewing out of the creature's body, I'll show, points to a sustained temporality of wounding in the early portions of the *Notebook*.

Before unraveling Césaire's discourse of wounding, I want to lay out my theoretical framework for working through questions of the body in the poem. Although I've alluded to it already, a closer look at Hortense Spillers's distinction between the flesh and the body, between the "captive and liberated subject-positions," is useful here. The flesh, she suggests in "Mama's Baby, Papa's Maybe," "registers the wound" of the African captive, representing the "primary narrative" in its "seared, divided, ripped-apartness, riveted to the ship's hold, fallen, or 'escaped' overboard." This wounded flesh forms a kind of "hieroglyphics," a series of "undecipherable markings on the captive body . . . whose severe disjunctures come to be hidden to the cultural seeing by skin color." And this hieroglyphics, she continues, has the potential to be passed from generation to generation as a kind of inscription of trauma transmitted through time, forming a distinct cultural code and sociality: "These lacerations, woundings, fissures, tears, scars, openings, ruptures, lesions, rendings, and punctures of the flesh create the distance between what I would designate a cultural *vestibularity* and *culture*, whose state apparatus, including judges, attorneys, 'owners,' 'souldrivers,' 'overseers,' and 'men of God,' apparently colludes with a protocol of 'search and destroy.'"[30] Blackness as wounded flesh, for Spillers, is marked by its "vestibular" position to the law and dominant culture: as near to, but decidedly outside of, normative subjectivity and personhood. The wounded flesh sets blackness apart through its "undecipherable" language and the social life formed in this undecipherability.

For his part, Fred Moten locates an analogous ontological positionality of blackness in the "nearness and distance between *Dasein* and things . . . off to the side of what lies between subjects and objects."[31] This liminal space, for him, is the space of fugitive movement, the space of persistent flight toward an unrecognizable form of being: "The lived experience of blackness is . . . a constant demand for an ontology of disorder, an ontology of dehiscence."[32] Moten's language of "constant demand," as I read it, is proleptic. That "ontology of dehiscence," bursting with refusal, is something to be desired, something yet to be lived. Indeed, Alexander Weheliye effectively reads Spillers's "cultural vestibularity" as similarly proleptic, as "simultaneously a tool of dehumanization and a relational vestibule to alternate ways of being." The wounded flesh, in other words, is the marker of subjection, but it also carries with it the potential for transcendence. In its generative capacity, the flesh "provides a stepping stone toward new genres of [the] human."[33] Like Moten's language of "constant demand," this "stepping stone toward" signals an anticipation of new life, that proleptic sense of being toward ontological transfiguration. The flesh occupies the precarious threshold separating annihilation and regeneration, the end of the world and a new order of being.

This fleshly dialectic of catastrophe and utopian flight resonates throughout Césaire's *Notebook*. If, as most Césaire scholars agree, the poem's structure can be separated into three implied parts—(1) the swelling of alienation in the return to Martinique, (2) the descent into introspection and a mythical Africa, and (3) the ascension toward a new life and world—it would not be incorrect to say that the first third focuses on registering the historical and experiential subjection of the flesh, and the final two thirds pivot to the fugitive utopian capacity of the flesh.[34] But this would be an oversimplification, given how violence and desire ebb and flow throughout the poem. The reading that follows, then, is less determined by the confines of the poem's implied sections than by the locations of Césaire's corporeal references. Similar to Weheliye's understanding of vestibular flesh, Césaire's hieroglyphics of the flesh is at once devastatingly violent and utopian.[35] And this dialectic of the flesh is very much evident in Lam's sprawling second drawing. Next to the blood-spewing wound in the beast's back are two huge leaf wings poised to lift this being out of this world, toward the glimmering star hovering over the stooped creature, the star bearing breasts with the promise of new life. As Lam's image suggests, the violence of the flesh is a crucial component of the poem's utopian impulse. We might even say that without his account of the historically wounded black body and the vestibular collectivity the wound instantiates, the vitality of Césaire's utopia would not be lost. As with my reading of *Sula* and *Beloved*, we need to unravel the *Notebook*'s temporality of wounding to fully grasp the contours of its fugitive time.

Part of what distinguishes Césaire's aesthetics here is his ascription of historical and phenomenological time in the wound. Through nouns, epithets, and their corresponding verbs, Césaire articulates a wounded flesh in which time ceaselessly expands as a kind of continually violent act. This temporality has the effect of perpetually deepening the wound, bringing the historical trauma on the black body to the fore of his poetics. The poet does this by describing literal bodies, but also myriad metaphors that stand in for the body, such as the land, the town, and even water. His language of the wounded flesh is constantly on the run, shuttling between metaphors and allusions. Take the poem's second stanza: "At the end of daybreak, the extreme, deceptive desolate eschar on the wound of the waters; the martyrs who do not bear witness; the flowers of blood that fade and scatter in the useless wind like the screeches of babbling parrots; an aged life mendaciously smiling, its lips opened by disaffected agonies; an aged poverty [*misère*] rotting under the sun, silently; an aged silence bursting with tepid pustules."[36] The eschar, wound, blood, lips, and pustules all evoke images of life—indeterminately human and animal, like the beast figure in Lam's second sketch. The attributes of the body in this passage are not just described but are also enumerated, as if the stanza were cataloging its devastations. And in this catalog is a coursing, phenomenological sense of time. The first clause here appears to occupy a suspended moment in time in its verblessness, yet the Latin-derived "eschar"—a dry, dark scab on the skin—implies a passage of time, that the "wound" has eroded the body (here, the body as *water*), and that healing is far from guaranteed, given the epithets "deceptive" and "desolate." "Rotting" carries with it a phenomenological sense of festering flesh, of time deepening the wound further and further, as does the phrase "tepid pustule," with pus accumulating over time, filling a blister in the flesh to its breaking point. And the sense of corporeal decay deepens further in the last three clauses through anaphora ("an aged") and the sense of continual action in the gerunds "rotting" and "bursting." In just one stanza, Césaire creates a network of bodily metaphors—the body of water, of a smiling person, of poverty and silence personified—all of which bear a certain hieroglyphics of violence. Time courses through their collective flesh—the collectivity that occupies the vestibule of blackness—as a kind of wasting away, as if time itself, as in Morrison's fiction, were the instrument of violence making the wound that continually eats away at life.

The wounded flesh and its phenomenological temporality are sprawling in the *Notebook*, with the body effectively migrating across the text from metaphor to metaphor. The two most persistent are the "town" and the "land," which become so entwined as to nearly become a single porous metaphor. This entwining begins in the first few pages with the iconic town "sprawled flat": "At the end of daybreak, this inert town and its beyond of lepers, of consumption, of famines, of fears crouched in the ravines, of fears perched in the trees . . . of piled up fears and their fumaroles of anguish."[37] The "inert town and its beyond" take on the debilitation of a formerly healthy, mobile body. The terms "lepers," "consumption," and "famines" all carry a phenomenological sense of the body deteriorating over time: leprosy in its effects on the skin and the nervous system; consumption, or tuberculosis, damaging the respiratory system; and famine as a kind of extreme temporal elongation of hunger and malnutrition that erodes the body like a festering internal wound. This latter term recalls the two-headed iguana's bared teeth and protruding ribs in Lam's cover image, the emaciated creature scanning about for elusive prey, having perhaps experienced an extended hunger analogous to Césaire's "inert town." With the metaphor of the body effectively fused to the environment, the *morne*—doubling as the Antillean French term for "hill" but also, aptly, as the French adjective meaning "bleak" or "dismal"—becomes the next prominent corporeal metaphor: "its malarial blood routs [*met en déroute*] the sun with its overheated pulse . . . slowly vomiting out its human fatigue, the morne alone and its blood shed, the morne and its bandages of shade, the morne and its ditches of fear, the morne and its great hands of wind."[38] The morne—repeated like "fear" above—takes on the explicit bodily elements of hands, blood, and fatigue. Disease courses through the blood of this morne body, spreading throughout over time. The flesh of the morne has been wounded, and the passing of time has brought the shedding of blood and a bandaging in a seemingly futile effort to stop the bleeding. The town, land, and different parts of the surrounding environment take on attributes of a body slowly wasting away as time elapses. Césaire's aesthetic opens us not to a static account of the hieroglyphics of the flesh but to a phenomenological account of those woundings as they deepen over time.

These *Notebook* passages open up multiple readings of Lam's second sketch. The image's two-headed figure appears most evidently to be a bull, but its stooped curvature might be read in other ways. Its outline, for one, almost looks like the oval shape of Martinique itself, which Césaire refers to derisively in the poem as "this little ellipsoidal nothing": the creature's head corresponds to Grande-Rivière and Mount Pelée at the northern end of the island, and the fallen additional head and posterior hand correspond to the inward-angled extensions of Cap Salomon and Sainte-Anne in the South.[39] But really what these previous passages from the *Notebook* most reveal is the likeness of the curvature of Lam's stooped creature and the morne. This creature literally has plants and leaves growing out of its back, but the blood coursing from the neck of its second head is not unlike the morne's coursing malarial blood or the bloodied wound that requires bandaging. Lam captures that deepening phenomenal temporality of wounding here in multiple ways: in the blood that seems to continually spatter from the creature, in the scab-like half-circles to the right of that spewing blood that evoke a clotting as a passage of time, and even in the hair of the fallen head that could itself be read as blood streaming onto the ground—or, indeed, streaming out into the Atlantic, if we read Lam's beast as the ellipsoidal outline of the island. Those streaming lines of blood and/or hair could also correspond to the "human fatigue" that the morne is "vomiting out," and the creature's massive hands holding and caring for the wounded head could be the morne's "great hands of wind" enacting that "bandaging." Lam, we might say, provides a shape-shifting, hallucinatory map of wounding in the poem, simultaneously evoking Césaire's phenomenally coursing poetic images while overlaying and extending them to create a new constellation of wreckage.

Continuing with the poem, along with this sense of phenomenological time is a larger sense of historical time in the wound, notably in the poem's actual human bodies. Take for instance Césaire's harrowing experiential account of the middle passage: "I hear [*J'entends*] coming up from the hold the enchained curses, the gasps of the dying, the noise of someone thrown into the sea . . . the baying of a woman in labor . . . the scrape of fingernails seeking throats. . . ."[40] The sedimented temporality in this passage hinges on the auditory, on what it means to *hear*. The poet/speaker is the one who hears, but what he hears is centuries removed: these are sounds articulated no later than the nineteenth century, yet the speaker "hears" them from his mid-twentieth-century moment of enunciation. What the speaker hears, we might say, is an audible trace of collective traumatic memory. Césaire's diction makes this clear: the chosen verb "to hear" (*entendre*) indicates the ear's perception of a sound—of the sound object, as it were, moving toward the subject—whereas the verb "to listen" (*écouter*) would have implied a more active attention to sound by the listener. Césaire's use of *entendre*, then, signifies an unexpected sound, one that rises up spectrally from another's past to rupture the speaker's experience of the lived (sonic) present. It resembles a kind of auditory register of the transgenerational transmission of the hieroglyphics of the flesh. "We might well ask," Spillers suggests, "if this phenomenon of marking and branding actually 'transfers' from one generation to another."[41]

But crucially, history in these auditory traces erupts into the speaker's present as phenomenal unfolding. He *hears* the undulating sounds of his ancestors' wounding: their chains repeatedly clanking against the steps, the pulse of their final heaving breaths. All of these spectral sonic traces are overlaid, swirling in the speaker's consciousness. And all of these phenomenological layers are further sedimented by the *durée* of historical time. Moreover, in this passage Césaire has buried these bodies under multiple layers of sensorial distance from the reader: the *sound* of the body instantiates the *materiality* of the body, but that sound is registered *lexically* on the page. Instead of silencing these bodies, however, this threat of (historical) erasure produces the opposite effect: it raises the flesh to the fore of the reader's consciousness, vividly rendering the image of what Spillers so graphically describes as the "lacerations, woundings, and fissures" inscribed onto black flesh. In this instance the body's absence marks its haunting presence.

Before moving to the poem's sense of anticipatory desire, I briefly want to turn to one of the more famous literal bodies in the poem. The descriptive account of the tramway nègre marks what Gregson Davis calls the poem's "nadir of being," the lowest point of the speaker's self-loathing and accountings of black subjection, before the poem shifts to a sense of profound humility and utopian desire.[42] Unsurprisingly, this figure is not unlike the stooped creature in Lam's second *Notebook* drawing, with its broad shoulders and huge arms—eliciting yet another way to read Lam's multi-being. The speaker, looking back on his time in metropolitan France, remembers with "cowardice" his loathsome appraisal of a "pongo"-looking nègre with "gigantic legs" sitting in a streetcar:

> His nose which looked like a drifting peninsula and even his négritude discolored as a result of untiring tawing. And the tawer was Poverty. . . .
> He was a gangly nègre without rhythm or measure. . . .
> A nègre whose eyes rolled a bloodshot weariness. . . .
> Poverty, without a question, had knocked itself out to finish him off.
> It had dug the socket, had painted it with a rouge of dust mixed with rheum.
> It had stretched an empty space between the solid hinge of the jaw and bone of an old tarnished cheek. Had planted over it the shiny stakes of a two- or three-day beard. Had panicked his heart, bent his back.[43]

Time can be measured here phenomenologically and historically. Poverty has wounded this body: it has incrementally eroded tissue, muscle, and bone, but this incrementalism has clearly taken place over the decades of this man's life. In this brief passage, in other words, Césaire demonstrates how the micro-intervals of phenomenological time expand into the larger intervals of historical time. As time has accumulated from moment to moment, day to day, year to year, Poverty has "dug" at this body, "stretched" it, "bent" it. The tramway nègre's skin has been worked over, or "tawed," like a piece of leather that is softened and rendered pliable through repeated beatings. Between the purposeful capitalization of "Poverty" (as if it were a given name) and the term's personification (as if it were enacting violence), Césaire effectively transforms the term into a kind of slave-driver figure who has steadily beaten and devastated this man's black body over years, ceaselessly deepening the wounds in his flesh.

That we can see a trace of this "pongo" figure in Lam's stooped creature demonstrates how Lam's surrealist drawing, like the *Notebook*'s traces of the body, is constantly on the move, mutating into different figurations depending on one's location in the poem. This is one of the crucial functions of Lam's three sketches. Their visual shape-shifting and multivalence signal how wounding in Césaire's epic moves stealthily across different metaphors and literal bodies, sometimes so subtly and fleetingly as to be unrecognizable. The poem's wounded body, we might say, is a fugitive figure in itself, shuttling in and out of the literal and the figurative, never settling into a single form, always moving from one to the next in an unpredictable projection. One can read the poem's language of the body as revealing a multitude of singular bodies, yet there's a way to read the many literal and figurative references to the body *cumulatively*, as if every time we encounter a trace of the human body in the text, each of those traces adds on to those that precede it, forming a simultaneously collective and singular image of the wounded black body, one that constantly changes shape. Lam's second *Retorno* sketch crystallizes this simultaneous singularity and multiplicity. And as this fugitive wounded body moves about, changing its guise in every stanza, the wound itself continually deepens in time. Historical time and phenomenological time overlay in the wound, creating a kind of temporal sedimentation that pushes the cut farther into the flesh. The deeper the cut—in time and in the flesh—the greater the sense of solidarity, of being with, among the *Notebook*'s many bodies, and the more, too, that these traces of the body accumulate to constitute an ever-transforming single being that resides in that vestibular position of blackness. It's this wounded collectivity that looks outward toward release. From this multifarious wounded body emerges a desire for new life, a leaning into the beyond.

FUGITIVE BODIES

This wounding reaches a critical juncture a third of the way through the poem. "By an unexpected and regenerative inner revolution," the speaker says, "I now honor my repugnant ugliness." Césaire shifts from the catalog of negative tropes to an effusive sense of humility and outward vision. Instead of disavowing the wound he has spent so many stanzas excavating, he embraces it: "I accept . . . totally, without reservation . . . my race that no ablution of hyssop mixed with lilies could purify / my race gnawed with blemishes."[44] With the speech act "I accept," the "blemishes" on this body effectively become generative. Historical debilitation becomes the potentiality for new life, and the deepening of time in the wound becomes a resource for anticipatory desire. The vestibularity of blackness is now directed outward.

We find this reconfigured wound throughout the *Notebook*'s final two thirds and indeed throughout Césaire's oeuvre. The corporeal metaphor of the "land"—earlier in the poem described as "malarial" and "hideous"— becomes an affirmative trope of deepening rootedness: "[My négritude] plunges into the red flesh of the earth." Even the term "wound" becomes generative: "And see the tree of our hands! / it turns for all, the wounds incised in its trunk."[45] The wounded tree body, here, as Abiola Irele notes, is a reference to the rubber tree: "Just as some plants . . . thrive on incisions made to their trunk to produce sap, so the black race is seen as having derived spiritual benefit from its painful historical experience."[46] But it's not merely "spiritual benefit" that the wound produces. It also generates a sense of outward desire, a kind of utopian anticipatory desire for disalienated life. We glimpse this desire in Césaire's play *A Season in the Congo*: "Comrades and brothers in combat," Lumumba exclaims, "may all our wounds be transformed into udders!"[47] Here the wound becomes a source of nourishment, a living organ from which to gather strength to move forward. Indeed, this is an idea that Wifredo Lam's second sketch draws out of the *Notebook* and brings to life, not just in the leaf wings and the moon-faced angel figure rising from the wounded creature, but also in that angel's breasts and in the full breasts of the star toward which it rises. As in *A Season*, Lam signals a certain proleptic function of the wounded flesh in the *Notebook*, where the "udder" is that which propels one toward new life rather than being the end in itself. The wound in the poem, we might say, "open[s] up imaginative worlds," as Francesca Royster frames the work of fugitivity.[48]

The most basic formation of this corporeal anticipation in the *Notebook* is a pervasive discourse on hunger, a discourse not unlike Ernst Bloch's on satiation in volume one of *The Principle of Hope*. In the context of his larger critique of psychoanalysis, Bloch suggests that what he calls the "self-preservation drive"—hunger being its "most obvious expression"—is the "most universal" among the drives, including the libido. The crucial connection to Césaire, however, is the relation that Bloch establishes between this fundamental drive and utopia: "The self-preservation drive ultimately means the appetite to hold ready more appropriate and more authentic states for our unfolding self, unfolding only in and as solidarity. . . . Our self always remains, with its hunger and the variable extensions of this hunger, still open, moved, extending itself." Hunger, in other words, is that which reaches out toward fulfillment. It's a physiological drive toward satiation but also a psychological desire for Bloch. And he understands both of these registers phenomenologically. Hunger "unfolds"; it "extends itself" in a kind of outward projection seeking that ideal physical and affective state. Furthermore, Bloch's self-preservation drive is a collective one, implying that true satiation cannot be attained in isolation. Like Césaire's poem, Bloch's notion of hunger—and indeed his larger utopian project—is about disalienation, attaining one's authentic self and being-in-the-world, however (im)possible that may be. And similar to Césaire, Bloch is unequivocal that this most fundamental of drives emerges from the materiality of the body: "The drive-instinct belongs to the economy of the individual body and is employed in so far as it belongs to it, in so far as the body does its business, fleeing from what damages it, searching for what preserves it."[49] At its most elemental level, the *Notebook* is concerned with this very idea of the body "fleeing from what damages it, searching for what preserves it."

A discourse on self-preservation commences on the first page of Césaire's poem, and it's woven in and among the poet's discourse of wounding and devastation. Like Bloch, Césaire's primary mode of the self-preservation drive is hunger. And, perhaps unsurprisingly, the poet's ascription of hunger shuttles between a literal human hunger and a metaphorical hunger of the land:

> for his voice gets lost in the swamp of hunger,
> and there is nothing, really nothing to squeeze out of this little rascal,
> other than a hunger which can no longer climb to the rigging of his voice,
> a hunger heavy and cowardly,
> a hunger buried in the depths of the Hunger of this famished morne.[50]

The "hunger" in this stanza is clearly embedded in the collective wounded body that Césaire spends much of the poem exploring. We don't get the outright utopian sensibility from the term that we find in Bloch. Instead, we have the sense that the hunger (of the child and the morne) is so longstanding that it threatens to deepen into starvation, a sense crystallized in the protruding ribs of the iguana figure in Lam's *Retorno* cover image. But there is still an outward projection toward satiation in Césaire's use of the term, however faint, particularly because he explicitly uses "starvation" elsewhere to articulate a kind of temporal elongation of hunger such that the body has begun to waste away. Starvation, in those instances, is akin to the sedimented wound discussed earlier. But the "heaviness" and even the "cowardliness" of the hunger in the penultimate line of this passage still imply an outward orientation, that drive toward the phenomenal moment of satiation and release, however Sisyphean it may seem here.

Just when it seems the speaker has succumbed to nihilism as hunger threatens to deepen into starvation, Christmas arrives. These few stanzas are like an island of respite in this early part of the *Notebook*. Ecstatic, hopeful, and filled with food, drink, and collective belonging, they evoke something akin to the transient ease in Morrison's early novels. Those ephemeral pockets gesture to the (im)possible, serving as reminders, promises even, of a more sustained, even permanent, coming release:

> It had first come in, Christmas did, with a tingling of desires, a thirst for new tenderness, a burgeoning of imprecise dreams. . . .

> At evening an unintimidating little church that would benevolently make room for the laughter, the whispers, the secrets . . . and the village turns into a bouquet of singing, and you feel good inside, and you eat well, and you drink heartily and there are blood sausages . . . and steaming coffee and sugared anise and milk punch, and the liquid sun of rums, and all sorts of good things which drive your taste buds wild or distill them to the point of ecstasy or spin them with fragrances, and you laugh, and you sing. . . .
> And not only do the mouths sing, but the hands, but the feet, but the buttocks, but the genitals, and the entire being [*la créature tout entière*] liquefies into sounds, voices, and rhythm.
> At the summit of its ascent, joy bursts like a cloud. The songs don't stop, but roll now uneasy and heavy through the valleys of fear, the tunnels of anguish and the fires of hell.[51]

Hunger and the "thirst for new tenderness" are momentarily sated here; Christmas provides temporary relief from the traumas of poverty and history. The sensorium enables the village's annual collective escape: the taste and smell of the most decadent food and drink, the sounds of laughter and singing constituting what Damien Sojoyner calls fugitivity's "alternative social vision."[52] This multisensory satiation courses phenomenologically and "liquifies" their "entire being," their "*créature tout entière*"—very much an embodied, material category that carries affective registers. However, Christmas vanishes as quickly as it came. The "joy bursts," and anxiety and fear return as the sight of ecstasy's end nears. Césaire then proceeds with his catalog of the "town sprawled flat."

The words "hunger" and "thirst" continue to appear intermittently throughout the rest of the poem, scattered across Césaire's accounts of historical trauma and utopian longing. The implicit desire of these terms accumulates—adding on to the undercurrent utopian energy in fleeting releases and ecstasies such as the Christmas episode—creating a persistent anticipatory desire to take flight from the sufferings of the body. By the time we arrive at the "acceptance" section of the *Notebook*, hunger and thirst are directed toward a deeper utopian vision:

> what I want
> is for universal hunger
> for universal thirst
>
> to summon it free at last

>   to produce from its intimate closeness
>   the succulence of fruits.[53]

Here hunger and thirst resemble more closely Bloch's self-preservation drive, the "appetite to hold ready . . . more authentic states for our unfolding self." These terms for Césaire are expansive, generative, searching outward for an all-encompassing idea of freedom. Indeed, hunger is the most basic utopian impulse in the *Notebook*, one that emerges from deep within the wounded body. Hunger in the poem may seem faint at times, satiation may be only a temporary escape in the Christmas episode, but the self-preservation drive is undoubtedly the foundation of the anticipatory temporality in the poem. It's the bedrock of Césaire's formation of fugitive time, that desire to rid the body of traumatic debilitation, where the dream of the "succulence of fruits" lies not in an expansive, determinate future but in the "intimate closeness" of the phenomenal moment just beyond the now, when release may at last consume the body.

But hunger is only the prelude to a pervasive feeling of phenomenological becoming in the *Notebook*'s language of the body. Here I want to draw a direct connection between the outward orientation of hunger and the myriad other instances in which we find an analogous sense of growth, expansion, and outward movement located in the body. Like the wounded body, these latter instances of becoming are inscribed across a series of bodily metaphors, many of which, in one way or another, relate to the environment. It's as if the continual movement and growth of nature were superimposed onto the body itself, undergirding the force of the body's expansion. One brief example comes in the moment when the poet/speaker announces that his "[négritude] plunges into the red flesh of the soil / it plunges into the ardent flesh of the sky."[54] Here a personified, perhaps even embodied négritude reaches down into the earth and up into the sky, the present tense "plunge" enacting a kind of simultaneous movement of deepening rootedness and heightening flight into the cosmos. The image seems to shed a different light on Lam's second *Notebook* drawing, allowing us to read the beast's hoof and hands on the ground as "plunging" farther and farther into the "flesh of the soil" and its leaf wings as plunging it increasingly higher into the "flesh of the sky."

One of the richest of these instances of corporeal becoming in the *Notebook* comes toward its conclusion, when the speaker takes to prayer to address his desire for a new form of being. The body in this sequence transforms into a pirogue, a tree that's been dug out into a canoe that cuts through the sea:

> grant me on this diverse ocean
> the obstinacy of the proud pirogue
> and its marine vigor.
>
> See it advance rising and falling on the pulverized surge . . .
> the pirogue rears up under the attack of the swells, deviates for an instant,
> tries to flee, but the paddle's rough caress turns it,
> then it charges, a quivering runs along the wave's spine,
> the sea slobbers and rumbles
> the pirogue like a sleigh glides onto the sand.
>
> At the end of daybreak, my virile prayer:
>
> grant me pirogue muscles on this raging sea and the irresistible joy of the conch of good news![55]

Here the materiality of the pirogue is directly superimposed onto the body. The speaker requests the pirogue's "obstinacy" and "vigor" in these first lines, and its "muscles" in the final, initiating its metamorphosis. Outward movement and expansiveness are unequivocal in the present-tense verbs and infinitives: the pirogue body "advances" and "charges" through the water; it "deviates" and "flees," moving in and out of the undulating waves. With grace and ferocity, the body in this metaphor embarks upon a quest for release, constantly battling against that which threatens to destroy it. The pirogue's phenomenological movement through the sea is akin to the wounded body's phenomenological search for release from moment to moment, breath to breath, its perpetual outward drive toward an ever calmer, freer world. Bloch's notion of the self-preservation drive remains apt, that desire for "more authentic states for our unfolding self." It's also important to note that this scene is a structure of desire. The poet/speaker wishes, he *hopes* to be granted the power to undertake the journey. He is, in other words, living and imagining it proleptically, in advance, moving in his mind toward that moment of unburdening. And as the metaphor indicates, the body's journey is not linear or future oriented. Reaching those utopian shores, wherever and whenever they may be, is far from guaranteed, requiring constant deviations and tactics of escape that may spin one in circles along that outward path.

Another crucial expression of embodied anticipation in the *Notebook*—one with multiple valences that I want to highlight across the range of Césaire's poem and Lam's drawings—is gender and sexuality. Of these, perhaps the more evident is (anticipated) phallic climax, which in fact is alluded to in parts of the text and images that I've already touched on. Rather than any single instance, it's the assemblage of these different moments and representations that combine to produce a sense of phallic penetration and climax. Again, I see their assemblage as akin to a desire for transient relief, like the fleeting respite of the Christmas episode, that evinces a desire for a (more) permanent release from subjection. This is indeed much like that anticipated transient ecstasy I discussed in the previous chapter between Sethe and Paul D early in *Beloved*. The clearest representation of phallic climax is that secondary fallen head in Lam's second sketch, which I noted suggests a head with hair splayed out or, alternatively, a head that's been violently beaten and with blood pouring out. But if we step back to read it anew, we see something like the ejaculating glans of a penis. Lam captures this creature right at the height of climactic release, in the wake, presumably, of rising desire and anticipation. This reading is buttressed by its resonance with specific moments in the *Notebook*, particularly the penetrative image that Césaire gives us of négritude as it "plunges into the red flesh of the soil" and "plunges into the ardent flesh of the sky"—lines that earlier I read as a desire for rootedness in the land and flight into the cosmos. Given this reinterpretation, even that line late in the Christmas stanza—"At the peak of its ascent, joy burst like a cloud"—reads like a thinly veiled reference to the momentary relief of orgasm, and all the celebratory indulgence leading up to it as climbing desire. The latter is not necessarily phallic, but the "plunging" lines certainly are, as is Lam's spraying glans. What's also interesting about the assemblage of these different images is that they may be masculine, but they're not necessarily explicitly heterosexual, although perhaps a normative heterosexuality might be inferred. In other words, that which is plunged into, and that which brings Lam's penis to ejaculate, is ambiguous. What seems clear, though, is that a climactic and penetrative reading is made possible through this inter-animation of image and text.

As in the previous chapter, this discussion of sexual pleasure is complicated by the history of black subjection in the Americas. One of the more pertinent texts here is the often-overlooked short chapter, "Pleasure and Jouissance," in Glissant's *Caribbean Discourse*, where he presents a historically inflected theory of Martinican (hetero)sexuality.[56] To be outside the control of the master, the slave was forced to have "hidden" sexual encounters in the cane fields, where males quickly and violently penetrated females, Glissant suggests, drawing on a series of creole proverbs to support this claim. The result, historically, is both an "obsession with orgasm" and a kind of "short-circuiting" of pleasure, manifesting in a "violent and uncontrollable need to go immediately to the act with resolute impunity . . . annihilating the pleasure in the orgasm."[57] Glissant's account is not entirely inapt to Césaire and Lam's phallic images—especially if we consider those stalks of cane in Lam's *The Jungle* to be phallic—but Omise'eke Tinsley's trenchant critique of Glissant's chapter, as laden with misogyny and black queer gender phobia, is indispensable. In Glissant's framing, Tinsley argues, the enslaved male seeks a "fleeting sense of power," using his penis as a "tool-cum-weapon," and the "penetrated orifice becomes a site of powerlessness and degradation." Any kind of nonheterosexual, nonmasculinist, gender-nonconforming figuration becomes "an impossible subject in [Glissant's] black masculinist landscape." If Lam and Césaire's phallic representations fit Glissant's masculinist account to a degree, that would indeed reframe how we understand anticipatory desire and climax in their work, given that such anticipation is at best minimal in Glissant's framing. Read through Glissant's optic, it would suggest a kind of rush toward the momentary escape of climax, but devoid of pleasure, climax would perhaps not be a fleeting escape at all. However, I'm not convinced that Lam and Césaire's representations of sexuality should be exclusively read through this lens. As I'll show, Lam and Césaire's aesthetics of sexuality are more complicated and multivalent, corresponding, perhaps surprisingly, more with Tinsley's broader investigation: "If those who have penises do not have to use them as the machetes that slavery constrained them to do, they can develop not only different kinds of eroticism but also different vehicles of resistance; they can decolonize gender and sexuality otherwise."[58]

Before I move to these otherwise formations, I want to pan back out to pivot from the question of climax to Césaire and Lam's aesthetics of reproduction more broadly, which I also see as instrumental to the structure of fugitive time in the *Notebook*. Like the creatures in all three of Lam's images, with their testicles and breasts, the *Notebook*'s literal bodies are often sexed and in turn are stitched into a reproductive discourse that implies a desire for generational expansion. In contrast to the poem's *actual* representation of children, who tend to be consumed by the woundedness of blackness, these moments of birth and sex are proleptic in the *Notebook*, as if in anticipation of a (literal) new being that might bear less of the physical and affective burden of trauma. The (implied) child, in a way, signifies a kind of utopian desire for a break in Spillers's notion of the intergenerational transmission of trauma (the "hieroglyphics of the flesh"). The descendant assumes the strength and generativity of the historical wound without—or *with less of*—the traumatic weight of direct and continued subjection.

The desire for the next generation to inhabit less trauma is certainly not utopian, but it is, perhaps, when one reads this desire as an infinite line, a ceaseless succession of generations incrementally moving toward that horizon of (impossible) unburdening. We might think of the small child in Lam's second *Notebook* sketch—which, depending on how we read it, is either resting on the back of the bull creature or tethered in some way to the winged moonfaced angel figure—as a literalization of this implied being, this utopian generational extension, in Césaire. This small figure is covered with, even protected by, leaves and vegetal growth, indicating that it's part of the poem's discourse of new life, not wounding. As I show below, to return to Tinsley, what most distinguishes Césaire's reproductive aesthetic is the flux between normative and nonnormative sexual formations. The unexpected fluctuation of reproductive roles and sexually specific physiology throughout the poem produces a utopian structure of time that cuts against linearity, creating a kind of alternative temporality of and begat by queerness.

Perhaps the most conspicuous images of reproductive sexual specificity in the poem, however, are the seemingly normative tropes of masculinity and femininity. Take the second stanza of the speaker's "prayer" discussed earlier: "And here at the end of daybreak my virile prayer / . . . / make me into a man of germination / make me into the executor of these lofty works / the time has come to gird one's loins like a valiant man."[59] To be sure, "virility" and "germination" imply a heteronormative articulation of the masculine, as do the connotations of power and dominance in the man's role as the producer, or "executor," of that which is generated. Césaire adds a similar gesture to heteronormative reproduction in the 1947 expanded edition of the *Notebook*, published by Brentano's of New York: "and you star please from your luminous foundation draw lemurian being of man's unfathomable sperm / the undared form / that the trembling woman's body carries such an ore!"[60] Here, again, the masculine sperm produces the "undared form," and the woman brings that germination to fruition. On numerous occasions Césaire's reproductive imagery appears decidedly normative. Man plays the role of the sower, woman plays the role of gestator, and together they produce a kind of heteronormatively generated being.

The other half of this dialectic, the moments of queerness, doesn't appear in the *Notebook* until the 1947 Brentano's edition—though Césaire completed the manuscript for this second edition in 1944—approximately one year after the release of the Cuban translation. There's a curious resonance between Lam's second drawing—if we read it in yet another way—and the queer passages in the Brentano's edition of the *Notebook*. Lam's images may very well have influenced Césaire's well-known revisions that resulted in a significantly expanded, and queerer, poem in 1947. A certain queerness emerges from that second drawing when we consider the relation between the leaf-protected child and that beast. What if the image were depicting that horned bull—an animal normatively considered male—giving birth to that child? Or, to complicate it even more, what if those lines pouring from the neck of the second head were read, alternatively, as blood, ejaculation, and even amniotic fluid? We arrive at a queer image indeed. We're left with either some kind of two-headed male animal that has given birth to a rabbit-eared child, a single-headed beast both ejaculating and giving birth, or a two-headed being that's both male *and* female, where each head represents a sex. In the latter case, the collapsed position of the second head might indicate exhaustion from labor. This is precisely the kind of surrealist-inflected queerness that appears in scattered traces in Césaire's 1947 revision, a queerness that in turn forms a crucial valence of Césaire's larger structure of fugitive time. Although this queer inter-animation between Lam and the poet remains speculative in the absence of any explicit acknowledgment of it, the possibility is only strengthened when Sergio Quintata asks, "In the corrections of the *Cahier* and in the introduction of new fragments, is there no dialogue with the work of Lam?"[61] The evidence that Quintata cites is the influence of Haitian religious practices on both in the mid-1940s—particularly Lam's 1943 *The Jungle* and the iconic snaking charming "voum rooh oh" section Césaire added to the 1947 *Notebook*. Though speculative, Quintata's query supports the possibility that Lam's work, including the images he drew for the Cuban translation, may have influenced Césaire's reworkings of the poem.

And so we come to the queerness in the 1947 Brentano's edition that stands alongside those seemingly heteronormative representations that remain in the poem through the final 1956 *Présence Africaine* edition. Similar to Lam's representations of sexuality, Césaire's expression of sexual difference beginning with the Brentano's publication comes to resemble his approach to the poetic image: "A can be not-A," which in turn produces "strange cities, extraordinary landscapes, worlds that are twisted, crushed, torn apart."[62] The poet at times turns sexual specificity on its head, "twisting" and "tearing apart" normative formations with his négritude-surrealist aesthetic. In other words, alongside Césaire's heteronormativity is a decided break from heterosexual reproductivity. Consider these lines at the end of the poem's catalog of black pathology in the Brentano's *Notebook*: "I am forcing the vitelline membrane that separates me from myself / I am forcing the great waters which girdle me with blood."⁶³ In the first person, the speaker—understood to be male in the poem—wills his own (re)birth, "forcing" the protective layer of his womb to break. Disalienation becomes a literal act of generating a new being from his own body, a being at once *self* and *other* not at all unlike the male birthing figure in Lam's second 1943 sketch. Similar to his poetic image contortions, here Césaire produces a "strange" and "twisted" image. Its queerness lies in its simultaneous singularity and multiplicity, and in the seemingly autonomous reproductive role assumed by the masculine. Framed another way, we might think of it as a kind of ungendered figure. And there is, I should say, a phenomenal temporality of emergence in this short passage, primarily in the verbs "force" and "separate," but also the coursing movement of the "great waters." This flowing bloody water refers to amniotic fluid—which our queer reading of Lam's image evokes—but it also recalls, as Irele suggests, the waters of the Atlantic forcibly crossed by the poet's ancestors.⁶⁴ Indeed, this child is fugitively ahead of itself: it "forces" against the waters, striving to escape them, but the waters consume and "girdle" it as if its very being depended on that girdling. It's a position analogous to what Tina Campt identifies as the fugitive desire to create "new possibilities for living lives that refuse the regulatory regime from which they could not be removed."⁶⁵ This is the queer fugitive time that emerges from Césaire's négritude aesthetic.

This step into queer discourses, I contend, is not at all a detour from Césaire's utopian poetics. Queerness, in Césaire's aesthetic, is another valence of blackness, that ontology which Moten says resides "off to the side of what lies between subjects and objects." For both Césaire and Lam, the inclusion of normative and queer sexual formations is simply the product of their surrealist-inflected aesthetics, the strategy of building an image only to explode it, invert it, reshape it. It's that constant simultaneous effort to create and take flight from meaning. This shuttling between the queer and the normative—otherwise understood as a fugitive evasion of recognition and the recognizable—is organic to Césaire's négritude poetics. And indeed in all of Césaire's reproductive images, whether normative or queer, the resultant new black life is the progeny of the wounded body. The *Notebook*'s discourse on reproduction is pivotal to the poet's larger anticipatory sensibility that emerges from that wound, the pervasive desire structured by that Blochian drive toward self-preservation.

Another salient moment of queer reproductivity comes a few pages later, when the poet inverts the cosmological signs of the sexes: "let the wolves come who graze in the untamed orifices of the body at the hour when my moon and your sun meet at the ecliptic inn."⁶⁶ For Lilian Pestre de Almeida, both the moon and the sun in this instance correspond to *both* sexes, instead of the typical masculine-sun and feminine-moon associations. The two androgynous beings then combine in the eclipse: "The end of the eclipse is the liberation," Pestre de Almeida suggests; "they make love, the one devouring the other, giving birth."⁶⁷ Here, as in the prior self-birthing passage, Césaire's surrealist-inflected reproductive mode not only indicates a newly generated being but also gestures to a kind of alternative experience of time, a proleptic temporality that moves against teleological expectations. These moments in the *Notebook* recall José Muñoz's characterization of queerness as utopian horizon, as "that thing that allows us to see that this world is not enough." The temporality of queerness, he proposes, sees beyond a present "impoverished and toxic for queers and other people who do not feel the privilege of majoritarian belonging, normative tastes, and 'rational' expectations." The reproductive temporality of Césaire's self-birthing and androgynous sex images disrupts what Muñoz calls "straight time," the time of progress and linearity, of "reproductive majoritarian heterosexuality," the time of "the state refurbishing its ranks through overt and subsidized acts of reproduction."⁶⁸ Straight time, in other words, is the time of the state apparatus that inscribes the wound on the flesh of blackness—the time of black subjection that I identified in chapter 1. It's a temporality enforced by those authorities of the state that Spillers identifies as the "judges, attorneys, 'owners,' 'souldrivers,'" operating under "a protocol of 'search and destroy.'"⁶⁹ The poet's queer fugitive time takes flight from straight time's privileging of whiteness and heterosexuality, with their putatively normal desires that remain sanctioned by the state.

The figure of the child in the queer passages of the *Notebook* poses a curious question about time. My reading recalls Lee Edelman's critique of "the Child" as the image, or "telos," that regulates a certain heterosexual reproductive futurity, the hope for a coming normative collectivity. He suggests that rather than contest the role of negation imposed on queerness, the queer ought to embrace that negativity, to dissolve the contract for which the child stands. Such a break from sociality, he says, "[does] not intend a new politics, a better society, a brighter tomorrow, since all of these fantasies reproduce the past, through displacement, in the form of the future." Instead, queerness ought to embrace the "jouissance" of its capacity to undo "fetishistic investments" that perpetuate the heteronormative order.⁷⁰ Edelman's polemic, in other words, is a kind of antiutopianism, running against the relational and open temporality of Muñoz's queer utopianism.

In Muñoz's extensive engagement with Edelman's *No Future*, he contests Edelman's refusal of hope, politics, and sociality, even if he agrees with much of Edelman's critique of "reproduction as a world-historical value." But what's most convincing in Muñoz's critique is his claim that Edelman's framework assumes a figure of the child that is "always already white": "In the same way all queers are not the stealth-universal-white-gay-man . . . all children are not the privileged white babies to whom contemporary society caters."[71] Edelman's framing denies a certain historical specificity, Muñoz says, of brownness and blackness—a history in which the lives of black and brown children are valued less than those of white children. Muñoz thus allows us to see that the figure of the child in the *Notebook*—the child of *both* queer and nonqueer reproduction—is critical. Its potential capacity to connect generations, to galvanize black solidarity, to engender hope for the end of violence on the black body, needs to be pursued.

Césaire and Lam's queer formations importantly also resonate in a wider (diasporic) Caribbean context. Again, Tinsley's work beautifully draws out these connections. "Fomented in Atlantic crosscurrents," she suggests in her essay "Black Atlantic, Queer Atlantic," as if in conversation with Césaire and Lam, "black queerness itself becomes a crosscurrent through which to view hybrid, resistant subjectivities—opaquely, not transparently." In the same piece, Tinsley's reading of Ana-Maurine Lara's novel *Erzulie's Skirt* also gestures to the layers and indeterminacies of the pair's queer aesthetic: "To think the black queer Atlantic, not only must its metaphors be materially informed; they must be internally discontinuous, allowing for differences and inequalities between situated subjects that are always already part of both diaspora and queerness."[72] Césaire and Lam's surrealist queer aesthetic similarly toggles and enmeshes the metaphorical and the material—in, for instance, their seamless poetic and visual melding of blood, amniotic fluid, ejaculate, and the waters of the Atlantic. Their queer images are also very much hybrid formations that refuse transparent, monolithic, singular readings. And indeed Césaire and Lam's implied intergenerationality gestures not just to that Muñozian queer temporal horizon but also to the sprawl of diaspora, to the dispersal of West Indian queer life throughout the hemisphere. We might even say that the androgynous and ungendered beings that Césaire imagines at mid-century prefigure and clear queer space for the artists and performers that Tinsley examines in *Ezili's Mirrors*, like MilDred "Dréd" Gerestant, the Haitian American, "multi-spirited," "gender-illusioning," "non-labeling woMan" drag star of 1990s New York City. Dréd, Tinsley maintains, evinces a "submerged epistemology of gender variance" in her insistence that "all people have the possibility to be simultaneously man and woman, Shaft and Foxy Brown. . . . Because they're always surrounded by multiple, multiply gendered spirits and may temporarily *become* any one of these spirits at any time." Moving seamlessly between Kreyòl and English, Dréd says, "Mwen gen tou le de: *I have both in me*. Nou tout gen tou le de andedan nou: *We all have both in us*."[73] Both Césaire and Lam's aesthetics, I argue, are subtle early deposits of this multi-spirited black becoming, this queerness of inhabiting both and all. It's stitched into their surging, surrealist formations of fugitive time.

All of the aforementioned modes of bodily anticipation in the *Notebook*, including these multivalent poetics of sexuality and regeneration, come to a head in the poem's final pages. The feeling of becoming accelerates in a series of dramatic interrelated images that elicit an ecstatic sense of swelling outward movement and anticipation. Returning to the 1939 edition that was Lam's muse, the body lies at the center of these final iconic stanzas:

> the old négritude progressively cadavers itself. . . .
>
> the horizon breaks, recoils and expands
> and through the shredding of clouds the brilliance of a sign
> the slave ship cracks everywhere. . . . Its stomach convulses and resonates. . . . The horrible tapeworm of its cargo gnaws the fetid guts of the strange suckling of the seas![74]

Césaire again disavows the idea of a pathological and subjected blackness with the images of a decaying body. But this "cadaverization" is a catalyst for his next move of outward lunging toward the "horizon," that elusive object of desire toward which the moonfaced angel figure in Lam's second sketch appears to pull the child and devastated beast. In Lam's image, that glimmering star hovering over the angel represents that horizon of escape and release, its full breasts ready to nourish imminent new life.

In the poem, this slave ship then becomes the body that breaks and decays from the inside out. The slaves in the hold—the "horrible tapeworm" of the ship body—have begun an insurrection. Suddenly, the ship has been reconstituted, and the cargo takes control:

> the seated négraille
> unexpectedly standing

> standing in the hold . . .
> standing on the deck
> standing in the wind . . .
> standing under the stars
>   standing
>   and
>   free
> and the lustral ship fearlessly advances on the overwhelmed waters.[75]

As we've seen, through the act of raising the body, Césaire transforms the derogatory *négraille* into a term of poise and strength. Lifting up the body is a critical initial step toward reconfiguring the wounded body as generative, outward striving. It is, we might say, a fundamental step in that Blochian drive toward self-preservation. But the ship's continued "advance on the crumbling water," like the pirogue battling the "raging sea," indicates that to be *debout* is not enough. The horizon of the breasted star demands insistent pursuance.

In the final stanza of the *Notebook*, the speaker is propelled into the air. We arrive, at last, at the interplay of Lam's final 1943 sketch and the poem's conclusion, the wind enfolding the body, galvanizing momentum and strength:

> coil, wind, around my new growth
> light on my measured fingers
> To you I surrender my conscience and its rhythm of flesh
> To you I surrender the fire in which my weakness smolders
> To you I surrender the chain-gang
> To you the swamps
> To you the non-tourist of the triangular circuit
> Devour wind . . .
> Embrace me to furious us
> Embrace, embrace US [*NOUS*][76]

The wind consumes the body, pushing it farther and farther outward, escalating the metamorphosis of disalienation. Like the négraille's act of standing debout and the ship's forward projection, the wind's swirling movement reads temporally as a kind of acceleration of prolepsis, of living in advance of oneself. Anaphora ("To you I surrender") deepens the intensity of anticipation. The speaker has taken flight and has demanded that the wind strip his body of the remnants of subjection: the "fire" of weakness, the violence of the "chain-gang." In the wind, the self dissolves into the vestibular collective ("US") that has discarded its imposed pathologies.

The scene plays out in Lam's final sketch with a masked figure tilted as if soaring in midair, having reached the height of the stars and a crescent moon, the latter doubling as its wings. Lam's figure flies alongside the rising dove of Césaire's lines:

> bind my black vibration to the very navel of the world
> Bind, bind me, harsh brotherhood
> Then, strangling me with your lasso of stars
> rise, Dove
> rise
> rise
> rise
> I follow you who are imprinted on my ancestral white cornea.
> Rise sky licker[77]

The imperatives "bind" and "rise" drive the intensity of flight. Lam creates his own sense of propulsion in the undulating lines streaming from his flying creature, the artist transforming the raffia hair of an African mask into a kind of jet stream that traces this figure's pathway through the sky. The speaker, the dove, and Lam's figure all rise farther and farther out in their endless search for release—a movement indeterminately directed upward and outward, away from the time and place that disposes of blackness. Lam extends Césaire's final lines with the horned mask, signaling not some futile nostalgic return to an African past but the pursuit of ancestrality located in the "white cornea," a kind of proleptic reinhabitation of Africanité en route to the cosmos, a metamorphosis of being among the stars as a reembodiment of the vitality of the poet's metaphysical idea of Africa. The leaves on this flying being tell us that it remains, even in outer space, *l'homme-plante*: the term Suzanne Césaire famously uses in a well-known early *Tropiques* essay to characterize the African's plant-like essential nature, one that "germinates, shoots up, blossoms, yields fruit and the cycle begins anew."[78] In Lam's image, that cycle seems to transform into a new species of cosmic plant man. And its full breasts portend new life in the sky, a promise that this masked plant creature's continued lunging toward release will be a vestibularly social one.

In Césaire and Lam's final images, the phenomenological microinterval of fugitive time—that anticipatory desire for the moment of bodily release—has accumulated and fomented to such a degree that the underlying trajectory has now launched into the sky, upward into the cosmos. Stripping oneself of trauma, it appears, now requires stripping oneself of the Earth altogether. Disalienated being and collective liberation—the elusive utopian object of fugitive time—still lie in that moment when the body and mind have finally found release, but now that release is to be sought on some other rock in the universe, however indeterminately located that extraplanetary site may be. Césaire and Lam, we might say, end where the American jazz musician and poet Sun Ra, whose work I take up in chapter 4, famously begins: with the idea that the time and place of black transcendence can exist only in another world, "beyond the limit of that which only always was," "other dimensions and planets."[79] And like that of Ra, Césaire's poetics is not about attaining that utopia but relishing the vitality of the journey, sustaining that imagined outward flight.

CÉSAIRE'S BEYOND

Unlike Sun Ra, however, Césaire had another side to his life's work that perhaps one might not expect of a utopian poet. For nearly five decades, Césaire was the mayor of Fort-de-France and Martinique's deputy to the French National Assembly. And he was the central figure who led Martinique from colonialism to departmentalism—not national independence. The 1946 law that Césaire sponsored led to the French West Indies (Martinique, Guadeloupe, and French Guyana) becoming departments of the French Republic. So where, we might ask, do we locate the poet's transcendent beyond in the pragmatism of the career politician? How do we reconcile his seemingly assimilationist politics and the radical aesthetics he shared with Lam? That the two sides of Césaire's professional life operated in tandem only intensifies the issue: Césaire repeatedly revised the *Notebook* throughout his political career; he wrote plays, collections of poetry, and his stridently anticolonial *Discourse on Colonialism* (1950) all during the decades that he traveled between Martinique and Paris as the island's elected representative.

One approach would be to reason that Césaire's political life and his utopian poetics ought to be thought of as two sides of the same larger project. Thinking outside the normative association between state sovereignty and emancipation, Gary Wilder shifts the conversation to how Césaire could have thought of departmentalization as a "creative anticolonial act." Reading Césaire's 1940s speeches at the National Assembly, Wilder identifies his call for departmentalization as an appeal to resurrect the mid-nineteenth-century ideas of abolitionist Victor Schoelcher, who demanded that all slaves in the Republic be granted freedom and full French citizenship. Like Schoelcher, Césaire sought to close the gap between "formal liberty and substantive freedom" by making all of France's overseas territories full departments of France, with the same laws as the metropole. Césaire envisioned a radically different nation, a radically different democracy, which, we know in hindsight, didn't take hold. His enthusiasm for departmentalism evaporated after the law was passed and it failed to live up to his ideals. Poverty persisted in Martinique, and Republican law remained unevenly applied in the Antilles. That notion of true freedom, freedom from all forms of subjection, remained out of reach. In the end, this failure only buttresses Wilder's insistence that Césaire's "revolutionary poetry [of] interruption, transformation, [and] emergence" aligned with his utopian politics.[80]

But again, what about the flight beyond the traumas of the Earth that animates his poetry? Are Césaire's politics and poetics really of the same utopian core? If we were to ask Marx, the answer would be clear: "Just when they seem engaged in revolutionizing themselves . . . , in creating something entirely new, they anxiously conjure up the spirits of the past to their service and borrow from them names, battle slogans and costumes in order to present the new scene of world history in this time-honored disguise and this borrowed language." Only when revolutionaries seek their own contingent path "without remembering the old," Marx says, can they fully chart their course toward liberation.[81] The ideologies and circumstances of the past cannot be allowed to shape the exigency of the present. At the very least, there's a decided tension between Césaire's two lives, between his perhaps nostalgic donning of Schoelcher's nineteenth-century clothes and rhetoric and his desire to flee the world.

Rather than wrangle a speculative resolution, I want to sit with the tension of this contradiction, recognizing that Césaire created these images charting an escape route from the world that subjects his people *while he sat in Paris trying to ameliorate that subjection*. We shouldn't lose sight of the fact that through his poetics, Césaire articulates a sentiment, not unlike Jared Sexton's, that "black life is not lived in the world that the world lives in, but it is lived underground, in outer space."[82] The tension of Césaire's political pragmatism and his aesthetics, I argue, produces an uncontainable energy akin to that which enlivens the anticipatory trajectory of fugitive time. Perhaps his poetic self is, and always has been, on the run from his political self, fleeing from Schoelcher's unrealized politics and the (failure of) departmentalization that kept him rooted in the past, escaping that which promised to keep his people grounded—literally—in a world that had considered them subhuman for centuries. Perhaps Césaire's ecstatic poetic self sought to escape the past that Marx warned only burdens revolutionary vision.

In Lam and Césaire's final collaboration, four decades after their first, this dogged flight from the devastations of the world gets one last reprise. In the poem "Passages" and the corresponding etching of the same title from their 1982 book *Annonciation*, we find a kind of extension and remixing of Césaire's epic.[83] If Césaire's final *Notebook* stanzas and Lam's final drawing gesture to a species metamorphosis as the dove escapes into the sky, that work has evolved, literally, by the first line of the poem "Passages" with "the necessity of speciation," the process of becoming another being altogether. The speaker calls on those listening—the dove, Lam's flying masked being, and their vestibular collective—to "pass on," imploring them to let "each bruise endure," not to "surpass living memories"—lines that recall the ever-deepening wounds pivotal to the (re)generation of new life in the *Notebook*. In the final lines of this short poem, as if gazing ahead in literal flight, the speaker announces, "already / in the distance emerges . . . / the tribulation of a volcano / the halt of a live termitarium"—Antillean-African-like topographical features, perhaps of that indeterminate promised world that just may bring them that long-awaited absolution.[84] In Lam's corresponding aquatint print, the kinetic energy of "passing on" is rendered in a group of beastly-looking creatures with long, rail-thin limbs reaching out and lunging to the left side of the frame, as if pulled by a gravitational force. A triangular horned mask similar to the one in Lam's third *Notebook* image leads the charge. An ellipsoidal celestial object hovering above bearing two twisted horns suggests that their journey has brought them deep into an African-mythologized cosmos, these beings scanning the surrounding landscape in flight, destined to go deeper as they continue their search for other worlds. We're left with an image much like the "contingent and mutable unfolding" that Zakiyyah Jackson attributes to the trans-species being in Octavia Butler's well-known story "Bloodchild"—one created in the "ever-expanding processual field of the relational dynamics of life in ceaseless flux and directionless becoming." Perhaps Lam and Césaire's metamorphized beings, like Butler's, are, as Jackson puts it, a "call for a praxis of being/feeling/knowing that can accommodate accommodation" as they search for other orders of black life that "might very well leave 'the human' behind."[85]

If we read these images of "ceaseless flux and directionless becoming" in *Annonciation* as an extension of the dove's flight into the cosmos, they also seem indicative of the continued nonmaterialization of Césaire's utopian political aspirations decades into his career in elected office. "Passages" evinces the sense that the poet's radical fugitive aesthetic self will never cease its flight, so long as realpolitik continues to render black life less than human. Decades into their search for another world deep in the cosmos, Césaire's fugitive speciating ontologies embody a kind of messianism, an expansive, obstinate will to bring new life and new worlds into being. Their quest recalls Derrida's notion of justice to come, unfolding in a moment "belonging no longer to history," where "emancipatory promise" comes from a "commitment to the event of what is coming . . . for justice beyond the law."[86] It's also reminiscent of the messianism that Bloch articulated during World War I, in which he spoke of a need to become open to the "outside," to maintain the "constant concentration of our waking dream on a purer, higher life, on a release from malice, emptiness, death and enigma."[87] Crucially, though, Césaire's messianic release is not to be found in the future. The new world sought out by the *Notebook*'s dove and the gangly creatures of "Passages" is not an earthly, future world constituted by the ideologies, laws, and institutions we know, but a beyond world to come. It's that utopian world that awaits in the coming phenomenological now moment that cannot but be imagined and lived in advance, somewhere out among the stars, among the horned celestial objects of deep space: an imminent world that has no particular location in time or space other than when and where pain disappears from the body and mind of black life.

This is Aimé Césaire's fugitive time. The *Notebook*'s excavated traumatic histories, its unraveled ideologies, its contorted meanings and images constitute the poet's singular version of this distinctly African diasporic experience of time. Césaire indexes this temporal experience in the materiality of the body, accounting for history's deepening wounds in the flesh of black life and the black body's endless search for release. And Lam is indeed with him each step of the way, illustrating, remixing, extending, perhaps even prefiguring the poet's radical fugitive aesthetic. With Lam's hallucinatory map, we see how Césaire's formation of fugitive time begins at that microcosmic level, where desire for release accumulates and swells in the flesh, the body eventually bursting in flight toward the sky, fleeing into the cosmos, all in the name of an as-yet-unrealized emancipation. Like many of the works examined in this book, Césaire's wound-less alter-world never arrives. His utopia, like that of Britain's Black Audio Film Collective, lies in the ecstasy of dwelling in prolepsis, in the vestibular pursuance of the continually receding horizon. From the mornes of Martinique to the streets of England, from the poetic image to the moving image, the next chapter continues the chase in anticipation of a world that's always one moment, one breath, to come.

3 BLACK AUDIO'S ARCHIVAL FLIGHT

In his essay "On the Borderline," Black Audio Film Collective founding member John Akomfrah considers a speculative photography exhibition that would feature "a notoriously public figure—the Black Body," "burdened by an excess of signs." The show would focus on images that would "flirt with the transcendental as a yearning," taking flight from the "scene of horror" of overdetermined blackness. These would be "impossible frames" of "protean" bodies, Akomfrah says, "floating, prodigal sensibilities" riotously playing with boundaries, disrupting the structure of the frame. As in the broader project of queer photographer Rotimi Fani-Kayode—one of Akomfrah's exhibition muses—to evince "traces of ecstasy," to "reveal hidden worlds" and "new visions," the bodies in Akomfrah's show would seek a "duress" that would "construct [them] anew," remaking the body's being-in-the-world.[1] As with this exhibition, fugitive, protean bodies saturate the work of the Black Audio Film Collective. Particularly in its early films, we find a similar ecstatic energy, a refusal of negation, a desire to free the body and mind of the "horror" of nonbeing. I want to show how this fugitive strain moves through Black Audio's chronicling of the black experience in 1980s Britain: how the collective centers the body to "flirt with the transcendental as a yearning" and, in turn, tease out the ways that memory, place, and identity mark the fault lines of what it meant to be black in the age of Thatcherism.

Between 1982 and 1998 Black Audio produced more than a dozen films, videos, and tape-slide texts that used various combinations of montage cutting, archival footage, interviews, tableaux vivants, electronic music, and voice-over narration to create an expansive image of black life in Britain and the larger African diaspora. As it happens, the group's foray into this experientialism was a multimedia performance of Aimé Césaire's *Notebook*, featuring projected tape-slide images, a low-frequency "rhythmic tonal rumbling," and three members of the collective on stage standing behind a screen in silhouette reciting cut-up fragments of Césaire's poem that were then manipulated, looped, and overlaid by the group's sound designer, Trevor Mathison, to create a swelling, improvised mass.[2] These experiments with form expanded as the collective soon settled into the essay film format for many of its works: a hybrid genre between fiction and nonfiction that both shapes, and is shaped by, critical thought, prompting the spectator "to shift her or his conceptual vantage point" and "glean otherwise elusive meanings."[3] The collective's earliest essay films focused on blackness in 1980s Britain, excavating the silencing of black voices in the media and dominant discourse on the one hand and black life's hypervisiblity as the contamination of Britishness on the other. Throughout, Black Audio sought to "develop an alternative visual grammar," as member Reece Auguiste put it, to build "a critical language . . . of movement and fluidity" so that "sound and image may assume new life."[4] In Akomfrah's words, this was an effort "to find and legitimize new versions of becoming."[5]

It's this "grammar of becoming," as it relates to figurations of the body, that I want to isolate in *Handsworth Songs* (1986) and *Twilight City* (1989), two of Black Audio's earliest experimental essay films.[6] On the surface they present two adjacent moments in the history of black British subjection: *Handsworth* centers on the black uprisings that took place in 1985 in the Handsworth neighborhood of Birmingham, and *Twilight* gives us an exposition of black precarious life in the "New London" of late-1980s financialization and development. Both, however, use archival newsreel footage from throughout the twentieth century to capture a sprawling view of disparate iterations of black life—from the postwar arrival of West Indian migrants to early twentieth-century footage of South Asian sailors on London's Isle of Dogs, generating what Tsitsi Jaji calls "an archive of transnational black solidarity."[7] I want to put these two films in conversation to show how Black Audio's juxtaposition of disparate images of desire and pain, memory and anticipation, reveals a distinctly black British fugitive life and sensibility, and indeed a singularly textured experience of time.

Specifically, I contend that *Handsworth* and *Twilight* present the black British historical experience as a condition of *thrownness*. With this term, I mean to indicate the heightened way these films articulate black life as always already subjected *and* always already thinking about escape, a dual inhabitation comprising an array of ceaseless fugitive operations set against an encompassing landscape of black disposability. In this immersive structure the persistence of subjection generates an ecstatic desire to exceed the immediacy of the present, an anticipatory consciousness of that phenomenal moment when one has fled the enclosure of the world and left behind its corporeal burdens. I'm adapting Martin Heidegger's use of the term wherein the human, or *Dasein*, is always already thrust, or thrown, into existence in the world, existing in a state of "anticipatory resoluteness" as "being toward one's ownmost, eminent potentiality-of-being."[8] Thrownness is integral to the fugitive structure of time in *Handsworth Songs* and *Twilight City*, where we encounter a persistent sense of being-toward-escape as a condition of ontological potentiality, of impending transcendence amid surrounding devastation. Certainly, many of the artworks I examine in this book present some form of this dual structure, but what thrownness names in this chapter is the *magnification* of this condition in Black Audio's films. As the visual, aural, and narrative registers of *Twilight* and *Handsworth* converge, constantly moving in and out of sync, deliberately scrambling any progressive sense of past, present, and future, the collective creates, on the one hand, a sense of all-encompassing antiblackness, a kind of surrounding, suffocating temporal-historical enclosure, and on the other, a sense of continuous movement, a persistent imaginative drive to flee this encasement. *Thrownness* refers to the intensified, multilayered way in which Black Audio presents this dialectic of surround and desired escape, capture and prolepsis. I intend the term in the Heideggerian sense of *already being thrown* into the world, of never being conscious of when one was not already thrown. If something does throw the black lives and aesthetic forms in these films, though, it's the sedimentations of antiblackness and the mechanisms of (neoliberal) capital that devastate black lives—sedimentations and mechanisms that feel like they've always been there and always will be. It's the insidious structures of our post-Enlightenment world that maintain, and indeed rely on, the subjugation of blackness.

My analysis of thrownness in this chapter concerns representation as well as form. I trace the encompassing enclosure of antiblackness established in these films through the use of archival footage and voice-over narration. And I home in on the presentation of literal bodies envisaging release, as well as the way the collective sutures this being-toward-escape into the cinematic architecture through montage cutting and nondiegetic sequencing. This is, altogether, Black Audio's fugitive filmic grammar, its cinematic formation of fugitive time. In their incessant sense of entrenchment and outward projection, we find in these films a black British fugitive time consciousness animated by a potential release from subjection that always feels imminent yet always remains just out of reach, necessitating the continual pursuance of the outside of the world.

ARRIVAL

Rather than read *Handsworth* and *Twilight* successively, as if the one begat the other, I want to put them in dialogue, allowing the fugitive thrownness of the one to speak to that of the other, in turn creating a larger historical and societal image of their fugitive temporalities. I begin with a sequence that lays out a critical moment in the prehistory of the 1980s crises foregrounded in both films: *Handsworth Songs*' representation of the June 1948 journey of 492 West Indians aboard the SS *Empire Windrush*. They were migrating to fill Britain's postwar labor shortage and fleeing an economic depression that reached the Caribbean years later than in Europe.[9] The voyage, as Stuart Hall suggests, "served as an important hinge between the large numbers of black men and women already represented in many walks of British social life before the war . . . and the later arrival (in significantly enlarged numbers) of black people as an identifiable group, to live, work and settle on a permanent basis."[10] Over the next decade, 125,000 West Indians came to live and work in Britain, forming a social group that indeed was identifiable to white Britons—identifiable, in large part, as a threat to the nation.[11] *Handsworth*'s filmic representation of this migration productively leads us into both films' larger construction of the thrownness of twentieth-century black British life.

Amid the 1985 uprising footage that predominates in *Handsworth Songs*, the film cuts against expectation by presenting an image of the postwar Atlantic crossing not as a moment of elated anticipation but one of decided anxiety. Generated in the friction of sound and image we find a kind of indecision about where to seek fugitive relief. A third of the way through the film, set against archival footage of men crowded on the deck of an ocean liner, a narrative poem offers an opaque lament to mark what seems to be the start of the Atlantic crossing:

They appeared in unison on the deck, summoned by the water. And they stood there brooding in collective silence. Suddenly a man in a black felt hat and a lively gabardine suit heaved hopelessly and uncontrollably, and his soul ran for the sea. But the winds rushed in and carried it back onto the deck. There it sat, abject and exposed. Without warning the water swept his soul from the deck. Zachariah looked at the water and felt the song swell inside him. It was said that each person recognized their fate in the song. As he stood there, the Caribbean sank into the water. The land was there, but he will not go to it anymore.

The voice-over narration describes an almost spiritual collective experience among the men on deck. Far from appearing elated about leaving the West Indies, their mood is anxious as the ship moves toward a new and contingent being-in-the-world. The water, endowed with agency as it "summons" the men and "sweeps" onto the deck, generates the movement in the narration, heaving them toward the horizon. Their departure seems to precipitate a feeling of alienation, a severing of body and soul as the latter is swept away by the sea, sinking into the West Indian waters filled with those who never made it through the first crossing. It's a sweeping away that also generates an anticipatory consciousness, a kind of prophetic "song" that these men "recognize" as their "fate," pushing their minds outward toward their new world.

What's striking about this poem, however, is its juxtaposition with grainy mid-century archival footage of hundreds of black men standing on deck *arriving* in Britain. The viewer recognizes this only when the voice-over and footage sequence end simultaneously and the phrase "the Caribbean sank into the water" is set against images of men in crisp suits preparing to disembark at an industrial dockyard, presumably in Britain. But before we notice this incongruity, the narration and footage converge to form a moment of filmic synchresis: panning close-up shots of stoic passengers coincide with the phrase "they appeared in unison on the deck"; images of men standing at the bow of the ship holding their fedoras in the wind match the phrase "but the winds rushed in." Within seconds, synchresis gives way to what Gilles Deleuze calls asynchrony: "two 'heautonomous' images, one visual and one sound, with . . . an irrational cut between them," creating a series of "contradictions" that "induce a system of unhookings and intertwinings which in turn determine the different presents through anticipations or regressions."[12] If *Handsworth*'s voice-over puts in mind the image of a group of men facing an island as it falls into

3.1 Still from *Handsworth Songs* (1986).

the horizon, the closing frame of what is likely London's Tilbury docks triggers this Deleuzian "unhooking" and an unexpected anticipation of those industrial docks. The jolt of asynchrony projects an accelerating effect on the passengers' time consciousness, as if their fixation on departure were suddenly fast-forwarded at breakneck speed, launched ahead in time and space, and transformed into a fixation on their imminent arrival, producing a kind of vertigo as their minds rush toward shore. This anxious arrival, I want to suggest, marks a critical threshold in the historical thrownness of black life in Britain. Thrown into a refigured subjection the instant they get off the boat, these migrants must navigate the exclusions, prejudices, and violence of a public that sees their presence as a threat even before they touch solid ground.[13]

The *Handsworth Songs* sequence that best exemplifies this initial navigation of antiblackness upon arrival is the train montage in which dozens of moving and still 1950s archival images appear in the span of a mere thirty seconds. We, the spectators, are the travelers in this fast-moving clip, which begins with the quick chugging sounds of a coal-powered locomotive and the camera directed through the train window to the outside, as if we're sitting and peering out. The grainy footage shows identical-looking brick houses quickly passing under a gray sky before the train enters a tun-

104 CHAPTER THREE

nel and the screen momentarily goes black. Suddenly, the camera is situated behind a woman as she steps off a train onto a station platform. The montage accelerates, now cutting every second or faster, showing a train spewing smoke, close-ups of white police officers and taxi drivers ("Taxi!" one hails), and black travelers walking the platform, many looking about, confused. The camera angles up at the imposing "way out" sign, and suddenly we are out on the street, buses and motorcycles speeding by, chimneys spewing smoke, car horns honking. Director John Akomfrah punctuates this short sequence with a close-up of a brick wall with the graffiti message "BLACKS GO HOME."

Here in *Handsworth* and throughout Black Audio's work, archival images function as "reservoirs of memory," as "one of the few sites that attest to the diasporic subject's existence" in the face of the erasures of British imperial archives.[14] In this sequence the collective crystallizes a crucial transition in the migrants' experience of fugitive time using those "reservoirs of memory" as raw material. If, as Deleuze suggests, cinematic montage is constituted by a "duration and time which flow from the articulation of the movement-images," then Black Audio's shift during this sequence to rapidly accelerating successive images suggests a kind of accelerated temporality and, I argue, an accelerated temporal consciousness of the migrant.[15] As the images rapidly succeed one another and anxiety builds in the moment of exiting the train, the experience of time pivots to a reshaped embodied urgency from moment to moment, of taking flight from whomever wrote "BLACKS GO HOME" on that brick wall. The fugitive desire for bodily release is no longer sought in the anticipation of Britain as a reprieve from West Indian poverty but in the anticipation of the immediate outside of the ideology that produced those three words. Black Audio's use of the archive to evoke this migratory and affective trajectory is reminiscent of Saidiya Hartman's readings in and beyond the frame of images of early twentieth-century black American life: "Images of *too fast* black girls trying to make a way out of no way, a serial picture of young black women rushing to the city to escape the plantation and intent on creating a free life in the context of a new enclosure." The historical analogue of the energies and desires of the Great Migration is certainly relatable to this moment of black life in Britain: "This collective endeavor to *live free* unfolds in the confines of the carceral landscape."[16]

This "BLACKS GO HOME" inscription that the migrants hurtle toward signals critical shifts in the structures of capital and ideology in mid- to late 1950s Britain. The defeat of Labour in the 1951 general election effectively marked the decline of the welfare state and the turn to a new conservatism of free enterprise and a discourse of "affluence" that sought to obscure older forms of class consciousness.[17] Underlying the appearance of a seemingly "healthy" economy, though, was a penetrating sense of social anxiety about society's changing structure. As the authors of the influential text *Policing the Crisis* (1978) maintain, that first generation of postwar West Indian immigrants was "destined to signify the dark side of the 'affluent dream'": "The black immigrant . . . entered this 'tight little island' of white lower-middle and working-class respectability—and, by his every trace, his looks, clothes, pigmentation, culture, mores and aspirations, announced his 'otherness.' . . . The symbolism of the race-immigrant theme was resonant in its subliminal force, its capacity to set in motion the demons which haunt the collective subconscious of a 'superior' race."[18]

Blackness threatened the white upward dream of affluence, but it also brought fears of the poor becoming poorer—of becoming, effectively, black. In Nottingham and the London neighborhood of Notting Hill, anti-black violence revealed for the first time in mainland Britain an "open and emergent racism of a specifically indigenous type."[19] With the economic slowdown of the early 1960s, black immigration was officially declared the problem, and the 1962 Commonwealth Immigration Act was passed, significantly limiting who and how many could enter Britain from the former colonies. Enoch Powell infamously played on the popular perception of blackness as menace in the late 1960s in his call for an end to black immigration, initiating the "formation of an 'official' racist politics at the heart of British political culture."[20]

What's so evocatively presented in *Handsworth Songs* and *Twilight City* is not simply the way that postwar West Indian migrants are cast into this divisive political culture but also the expansive historical temporality they enter upon arrival. *Handsworth* and *Twilight* give us an image of the postwar migrant entering an all-encompassing historical wreckage: a decades-long, even centuries-long past of black precarious life in Britain, on the one hand, and a kind of predetermined future of black precarity in the decades that followed the arrival of the *Windrush*, on the other. What I'm calling the condition of thrownness refers to how these films represent—across multiple cinematic registers—the migrant as inhabiting this seemingly inescapable historical surround of subjection while constantly scheming for an exit, anticipating another world.

NAVIGATION

Handsworth Songs and *Twilight City* both provide this sprawl that the migrant enters at mid-century, but *Twilight City* presents a particularly expansive terrain of historical subjection. As in *Handsworth Songs*, we encounter this sprawl in the relationship between *Twilight City*'s moving images and voice-over epistolary narrative. The narrative, written by Edward George and John Akomfrah, is structured around the letters of a young researcher, Olivia, to her mother, who wants to return to London from Dominica, where she had moved "after 35 years of trying to belong" in London. The majority of Olivia's narration traces her own study of "wealth creation" in London, telling her mother how London has become increasingly suffocating for people of color while also chronicling a history of black disposability in the city. The film chronicles, as director Reece Auguiste's notes suggest, the lives of "the city's dispossessed entrapped in the New London."[21] Set against Olivia's narration—in addition to brief nondiegetic scenes, interviews with activists and scholars recalling their London childhoods, and shots peering outside a car as it navigates the London streets—is a scattered series of grainy black-and-white archival footage sequences of particular moments in London's twentieth century. In the interplay between these archival shots and Olivia's narration, we find the expansive past and future of black violation that the migrants of *Handsworth* effectively enter when they set foot on solid ground, their minds racing toward that moment of unburdening.

Two particular threads in *Twilight City* give us a deeper sense of the black historical presence in Britain that predates the *Windrush*, implicitly speaking to the ideology that produced that "BLACKS GO HOME" graffiti in *Handsworth*. The first is the film's allusion to the black experience in London during World War II, the sense of exclusion felt years before the postwar migratory rush. We find this in a letter written by Olivia's father after the Blitz, an excerpt of which Olivia includes in her own letter:

> I walked through the ashes and the black smoke. They were pulling bodies from under the rubble. I tried to be of help. People would look at me as though they'd seen a ghost. Then the look would disappear. I walked around London watching them mourn, and I wanted to mourn with them. And then I noticed that the first apprehensive look took longer to disappear each time. When the bombing stopped and the smoke cleared the look was still there, frozen and fixed on a thousand faces. I tried to continue my job as a fighter pilot, but every time I look down I see the blue ice of that look.

Set against these words is footage of a recently bombed-out London, the film cutting between clips in a steady three-second tempo. As we imagine the West Indian man walking through the ashes and smoke, the frame gives us successive stationary shots at street level of overturned buses, piles of concrete and glass, and rescue workers in hard hats searching through debris. With stoic armed soldiers monitoring the scene, men and women, nearly all white, file determinedly through the rubble and military tanks, going about their daily business in their dresses, pressed suits, and polished shoes.

In the juxtaposition of sound and image, Black Audio invites us to imagine Olivia's father walking through these images, among those filing through the rubble. We imagine them giving him "the look," refusing his desire to belong. The phrase evokes the iconic line in *Black Skin, White Masks*—"Look, a Negro!"—when Fanon recalls his own (non)interpellation as an "object" in the world, as a figure of "nonbeing."[22] The way "the look" ceaselessly haunts Olivia's father, "frozen and fixed," elicits that objectification, that rendering as immanently other and less than human. His observations also call to mind the metropolitan-based West Indian servicemen whose experience Hazel Carby examines in her recent work on black British identity, arguing that their presence in Britain corresponded to a "racialization of subjects during World War II" that "prefigured the formation of postwar black British subjects," a racialization that "occurred in the context of the expression of particular fears and anxieties which had developed about 'race' in the colonies and in British cities."[23] "The look" that follows Olivia's father, we might say, is the consequence of these sedimented anxieties.

Carby is certainly right to highlight the racialization of blackness during the war, but *Twilight City* gives us an instance of black exclusion in Britain that prefigures even this—one that further entrenches the structures of subjection that *Handsworth Songs'* postwar migrants encounter upon arrival. It appears in Olivia's letter when she recounts her realization that in the nineteenth century a community of Lascars lived on the site of her family's former Isle of Dogs home: "They were seamen from Bombay and Calcutta, brought here by the East India Company and abandoned to misery." Accompanying this narration is a striking montage that cycles through three types of sequences: contemporary still shots of a graveyard with toppled tombstones, archival footage from the 1920s of South Asian seamen sitting on paved ground cutting one another's hair, and darkly lit sequences from the 1980s of a camera panning across dozens of people sleeping on the London sidewalks in sleeping bags and cardboard boxes.

Olivia's phrase "abandoned to misery" coincides with an image of a tombstone overrun with weeds followed quickly by images of London's sleeping unhoused. And the moment we hear her words "covered by three inches of snow," the film cuts to a person lying next to a storm drain in a box labeled "IBM" in large letters.

Olivia's words bridge the precarity of the seamen, the decay of the cemetery, and the men and women cast aside by Thatcher's neoliberal order, articulating a common structure of "abandonment" across the three, despite their seeming dissonance. Her voice-over soon gives way to historian Rosina Visram describing how eighteenth-century Lascar sailors, after being discharged by their employers upon arrival in London, "roamed around the metropolis . . . [without] shoes, shivering, starving, many of them dying in the streets." Visram's authority on the subject buttresses Olivia's revelation during her visit to her childhood home, serving as a kind of citation for Olivia's research as well as for Black Audio in the collective's use of the essay film genre to sketch a prehistory of Thatcherist London. That's effectively what this montage sequence accomplishes: positioning the figure of the "abandoned" Lascar against the image of the person sleeping in the IBM computer box implicitly articulates a kind of centuries-long Thatcherism in the making, a genealogy of what Hall calls Thatcherism's "assault . . . on the very principle and essence of collective social welfare" in favor of "competition," "profitability," and "personal responsibility."[24] In this way we start to get a sense of how *Twilight City* doesn't just articulate a *past* of subjection encountered by *Handsworth*'s migrants at Tilbury docks but also a *future* prefigured in their arrival.

The missing link in this discussion, of course, is the Lascars' proximity to blackness. This requires consideration of the next generation, the children of the "Windrush generation" born and raised in Britain. When Powell argued in the late 1960s for "repatriating" blacks, it was this second generation that formed the British Black Panther Party and the Black People's Alliance with a "degree of politicization and organization *in depth* hitherto unknown in the post-war history of black migration."[25] And it was this generation that became the symbol of growing crisis as economic recession deepened into the 1970s, with "crime" and "mugging" becoming synonymous with blackness as youths sought alternative survival methods beyond the wage-labor system denied to them.[26] "If we were invisible, marginal and silenced by subjection to a racism by which we failed to enjoy equal protection under the law as common citizens," Kobena Mercer incisively suggests, "this was because we were all too visible, all too vocal and all too central, in Britain's postimperial body politic, as a reminder and remainder of its historical past."[27] This (in)visibility erupted during the uprisings of 1981 in South London and Liverpool, and in the 1985 uprisings that Black Audio foregrounds in *Handsworth Songs*, all of which were the culmination of years of aggressive policing, far-right antiblack violence, and concentrated poverty.[28] The fugitive anticipatory consciousness that we find in *Handsworth* and *Twilight*, of proleptically taking flight toward another world, emerges from this entrenched racialized system.

It was amid this fraught climate that a new notion of blackness took shape. From the 1970s into the 1980s, the idea of blackness in Britain came to encompass West Indians, Africans, and South Asians. Certainly there was immense diversity within and among these communities, but what brought them together was their common racial exclusion from British society and their related historical experiences under colonialism and slavery.[29] Within these black groups emerged "new, hybrid and crossover cultural forms of tremendous vitality and innovation" as many elements from their "traditional" cultures were modulated to fit their new lives in Britain.[30] With members of West African, South Asian, and Caribbean descent, Black Audio stood at the forefront of this coalitional politics, conceiving of black filmmaking in Britain as "structured by pluralism," undergirded by "diverse histories of exclusion and emigration; by cultural experiences emanating from the historical conditions of the New World, Asia and Africa."[31] And so we find the Lascars in *Twilight City*. Certainly in their time these seamen would not have considered themselves black, but the 1980s identity politics from which *Twilight City* emerged brought them into the fold of the coalitional blackness of that moment. In this way I'm positioning the Lascars in the film as part of the history of black subjection encountered by the postwar West Indian migrants in *Handsworth Songs*. Black Audio, in a word, recodes the experience of the Lascars as black—a group refused inclusion, subjectivity, and being.

This recoding becomes all the more evident when we consider *Handsworth Songs*' framing of this coalitional blackness. The film demonstrates how both West Indians and South Asians were criminalized for participating in the 1985 Handsworth uprisings. The latter, like their West Indian counterparts, are interviewed throughout the film. They argue for increased scrutiny of policing, providing anecdotal evidence of police abuse. Black Audio even establishes this coalition cinematically in *Handsworth*, particularly through sound. In one sequence, after focusing for half a minute on an Indian classical music performance featuring tabla, harmonium, and a group of men singing in unison, the image cuts to a group of people of South Asian and African descent walking through the streets of post-uprising Handsworth holding flowers to honor those lost during the uprisings. But, crucially, the Indian music continues across the filmic cut, bridging the performance's connotative feeling of sacred intimacy with the feeling of insistent solidarity among the people walking past burned-out buildings. If, for Mercer, "Mathison's compositions play an important 'binding' role in melding [Black Audio's] disparate visual materials," then this sequence, I argue, shows us how Mathison's sound design also "binds" cultures, "melding" the disparate components of blackness into a collective lament for those lives lost.[32]

There's one last component of this emergent blackness that I want to introduce, one that comes to the fore in *Twilight*. The intersection of sexuality, specifically queerness, played a crucial role in further opening up this coalitional identity in the 1980s, even if it was very much contested ground. The film *The Passion of Remembrance* (1986), produced by another celebrated black British collective, Sankofa Film and Video, usefully stages a kind of front-lines debate among black youths on the subject, addressing it during an informal viewing session of pride demonstration footage shot by one of the young women gathered. Using Jamaican homophobic vernacular, one of the young men asks the filmmaker, "Is it true that you're a lesbian? You had images of batty men and lesbians in your footage," after which another claims that homosexuality is a "white informed" concept, that "those white directions can't add anything to our struggles except hindrance." These layered comments feel very much conversant with the work of scholars such as Marlon Ross and Phillip Brian Harper, who identify how, in the American black nationalist context, "Amiri Baraka and other black cultural nationalists sling heterosexist (and sexist) lines as though homosexuals (and implicitly women) were the enemy, rather than the white system of domination."[33] But in this film, cowritten and codirected by Maureen Blackwood and Isaac Julien, the queer youths in the group challenge the young men's hypocrisy of resisting Babylon while being "well content . . . to call me batty." The young filmmaker insists, "You're not *really* hearing anyone else. *The black community*. You can't even talk about communities. It's always homogenous." Alongside other films like *The Attendant* (1993) and *Looking for Langston* (1989), this scene in *Passion* affirms Rinaldo Walcott's observation about the function of Julien's larger body of work as "black queer diaspora communicative tools."[34] *Passion*, which premiered in 1986 alongside *Handsworth Songs* at London's Metro Cinema, pushes against monolithic, heteronormative, and masculinist formulations of blackness, revealing another valence of this 1980s pluralist identity—one that I'll show happens to lie at the center of the formation of fugitive time in *Twilight City*.

Before moving on to *Twilight* and *Handsworth*'s principal modes of fugitive time consciousness in their use of montage cutting and nondiegesis, I want to provide a closer view into how Black Audio presents the black body's navigation of this expansive past and future of subjection that *Handsworth*'s postwar migrants encounter. In a way, this navigation serves as a kind of "first order" of flight in the two films: that more obvious register of longing for an outside of the world that engenders and buttresses their cinematic grammars of fugitive time. This first order, in other words, is the level of *literal bodies* searching for escape; the second is the order in which this bodily flight and its attendant time consciousness is inscribed into the cinematic architecture, sutured into editing strategies.

Several sequences in particular evoke this essential feature of thrownness, this unequivocal embodied desire to escape an antiblack world. Take the following repeated sequence in *Handsworth Songs*. After brief shots of post-uprising Handsworth streets, with papers, glass, and concrete chunks scattered along the roadside, we see a black youth running toward the camera with riot police behind and in front of him.[35] A minimalist baton clanking echoes and repeats in the background. The youth cuts to his left to avoid an officer's grasp, using his hand to push off from a brick wall to avoid the officers approaching from his right. He then stumbles in the middle of the street, and a half dozen police descend on him with riot shields, pinning him against the wall. This same sequence reappears toward the end of the hour-long film, following, fittingly enough, a clip of a smirking Margaret Thatcher, saying, "People are rather afraid that this country might be rather swamped by people of a different culture. . . . The moment a minority threatens to become a big one, people get frightened." Immediately after these words, the film cuts back to the same youth running up the street, but this time Akomfrah retimes it at half the speed. We see very clearly each of the youth's steps, one white shoe placed before the other as he cuts left and pushes off the wall. The slow motion gives the viewer a phenomenal sense of the youth's movement—dreadlocks flying above, arms stretched for balance, his gaze looking ahead for a clearing. The clanking baton now sounds like a slow-metered, incarcerating pulse, akin to what Frank Wilderson calls "the gratuitous violence of sound," the way a film's "acoustic strategies . . . evoke this structural position of the Black as one of unmitigated vulnerability to violence." If, for Wilderson, the sound of the voices heard in the mind of Dorothy in Haile Gerima's film *Bush Mama* (1979)—voices of welfare agency workers demanding that she abort her pregnancy—position her as "one of the 35 million accumulated and fungible (owned and exchangeable)

3.2 Still from *Handsworth Songs* (1986).

objects living among the 230 million subjects," then we might say that this sound of the carceral clanking baton analogously positions this running youth as a figure of subjection, as "accumulated and fungible" in the way that the British state polices and criminalizes blackness under Thatcher.[36] Saliently, Black Audio slows down the fugitive chase, demanding that we gain a closer sense of the youth's terror as we watch his body contort from one motion to the next, eyeing for an opening, chasing the promise of that elusive phenomenal moment of the body's nonfungibility.[37]

Twilight City also includes crucial scenes of embodied navigation of subjection, one of which comes early on in the film when Olivia recalls a recent dream. "I wandered through the ruins of an old city, searching for your love," she writes to her mother. "I wandered aimlessly, like a figure torn from a forgotten body. . . . I saw your love searching for a glimpse of my face. I tried to call to you but the words were drowned in the silence of the ruins." Set against these words are haunting night images of London during the 1940 Blitz: smoke rising from rubble, panning aerial images of leveled neighborhoods. The juxtaposition of image and text reminds us of Olivia's father walking through the post-Blitz rubble, where he encounters that Fanonian "look." In this sequence it's the ruins that negate Olivia's being, tearing at her body, silencing her voice. Her searching, however, intimates a structure of anticipation, a longing for the outside of her alienation in the present, an outside constituted by the peace and belonging of her mother's love. Her dream recalls influential theories of movement in African diaspora studies, such as Édouard Glissant's notion of errantry: that movement of the dispossessed out and away that's always formed in relation to other life experiences, cultivating sociality and identity in the act of motion.[38] Or Sarah Cervenak's meditations on wandering: moving along "unsurveillable paths" of the mind, oriented toward "the other side" of "violent stares, and vicious (mis)readings." Like Olivia's movement in search of her mother, "wandering," Cervenak suggests, "might get you home."[39]

Twilight's other mode of bodily navigation of subjection is altogether different. It comes in the repeated sequences in which the camera is situated on the dashboard of a car, directed out the windshield as the car navigates the nighttime streets of late-eighties London, shooting with a wide-angle lens to give us a sprawling panorama. We cruise past neon signage and illuminated storefronts, underneath an endless succession of dim streetlights, down both deserted streets and streets crowded with the glaring lights of oncoming traffic. We speed and slow, turn and continue on with the car as it navigates the structures of subjection in the New London that Olivia narrates in her voice-over letter. These night car sequences appear at steady intervals throughout the film, accompanied by Mathison's low pulsing electronic music and occasionally Olivia's voice reading her letter. Their regularity amid the constant barrage of facts, anecdotes, and images of subjugation gives the sense of the car moving in, out, and through not just the traffic but also through the sprawling debris of historical subjection the film presents. The fluid, continuously moving car begins to feel like a body engaging in stealth "tactics of evasion," longing to escape this dark, precarious world.[40]

What this car navigates, or indeed is thrown into, is the lineaments of subjection and dispossession that *Twilight City* presents: the histories and futures of precarious life that *Handsworth*'s postwar migrants encounter when they step off the *Windrush*. The stealthy, uninterrupted movement of the car gestures toward a fugitive structure of time, a desire for the moment when the physical and mental effects of the suffocating world have vanished. I want to turn to the ways that Black Audio registers this anticipation of bodily release in the filmic structure—in the cut, in the movement between frames, in the relationship between diegesis and nondiegesis. This cinematic inscription is where we find the singularity of Black Audio's filmic grammar of fugitive time.

TOWARD THE THIRD SPACE

My larger focus, moving into this different mode of cinematic reading, has to do with how Black Audio's "alternative visual grammar," as Auguiste puts it, intersects with what Akomfrah refers to as the collective's "search for new versions of becoming." In the interplay of these two ideas we find the sense of anticipation of embodied flight central to this study's larger conception of fugitive time—an anticipatory sense, that is, built right into the editing strategies of these two films. I'll begin with what I understand to be the phenomenal fugitive movement in the succession of images in *Handsworth Songs*: the sense in the film, from moment to moment, of a longing for release in that next moment from the immediacy of embodied trauma. The desire to escape the persistent haunting of violence that nonetheless always remains constitutive of that phenomenal flight.

The specificity of this temporality in *Handsworth Songs* lies in its structure of montage. For Akomfrah, cinematic montage corresponds to a search for the "third meaning": "that somehow when . . . two opposites collide in this dialectical way, some sort of synthesis is engineered . . . and in that a new form, a new meaning, a new way emerges which you can chase ad infinitum."[41] This dialectical structure is the fulcrum of *Handsworth*'s fugitive temporal grammar, this Eisensteinian principle of montage as a "collision of independent shots" from which "arises a new, higher dimension."[42] Deleuze suggests that this structure is produced through a "dialectical yearning of the image . . . to leap formally from one power into another."[43] However, what makes Black Audio's mode of montage distinct is its fugitive valence. In *Handsworth Songs* the dialectical synthesis, this "third meaning," signifies that indeterminately located utopian site of release from the traumas of an antiblack world. Put another way, if the two images of the dialectic emerge from *within* the world that subjects black life, then this third space signifies the *outside* of that world, that Deleuzean yearned-for space. The other critical dimension of *Handsworth*'s fugitive montage structure lies in Akomfrah's idea of the "chase ad infinitum," the relentless fugitive pursuit of that utopian third space that always seems just out of reach. In Black Audio's first feature-length essay film, the movement and collision of images produce an infinite, ecstatic energy that lunges out toward that third space.

To understand *Handsworth Songs* in this way requires that we allow the film itself and its discursive apparatus to stand in metaphorically for the body, the same black body that Akomfrah centers in his speculative photography exhibition: "a particular body burdened by an excess of signs; a body literally framed as a figure of torment and bliss."[44] I'm thinking of this filmic body in the way Jean-François Lyotard understands a film as "the organic body of cinematographic movements," the way that a given single film is made possible by "the subordination of all partial drives . . . to the unity of an organic body."[45] But what distinguishes the corporeality of *Handsworth Songs*, of course, is its blackness—the way that this film might be thought of as representing the historical and cultural specificity of the black body and the embodied desire, as Akomfrah suggests, to "flirt with the transcendental as a yearning," thereby stripping itself of trauma (experienced, remembered, even unconsciously perceived trauma). I want to stay with the language of the "black body" in this analysis, given Akomfrah's deliberately discursive cultivation of the term in his "On the Borderline" essay, but in my evocation of it in *Handsworth* I do read a valence of Spillers's "flesh," even if it's not named as such. The flesh is that "zero degree of social conceptualization" of black trauma. As with Césaire's *Notebook*, Spillers's influential distinction between the body and the flesh doesn't neatly translate in Black Audio's work at each turn. However, I maintain that in Akomfrah and Black Audio's naming of the black body there's a strong resonance with that "primary narrative" of the flesh, "[the] seared, divided, ripped-apartness," that which has historically rendered black life a "prime commodity of exchange."[46]

In *Handsworth Songs* the trauma lies principally in the dominant discourse on race shown in the film's newsreel footage, in which blackness is represented as pathological, irrational, and inchoately violent. These clips in turn elicit memories of past experiences of racism and violence, but they also elicit the attendant unconscious hauntings of traumatic experiences that, as trauma theorist Cathy Caruth frames it, manifest belatedly and repeatedly, despite "an absolute inability to know it."[47] These news media headlines and clips threaten to enact a kind of violent erasure of black life, indeed of the black body, rendering it, as Kobena Mercer would put it, paradoxically invisible to the law yet hypervisible as the blight of the Powellian nation. If, then, the entire discursive montage of Black Audio's film represents the black body, then those racist news clips are constitutive of this body, inscribed, we might say, into that "primary narrative" of wounding. Understanding the filmic amalgam of *Handsworth Songs* as metaphorically standing in for the wounded black body allows us to see how Black Audio configures its fugitive filmic grammar.

Crucial to this wounding, however, is the way that the film moves through time by means of disparate successive images, each colliding with and disrupting the next. Despite the achronological succession of many of *Handsworth*'s archival images (leaping between the 1980s and 1950s), the film unfolds phenomenologically over a set duration. The energy of what Jacques Aumont calls cinema's "time of projection" engenders a sense of fugitive thrownness away from the racist discourse that has become part of that body.[48] There's a way, in other words, in which the temporal projection of *Handsworth* suggests a kind of lunging toward that utopian "third meaning" of montage, that longed-for site of release that lies just beyond the now and just outside the world. In my example below, the two types of montage sequences of concern—those of blatant antiblackness and those of black discursive power—are bound together in this singular filmic projection (this singular black body), yet the radical political and affective disparity between the two reveals a volatile fault line, a sense that those sequences of black discursive power threaten to escape the rails of the film's temporal projection, breaking from the filmic body in search of that utopian third space beyond representation, beyond that originary narrative of wounding.

One of the more prominent instances of this cinematic grammar of fugitive time comes just minutes into the film, beginning with footage of the British home secretary walking through an incensed crowd of black Handsworth residents. An omniscient narrator fills us in on the conversation: "The masses saw him struggle for composure, and they heard him mutter to journalists: 'These are senseless occasions, completely without reason.' Somebody said behind him, 'The higher the monkey climb, the more he will expose.'" The film then cuts to several other deserted postuprising street scenes before we see the previously discussed sequence of the dreadlocked youth running toward the camera attempting to evade riot police—the speed and vitality of the youth contrasting sharply with the stationary and slow-moving shots that came just before. The film then cuts to interviews with several West Indian youths, with one saying: "You hear in the news . . . it's black against Indian. Rubbish, that talk. Seen? It's just police and them stupidity. . . . And black people *have had enough.*" The film then cuts to a series of still images of national newspaper headlines:

"Racial Fights Could Take Over City," "The Face of a Bomber" (next to the face of a West Indian man).

The fugitive temporal grammar of this series lies in the succession of images that separate the two sequences of overt discriminatory bias: on the one end, the home secretary's pronouncement that "these are senseless occasions," and on the other, the headline stills that unequivocally indict (only) blacks for the uprisings. In the temporal flow of the film, the home secretary's sequence is cut off abruptly, denying him further discursive power, by a series of scenes that give more discursive weight to black voices and presence. But the interview of the West Indian youth is also cut short by the newspaper headlines' claim to discursive authority. The sequences in which blacks have discursive power, I want to suggest, stand in such evident political contrast to those antiblack scenes that the former enact a sense of fugitive propulsion—made possible by the momentum of the film's temporal projection—away from those sequences in which the state and the media assert their antiblack biases. Reading the movement of the running black youth in the context of the larger montage, Nina Power suggests that "as they grasp at him and he manages to break free, if only for a moment, you long for him to make it through, to escape the inevitable punishment and media stereotyping, to be part of a better history that never was, but that might still be."[49] To "make it through" is not simply for this youth to break free from the police but, as Power suggests, to break free of the discursive cycle that subjects blackness and to break out of the film's projection that maintains the woundedness of blackness, to shatter the dialectical montage in order to find some kind of freedom in that third space where trauma and violence have vanished. In Power's reading, too, there's a suggestion that the young man may have eyed an opening, that he somehow anticipates the possibility of that outside, as if to inhabit that third space, impossibly, in advance.

The sequence of the dreadlocked youth running away from riot police holds a central place in this fugitive desire to break away from the filmic projection and the larger filmic body. In contrast to the montage cells surrounding it, which are either still images (of newspaper headlines) or subtly moving images (like a boy pulling a milk cart), this running sequence exudes an uncontainable energy and velocity. Indeed, it threatens to become what Malin Wahlberg calls a "frame-breaking event." Extending Erving Goffman's phenomenological theory of everyday life to the study of experimental documentary film, Wahlberg explains that such an event corresponds to those "unexpected modes of representation" in a film that disrupt the expected patterns of timing and representation, jolting the "constructed meter": "The frame-breaking event is often propelled by a combination of manipulated space-time (duration, tempo, rhythm, and repetition) and the enactment of the sound-image record as a trace of a historical and social realm."[50] The combination of three critical elements in this running sequence—its relatively quickened tempo, its archival status as a historical record of black refusal, and the suggestion of this figure's proleptic inhabitation of the outside—makes this sequence leap out at the spectator from the surrounding montage cells, its speed and (historical and discursive) weight threatening to escape the frame (and the bodily wounding) that constitutes *Handsworth*'s pro-filmic world and the film's temporal projection.

It's important to understand the larger montage I've isolated—of which this running youth is but one cell—as a continual oscillation between antiblack sequences and those of black discursive power. The running-youth sequence ultimately doesn't shatter the film and escape the film body, as much as its energy suggests it might. After this running event nearly breaks the frame, the film reconstitutes its rhythm and tempo, showing us those stills of antiblack newspaper headlines ("Riot of Death," "The Face of a Bomber"). As much as *Handsworth*'s black discursive power sequences register a kind of symbolic stripping away of that racist discourse and a desire to flee the temporal projection of the film body and find the third space, those racist sequences continue to reemerge throughout the film like a persistent haunting of subjection. A back-and-forth between the two types of montage sequences becomes clear after the "Riot of Death" headline, when the film again pivots to the side of black social life with a new tableau of still images: "images of a 'happy' past," as Coco Fusco describes them, of West Indian couples cutting wedding cake in tuxedos and flowing white gowns, images "that are a precious part of the black immigrants' collective memory."[51] This tableau renews the fugitive temporal pulse of the film, bringing discursive power back to the side of blackness, leaving open the hope that black life might yet break out and find that utopian third space, harnessing the escapist energy of its thrownness, freeing itself from those wounds that have rendered black life a "prime commodity of exchange."

This reading of *Handsworth Songs*, I should say, complicates some of the critical interpretations of the film. In them, the relation between antiblack media sequences and those sequences of black discursive power is read as a "counter-discursive" relation, whereby the latter sequences effectively resist the hegemony of the former. For Mercer, this relation "interrupts the amnesia of media representations of the 1985 conflicts . . . [creating] a space of critical reverie which counteracts the active ideological forgetting of England's colonial past in media discourses on Handsworth."[52] More recently, Simone Sessolo has argued that *Handsworth Songs* "counters the representation of immigrant minorities as peripheral and extraneous entities to the national, social discourse."[53] Although I don't disagree that the film undermines the discursive hegemony of media biases, these readings don't account for the temporal movement of the film in that negotiation of discursive power. The film's juxtaposition of images is not stationary, as if it were presenting a series of still images mounted on a gallery wall. The film's images continuously move through time as "fluid movements, the gradual congealing and dissolution of meaning," and this temporality needs to be understood as integral to the film's discursive negotiation.[54] This temporal projection, I argue, enables a reading of the black discursive position in the film as a "refusative escape," as Marquis Bey characterizes the practice of fugitivity, as a *kinetic* refusal of the interpellation of those antiblack media sequences rather than a simply a contestation of interpellation.[55]

The final component of the film's grammar of fugitive time has to do with another category of traumatic frames from which the others take flight. There are two grainy, presumably early twentieth-century footage sequences of black figures laboring in the West Indies that recall an older, larger structure of black historical violation. Between shots of 1950s mixed-race dance parties are two fleeting three-second shots of a shirtless man throwing an armful of cut sugarcane into a pile and a woman pounding fish in a dugout canoe. In both shots, their bodies shine under the equatorial sun as unequivocal reminders of the violence of slavery. Indeed, these shots stand in stark contrast to the relatively affluent blackness in the dance sequences that surround them. In its temporal projection, the film moves on from these historically fraught shots, to be sure, taking abrupt flight from them, riding, it seems in part, on the film's affective residue of the escapist energy of the youth running from riot police searching for an opening to that beyond world. But there is also an affective residue of these West Indian shots that remains for the duration of the film, forming a kind of (un)conscious memory of historical subjection that lingers in the projection of the film's fugitive thrownness. The tension produced by this persistent haunting of black embodied violence ensures that "chase ad infinitum," generating a vitality that animates that movement toward absolute release. Indeed, Black Audio reminds us that fugitive time is not about attaining a definitive utopian life. In *Handsworth Songs* the collective demonstrates how this temporality can be stitched into the layers of cinematic editing, proposing a kind of perpetual lunging toward that ever-deferred utopian third space of montage, a celebratory and ongoing effort to imagine that moment when the wounds of the body might at last be no more.

If in *Handsworth Songs* the structure of dialectical montage gestures toward the utopian freedom of the third space, in *Twilight City* we seem to get a glimpse, albeit an ephemeral one, of a potential version of that freedom. In the latter we get a similar sense of lunging toward that outside, a kind of kinetic propulsion toward release, but its grammar of fugitive time lies in another location of the film's architecture: its nondiegetic content.

NONDIEGETIC DREAMING

If Gérard Genette defines the diegesis of literary narrative as the "universe in which the story takes place," then nondiegesis is simply that which lies *outside* the story's universe.[56] Film critic Edward Branigan refers to this relationship as "two simultaneous worlds." For him, diegesis in film "extends beyond what is seen in a given shot and beyond even what is seen in the entire film.... The diegesis, then, is the implied spatial, temporal, and causal system of a character—a collection of sense data which is represented as being at least potentially accessible to a character." Nondiegesis, on the other hand, is those elements "not taken to be part of the character's world, and hence not subject to its laws, but instead are taken to be *about* that world and are addressed only to the spectator."[57]

In *Twilight City* the diegesis is Olivia's world: the research, the dreams, and the personal histories she references in her letter, as well as the interviews, historical footage, and contemporary images of the city that correspond to those references. *Twilight*'s diegesis, in short, is the world she critiques, the world that subjects, the world of twentieth-century London within which she locates the precariousness of black life. The nondiegetic moments of the film, on the other hand, lie outside this world. They represent another—to read Branigan's language literally—that is, "not subject" to the "laws" of the subjecting diegetic world. These moments lie outside Olivia's frame and consciousness, yet the existence of this other world stands in relation to hers as a kind of response to the subjections she chronicles. Put another way, nondiegesis consists of *freedom glimpses* in *Twilight*. I borrow the term from Walcott's recent work, where he identifies black creative expression as a critical site in which to "glimpse the possibility of Black freedom . . . moments when Black people are responding to themselves, unintruded upon by the white gaze." Such glimpses, he maintains, lie beyond normative post-civil-rights and postcolonial discourses of freedom.[58] In *Twilight* we glimpse quiet moments of relief in body and mind beyond the reach of the law's interpellation; they're glimpses because, though ecstatic, they're fleeting, and the diegetic world interdicts their permanence at every turn. The law is never far enough removed. Nondiegesis in *Twilight*, however, brings with it a promise of a more sustained release, specifically the potentiality of a queer utopia that would transform the body's being-in-the-world. Structuring this relationship between diegesis and nondiegesis—between the subjecting world and these glimpses of freedom—is a back-and-forth movement akin to Fred Moten's notion of "fugitive movement in and out of the frame, bar, or whatever externally imposed social logic" that animates much of this book.[59] We find a shuttling in and out of the world in *Twilight City* that produces a kind of vital thrownness, an ecstatic promise of a more lasting utopian release.

There are three sequences of nondiegesis in the film, each featuring the work of Nigerian-British photographer Rotimi Fani-Kayode. Though separated and scattered throughout the film, all three consist of tableaux vivants, or reenactments, of well-known Fani-Kayode photographs. The tableaux are still and quiet, each made up of multiple composed scenes of nude or partially nude black men set against a pitch-dark background. In this darkness their bodies hover in the glow of a focused studio light, alternately at rest and moving about with measured assertiveness. The affect in these sequences is radically different from the world that Olivia narrates. They mark a "suspended time," Kodwo Eshun suggests, moments in the film in which "montage and chronology give way to reverie."[60] In them we find calm and self-assurance in one's embodied presence, a world far flung from the layered violence of Olivia's world, one very much "unintruded upon by the white gaze." A world, in short, filled with ecstasy: a "reprieve from injury," a "state of intensely heightened sensual feeling [that] creates a space of timelessness, of suspension in the space where the material and immaterial commingle."[61] In his manifesto, "Traces of Ecstasy," Fani-Kayode explains how he seeks in his work to translate his "rage" and "desire" into "new images," "reveal[ing] hidden worlds" through an "imaginative investigation of Blackness, maleness and sexuality."[62] It's Fani-Kayode's queer photographs that inspired Akomfrah's speculative photography exhibition that opens this chapter. Situating these tableaux in the nondiegetic spaces of *Twilight City*, Black Audio deepens the utopian impulse of Fani-Kayode's work, sustaining his quest for "new visions" of black life.

An energy-generating dissonance develops, I argue, in the film's back-and-forth between diegesis and nondiegesis, which in turn maintains a continual anticipation of Fani-Kayode's tableaux. This occurs visually in the juxtaposition of, say, the images of people sleeping in boxes on London's streets and the reenactment of Fani-Kayode's well-known "Milk Drinker" photograph. But this dissonance also occurs in the audiovisual relation, in the way that the diegetic narration of London's structures of subjection (whether provided by Olivia or an interview subject) bleeds into the nondiegetic tableaux. In one nondiegetic sequence, for example, as we look at a close-up profile view of three nude male torsos, Olivia recounts a dream in which she "saw a weary black man stumbling through Shadwell High Street to be found dead in the morning." In these nondiegetic sequences, traces of diegetic trauma incessantly remind us that lasting utopian release hasn't fully arrived, that the world of antiblackness and antiqueerness is not far enough removed from Fani-Kayode's sites of desire.

These tableaux gesture toward a fugitive queerness to come. As Mercer puts it, the distinctiveness of Fani-Kayode's images lies in their "invitation into a subterranean escape route from worldly experiences of racism and homophobia" and their "subtle and subversive miscegenation of the visual codes through which it articulates black gay male subjectivity."[63] Steven Nelson similarly argues that Fani-Kayode uses homoeroticism as a tool of "transformation" to "[question] the very ability of the body to retain its position as a coherent signifier of identity and experience."[64] The photographer's work, in these readings, constitutes a fugitive space in which the black male body escapes its place in the world, taking flight from the world's exclusions and violence. These notions of "transformation" and "escape," in conjunction with Fani-Kayode's own characterization of his work as "ecstatic" and revelatory of "hidden worlds," also recall the valence of queerness as potentiality that I address in the context of Césaire's *Notebook*. Pertinent here is José Muñoz's understanding of queerness as a "structuring and educated mode of desiring that allows us to see and feel beyond the quagmire of the present." "The present is not enough," he maintains. "It is impoverished and toxic for queers and other people who do not feel the privilege of majoritarian belonging, normative tastes, and 'rational' expectations." Queerness "promises a human that is not yet here"; it takes on an "ecstatic and horizontal temporality [as] a path and a movement to a greater openness to the world."[65]

As in the previous chapters, especially chapter 2, the question of sexual climax and its presumed anticipation is critical to account for in the queer "horizonality" of Fani-Kayode's tableaux. Although Ian Bourland rightly suggests that "sex is only ever implied" in Fani-Kayode's work, homoerotic and orgasmic insinuations at times seem unequivocal, especially in *Twilight*'s reenactment of "Milk Drinker."[66] Reading the original 1983 photograph, Mercer maintains that the gourd appears like a "metaphorical penis," and "a connotation of fellatio inescapably arises by virtue of the way it looms above the mouth."[67] However, I would argue that mere "connotation" is exceeded in the five seconds of the *Twilight* reenactment: with the camera focused on the drinker's upper body, the gourd certainly looms, but as a moving image it also pours milk, the figure gasping for breath as he consumes, much of the milk streaming down his face, chest, and stomach with each pulsing gasp, streaking rivulets running down his body. The focused care of the drinking figure as he holds the gourd and takes in the liquid certainly evokes fellatio, the gourd-phallus reaching the fleeting ecstatic release of climax, ejaculate running full and everywhere. Crucial in this brief shot are those heaving gasps that punctuate the tempo of ejaculation, almost making the shot seem like it's slowed down, even retimed in slow motion. The viewer watches these full, pulsating moments, sitting with them for those five full seconds, witnessing that pleasure as it stretches out, as if time in this ethereal black queer space were momentarily suspended and elastic. The way Black Audio sits with the intimacy and immediacy of the moment feels like a deliberate effort to embrace this queer orgasm, to stretch the temporal limits of homoerotic pleasure, in a way that runs counter to the manner in which Annamarie Jagose keenly observes the experience of orgasm as decidedly "not an eidetic phenomenon": "Despite its apparent indenture to the present moment, the now of embodied experience, orgasm can seem more immediately historical or futural, hard to recall or summon in any specificity, belonging to some moment whose distance from this reflective one marks the impossibility of its full interpretive recovery."[68] In the slowness and stretching duration of the "Milk Drinker" reenactment there almost seems an intent to make that orgasm eidetic, lasting, full, and immanently recoverable—something longer than just a glimpse. Or at least to gesture to the possibility, the queer promise, of that fullness. This effect has everything to do with Black Audio's decision to include Fani-Kayode's images as tableaux vivants, as *living pictures*—living, breathing, and moving in ways that still photographs cannot capture. Fani-Kayode's tableaux may not be a lasting utopian release,

3.3 Still from *Twilight City* (1989). Reenactment of Rotimi Fani-Kayode's "Milk Drinker" photograph (1983).

but that promise of care, ecstasy, and unburdening for black queer life is unmistakable.

To pan out more broadly, these queer frames in *Twilight* open us to distinctly black formations of queer time and desire. Especially apt here, with these tableaux set against neoliberalism's devastations, is Kara Keeling's notion of "black futures," which she characterizes as a "political imagination that posits radical socioeconomic and geopolitical transformations." "Ungovernable" and "anarchic," "animated in queer times and inseparable from queer relations," black futures, for Keeling, cut against and through the mechanisms of financial derivatives and calculations, naming "what remains unaccountable."[69] The unaccountable—that which remains illegible to the neoliberal logics of finance capital—is located in that suspended space and time of nondiegesis in *Twilight*, a site where Alexis Gumbs and Julia Wallace's distinction between "security" and "safety" in relation to black queer life resonates. Security, they say, often means "having access to the violent means that the state uses to defend itself, the police, the national guard, the private security forces that companies use to protect their wealth. For those of us, black, queer, young, radical, and grassroots, who are not often seen as part of the state's project to reproduce itself . . . those sources of security are not dependable." By contrast, safety, Gumbs and Wallace insist, is what black queer youth strive for. Indeed, it's as if

BLACK AUDIO'S ARCHIVAL FLIGHT **125**

they're describing the utopian extensions of Fani-Kayode's queer scenes: "Safety, to us, means being able to be comfortable in our skin, having the freedom to move, being able to sleep restfully and wake renewed and excited about the journey. Safety comes from knowing that we are held by a community."[70] Crucially, though, in *Twilight City* this safety has not yet come. It remains a promise. It resides in that next moment, in the not yet here of another embodied being-beyond-the-world.[71]

An example best shows how this queer fugitive time structures the film. The sequence I have in mind, which appears a third of the way through, emerges from the diegetic components that lead up to it. Following Homi Bhabha's narration of the parasitic structure of development in the new London, the frame cuts to the car navigating the deserted nighttime streets, which in turn triggers a shift in Mathison's sound score: a low synthesizer drone sounds against a male voice repeating a flourish of half steps and quarter steps, a kind of nervous, ritualistic swirling sound resembling part of a muezzin's call to prayer playing over and over. Olivia reads from her letter during this fifteen-second car navigation sequence: "You say you hope I've not joined the city's lost souls, those who shuffle in the shadows, always waiting for the darkness to melt the autumn evening light. You ask if the winter evenings still last forever. Yes, they do. And as the Old London dissolves, your lost souls are becoming more visible." When Olivia reaches the words "always waiting," the image cuts to a close-up of a lit candle held in a clenched black fist. This is the first of several five-second shots that together form the first tableau. When Olivia's narration reaches the phrase "last forever," the image cuts to a profile view of a man holding a tray on which rests a large, pink-hued fish. Five seconds later, the frame cuts to a man lying down, resting his head on the stomach of another. After five more seconds, at the phrase "more visible," Olivia's narration stops, and the image shifts to the "Milk Drinker" reenactment. The final frame of the tableau is a return to the man holding the candle, this time with his entire body situated in the frame, sitting on the ground and holding the candle with determined stillness. All of these sequences are set against a deep black background, the men's bodies illuminated by the studio light. There's a profound calm in each of the frames, again like subtly enlivened still photographs. Throughout these sequences, Mathison's soundtrack of the low synthesizer drone and muezzin-like vocals continues to loop in the background. The tableau concludes as the frame cuts to shots of men eating in a London Somali center, the drone and vocals persisting as Olivia

3.4 Still from *Twilight City* (1989).

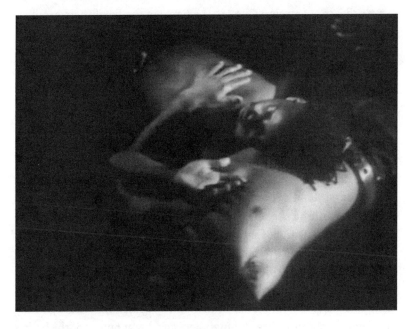

3.5 Still from *Twilight City* (1989).

restarts the narration of her letter, telling her mother, "I suppose, in one way or another, most of my friends are the people you warned me about."

Audiovisually, a kind of tension is generated as the car cruises through the dark streets, which in turn produces a sense of anticipatory flight toward Fani-Kayode's nondiegetic queer world. This upward and outward thrownness is created by sound that "vectorizes" the images, as Michel Chion puts it, where the movement in the sound combines with the movement in the images to create a "feeling of imminence and expectation." This particular *Twilight* sequence corresponds to Chion's example of how a "regularly cyclical" sound combines with an image's "microrhythms," those "rapid movements on the image's surface caused by things such as curls of smoke" that "create rapid and fluid rhythmic values, instilling a vibrating, trembling temporality."[72] Thus we have the energy of the muezzin-like singing voice looping against the low-pitched synthesizer drone that merges with the energy of the car moving through London's night streets, signage and shops flying by. The combination produces a sense of "imminence," as if the car were stealthily gathering energy in order to lift off into Fani-Kayode's parallel world, creating a "vibrating, trembling temporality" that takes flight from the precariousness of those streets to chase the fugitive's "dream of an elsewhere" in the flame of the firmly held candle.[73] Once we see that hand, we immediately sense an affect of rest and comfort, in stark contrast to the earlier footage of the Lascars and the unhoused lining the sidewalks. It signals "other terrains where black life can amble unharmed . . . where bodies are no longer the grounds for others' becomings, others' vicious expressions of neoimperial, homophobic, transphobic, racist, sexist, classist, and ableist desire."[74]

But the film's audio track reminds us that this relief and calm are just a glimpse of freedom. Mathison's cryptically looping sounds and Olivia's account of the "city's lost souls" bleed into Fani-Kayode's freely queer frames. If film sound "bind[s] the flow of images . . . through sound overlaps," then here Mathison's score and Olivia's text tether, as it were, diegesis to nondiegesis, the world of subjection and that glimpsed ethereal world.[75] Those sounds begin before the tableau and continue on after, indicating that the subjugating world threatens to contaminate the temporary safety of that nonconforming space. This auditory haunting of subjection is critical to this sequence's grammar as the fugitive search for release in body and mind advances outward, lunging toward the moment of the body's unburdening. And just as the car took us out of the frame of the world and into Fani-Kayode's nondiegetic glimpse, the film ushers us back into the diegetic world when we see the images at the Somali center. The reentry establishes the fugitive movement in and out of the frame found throughout the film, the ongoing rush for that sustained nondiegetic freedom.

In the other instances of this back-and-forth, Fani-Kayode's queer frames are juxtaposed with diegetic sequences that focus explicitly on the persecution of lesbians, gays, and gender-nonconforming people under Thatcherism, specifically Section 28, which prohibited the "promotion of homosexuality" in the United Kingdom until its repeal in 2003. In one interview, Femi Otitoju, an equal opportunities consultant, warns that the "proactive legislation has made people feel they can just attack me on the street corner whenever they wish." Lifting us away from this site of attack and into Fani-Kayode's all too ephemeral alter-world, the wandering night car appears in the seconds before each tableau, cruising along as if gaining velocity to flee into the dark sky, pursuing "dreams of lives unencumbered by state-sanctioned homophobia."[76] "Queers need fabulation," Keguro Macharia insists. "We need to imagine and theorize and practice strategies that make our beings possible."[77] These tableaux in *Twilight* are one such fabulation: fleeting imaginings where one can almost taste the promise of a ceaseless break from the impositions heaped on blackness and queerness, the burdens that bear down on the black body, promising "a human that is not yet here." In each instance, Mathison's score precedes and exceeds the nondiegetic cells to reveal a kind of slippage between worlds, the sense that their limits are not clearly marked, that one must savor the fleeting moments of reprieve before they recede. Mathison's synthesizer moves us in and out of the frame, returning us to the world to rejoin the film's study of black disposability, to plan and anticipate the next escape. His sounds allow us to trace a counterpoint much like the one we find in *Handsworth Songs*, an interplay between disparate frames that generates the film's kinetic lunging toward release, however elusive that release may be, inscribing the phenomenal experience of fugitive time into the structure of the film itself.

....

In *Twilight City*'s nondiegetic sequences and *Handsworth Songs*' montage editing we find figurations of what Akomfrah describes in his speculative photography essay—frames that "flirt with the transcendental as a yearning," frames that center on that "notoriously public figure," the black body. On the surface, this embodied yearning speaks to their 1980s moment of production—the hyperfinancialization of the metropolis, the police occupation of black communities, the uprisings in Brixton, Toxteth, and Handsworth, the persecution of LGBTQ communities, the coalitional blackness assembled by the children of the Windrush generation. Black Audio's "alternative visual grammar," in a way, was a grammar of its time, a grammar of black entrenchment and refusal amid the onslaught of Thatcherism. But this alternative grammar and the embodied yearning it indexes is just as much about histories and futures. It charts the disparate historical experiences that brought it into being—the Lascar sailors on the Isle of Dogs, the London Blitz, the mid-century collapse of West Indian agriculture, the arrival of the *Empire Windrush* at Tilbury. It's also a grammar indebted to prior black British grammars, including dramatic narrative films such as *Pressure*, directed by Horace Ové and written by novelist Samuel Selvon, or Menelik Shabazz's *Burning an Illusion*—both among the earliest screen representations of that second generation.

Perhaps most urgently in our own moment, we might also see Black Audio's grammar as prefigurative, gesturing to fugitive aesthetic languages to come. Writing at the cusp of the new century, soon after the members of the collective dispersed in different creative directions, Stuart Hall suggested that Britain had entered a moment of hollow, uneven multiculturalism. Outside of sterile celebrations of diversity, "the practices of racialized exclusion, racially-compounded disadvantage, household poverty, unemployment and education under-achievement persist—indeed, multiply." From 1958 to the turn of the century, Hall insisted, "black people have been the subject of racialized attack, had their grievances largely ignored by the police, and been subjected to racially-inflected practices of policing."[78] Indeed, these trends have hardly abated since Hall wrote these words: in 2020 Scotland Yard continued to disproportionately target black Britons, and police brutality and killings of unarmed black folks have persisted with devastating frequency.[79] And, of course, on the other side of the Atlantic we find in America a haunting repetition of an analogous police brutality, police militarization, and black invisibility to the law that carries its own harrowing legacies. In the historical conjuncture that has seen the murder of Mark Duggan, Breonna Taylor, and Chris Kaba, we need fugitive grammars now as much as ever. The next generation—the Otolith Groups, the Danez Smiths, the Nest Collectives, the Grace Ndiritus—are tracing the further evolutions of fugitive desire into the twenty-first century, the mutations of that thrownness, giving voice and language to those lives that matter. In this next chapter I want to move further toward the contemporary with a study of two radically imaginative multidisciplinary artists from disparate diasporic locations whose lives together span nearly a century. Triangulating Europe, North America, and West Africa, there's a kinship connecting the Black Audio Film Collective, Sun Ra, and Issa Samb. Ra and Samb take that desire for unrecognizability and safety in the third space of montage and the outer world of nondiegesis and explode it into seeming chaos: inhabiting what the world reads as madness as their fugitive vessel that just might lead them into the beyond.

ness
4 SUN RA, ISSA SAMB, AND THE DRAPETO-MANIACAL AVANT-GARDE

In "the muscles, the tendons," in the "brain and nerves," Samuel Cartwright wrote in 1851, lies the difference between the "African race" and all others. Like the skin, he explained, the insides of the black body are "tinctured with a shade of the pervading darkness." Read today as emblematic of pro-slavery pseudoscience, the American physician's "Diseases and Peculiarities of the Negro Race" contains his now-infamous pathologization of black freedom. "Drapetomania," he called it, was a "disease of the mind" that drove the slave to become fugitive, to "abscond from service." It apparently emboldened African-descended enslaved people to defy the will of the "Almighty," for it was God who had made them "more flexed or bent . . . than any other man," making "submission" their natural physical and societal position. If the slave was not deprived of basic necessities or beaten too close to death, but was also not treated as an equal, Cartwright insisted, the disease could be effectively contained: "The negro is spellbound, and cannot run away."[1]

To be "spellbound" is an obstruction of the premise of this book—that desire for the phenomenal moment in time when the body and mind are at last *un*bent, freed of historical submission. In Cartwright's account of the disease, we find a curious melding of theology and science, as if an apparent dearth of medical evidence required the compensation of divine law, producing, as Calvin Warren aptly puts it, a kind of "mysticism" designed to keep the enslaved in their place.[2] That the disease functions as a mechanism of power seems clear. My interest in Cartwright's racist theory, however, moves toward a different end. What if this pseudoscience were reimagined as a condition of possibility? How might it veil one's desire to "imagine a black world"?[3] What would a drapetomanic time consciousness entail?

Fast-forward a century to two multidisciplinary artists living, working, and reenvisioning the world in discrete nodes of the global diaspora. On the surface, the Senegalese painter, sculptor, playwright, and poet Issa Samb and the American jazz musician, composer, and poet Sun Ra have little in common. Born in the 1940s to a Lebu family in a small fishing village on the Senegalese coast, Samb lived most of his life in that country's capital of Dakar; Ra, in turn, was born more than three decades earlier in Birmingham, Alabama—although he famously insisted his time on Earth was a "visitation," that he was originally from the planet Saturn. Samb and Ra, however, were kindred spirits. Both bore a subversive proximity to drapetomania. Their work was read by many in their time as illegible, even crazy, but that coding of madness belied a cultivated opacity and indeed a radical potentiality of fugitive visions and alternative worlds. For Samb and Ra, full legibility in the eyes of the world was regulatory and constricting. Opacity, in turn, what Édouard Glissant identifies as "irreducible singularity," was for them a kind of freedom—or at least *pointed the way* to freedom.[4] Nontransparency signaled a coming release, a refusal of the world's impositions. And this illegibility manifests in their work both formally and conceptually. Sun Ra's opaque form was in the dissonant sounds of the band he led for decades and in his constant poetic wordplay. Samb's took the shape of a constant shuttling between disparate ideas in his writing and in the heaving layers of artworks and ephemera assembled in his Dakar installation/courtyard. Conceptually, each was driven by a desire for a host of indeterminate states and ideas: "infinity," "perpetual errancy," the "unknown," the "impossible." For them, opacity saturated the operations of escape (the path and method to the outside) and also the site of escape itself, what they imagined that outside might be like. And the body, for both, undergirded it all: at times buried in a poem or an anecdote but always at the fore in their performative presence.

My interest lies in how Samb and Ra turned accusations of craziness, even insanity, into an insurgent aesthetic practice and anticipatory consciousness. As one writer in the *Atlanta Daily News* asked in 1992: "Is Sun Ra crazy? Or is it all just an act by a brilliant artist born of the same African-American tradition . . . [that ultimately led to] rock and roll? It's unlikely anyone but Sun Ra will ever know." Likewise, an article on Samb ahead of the 2010 Dakar Biennale praises the artist but notes that "almost everyone thought he was weird, strange, even crazy."[5] These views expose, I want to suggest, what La Marr Jurelle Bruce calls "psychosocial madness," an ostracism that "unsettles reigning regimes of the normal" and "hegemonic common sense," indexing less a person's actual psychological state than how "avowedly sane majorities interpellate and often denigrate difference." I'm interested in what Samb and Ra do with this breakdown in social processing, this inability of the putatively "sane majority" to make sense of their "radical difference."[6] Consciously or not, they took advantage of these dismissals and the cover they afforded from that majority's invasive gaze. My contention centers on the work itself: that Samb and Ra's sprawling oeuvres mine the liminal space exposed by their relegation to madness and that they use this space to cultivate their fugitive time consciousness, envisioning in advance escape routes to otherwise worlds and existences.

To be clear, this chapter is not a study of mental illness or disability. It's not about placing either Samb or Ra in the context of Frantz Fanon's work on psychopathology, for instance, including the last chapter of *The Wretched of the Earth*, where Fanon is preoccupied with "the psychic effects of colonial war" and how "colonialism is the catalyzer of mental illness."[7] Instead, I'm interested in the ways nonnormative thought, *externally ascribed as madness*, instantiates dream consciousness, a frame of mind that anticipates otherwise worlds. As I see it, this occupation of the space of putative madness has a host of analogues in black studies and black experience. We read it, for one, in Glissant's account of the West Indian enslaved people's manipulations of the creole language, the production of sound and meaning in excess of the master's comprehension: "Slaves camouflaged the word under the provocative intensity of the scream. No one could translate the meaning of what seemed to be nothing but a shout . . . the apparently meaningless texture of extreme noise."[8] And in a broader scope, what I'm getting at in this chapter runs alongside Fred Moten's theorization of the position of anticolonialism as one that "disorders" the regulatory capacity of settler colonialism. For him, the anticolonial demand for disorder can be read only as "cacophony," as "multiphonic delirium," from the normative colonial perspective. "No," he says, "let's look at this shit from our perspective, from the perspective of the ones who are relegated to the zone of the crazy." Excavate it, cultivate it, allow its radical "non-normative form of cogitation" to generate possibility, to reach for new forms of existence.[9]

This is the position from which Issa Samb and Sun Ra articulate their formations of fugitive time. Their improvisatory delirium and camouflaged screams constitute a world-building, generative force, a mass of catalyzing experimental imaginings that proleptically envisage an expansive refuge in the opaque. Opacity, in short, as open flight, an open set. Their aesthetics anticipate the open, in the hope of fleeing beyond the threshold of any trace of recognition, where they might at last discover the freedom of absolute illegibility, realizing their own unique genres of an utterly singular, incomparable, ungovernable black life. This shroud of nonreason, of delirium, is for Samb and Ra a kind of fugitive antechamber, a site of strategic planning with the potential to open out—even if fleetingly—to a utopian opacity where blackness has been rid of all preconceptions in the eyes of the world. An opacity where black life, as Nahum Chandler might put it, is "an exorbitance for thought," and no logic of settler colonialism, antiblackness, police brutality, misogyny, homophobia, structural adjustment, apartheid, or pseudoscientific racism can contain it.[10] In short, an opacity where black nothingness is everything. Where blackness, at last, in the beyond, can *be*.

In what follows I take up a kaleidoscopic study of these two influential artists. The sprawling aggregation and seeming chaos of their bodies of work necessitate a focus not on one or two works but on an amalgam of poems, audio recordings, cell phone videos, films, liner notes, installations, and polemic essays. Such an archive requires an approach conceptually guided by their respective formations of opacity and fugitive time consciousness, not an attempted comprehensiveness guided by objects. A conceptual approach opens up a map, a way of seeing a landscape, while letting the ungraspable remain ungraspable. "Opacities can coexist and converge, weaving fabrics," Glissant insists. They just can't be reduced to a shell of their former selves in order to be compared to, or judged against, an existing norm: "One must focus on the texture of the weave and not on the nature of its components."[11] This chapter ventures into the texture of the weave that moves in and through Samb and Ra's work. It undertakes not a systematic decoding but a speculative practice that limns, identifying the sites and forms of opacity that allow these artists to proleptically glimpse the open of unrecognizability, such as Samb's manipulations of montage form and Ra's inscrutable use of ellipses. The fugitive time of Samb and

Ra is an ungovernable drapetomanic time consciousness. Their temporal modes forge new worlds out of seeming madness, each in his own way anticipating the unanticipatable, lunging after a life, impossibly glimpsed in that next phenomenal moment, that refuses to be known.

(UN)COMMON FORMATIONS

Both of these artists came of age in the aftermath of two world wars, in societies consumed by white supremacy. Jim Crow and French colonial occupation were regimes of racialized subjection that together constituted critical nodes of the global color line that W. E. B. Du Bois, at the turn of the twentieth century, famously identified as the new century's problem.[12] Samb and Ra also witnessed the expansion of global capitalism, as well as the Cold War's ever-looming threat of nuclear holocaust. For both, the 1960s was a threshold decade. The passage of the 1968 US Civil Rights Act brought an end to legalized segregation and state-sanctioned discrimination, although racialized exclusion and violence continued under new guises, of course. And Senegal's independence from France in 1960 was monumental, but it ushered in a new era of widening wealth disparities, corrupt governance, and state violence. Through all of this, Ra and Samb's careers together spanned three-quarters of a century, from when Ra began to find his musical and political voice in Chicago in the late 1940s to Samb's death in 2017.

Before launching into their respective bodies of work and their arrangements of fugitive time, I want to provide a sense of how these artists came into their own. For Samb, because it so shaped his worldview and artistic practice, his Lebu background is crucial. Historically located on Cap-Vert, the peninsula in the northern section of Dakar, the Lebu are an ethnic group that for centuries have been known for their mastery of fishing, for their stratified system of law and politics, and for retaining much of their indigenous religious beliefs even after the arrival of Islam from the Maghreb in the sixteenth century. Of particular relevance in this history is the way that Samb's Lebu identity—being the "son of a Lebu dignitary," as Simon Njami tells it, "and close to his grandfather who initiated him into the hidden nature of things and into the power of symbols"—positions him within a centuries-long genealogy of fugitivity.[13] Since the fifteenth century, the Lebu have comprised people from diverse West African ethnic groups fleeing persecution, "refus[ing] to be dominated politically or culturally."[14] This was a refusative inheritance, I'll show, that Samb carried on.

From scatterings across several interviews and essays, we get a sense of how Lebu metaphysics figure into his work and thought. Central to that cosmology is the role of the group's ancestors, who are believed to actively remain among the living after passing on. More broadly, the Lebu religion, Douglas Thomas explains, is organized around an assumed direct relationship between the physical and spiritual worlds, where ceremonies and rituals work to negotiate a desired balance between the two ontological orders. Objects and entities in nature, such as trees, are connected to the living and the departed through a larger cosmological order, giving the sense that "everything one experiences with his/her five senses is just a manifestation of a greater reality hidden from the natural eye."[15] Although Islam and Sufi thought have become integrated into this Lebu worldview, it seems they had less influence on Samb than this Lebu cosmology. In conversation with Koyo Kouoh in 2013, he describes how his various "totems" to his deceased artistic collaborators don't signify the past but a "sacred present": "I see them come to me, and it's got nothing to do with dreams." Samb then immediately confirms the Lebu notion of material-immaterial interrelationality: "Maybe someone might not consider the rock I put there to be a work of art. I know why I put it there. . . . I know how to give it an emotional charge."[16] Just as the Lebu's freedom-searching history has been sutured into his own fugitive thought and practice, so too has this larger cosmology. This is one of the vectors of supposed madness that I want to unpack in Samb's thought and work, one that, I argue, is not far removed from the way Jayna Brown conceives of the thought and practice of Sojourner Truth, Zilpha Elaw, and other nineteenth-century black women mystics who sought out "spirit and temporal impulses not fettered by the cycle of life and death," cultivating an "autonomy from dominant sociopolitical regimes."[17]

Politics was also central to Samb's coming of age. He was twenty-three years old in 1968 when students protested the Senghor government's decision to cut student funding, drastically limiting who in the country would have access to higher education. The protesters opposed the president's de facto single-party political system and his sanctioning of continued French influence and capital in the country, including at the University of Dakar, where French curricula—and French faculty—had largely remained in place since Senghor became the country's first independent leader eight years earlier.[18] In this mid- to late-1960s moment, while studying philosophy and law at the University of Dakar and art at Dakar's National Institute of the Arts, Samb was among those who demanded the "Africanization" of the university. In 1974, in the waning days of those student protests and in the aftermath of the killing of student activist Omar Blondin Diop, he became a founding member of Laboratoire Agit-Art, the group he would go on to lead until his death. Diop, who had returned to Dakar from Paris to lead the Marxist-Leninist Youth Movement, which Samb was also involved with, was one of many young people arrested by the government around this time.[19] But Diop was killed in prison on Gorée island, the infamous outpost of the Atlantic slave trade off the coast of Dakar. The government insisted that he had committed suicide, but Diop instantly became a martyr, and the laboratoire was founded to continue in his anticolonial and anti-Senghorian spirit.[20]

The laboratoire marked a radical break from established art-making practices in independent Senegal. Comprising a core of artists working in a range of media, from painting to drama to music to design, Laboratoire Agit-Art created collaborative, often improvisatory projects that sought, as their name suggests, to shake up the existing political-aesthetic order. Their primary target of refusal was Senghor and the modernist formalism that had emerged through his patronage since independence, particularly at the National Art School of Dakar, where French-trained artists such as Papa Ibra Tall and Iba N'Diaye taught and integrated the ideas of Senghorian négritude—notions of "return to sources" and African "authenticity"—into their work. But Samb and his colleagues insisted that this older generation's images of Africa were European, exoticized, and manufactured. They pushed against their use of imported materials and their reliance on European models of technique and commodification. The laboratoire's work, as Samb bluntly put it, was an "unseizable."[21] They were driven by process, ephemerality, community engagement, and collective experimentation, not patronage, the fetishized art object, or individual authorship.[22] However, they were not shy about incorporating European thought and avant-garde practices into their work, particularly Antonin Artaud's theatrical techniques, so long as "these borrowings would not become the primary criteria by which to judge [the work]."[23] Much as described in Chika Agulu-Okeke's discussion of the Art Society—a group of young modernist artists working in 1950s and 1960s Nigeria—the laboratoire practiced a "natural synthesis." Suspicious of both romanticized nativism and the strictures of European formalism, the laboratoire and the art society alike were intent on cultivating an artistic autonomy through "purposeful blending of distinctive, disparate, yet mutually entangled heritages," recognizing "the historical reality of postcolonial society as constituted by indigenous, premodern, and Western elements."[24] Under these circumstances and with these politics, the laboratoire took up the struggle against Senegal's postcolonial autocracy under the guise of the aesthetic.

Over the years, Samb moved in and out of collaborative work, retaining the "preeminence of idea over form" characteristic of African conceptualism.[25] He still produced group projects, but he also put on performances under his own name and wrote his own uncategorizable texts.[26] It's largely this more individually crafted work that I focus on in this chapter. In this material his social critique retains the fierceness of the laboratoire, such as in his more recent essay *On the Art of Recording Trivial Ideas*: Samb laments the 2002 capsizing of the Senegalese government-owned ship *Le Joola* that killed more than 1,800 people while carrying nearly three times its design capacity; he digs in at the Senghor government for having "pursued the very policies of domination which they accuse[d] the colonizers of imposing"; more indefinitely, he suggests that "Africa isn't faring well. . . . They have lost their harmony and accord because we are in discord with ourselves. . . . We are in a realm of predators and speculators." This type of expansive, all-encompassing critique of the world runs through Samb's oeuvre, like in the multi-genre work "Poto-Poto Blues": "Consternation reigns throughout the universe. The people of the earth have, in just a few centuries, polluted what, for millennia, our ancestors had honoured. . . . The future looms like a coincidence, an elusive dream."[27] Indeed, with these views of the world it's not surprising that Samb was drawn to fugitive aesthetics.

If Samb was focused largely on the immediacy and ephemerality of his work, Ra was far more inclined to create a lasting impression, leaving for posterity dozens of recorded albums and hundreds of published poems, essays, and interviews. Like Samb, however, Ra's early spiritual and cultural upbringing led him to social critique. Attending church as a child with his grandmother in Birmingham, Herman Blount, as Ra was originally named, soon settled into a questioning mode: "The most difficult task," he recalled, "would be to find out the real meaning of the Bible."[28] And so an early seeming piety evolved into a lifelong quest to decipher the Bible, to seek out its hidden meanings and the esoteric intellectual traditions that shaped the text over centuries. Soon after his arrival in Chicago in 1946, his apartment was teeming with books as diverse as the ancient Egyptian *Book of the Dead*, David Livingston's *Missionary Travels and Researches in South Africa*, and *A New Model of the Universe* by the Russian esotericist Pyotr Ouspensky. Ultimately, as I'll show, despite the formative influence of Christianity, "Ra's philosophy and practices of escape are past the bounds of religious understanding," as Brown aptly puts it, "with the Hebrew exodus from Egypt in the Christian Bible a metaphor fitted to a deeper trope of black fugitivity."[29]

Eventually, with a group of like-minded Chicago-based intellectuals, Ra started Thmei Research, a discussion group covering topics ranging from theosophy, ancient history, and speculative evolutionary theory to advanced technology, numerology, and astrology. For Alton Abraham, Ra's close friend and eventual business manager, the group sought another way to exist in the world, intent on "prov[ing] to the world black people could do something worthwhile." With the black community as their target audience, the group wrote and distributed leaflets on Chicago's South Side with topics such as apocalyptic prophecies, biblical (mis)interpretation, and the historical subjection of black people. For Ra, these sprawling studies confirmed that a demystified, contextualized Bible was central to navigating the turmoil of twentieth-century America. And more broadly, he became convinced—not unlike Samb—that "the universe was organized hierarchically, with forces or spirits which moved between the levels and affected life on earth."[30] With this intellectual foundation, music would become a kind of science for Ra, a medium, a method, and a process through which to seek out alternative dimensions and cosmologies.

As with his intellectual training, Ra's development as a pianist and bandleader was largely informal and collaborative, playing and performing regularly throughout Birmingham and Chicago. In the early 1950s Ra started experimenting with his own bands and compositions, first with the small group he called the Solar Trio, named for his increasing interest in all things technology and outer space. For Ra to have his own work and projects, as a black man and a musician, was a way to "create something that nobody owned but us," he said, a kind of autonomous space of uncompromised study and experimentation.[31] This mission would soon manifest on a larger scale in his iconic Arkestra, the large ensemble that simultaneously served—again, not unlike Samb's laboratoire—as a workshop and community center that Ra would go on to lead for nearly four decades. The band members, several of whom lived in the rehearsal house, were devoted to Ra's music and eccentric studies, gathering at any time of day or night to listen and rehearse, taking seriously Ra's firmly held tenets of discipline and precision. Over the years, the band's name changed dozens of times, reflecting the subtle evolutions of their leader's interests in science, outer space, and the ancient world: the Intergalactic Myth-Science Arkestra, the

Solar Hieroglyphics Arkestra, the Transmolecular Arkestra, the Omniverse Arkestra.

The band's 1957 record, *Jazz by Sun Ra*, was not just the Arkestra's recording debut but also an announcement. Part manifesto, part explanatory statement, part instruction manual, the album's liner notes are a kind of key to the map of Ra's music and thought at that moment: "All of my compositions are meant to depict happiness" and "reach for a better world"; "by listening you will learn to see with your mind's eye." The notes also announce the debut of the *poet* Sun Ra, explaining the inclusion of several poems while insisting that "music is only another form of poetry," a "tone poem." Named after one of the album's compositions, the poem "New Horizons" marks this convergence: "Music pulsing like a living heartbeat, / Pleasant intuition of better things to come . . . / . . . / Music rushing forth like a fiery law / Loosening the chains that bind, / Ennobling the mind / With all the many great dimensions / Of a living tomorrow."[32] The sound of the Arkestra was to be the driving force of a quest into the beyond, a lunging after something that exceeds this world.

Already in "New Horizons" we get an intimation of the scathing critique of the world that animated much of Sun Ra's work, although that critique was perhaps confirmed decades earlier in his now-famous alien encounter. Throughout his life, with complete sincerity, he insisted that in 1936 a light beamed him up to a spacecraft, and his "whole body was changed into something else." Transported to Saturn, he was told that "the world was going into complete chaos" and that he needed to return because "the world would listen."[33] And so Ra's story of coming from Saturn, and of not being human, was born, as were the various accusations, however veiled in praise, of his supposed madness. The abduction account, I want to suggest, was also foundational to the unsparing view that Ra would have of society for the rest of his life. It would serve to confirm his abhorrence for the racialized, segregated world that brought him up but also, more broadly, his sense of the imbalance of life on Earth. In his Chicago leaflets, after more than a decade of study, Ra's criticism is targeted and uncompromising, most of it focused on how biblical misreadings have caused the world's disorder. Black people aren't just the intended audience of these papers but their principal target as well. He acknowledges the history of black subjection, how "their present condition is a condemnation upon the governments of the world," but he lays in: "It is time for you to wake up! Jesus placed a terrible punishment upon you. By now you should be aware that you are not saved."[34] Importantly, as Brent Edwards has suggested, Ra's seeming dismissal of black life in these broadsheets is perhaps best understood less as a rejection than as a call for renewal and self-determination.[35]

Over time, Ra's social critique would become more sweeping but no less scathing. The scale became planetary, pertinent to all races, modulating into a kind of all-encompassing ideology critique. In a 1967 interview, for instance, after suggesting that the "planet is in such a bad condition" with its "wars" and "confusion," Ra explained that "some intelligence set up words, and enticed the people to be part of that word. . . . If something is wrong, it must be the educational system and what it teaches them to think."[36] Occasionally he would mention contemporary political events of his time, such as his reference to Iranian students ("They're the products of religion. They're not really the products of themselves") in his 1980 essay "Your Only Hope Now Is a Lie." But his mention of the Iranian Revolution is a fleeting point of entry into his larger criticism of a global crisis of normative thought and belief. "This planet really has been hoodwinked," he says in the same essay, quoting the Bible as saying, "'God will send them a strong delusion in order that they might believe a lie.'" The lie was, for Ra, that "freedom" and "righteousness" equal "obedience."[37] Not altogether unlike Samb's sweeping sense that "consternation reigns throughout the universe," the far-reaching political impetus of Ra's work was to refuse an "unfortunate planet" "poor in spiritual values, void of natural contact."[38] His response was to turn to music, poetry, and, indeed, the openness of the cosmos.

MUTABLE BLACKNESS

Before turning to Ra and Samb's fugitive time and aesthetics, I want to discuss the question of race, given that neither held a straightforward identification with notions of blackness. Even Ra, whose audience is often assumed to be black, sent mixed messages early in his career. At roughly the same time *Jazz by Sun Ra* debuted in 1957—where he explicitly identifies his audience as "all of the people of different nations who are living today"—Ra was out on South Side street corners distributing his radical leaflets almost exclusively to the black community. This deliberate engagement with black audiences was more the norm at this point in his career. After all, the leaflets themselves demonstrate how Ra's interest in ancient Egypt was about black life and culture, about revising white received histories of the ancient world and placing Africans in their rightful historical place as creators of civilization. "The Negroes now in America," Ra explains in one of these broadsides, "were all inhabitants of ancient Ethiopia when they were captured and brought to America." Here he uses the term "ancient Ethiopians" to mean Central Africans, the people he believes built ancient Egypt.[39] The leaflets also describe the "fall" of blackness from this ancient greatness; how, since biblical times, blackness has come to be understood as nothingness: "Now the world know them as the blamed Etiops/Ethiop"; "Negroes are in the low places. . . . There are nnone [sic] beneath them."[40] With his persistent invocation of ancient blackness, Ra spoke to black audiences about the need to "wake up," to seek a new world beyond that nothingness.

Blackness, for Ra, was also experiential, lived, and embodied. In his 1968 essay "My Music Is Words," we get a fleeting sense of how he understood his own marking in a deeply racialized America: "Because of segregation, I have only vague knowledge of the white world and that knowledge is superficial; because I know more about black than I do white. . . . I know my needs and naturalness."[41] Ra would later turn to theoretical physics to make sense of this black naturalness, arguing in one of his 1971 lectures at UC Berkeley that black and white bodies have distinct measurable frequencies, or "vibrations."[42] If the wind, he contended, as it hits and moves around an object, produces micro-sounds that are distinct to that object, then human bodies, with their different proportions, different skin colors, and other physical features, would likewise produce distinct sounds: "Color itself is really like music, you can hear it."[43] A crucial way to know yourself, he suggests, is to know your own singular sound. Thus blackness is not just about a history of subjection, or even a vaunted ancient civilization, but a verifiable materiality, something that speaks and sounds to the world.

Curiously, Ra seems to come full circle on notions of blackness by the latter decades of his career, turning to the more general audience he addressed in his 1957 album notes. In a 1982 interview with a British journalist, he says that he "tried talking to black people, but they weren't listening." "I'm telling you now," Ra says in response to Andy Gill's question "So who do you tell next?": "You tellin' England. You're the pivoting point."[44] This pivot, interestingly, while perhaps more identifiable in Ra's essays and interviews, is somewhat veiled in his poetry. A surprisingly small percentage of his poems directly address black culture and people. Particularly in the last two decades of his career, Ra leans heavily in his poems on indeterminate pronouns like "you" and "we" to address his reader. And many of these are interpellative, calling the reader out, imploring them to "wake up" to the world's crises and join him on his fugitive quest. "There is something in the cosmos / called Fellowship," he writes in "Calling Planet Earth." "Reach for it. / . . . / you will get what is due you on an / infinite eternal plane of being."[45] Even if this call to a planetary social collective is more apparent later on, it may very well connect back to his 1936 alien encounter. After all, that was an event that led him to understand his time on Earth as a "visitation," to repeatedly declare himself "another order of being."[46] To claim to reside outside of the human race altogether, as I read it, is a kind of strategic drapetomanic maneuver: it suggests a discursive circumvention of normative racialized difference, a way for Ra to see through and beyond it in order, perhaps, to foreground his larger, more opaque interests in "continuation-living-being" and the "unknown." Indeed, it's his avowed alienness that leads Rinaldo Walcott to identify Ra as a leading figure of black "funk"—an aesthetic and ethical mode that "turns European modernity inside out, on its head, and calls its claims of rationality and logic not just into question but also into disrepute," initiating a "epistemological break" that allows us to "conceive and to think new life-forms."[47]

Like Ra's positions on race and blackness, Samb's are complicated, but in very different ways. For one, race as a social category in West Africa requires a distinct lens. If there's anything resembling an American racialization, it's the racializing logic produced through the Manichaean structure of colonialism: the French historical subjugation of the Senegalese. But colonialism certainly didn't produce an identical racialization and black consciousness in Senegal. Instead, ethnicity—cultural, historical, and linguistic differences among Serer, Wolof, Fulani, and other indigenous groups—is often understood to be more of a differentiating category in the country. And Samb seems to confirm this in various interviews and essays by emphasizing his Lebu worldview and dismissing race *tout court*. Speaking with Kouoh, Samb explains that he and his artist comrades were against Senghor's postindependence politicization of négritude as a kind of nationalist ideology, refusing the president's enlistment of artists to legitimize that politics. He then, it seems, comes to the heart of the matter: "We decided that négritude was a form of racism. Not only were we against racism, we knew that the very question of race held no water."[48] Salient though fleeting, Samb's distancing from questions of race is clearly deliberate. But what's curious is the persistence of his critique of Senghor and political négritude even decades after the president's death. It's a persistence, I argue, that reveals a kind of veiled preoccupation with racial difference, and it gestures to the subtle ways that race structures his thought and work.

Beneath all of this is the long-standing reluctance by many Africanist scholars to engage with conceptions of race in postcolonial Africa, except in southern Africa, where settler colonialism and apartheid extended later into the twentieth century.[49] But if it's widely held among scholars that the European former colonial powers in many cases continue to hold significant economic, military, political, and social influence on the continent—to the point of naming this influence *Françafrique* in the francophone context—then how is it possible that colonial logics of race *don't* shape social life in the postcolonial moment? Jemima Pierre makes this case in *The Predicament of Blackness* (2012), arguing that colonialism's dependence on "a racial hierarchy that 'nativized' Africans through the simultaneous consolidation of 'tribal' difference and White racial and cultural and political supremacy . . . did not disappear with independence."[50] I wouldn't claim that Samb's emphasis on his Lebu identity is the result of colonial ideological manipulation, but Pierre's argument would suggest that Samb, who grew up in the capital of French West Africa, would surely have been exposed to and conditioned by colonial formations of race even after independence. What I'm saying is that in his persistent work of negation—consistently, over decades, criticizing Senghor's racialization of politics—Samb implicitly reveals a preoccupation with the politics of race: a kind of keen awareness of its operations both in Senegal and indeed the larger world. Not insignificant to this claim is Samb's bitter acknowledgment in *On the Art of Recording Trivial Ideas* of the residue of colonial racism and racialization that came to the surface in Nicolas Sarkozy's 2007 speech at the University of Dakar. Resuscitating the ghost of Hegel's lectures on the philosophy of history, the French president suggested that "Africa's challenge is to enter to a greater extent into History . . . to realize that the golden age that Africa is always recalling will not return because it never existed."[51] Such a racialized view of the world, which denies Africans coevalness, relegating the continent to a kind of prehistoric twenty-first century, is likely just the tip of a more pervasive logic of white supremacy that continues to shape Senegal's position in the world today. Indeed, it's a view often framed in economic terms in the contemporary discourse of Africa's "emergence" on the world stage—a notion, keenly exposed by Felwine Sarr, which assumes that the continent has somehow long been "submerged," effectively reducing "African societal realities to the deficiencies of their economic dimensions alone."[52]

This larger racialization manifests in various ways in Samb's work. One piece, for instance, perhaps appears racialized only when placed in relation to Ra's writings. If in one of his Chicago pamphlets Ra describes the position of blackness in American society as nothing, as the lowest ("there are nnonc beneath them"), Samb, interestingly, makes an analogous rhetorical move in his essay "Life Has Long Legs," describing his affinity for the lowest in society, the "most deprived" ("*les plus démunis*"): the poor and difficult lives that, in his words, "favor refusal." Samb admittedly doesn't name this social position, let alone call it black. But the juxtaposition of his and Ra's respective identifications with the most subjected discloses in Samb's language if not an implicit blackness, then something more opaque—a *blackenedness:* a social and ontological category that threatens to veer toward the nothingness that Ra calls blackness. At the very least, Samb's language suggests a structure of radical alterity, a polity stratified by dominance and subjugation. And the politics of Samb's social category further underscores the point. Not unlike Moten's characterization of the "fugitive, radically imaginative sociopoetic work of refusal" immanent to black life, what distinguishes Samb's "most deprived" is their innate desire to refuse the world given to them.[53]

My other example of race in Samb's work gives credence to this reading of *les plus démunis*. It comes from "The Best Marxist Is Dead," a 2013 six-hour solo performance in Chicago featuring Samb simply sitting in a wicker chair. Wearing a black leather jacket and beret, holding a spear and a rifle, Samb re-created the iconic 1967 photograph of Huey Newton that—originally accompanied by the caption "the racist dog policemen must withdraw immediately from our communities"—became a searing symbol of 1960s black radicalism. Held in the storefront window of a former Harold's Chicken Shack on the South Side, Samb's show was part of Jean Michel Bruyère and LFKs Collective's two-month-long series of events reflecting on the legacy of Fred Hampton and the Black Panther Party. The performance was, as Cedric Johnson puts it, "a call for the renewed critique of capitalism within black public life." But it wasn't simply a facsimile: "Samb's grey beard and locks contrasted sharply with Newton's clean-shaven, youthful appearance. And where Newton sits with his feet firmly planted, meeting his onlookers with a militant, unflinching gaze, Samb's legs were crossed and his countenance was more introspective, his eyes sullen. He was the old man who has outlived the revolution, or maybe a ghost."[54] And so we find the artist who once said that "race held no water" performing a kind of militant American blackness in the final years of his life. Like Ra, Samb's

4.1 Street view of Samb's performance "The Best Marxist Is Dead" (2013), re-creating Blair Stapp's 1967 photograph of Huey Newton. Performance in collaboration with Jean Michel Bruyère and LFKS Collective. Courtesy of Jean Michel Bruyère.

relation to blackness is at times confounding, and it is perhaps more about the flux and evolution of political consciousness than the hypocrisy of contradictory positions. What Johnson doesn't mention is the diasporic relationality: the confluence of Senegal and the United States, Africanness and blackness, two historical diasporic nodes separated by the ship's hold. If Samb is Newton's aged ghost, he's also a comrade from across the Atlantic whose own anticolonial, anticapitalist militancy ran through, around, and alongside Newton's.

That is where "The Best Marxist Is Dead" leaves us at the edge of Samb and Ra's formations of fugitive time. Convergence and divergence. Relation and incommensurability. It's the notion of diaspora that Edwards articulates as a searching for solidarity across difference—the very glue connecting the diverse tissues of this book.[55] In a way, Samb's performance is the quiet anchor of this chapter, the symbolic node of revelation that makes this juxtaposition of Samb and Ra's work generative of new vectors of diasporic solidarity and imagining. It's the point at which their seemingly disparate aesthetics, politics, and mysticisms emerge as a heaving mass of inchoate diasporic radicalism—indeed, a sprawling confluence of seeming madness. If Samb's performance is less a reproduction than an approximation, representative of all the imperfect translations that constitute the African diaspora, that gap between Samb's performance and Newton's image represents a kind of experimental space where identities are tested, where blacknesses disperse and congeal, where solidarities are made, unmade, and remade. A place to dream and try and fail and revise and do it all over again, in the hope of conjuring something otherwise.

ISSA SAMB'S EXIT FROM THE WORLD

Part of what makes a kaleidoscopic approach, as I'm calling it, suitable for this study of Ra and Samb's work is that it doesn't entail a comprehensive treatment of their oeuvres. Instead, it isolates the terms and ideas that ground Ra and Samb's creative practices, then proceeds to examine how those fundamental concepts modulate across a selection of essays and artworks. It's a method that holds on to opacity, ensuring that the inscrutable remains inscrutable. A kaleidoscopic approach, in other words, allows us to move back and forth inside that Glissantian texture between the macro and the micro, between the sprawl of their oeuvres and a series of telescopic

PLATE 1 Detailed installation view of Shikeith's *The Moment You Doubt Whether You Can Fly, You Cease Forever to Be Able to Do It* (2014). Courtesy of the artist.

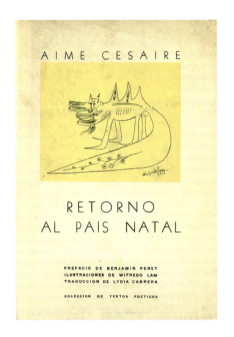

PLATE 2 Cover of Aimé Césaire's *Retorno al país natal* (1943), featuring the first of three illustrations by Wifredo Lam. Courtesy of the Latin American and Caribbean Collections, George A. Smathers Libraries, University of Florida.

PLATE 3 One of six illustrations by Wifredo Lam accompanying André Breton's *Fata Morgana* (1942). Source: Rush Rhees Library, University of Rochester.

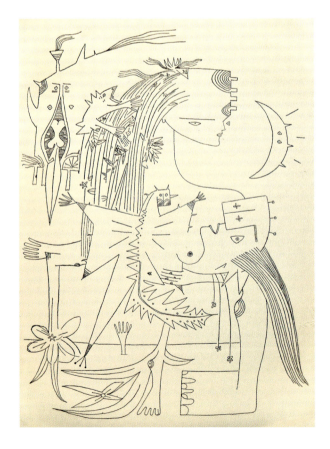

PLATE 4 Wifredo Lam's *The Jungle* (1943).
Source: Museum of Modern Art.

PLATE 5 Wifredo Lam's second illustration for *Retorno al país natal*, appearing opposite the first page of Césaire's text. Courtesy of the Latin American and Caribbean Collections, George A. Smathers Libraries, University of Florida.

PLATE 6 Wifredo Lam's third and final illustration for *Retorno al país natal,* appearing opposite the final page of Césaire's text. Courtesy of the Latin American and Caribbean Collections, George A. Smathers Libraries, University of Florida.

PLATE 7 Wifredo Lam's *Passages* (1971), which accompanied Aimé Césaire's poem of the same title in Césaire's 1982 collection, *Annonciation, Les poemes d'Aimé Césaire.* © 2022 Artists Rights Society (ARS), New York / ADAGP, Paris.

PLATE 8 Issa Samb in performance at his courtyard studio in 2016. Source: Amy Sall.

PLATE 9 Sun Ra at his keyboard in 1973. Source: Impulse! Records and ABC / Dunhill Records.

PLATE 10 Samb next to his courtyard's sprawling rubber tree. Source: Bastien Defives.

PLATE 11 Detailed view of Samb's courtyard installation. Source: Margaux Huille.

PLATE 12 Back cover of Sun Ra's 1965 album *The Heliocentric Worlds of Sun Ra*, vol. 2. Source: ESP-Disk'.

views into select objects and locations. The first move, then, is to read the conceptual framing of fugitive time that gives us access to that sprawl, as resistant to full disclosure as it may be.

For Samb, the essay that most reveals that frame is his "Life Has Long Legs" manifesto.[56] This blistering statement on what it means to live and create authentically as an artist is where his singular confluence of anticipatory consciousness, opacity, and seeming madness is most directly expressed. "My actions as an artist," he writes, "are entirely driven by the definitive refusal of all forms of existing society." Instead of contesting, which, he says, is to accept the premises of the other, he "detaches" from the world: "I implicate myself in nothing," "I give my destiny over to an uncertain path of perpetual errancy . . . on the surface of the earth and in myself," enacting a "constant escape for preservation." Knowingly or not, Samb's language feels very much in step with contemporary black fugitive thought, whether it's Moten's insistence on the fugitive's duty "to run away from the snares of recognition" or Saidiya Hartman's idea of fugitive consciousness as a "dream of an elsewhere," an "ongoing struggle to escape."[57] Opacity and proleptic thought fuse here, converging in the "uncertain" trajectory of his "destiny," the desire to wander infinitely in search of that indefinite "preservation," a kind of militant insistence that some outer unknown must be better than this world. And indeed there's an insurgent drapetomanic valence here. Confounding normative reason and rationalism, for Samb to deliberately "detach" from the world and seek out contingent errancy is effectively to "abscond from service," as Cartwright characterizes the "diagnostic symptom" of the supposed disease.[58] What Samb absconds from, though, is any role in the service of the neoliberal state and world order, refusing the capitalist chase built on the backs of those whom Cartwright deemed mentally diseased for daring to dream of freedom.

These drapetomanic temporal operations manifest in Samb's work in a couple of ways. The first is the errant movement among disparate objects, ideas, citations, and parables that effectively structures his writings and his iconic courtyard. It's not uncommon for a short length of text to deal with radically divergent subject matters, such as in *On the Art of Recording Trivial Ideas*, where he moves stealthily from the legacy of Aimé Césaire to French cultural conservatism to the societal role of the internet to ruminations on walking all night to the sinking of *Le Joola*—all in the span of two pages. Samb's work is restless, refusing fixed meanings and linear thought. Its energy is restless, each fragment breathlessly anticipating the next, fugitively in advance of itself. The reader moves through the mass of fragments that make up a single text, encountering a pulsating though opaque constellation of thought and experience. It's akin to the production of thought through montage, something like the historical materialist organizing principle of Walter Benjamin's *Arcades Project*, which the German thinker describes as "assembl[ing] large-scale constructions out of the smallest and most precisely cut components."[59] Benjamin's famously unfinished work enacts a "philosophic play of distances, transitions, and intersections," the project's translators suggest, an endless series of "perpetually shifting contexts and ironic juxtapositions," the amalgam of which was meant to jolt society into a new political and historical consciousness.[60]

Samb's opaque fugitive time consciousness also manifests in what I call escape cuts. These are elusive but deliberately articulated scenes of escape, most ostensibly in his writings, such as in "Poto-Poto Blues," where Samb digressively relates a brief tale that features an artist who literally escapes into one of his paintings. The escape-cut mode is an enactment of the "constant escape for preservation" that animates his creative and political practice. They involve a kind of proleptic visionary consciousness, a look ahead in time and space to an outer opacity. These cuts almost seem to signal to his readers a way they might slip out beyond the immediacy of a crisis-ridden world, transporting them, and perhaps him, to some kind of indefinitely located or lasting release. An escape, however fleeting, away from the world's material devastations and into the imagination, where new existences can be conjured. Beyond Sun Ra's desire to escape into the cosmos, there's a kinship between Samb's escape cuts and many of the ideas and artworks discussed in this book, such as Fanon's use of *dépasser* as a leap outward to an excessive, otherworldly black social life or the fugitive momentum of the night car in Black Audio's *Twilight City* as it accumulates energy to be lifted off toward Fani-Kayode's nondiegetic queer world.

Let me share a couple examples of Samb's montage form. The first comes from "Deconstructing Time," an essay of scattered thoughts devoted, elusively, to "dematerializing the WORD that penetrates and invalidates us," to destroying the discourses of "Capital-time" in order to "get rid of the clingy hands of the master."[61] Each page of this short piece is a montage cell, its own opaque world. Some have as few as three words; others have dozens of sentences. Some have lines arranged in stanzas with unpredictable breaks, spaces, and indentations; others have sentences organized into paragraphs of varying lengths. Part of the reader's task is to find the connecting nodes among the cells: most, for instance, are located in Dakar or in Senegalese history more broadly; many are narrated by a searching first-person singular voice.

There's a fundamental dialectic in this essay that generates a movement between cells and a larger, proleptically refusative opacity. At the one end is a sense of pervasive devastation—of society, of history, of the body. Abetted by the "avarice of the masters," he writes, capital "invades the body" through Dakar's "factories, banks / and shops." Gorée Island, he indicates elsewhere, is where "the barbarous West lit, for the first time in the 'history' of humanity, the fire that would supply Capital with human wood."[62] The other side of this dialectic contains frequent though scattered thoughts on wandering and opting out of the world, as if seeking and anticipating flight from the essay's images of ruin. In one cell, walking is an act that both destroys and generates: "For us on the footpath, the make-believe that lies in wait for each reconstruction of the landscape. Each step, each stop. / There is no longer a succession of days. / Only the madman [*l'homme fou*] seems to escape by refusal. . . . He invents, reinvents, he imagines, he imagines again diverse pleasures while WALKING."[63] Here, errantry dissolves the world just as a new one, along with a new experience of time, emerges. Given that this cell directly follows the reference to "human wood" at Gorée, the phrase "lying in wait" and the proleptic work of the imagination evoke a desire to escape devastation, a phenomenal anticipation of the moment when the body is no longer wood for capital's burning in the Americas. Samb also gives us a literal drapetomanic figure in the world-building "madman" who appears to use his illegibility in the eyes of the world to conjure freedom, seeing beyond the limits of past, present, and future to search for an otherwise life.

In several of the cell pages that follow, this walking figure is referred to obliquely in the first person, effectively dissolving any distinction between the madman and Samb himself. "Sitting on the curb," he writes in one, "I began my second night journey."[64] And just a few pages later: "I got up from the curb. . . . Hours of walking without a destination . . . / this desire to walk, to dream, to speak with the people."[65] Samb almost seems to play coy with the accusation of his own madness, his own perceived illegibility, and in the process articulating a practice of errantry as a kind of anticipatory dream consciousness of escape. Certainly an element of the seeming madness here is the aimlessness of the wandering, which Samb presents as generative, not alienating or dysfunctional. The latter is how Tejumola Olaniyan frames "perambulation" in the Nigerian context and specifically in the lyrics of Afrobeat performer and activist Fela Anikulapo-Kuti and his critique of the "rudderless, directionless [postcolonial African] state" that filters down through society. "Change, but no progress," Olaniyan insists. "Motion, but no movement."⁶⁶ Where Fela's critique is far clearer and identifiable, though, Samb's is shrouded in the opacity that gets him labeled "crazy." Samb's version of perambulating is a drifting and searching for sociality, for a greater sense of belonging, without knowing where, when, or even if that desired sociality will come. He turns what might be alienating for some into a potentially *dis*alienating force. It's a proleptic fabulation of a new world: "the make-believe that lies in wait for each reconstruction of the landscape."

There's a visual analog to this errant movement in many of the videos of Samb in his courtyard at 17 Rue Jules Ferry in central Dakar. For more than a half century, this courtyard served as Samb's personal studio, library, and living room, as well as a performance space for solo and group shows. Surrounding the massive tree at the center of this mostly open-air space were "archaeological layers" of projects spanning decades: sculptures, paintings, murals, textiles, newspaper clippings, exhibition monographs, chairs, tables, publicity posters, and countless found objects, all deliberately arranged by Samb and exposed to the elements.⁶⁷ Rusting, molding, gathering dust and debris, until the moment the artist decided to reshape a particular area of this experiment in sedimentation and ephemerality. Indeed, Samb remains best known for this heaving rebuke to a world that commodifies, fetishizes, and worships its art objects. It's undoubtedly his magnum opus: at once confoundingly chaotic and meticulously curated, simultaneously a massive, singular installation and a constellation of ever-changing, innumerable installations.⁶⁸ It also reads as a refusal of the colonial logics of civilization, expansion, and order unassumingly assimilated into the street name: among other imperial endeavors, Jules Ferry, the nineteenth-century French politician, played a leading role in Europe's partition and seizure of the African continent at the infamous Berlin conference of 1884–1885. Writing on women's political protest and resistance across the continent, Naminata Diabate's sentiment resonates with this irony: "Colonial ideologies in Africa did not foresee the resilience of 'irrational' ways of being."⁶⁹

Samb's courtyard installation has not existed since the artist's passing in 2017, but there's a substantial documentary record, mostly of photographs, films, and videos of variable quality shot by many of the artists and intellectuals who visited Samb over the years. This archive of course fails to replicate the immersive feeling of walking into Samb's space, but it nonetheless affords a sense of the courtyard's cacophony, Samb's physical presence, and how the space might be thought of as an extension of the proleptically fugitive montage form in his writing. The courtyard's discrete objects, however entangled with one another, are akin to the montage cells of Samb's writings—the disparate objects, ideas, and citations that make up a given text. And Samb's constant literal movement in these videos is analogous to the sense of fugitive errantry that saturates these texts. Consider the video shot with what's likely a cell phone by Tamsir Ndir in 2012.[70] The sun shines through the courtyard's towering tree, muffled talk radio sounds in the background, and dozens of objects dangle five feet off the ground from a sprawling web of string that spans the yard. Smoking his signature pipe and wearing a colorful quilted jacket, Samb moves from object to object, the camera following his every motion. He silently walks past a plastic doll sitting on a pillow and an X-ray of someone's (his?) lungs, both swinging with the breeze. He arrives at a decayed newspaper editorial clipped to a thread and reads the title, which criticizes then-president Abdoulaye Wade: "The Smallest Senegalese Could Replace Wade." "That's not the question," Samb curmudgeonly responds, setting off to exhibit for the camera a series of seemingly random hanging objects in quick succession: a bamboo pole with a scarf tied to it, a Nokia cell phone with a knife stuck in it, a dirty red plastic horn in the shape of a trumpet's bell. He then runs to the indoor portion of his space and emerges with a white T-shirt on a coat hanger bearing the image of Omar Blondin Diop next to the quoted words "We learn to think with our own heads rather than be deceived by those of others."

The admittedly poor, indeed opaque, quality of this six-minute video—moving in and out of focus, the shaking, the narrow vertical alignment—has a paradoxical affect: the single continuous shot establishes an informality that feels intimate and immersive, giving the sense, real or not, that Ndir has pulled out his phone on a whim to accept the artist's spontaneous offer of a tour. Ndir captures Samb's improvisatory energy, his acerbity, his immersive aesthetic. He reveals the courtyard's cacophony of objects, the way time has worked over them with mold and dirt. And he shows Samb shuttling between objects as if in performance, briefly holding each for the camera's gaze before fleeing to the next, never settling into a single object, meaning, or world. In his assertive movement, Samb demonstrates that he can navigate the cacophony, anticipating the next fragment/object/world before he arrives at it. As in his writing, he's fugitively ahead of himself, in both time and space in this case. His mind is on that Diop T-shirt and its message of warning as we watch him dart inside for it. By way of Ndir's phone, Samb is curating our experience of his installation, ensuring that we dwell in his critique of the state, in his chosen citations, in his history of Senegalese radicalism, and, most of all, in his singular opacity. What exactly are we to make of that plastic horn filled with debris, hanging by a thread? Does it have some connection to Diop? Or the X-ray? Like his writings, this video reveals Samb's Benjaminian method of "perpetually shifting contexts and ironic juxtapositions." He's the drapetomanic wanderer, like the figure in "Deconstructing Time" who has the desire to walk and dream with no destination in mind, in search of an exit. Samb seems to draw on the opaquely proleptic temporal operations of the "uncertain path of perpetual errancy" that he calls his "destiny" in "Life Has Long Legs." There's a waywardness in all this work, a desire, as Hartman says, to inhabit "the world in ways inimical to those deemed proper and respectable. . . . [To] wander, to be unmoored, adrift, rambling, roving, cruising, strolling, and seeking. To claim the right to opacity."[71] In Samb's case, the artist's mercurial wandering energy builds the sense of his always potential vanishing, certainly from the cell phone's frame but perhaps also from the time and space of the courtyard altogether.

If Samb is searching for an exit, we might locate a proleptically inhabited beyond-world specifically in the teeming, century-old rubber tree that dominates the yard. In Lebu cosmology, trees, among other objects in nature, are often said to be occupied by divine spirits known as *rab* (recently departed ancestors) and *tuur* (more ancient spirits), transforming the tree into a sacred inhabitation maintained by the living through ceremonies and rituals.[72] What if Samb's constellation of objects and sculptures in the courtyard were an altar, a kind of celebratory offering to this rubber tree? In its singular massiveness, but also its multitude—its uncountable tangled branches and roots that dive in and out of the earth around it—the tree establishes the courtyard's energy; it structures Samb's errant movements; it determines which objects are placed where. Although we know that Samb was a practitioner of the Lebu *Ndeup* ceremony, making him a healer figure who could "communicate directly with the tuur/rab," it's difficult to say precisely how he conceived of this rubber tree.[73] He did, however, speak of a corresponding vitality of stones, how they "breathe, displace and take up space."[74] And it's evident enough that Samb cultivated an intimate, if not a spiritual, connection to this tree. In other videos of the courtyard, like the 2016 wide-angle footage shot by performance artist Sara Maurin Kane, Samb meticulously attends to the tree's fallen dried leaves that cover the ground, at one point filling a corpse-shaped plastic bag with them, at another carefully arranging them in curved lines on the ground, framing the diverse montage cells that populate the yard.[75] As Samb asks in "Poto-

Poto Blues," "Who would have me believe that the dead leaf that falls in my garden is not my sister?"[76] Perhaps when Samb cares for this tree and its leaves, he's anticipating and caring for a world just beyond the visible, just beyond his immediate present, one inhabited by that ancestral force, a world where he might find his refuge from a future that "looms like an elusive dream." Perhaps this tree was his portal through which, at any moment, to step into the open, outside of time.[77]

To conclude this tour of Samb's opaque fugitive time, I want to turn to his more explicit routes into other realms. In several works, appearing amid thoughts on fugitive refusal and the shuttling montage movement characteristic of his writings are sudden moments of desired vanishing, moments of imaginative fancy in which the speaking voice of the text briefly imagines in advance what it might be like to step out of this world. Take the principal escape cut in "Poto-Poto Blues," an essay organized around a series of remembered conversations between Samb and his former mentor, Pierre Lods, on the nature of art, politics, and freedom. Amid fugitive ruminations on how to create "the image of a constant and uninterrupted search," Samb recalls Lods asking him "for news from Marguerite Youcenar and the painter Wang Fo whom the emperor wanted to kill because the universe was less agreeable than in his painting." Samb tells the story of Wang Fo not as a retelling of the Belgian novelist's actual 1936 short story, "How Wang-Fo Was Saved," but as an ambiguous parable that troubles the line between fact and fiction. Before putting the artist to death for painting the world more beautiful than it is, we're told, the emperor asks Wang Fo to paint one last piece: "The old painter sat in front of his canvas, traced the first lines of the setting: a high-vaulted sky and a sea that was initially calm, a boat, some dancing waves and then, in front of the cruel prince . . . he embarked himself aboard the ship he had just drawn." "Isn't reality really situated in this flight," Samb comments after remembering Lods's retelling, "in this transmutation barely perceivable?"[78] Certainly, some familiarity with Youcenar's actual story would make the inclusion of this passage less startling, but to stitch it so ambiguously into the events of the essay without citation is jarring and is indeed consistent with what Clémentine Deliss identifies as Samb's interest in "the manipulation of confusion."[79] And Samb's validating commentary gives it an added force, as if to propose the realistic possibility of "transmutation," of literally envisioning the scene of escape in advance by bringing it into being, then fleeing into the self-generated world of utopian representation in order to "get rid of the clingy hands of the master." What precedes transmutation, in other words, is anticipatory consciousness: a kind of fore vision of the potential of transmutation and its promise of change from one form to another. This Wang Fo piece reads like an invitation to imagine otherwise, in particular to consider this prefigured flight in the context of Samb's larger body of work—to imagine how one might escape into the ecstatic promise of representation, whether into the world of his Diop T-shirt or his ancestral rubber tree. Such a proleptic escape into the aesthetic also seems very much embodied, as if Wang Fo's painting, like Samb's tree, were some kind of literal trapdoor that would allow the body to enter another realm, however indeterminate that realm may be, like a utopian literalization of Samb's insistence that art pursue a "constant escape toward preservation."

To get a sense of the diversity of these escape cuts, I want to provide another example from the essay/pamphlet mentioned earlier, the full title of which reads: *On the Art of Recording Trivial Ideas, in the Form of a Project of Placing, Displacing, and Replacing the Concept in Its Environment with a View to Precipitating Its Fall.*[80] Just in the title there's a kind of opaque fugitive temporal operation: the anticipatory promise of the appearance and vanishing of a "concept." We get the sense that the essay is less about that concept—if indeed we can identify one—than the tandem fugitive operations of creation and destruction, revelation and erasure. The piece's escape cut comes not as a single discrete location like in "Poto-Poto" but as an accumulation of a multitude of short, scattered thoughts on "displacement" as a kind of hypnotic practice of self-effacement and self-searching. Placed among references to incompetent politicians, young people rising up, and other crises and volatilities, these micro-cuts accrue, creating a sense that any one of them could be torn open to reveal a new, unknown, unanticipatable world. A kind of expansive openness of possibility. Navigating this accrual, we have a curious sense of anticipation that a deep chasm could open up at any moment, even though what's anticipated on the other side, in the beyond, is utterly unknown and seemingly unanticipatable. Some of this text's escape cuts are animated by a confluence of his signature perambulative drifting and a sort of psychic spinning: "I decided to move about, to set out on a quest, to turn myself around, to put myself at the center of my conscience, to exit from my memory—to *unmemorize* and to see my mind enter inside the mirror, and to introduce doubt therein."[81] Others, like the following three fragments, evoke more ambiguous notions of imagined flight and erasure:

> As for what energy remains to us, it is necessary to study what the rules are based on—displace them. DISPLACE THE LINES.

> To let my imagination carry out its journey like a fisherman among dangers and currents. To endlessly displace myself. To displace, to place myself, to replace myself.
>
> Something tries to break apart. Something in this city which constantly defies the atom. But how to pass beneath the wave?[82]

Together these read like an attempt to conjure an exit from this world, which feels like it could happen at any moment, like Samb's stealth movement through his courtyard. As if the cycling displacement of himself and his material surroundings were generating some sort of wormhole to another dimension, allowing Samb to see through space and time in advance, into the beyond. This isn't an escape into representation like Wang Fo, but there's a decided desire for, even anticipation of, "transmutation" in these collective micro-cuts: a proleptic consciousness of inhabiting something else, another order of being, another order of time, that's been stripped of all vestiges of this world.

The way that Samb takes on this otherworldly vision—eyeing these different escape cuts, and even that potential alter-world and alter-time in the towering rubber tree—recalls my discussion in the introduction of Fanon's *dépasser*: the desire for beyondness. There I read the implied threshold that opens, or cuts, out toward Fanon's beyond freedom as a kind of utopian reconfiguration of Dionne Brand's notion of the "tear in the world" as the enslaved pass through the Door of No Return. Except that rupture, for Fanon, and, I would argue, for Samb, gives way to a third, unfathomable yet seemingly (un)anticipatable world far removed from the subjections of this one. If amended to fit another diasporic context, we might also frame Samb's capacity to see what others cannot see—and what they therefore would deem crazy—by way of La Marr Bruce's reading of Du Bois's enduring double-consciousness formulation. If the one line of consciousness gives black Americans a view on the larger scope of racialized America, the second makes them "privy to the backstage content of black life." For Bruce, double consciousness is an "instrument of insurgency": "a scopic tool and radar technology to secretly seek black horizons of being that are hidden from white surveillance."[83] Samb's "secret" second vision, on the one hand, might be thought of as the sight he has access to by virtue of Lebu cosmology and related West African metaphysical systems that conceive of worlds and ancestors in trees, stones, and other entities. These are systems of thought that see far less distinction between the living and the dead. But in the case of the different escape cuts—such as Wang Fo's design to flee into the painting or Samb's desire to "exit from his memory"—they seem like Samb's own singularly opaque desire and vision, although we might say that that vision is allied with those of Ra, Fanon, Equiano, and many others in and beyond this book. There's a structure of solidarity in their respective desires for the seemingly impossible, for the seemingly crazy. In either case, Samb seeks out a line of sight hidden not simply from the white gaze but also from the colonial gaze, from the hypercapitalist artworld's gaze, from the neoliberal postcolonial state's gaze. To all of these worldviews, Samb's insurgent cuts and fugitive imaginings would likely be the incoherent ravings of a madman.

In the end, we see the disparate pieces that make up Samb's practice. We can identify his montage form, his subtle integration of escape routes. We sense the undercurrents of anticipation and imminence that run through his work. But the final analysis of his aesthetics is indecipherable—as it should be. His fugitive time consciousness resides in the necessity of not granting full access to his view on this and other worlds. That's where he cultivates his refuge, however possible, tenuous, or fleeting. And this same limited access holds for Ra, Samb's perhaps unlikely transatlantic comrade in drapetomanic time. Panning back out in this kaleidoscopic method from the specificity of Samb's work and practice, I want to turn to some kind of unraveling of the ideas that distinguish Ra's aesthetics.

SUN RA'S LIMITLESS MYTH

If Samb's opaque fugitive time is distributed across a cluster of ideas, Ra's is more precisely located in a single term. But myth, for Ra, is deceptively complex. Like Samb's mode of proleptic consciousness, Ra's is elastic, multi-vectored, often presented through metaphor, association, and allusion. The deeper we get into his work, the more his myth becomes apparent, although there are pockets of concentrated attention, particularly in his poetry. In "We Hold This Myth to Be Potential," Ra describes a "Bridge-doorway / . . . / To another kind of unknown Living Live-Life / . . . / the knowledge beyond the knowledge / For beyond the knowledge is the infinity: / The uncharted ignorance."[84] Another, "Wisdom-Ignorance," adds more layers to this infinite tilt:

>   the hope
> Of continuation-living-being is myth. . . .
>   The myth is the seemingly false
> and the seemingly impossible. The
> borders of the realm of myth are vast
> and nonexistent because
> There is no limit to the imaginative
> realm-idea of the myth. . . .
>   Out upon the planes of Myth
> strange non-realities dwell,
> strange because they are not
> according to the propagated accepted
> "law."[85]

Myth, we might say, is an outside consciousness, an opaque ideal of "ignorance," "infinity," and "nonreality": a frame of mind that paradoxically cannot be known in advance yet is somehow potential and imminent, driving a sense of anticipatory desire. For Ra, traces of this (in)conceivable idea of myth reach those who remain in the world of subjection, giving them some perceptible sense of myth's transfigurative potentiality, keeping that hope and anticipation alive. Ra's myth, in short, is both the utopian ideal of ungoverned, unsubjected being, but also a driver of proleptic consciousness, feeding those in search of the temporal moment of transcendence, that indeterminately infinite life.[86]

Ra's work may cut away at coercive and constraining ideologies, but its fundamental concern is mythic escape.[87] "I'm opening an exit for you," Ra says in one essay, "to get out of this before it's too late."[88] This exit is about a deeper collective existence beyond the given, a utopian yearning that aligns with what Paul Gilroy identifies as the "politics of transfiguration" in African diasporic cultures: in contrast to the "politics of fulfillment," which "demands that bourgeois civil society live up to its promises of its own rhetoric," transfigurative desires and solidarities look beyond the political inheritances and racialized presuppositions of modernity, "striv[ing] in pursuit of the sublime, struggling to repeat the unrepeatable, to present the unrepresentable."[89] Gilroy's idea of black utopian desire certainly saturates *Fugitive Time*, but we find a distinct genre of it in Ra's long-held renunciation of "freedom" and "equality," his insistence that persistent inequity and unfreedom demonstrate that the "demands" of "bourgeois civil society," as Gilroy puts it, can be absolute only in death. Ra even went so far as to sever himself from the idea of linear, progressive time that governs modern life, suggesting instead an "alter-destiny." "My music is reaching outwards," he often repeated, "not being part of the past, or the present, or the future."[90] To exceed what's known as time and space, to exist beyond the broken promises of liberal democratic values, is to escape into myth. Ra's fugitive time—his drapetomanic time consciousness—is about envisioning this myth *in advance*, however opaquely or faintly, by way of the artist's sounds, words, and performance.

Ra distributes these disparate mythic vectors across his multilayered aesthetics, making his ideas, his music, his poetry, and his performative presence effectively inextricable. The colorful capes, the sequins, the hats that constitute the Arkestra's costumes, he says, are music: "Colors throw out musical sounds . . . vibrations of life."[91] The music, in turn, is a form of language that shapes and drives his proleptically mythic ideas: "In my music I speak of unknown things, impossible things, ancient things, potential things"; it "motivates, stimulates, and compels to turn loose things that are not probable."[92] Undergirding all of this is Ra's fusion of the ancient world and outer space, a kind of amalgam of his accumulated knowledge of the cosmos and ancient Egyptian culture that manifests in a unique configuration of aesthetics and ideas.[93] The opening minutes of Robert Mugge's documentary *A Joyful Noise* present it well: the film begins with Ra walking through the Egyptian section of the Philadelphia Museum of Art, placing his hand on a hieroglyphic-engraved pharaonic statue, saying, "All planet Earth produces is the dead bodies of humanity. . . . Everything else comes from outer space, from unknown regions." He says this while wearing one of his flamboyant faux-Egyptian space-age costumes—a metallic gold skull cap with beads draped over his forehead, an iridescent shirt, a flowing red cape. The film then cuts to the Arkestra wailing in free form on a Philadelphia rooftop, each member wearing some version of Ra's colorful sequins—blacks, greens, blues, golds. When Ra enters the rooftop scene magnanimously in his flowing gown and wire-sculpture hat to singer June Tyson's lyric "the living myth," proceeding to conduct the screaming band with his arms outstretched as if in flight, there's no doubt that his embodied presence lies at the center of this entire myth project. If, as he says in *Joyful Noise*, "there's an unknown [that people] need to know in order to survive," Ra is the designated guide to usher them toward that unknown—sequins, purple wigs, flailing arms, and all.

As I did with Samb's work, I want to look at some of the ways Ra's drapetomanic fugitive time—the proleptic inhabitation of this multifarious myth—surfaces not just conceptually but also more subtly in the formal architecture of the work itself. In the following I consider two especially prominent formal modes that traverse Ra's poetry and music. The first are the "accumulations," the ways he layers thought and sound to create pockets of swirling, generative cacophony. This is Ra's version of Samb's sedimented montage form, that multi-vectored movement through disparate objects and lines of thought. For Ra, it's an overlaying of tonalities, melodies, terms, and what he calls "equations," all intended to awaken audience consciousness and catalyze it toward myth, into the open. "Spacings," the second category, lies on the opposite end of intensity but is no less generative of an outward-oriented fugitive time consciousness. This formal mode corresponds to the frequent, seemingly inscrutable silences, breaks, lulls, sustained pitches, and other iterations of openness that saturate Ra's poems and recordings, which together generate a sense of anticipation, gesture to imperceptible fugitive pathways, and evoke the openness of flight.

Both of these aesthetic operations, I would argue, fall under the larger rubric of Ra's "funk"—that ethical and especially musical mode that flouts European modernity's claim to reason and order, allowing one to glimpse through time at new worlds and new forms of black life. "Funk is pure thought," Walcott suggests, "brought to us by those whose experiences are still understood as alien expressions in a world made by them but launched against them."[94] Understanding Ra's aesthetics as "alien expressions" coincidentally converges with Cartwright's characterization of drapetomania not just as a "disease of the mind" but a form of "mental alienation."[95] It's as if that will toward freedom, for Cartwright, were an aberration in need of correction, a kind of psychological severing from the putatively normative (antiblack) order of things. But Ra owns that aberrational status. As Walcott bluntly puts it, "Sun Ra was an alien." Ra spins Cartwright's language and racist logic on its head and turns alien(ation) into an insurgent force that operates under the cover of what the world deems madness. The underside of the world's unsettled gaze is his secret lab where he experiments with sound, language, technologies, mysticisms, and, most of all, proleptic dream consciousness. It's not just Ra's Saturn origin story that gives him the funk and makes him alien. It's also the *delivery* of that funk, his "alien expressions."

The first of these aesthetic modes of drapetomanic temporal funk—what I'm calling "accumulations"—saturates Ra's verse and music, although they take on very different shapes in each. In many of his poems, Ra uses convoluted wordplay to create a vortex of meaning and enunciation. He'll scramble word sequences, recombine the letters of words several times over, and riffle through disparate ideas with a quick succession of homonyms. So many of these "word equations" are "as much *sight poetry* as sound poetry," a turning over of phonemes and graphemes to create new orderings, new associations, new lines of thought.[96] "It's alright to permutate things," Ra explains, "if alpha is equal to omega." Indicative of the humor that saturates much of his work, he gives the example of recombining the letters in "Earth" to form "the ra": "If you change the name of the planet then it won't be here when God gets ready to destroy it."[97] Recombining, then, is a way to move from one valuation to another, to evade interpellation, to escape the seemingly inevitable tide of history.

Take the homonymic play in "The Three Dimensions of Air": "Because 'to word' something is to state it. / To word To state / Word State / Word Ward / To word Toward / To word Toward on."[98] There's an auditory-semantic slippage that occurs at "Word Ward," resulting in a blurring of enunciation and prolepsis, though "word" and "toward" remain in tandem in the poem, as if the voice of the "word" were announcing the anticipation-saturated tilt of "toward." In "From Another Forever," permutation takes the form of lexical scrambling:

"Out" Is The Way Of The "Outer" And
"In" Is The Way Of The "Inner"
The End Of The "Inner" End Is Different
From The End Of The "Outer" End, Because
The Outer End Is The Outer On
Yes, Out Is The "Outer" And In Is The
"Inner."[99]

Here Ra provides a series of dialectical equations, or balanced oppositions, reconfiguring the phrase slightly each time as if he were testing out a problem or trying to sever sign from signifier in order to usher us into the unknowable. This mode of defamiliarization—of "alien expression"—is not unlike Samb's wandering and conceptual spinning, his desire "to displace, to place myself, to replace myself," repeatedly modulating words, loosening them from normative conceptual ground. This mode and these poems also quite directly recall Olaniyan's discussion of the "perambulating" postcolonial state in Fela's music, especially in the lyrics he examines from Fela's "Perambulator": "He must start to go; start to go for / nothing / Start to go / He must to come, come down; come / down for nothing / Come, come down / He must to turn, turn round; turn round / for nothing/ Turn, turn round." As Olaniyan says of these lyrics, Ra's equational poems are filled with redundancy yet are somehow generative of a kind of kinetic energy.[100] In "From Another Forever," a kindred vortical spinning operation unfolds, but in Ra's case it's one that gathers momentum with fugitive anticipatory energy, marking out in advance, we might say, multiple escape routes: to the "end" or the "on," the "inner" or the "outer." The perambulations of Ra's verse accumulate vitality; they generate opacity and seeming chaos; they gesture, as in this poem, to myriad routes that might lead us to his mythical alter-world.

This mode of accumulation also structures much of the Arkestra's music, specifically their practice of collective improvisation. Throughout Ra's career the band played a stunning array of genres in the history of jazz, performing, especially in live shows, works by Billy Strayhorn, Jelly Roll Morton, Thelonious Monk, Fletcher Henderson, and others. But beginning in the mid-1960s, the Arkestra became known for increasingly free structured and dissonant sounds, pieces that blended group improvisation with Ra's own composed material. The title track on the band's 1965 record *The Magic City* is a landmark of the latter approach. A twenty-seven-minute recorded rehearsal, it's nearly entirely collectively improvised, although Ra did sketch out a rough sequence of small- and full-group improvisations, conducting the band with hand gestures. This piece may have no tonal center or metered tempo, but the result is remarkably cohesive, a balance of individual instrumental voices and a clear collective development and texture. "In my music," Ra suggests in one late interview, "there's lots of little melodies going on. It's like an ocean of sound. The ocean comes up, it goes back, it rolls. . . . It might go over people's heads, wash part of them away, reenergize them, go through them, and then go back out to the cosmos and come back to them again."[101] Ra isn't describing *The Magic City*, but he may as well be. The piece ebbs and flows, fluctuating in volume, pitch, and intensity, from Ronnie Boykins's bowed bass to the sustained high register of Ra's Selmer Clavioline electric keyboard to Marshall Allen's fluttering piccolo. The individual voices swirl, feeding off one another as if in conversation, cumulatively building a world piece by piece. Halfway through, the band gets the signal to let loose: saxophones squeal and honk, cymbals crash, the piccolo soars, the theremin-sounding Clavioline screeches. It sounds, at first, like utter chaos. But then one finds those individual voices threading in and out of one another, like hydrogen and oxygen molecules piecing together that "ocean of sound." The entire track is an ocean, the tide fugitively rolling in and out, from the Earth to the cosmos and back, the swinging contortions eliciting in the listener that proleptic inhabitation of Ra's infinitely mythic world. If, in improvisation, "you need to look ahead with a kind of torque that shapes what's being looked at," what we find in the Arkestra's heaving improvisatory accumulations is a generative force with an outward eye that just might bring that alter-destiny into being.[102]

Just as myth catalyzing and funkifying as his louder, denser accumulations is Ra's deliberate cultivation of space and openness. Silences—which "speak," Ra says, each occupying "a world all its own"—are a crucial manifestation of open space in his work, but so are related devices such as lulls, hesitations, and tapers.[103] Musically and poetically, they conjure the necessity of breath and considered thought; they evoke a sense of anticipation, weightlessness, and unseen pathways. These spacings saturate Ra's poetry, particularly his later verse, in the form of ellipses of variable lengths and placements.[104] Take this excerpt from the middle of "Lightning Realities":

> We can move to spheres in the vast endless abyss . . . .
> The vast endless abyss of Outer Space . . . .
> The approach of the Eon of adjustment is at hand
> Transition-adjustment . . alter interpretation . . . . . .
> Equational-precision
> Cosmo-Visions Magic . . . abstract translation
> To other waves of thought-feeling-attunement . . .
> "The lifting up shall be the casting down,"
> 'Tis thus it is written . . . .
> Look outward at the eternal pit of Out-Space . . . . [105]

Here ellipses give the poem an undulating visual contour. The differential effect of six, seven, and fifteen dots on the meaning of the words and the poem's spoken cadence is ambiguous, although Ra, a student of numerology, likely gave the numbers careful consideration.[106] An ellipsis typically signifies an omission, something missing though implied by context, but these feel just as much like pauses, breaths, or silences—that is, *deliberate* silences, as if we were meant to think and search after an image of "Outer Space" just a moment longer than for the image of a "vast endless abyss." Ra wrote dozens of poems with these opaque and uneven ellipses, some inserted midline but most added as extensions at a line's end, like some kind of synesthetic echo of that final poetic image, as if to stretch the proleptic inhabitation of that "eternal pit of Out-Space" just a bit further toward the cosmic myth.

It's also common for Ra to place an epic run of ellipses after the final line of the entire poem, as if to blast out the frequency of his final resounding mythic image into deep space.[107] "The Fantasy" is not uncommon:

> Yes . . . I am a spirit-stranger from the sky
> Far away . . . . farther than the eye can see
> Is my paradise
> A mythical world
> In Outer Space . . . .[108]

This is Ra's version of Samb's trapdoors, his escape cuts into other realms. These twenty-six dots are like a jet stream tracing the path to that mythical outer space for those on Earth. They lay the groundwork for proleptic thought, seeds to begin to envision the outside in advance. Many of Ra's poems conclude with similar elliptical extensions, but few are quite like "The Outer Darkness." Before content and meaning, this poem is a visual form. The incrementally indented six-point ellipses at the start of several lines make it relatively unique among Ra's poems, but it's the final thirteen lines of streaming ellipses, emerging from the undulation of those initial six-point lines like some cryptic Morse code–like enunciation, that sets this poem apart. That final shape almost resembles a V-formation, a social act of flight that both emerges from and lunges out in anticipation of that final resounding "Dark Unknown Eternal." This elliptical formation and the many that traverse Ra's poetry are reminiscent of the "suggestive opacity" that Anthony Reed attributes to the work of Umbra poet and Ra contemporary Norman Pritchard, "the sense of something just beyond articulation." Like Ra, Pritchard often employs trailing dots that "continually defer the possibility of a final, transcendent referent, defer[ring] the possibility of an ultimate meaning."[109] That "The Outer Darkness" concerns sound and music is crucial, too, to any speculative reading (speculation, to be sure, is the only way to read this poem's opacity). Music, the language suggests, infinitely projects, disperses, and quickens myth. As sound, the concluding shape reads like a deep reverberation, an ever-deferred taper, the sound wave of a scream moving through that darkness in search of further diffractive vectors. Indeed, the term may not be used, but Ra's myth saturates this poem. And in that "quickening spirit," in the immeasurability of its "multiplicities and potentialities," its myth bespeaks a fugitively proleptic inhabitation, a line of advance sight toward new life-forms and new consciousness.

I want to close this kaleidoscopic tour of Ra's work equationally, as he would have it, with some thoughts on how these extensions and deferrals correspond to his music. I have in mind literal silences, collapses in volume, sustained pitches, and tapers that do a similar sort of work as the poetic device—providing space for breath but also for proleptic vision,

THE OUTER DARKNESS

Intergalactic music is of the outer darkness
Therefore it is of the greater Void-Blackness
And from that point of view:
..........It is Black-Infinity:
............And from that point of view:
................It is Cosmo-Nature's music... ...
....It is the music of natural-spontaneous Infinity
....It is unlimited in scope....................
Immeasureable in it's multiplicities and potentialities.
Natural dark-black music projects the myth of ever Is
And he who is not dark in spirit will never know
That these words are true and valid forever.
I speak of a different kind of blackness,
The kind that the world does not know.............
The kind that the world will never understand.
......It is rhythm against rhythm in kind dispersion,
......It is harmony against harmony in endless coordinate
......It is melody against melody in dark-enlightenment
......It is Nature's voice in Cosmo-Sound
......It is the everything and the subtle nothing
         Of Omni-All
.::::It is the ever quickening-presence of The Living Spirit
...It is the Cosmo-bridge to the Dark Unknown Eternal.
....
....
....
....
....
....
....
....
....
....
....
....

4.2 Facsimile from Sun Ra's typewriter of "The Outer Darkness."
Source: Sun Ra, *The Immeasurable Equation* (Waitawhile, 2005).

flight extension, and mythic limitlessness. The amalgam of Ra's poetic and sonic spacings ought to be understood as integral to his larger mythmaking, of interpellating audiences and cultivating a sense of anticipation of the expansive openness of the unknown. If, for Walcott, "what funk offers us intellectually is an epistemological break . . . allowing us to conceive and think new life-forms," then we might think of these different forms of space across Ra's work as the sonic complement to that thought that expands outward, opening up a field of possibility, simultaneously, in their drapetomanic funk(tion), breaking away from putatively rational expectations of thought and sound.[110] Take the track "Extension Out" on the band's 1973 release *Pathways to Worlds Unknown*, which includes a brief interlude by Ronnie Boykins on upright bass slowly playing a series of open, spacious intervals. It's perhaps less the bass sequence itself than its severe contrast in intensity against the sounds of a freak-out Marshall Allen alto saxophone solo on either side of Boykins's intervals that makes his warm, round notes feel like a breath, a moment of anticipatory reprieve before Allen attempts another combustive "extension out" into the mythic cosmos. By contrast, the title track of the Arkestra's 1969 *Atlantis* begins with a full minute of nothing but Ra playing sonar beeps on his "Solar Sound Organ"—slow-metered single notes that echo tightly like underwater navigation. The articulations feel as close to a direct transposition of his poetic ellipses as one could imagine, setting up the steady climb of a famous freak-out solo of his own with a series of evenly spaced submarine breaths. As if in search of a "dreamless Atlantean sleep," as Nathaniel Mackey might put it, or Equiano's "inhabitants of the deep," those Drexciyan aquatic dwellers I discuss in the introduction.[111] Once it becomes apparent that these beeps are the calm beginnings of an epic run—where Ra, for fifteen minutes, "slash[es] and beat[s] at the keyboard, spinning around and around, his hands windmilling at the keys"—those sonar beeps recode more like an initial gathering of anticipatory energy, a conjuring of the pathways, in advance of an explosive blastoff into space.[112]

My last example of these sonic spacings is a kind of musical version of his "Outer Darkness" poem. "The Sun Myth," on *The Heliocentric Worlds of Sun Ra, Volume Two*, recorded the same year as *The Magic City*, is a nearly twenty-minute-long double concerto for Boykins on bowed bass and Ra on piano and Clavioline, with periodic collective screams, honks, and rumblings from the rest of the band. One of its principal features is the drawn-out ending: the track slowly peters out over the course of two full minutes, with a seemingly endless succession of pauses, ghost notes, breathy growls, and sotto voce screeches. The final thirty seconds is a slow unedited fade-out, a tapering of percussionist Roger Blank softly brushing and scratching his cymbals amid intermittent full-second pauses. It's as if the cacophonous horns and Clavioline from the previous fifteen minutes have lifted us out into the unknowable infinity of the cosmos, and we're now soaring in outer space, floating weightlessly in the Earth's ellipsoidal orbit, waiting in keen anticipation of the moment to fire back up and reach farther into the "uncharted ignorance" of deep space. The entirety of the track lifts us up and out as if we're already there and then, living and breathing Ra's myth in advance. This kind of elongated, slow-moving musical taper ought to be read alongside the concluding ellipses of poems like "Energies," "Vibration of the Ray," and "The Other Otherness." Sonically and poetically, they make no sense to anyone searching for rational, concrete, earthly meaning. Instead, they evince a pathway, a fugitive tilt, a proleptic inhabitation of a far-out world.

If, for Ra, the Arkestra's music is meant to transport listeners, "like a spaceship [that] lift 'em on out there," so, too, do the images, permutations, and open spaces of his poetry proleptically lift his readers out toward his myth.[113] Music and poetry are his dual engine, his two-chambered funk ship. Together they turn alien(ation) into a generative underground force that throws normative reason and common sense aside, using the veneer of madness to conjure the interstellar pathways of escape. Central in this vessel, though often out of sight, is the body. Unlike Samb's writings, where embodiment is explicitly foregrounded in his fugitive wanderings, in Ra's work the body is most often couched in an opaque noun ("continuation-living-being") or a fugitive verb ("We can move to spheres in the vast endless abyss . . . ."). It's the body of the spaceship itself, encompassing Ra, as well as all the people to whom he delivered his message of unknown, mythic horizons. It's this outward-lunging ship body that seeks the fugitive lightness of being essential to fugitive time: the moment when the ship has passed through the "cosmo-bridge" and its collective corporeality has been washed of earthly devastation. The body, too, is in the music: in the Arkestra's practice and performance, blowing horns, beating drums and cymbals, in Ra's "spinning around and around, his hands windmilling at the keys," all done to keep the engine fired up and the ship on its fugitive course. Ultimately, Ra's mythic other-order-of-being body is at the fore. As with Samb, Ra's flamboyant performative presence makes him the front man, guiding the ship, leading the world into the vast openness of his utopia. This is Ra's drapetomanic fugitive time: illegible to the normative world, he steers the ship toward a new order of freedom while cultivating an anticipatory consciousness of mythic transcendence, knowing that the ecstasy is in the infinite permutational quest for that ultimate unknowing/unowning/unowing.

FUGITIVE CONFLUENCE

In their distinct ways, Ra and Samb pursue the sublime, the transfigurative possibility of otherwise being, by seeing and cultivating worlds in advance. They do so through genres of the drapetomanic, striving to "abscond" not from the "service" of bondage, as Cartwright would have it, but from a world that has devastated African-descended lives for centuries. They inhabit what Cartwright calls "mania," but as a cover, a face to a normative world unable to think outside the hold of its reason. As Bruce says of Lauryn Hill's own inhabitation of psychosocial otherness, Samb and Ra demonstrate that madness can be insurgent, teeming with possibility, that it need not be a descent into abjection but a bridge beyond it, where they might at last find their own terms, their own existences.[114]

To be sure, Samb and Ra share common ground. They both forged their work collaboratively, shaping and devising with others. They worked across a range of aesthetic media, seeking out the forms that might best reveal, and simultaneously obscure, their vociferous critiques and operations of fugitive time. For both, those operations bore fugitivity's hallmark of refusal, the denial of participation, the avoidance of governance: the opting out of society, for the one, and the planet, for the other. What perhaps most makes them kindred spirits, I've suggested, is the density of the work, the opacity of their aesthetics of fugitive time. But they share not just a generic desire to remain not fully legible to the world. Opacity, for them, is an insistence on impossibility, uncertainty, and the unknowable. It's a perpetual project, a restless proleptic vision in search of infinity. An operation in which the only certainty is that it won't be of this world.

From the start of this chapter I've walked a tightrope, reading the contours of opacity but trying not to reduce, identifying the texture of the weave but trying to refrain from the appropriative measure of grasping, of owning. Despite their allied transatlantic operations, Samb and Ra each remain uniquely inscrutable. They give us traces of their worlds, their desires, their objectives, but we've arrived at the end of this tour still not knowing. As we were meant not to know. Ra's "dark unknown eternal" remains elusive. Samb's refusal of "all forms of existing society" still seems unfathomable.

And we still have little sense of what it means to live in perpetual errancy or to seek infinite, uncharted ignorance. Even if we intuit pieces of the aesthetic architecture—the ellipses, the montages, the sedimentations—the full extent of Samb and Ra's fugitive time remains fundamentally inaccessible, even to those who respect it, who want to feel with it. However, "Giv[ing] up this old obsession with discovering what lies at the bottom of natures" does not preclude solidarity. Opacities coexist and converge, Glissant insists. They remain open to relation. One doesn't have to grasp the other "to build with" the other: "Nothing prohibits our seeing them in confluence, without confusing them in some magma or reducing them to each other. This same opacity is also the force that drives every community: the thing that would bring us together forever and makes us permanently distinctive."[115] Likewise, for Alexander Weheliye, if the idea of singularity is thought of as "always already relational," then we might ascertain "the specificity of the cultural performance in question and potentially [network] it with everything else in the cosmos."[116] Ra and Samb, we might say, meet somewhere in the cosmos. There are junctures where their opacities intersect, brackish waters where they converge, speaking, mixing, stirring together, relationally, in their singular, refusative density.

If opacities can build with and alongside one another, though, what is it that Samb and Ra together build, or signal, that they don't individually? What does their confluence, their mis-en-relation, generate? Together, without coordination, they built a sphere of influence, a passing down of the tradition, a transmission of aesthetic opacity to the next generation. What comes to mind is the cohort of self-styled Afrofuturists that includes electronic music artist Ibaaku and fashion designer Selly Raby Kane. At the vanguard of Senegalese and global black aesthetics, citing Samb and Ra as formative influences, their collaboration on the 2015 music video "Djula Dance," part of their sprawling multimedia project *Alien Cartoon*, is filled with opacity in the spirit of Ra and Samb: percussive electronic repetitions, pulsating bass, giant bug creatures, floating soap bubbles, transparent kaftans, ritual masks, interpretive dancers swirling underneath a huge, telescoped view of the cosmos. There's a constant choreographic reach, literally, for other worlds: at one point a figure walks up a wooden ladder, escaping the frame, and into outer space.[117] It's just the sort of disparate, generative, and cacophonous confluence we might expect to emerge from Ra and Samb's amalgamated legacies.

But the confluence of Ra and Samb's fugitive time consciousness also gestures to a larger sphere of politics, aesthetics, and diasporic belonging.

Their convergence shows that aesthetic disorder is a critical mode of praxis for black life on both sides of the Atlantic. That to live in the wake of settler colonialism, the transatlantic slave trade, chattel slavery, and myriad other historical devastations is to inhabit an enduring wreckage, one that requires what the normative world variously calls noise, scream, crazy, delirium, madness, insanity, and irrationality, but what these artists, in turn, might call desire, possibility, or the beyond. Crisis, Ra and Samb's work suggests, requires crisis aesthetics: a scrambling of the known and the given so that one day a new world might emerge. It's a scrambling that also drives and cultivates community, as Glissant might say. Together, their aesthetic worlds signal that diasporic solidarity can be forged from afar, across oceans, histories, ethnicities, languages, art forms, and opacities, traversing disparate metaphysics and disparate burning worlds. If, as Keguro Macharia reminds us, "practices of difference suture the black diaspora," Samb and Ra's inchoate worlds together hold the edges, threading the needle of belonging.[118]

In a way, all the aesthetic works studied in *Fugitive Time* refuse full disclosure. To move toward that moment, wherever and whenever it may come, when pain at last has vanished from the body and mind, is nothing if not opaque. To continually desire and pursue something that is by definition unattainable bears its own mystification. Such is fugitive time, the ecstatic proleptic inhabitation of contingent possibility. Holding out for the promise, the moment, when one might at last be unburdened and unowned. Turning to this book's final movement, I want to remain on the African continent and with this desire for the impossible. Here women return to the fore, dreaming of new bodies, new lives, and new worlds, leading a nation out from the ruins of settler colonialism. It begins in the late nineteenth century with a prophet vanishing into thin air.

5 YVONNE VERA, NOVIOLET BULAWAYO, AND THE IMMINENCE OF DREAMING AIR

> She feels that gaping wound everywhere. The wound has been shifting all over her body and she can no longer find it. She raises her hands above her head as though supporting a falling roof. She gestures into the sky with frantic arms. She laughs. The skin tears away from her, and she knows that the damage to herself is now irreversible.
>
> **Yvonne Vera, *Nehanda***

Yvonne Vera's 1993 novel *Nehanda* is an antihistory. It chronicles the life of the prophet and spirit medium Nehanda as the author remembered it being told to her, passed down from generation to generation in what Vera calls a "mythical consciousness of history."[1] If the British claimed in 1898 to have hanged the historical figure Nehanda for inciting the first Zimbabwean revolt against colonial rule, in Vera's account Nehanda doesn't die—she *departs*. "She refused that," Vera explained in a 2000 interview of the woman whose singular connection to her ancestors and land galvanized the nation's First Chimurenga. "She surpassed the moment when they took her body, and when they put the noose upon it, she had already departed."[2] In the novel, Nehanda takes flight from the "gaping wound" on her body, the wound that has been inflicted on her people. She seeks the "ecstasy" of "healing" and "release." Sitting in her jail cell awaiting her fate, she has "hope for the nation," foreseeing "new languages," "new existences com[ing] out of the dreaming air."[3]

Nehanda's final moments of life are decidedly fugitive. She escapes execution, that ultimate enactment of colonial subjection, "run[ning] away from the snares of recognition."[4] Physically suffering, she finds her ecstatic release by escaping her body altogether, taking flight from those mortal scars, burdens, and sensations, letting her "skin tear away from her." And like Sethe's vision of stealing away "through the veil," this is all done in anticipation. For Nehanda to depart before the noose is placed around her neck, she must see her path to escape. Surrounded by a "dreaming air," she lives in advance that moment when she will finally be at rest, beyond the reach of colonial interpellation, in that time and place in which her people will once again flourish in their own cosmology, reborn into "new existences."[5]

In this final chapter I want to stay on the continent, moving to the South to consider the literary and historical afterlives of Nehanda's fugitive time consciousness—the effect and force of that "dreaming air"—in late twentieth- and early twenty-first-century Zimbabwean fiction. Vera's *Without a Name* (1994) and NoViolet Bulawayo's *We Need New Names* (2013) also feature women who seek to shed their bodies and minds of alienation, women through whom we can glimpse a larger view of a nation as it seeks to terminate violence and subjugation. Vera's *Without a Name* does so in 1977 during the country's Second Chimurenga, at the precipice of national independence from white settler rule; Bulawayo, in turn, sets this desire for self-transformation in the early twenty-first century, a time when thousands of Zimbabweans fled their collapsing country for foreign lands. If the fugitive anticipatory desire to strip the body of subjection can be understood as a Zimbabwean historical longing that begins with Nehanda's 1898 departure, *Without a Name* and *We Need New Names* each take up distinct moments in the evolution of this desire. Like *Nehanda*, these two novels establish a discourse of dreaming, of imagining in advance new configurations of the body that stand allegorically for a larger societal yearning. Their allegories, however, reveal the fault lines of national belonging, showing us women who strive to intervene in a historically masculinist nationalism and revealing a shifting conception of belonging to one's ancestors and land. This chapter extends Susan Andrade's influential study of earlier-generation African women's fiction and the ground she broke when she argued that in African literary studies, "women have not often represented explicitly national-allegorical feminine figures," that it's the *reception* of their work that's been flawed. Focusing on the more recent generation, my task here is similar to Andrade's: to "juxtapose a form of feminine coming into being in the world . . . against and within the national narrative."[6] In our own moment, in which the question of the nation has perhaps become out of fashion in postcolonial studies, Vera's and Bulawayo's formations of fugitive time demand to be read through the lens of Zimbabwe's last four decades of societal crisis.

Working through questions of fugitivity in African contexts, particularly in Vera's and Bulawayo's fiction, opens up distinct ways of reading African fiction as well as new valences in theories of fugitivity. For one, questions of indigeneity, of belonging to an ancestral home, bring a paradoxical layer to notions of black fugitivity: a discourse premised more on diasporic notions of rootlessness than on rootedness. In contrast, say, to the Caribbean in Black Audio's *Handsworth Songs* or the Kentucky plantation in Morrison's *Beloved*—both of which largely are presented with antipathy, as sites of trauma and nonreturn—in Vera's and Bulawayo's novels, Shona ancestral land is a more complex spiritual force around which fugitive movement and time consciousness revolve: in the former, it's the source of both belonging and violence, anchoring a distinct cyclical structure of fugitive time; in the latter, only the residue of this cyclical structure remains, and this ancestral force evolves, through transnational migration, into a melancholic trace that beckons its people to return. At the same time, if fugitivity lends itself to a phenomenological conception of time consciousness as an interweaving of anticipation and traumatic memory, then the frame of fugitivity opens up a distinct lens into the African novel. Indeed, Vera and Bulawayo show us how the micro-optics and micro-movements of phenomenology, an analytic rarely brought to bear on African literature, can reveal new ways of reading fiction from the continent. As I've shown throughout this book, it's an analytic that exhibits a telescopic view of the body—its sensations and perceptions, its desires and pains—revealing in the Zimbabwean literary context how fiction registers history's woundings and desires in and on the body.

In what follows I attend to the constructions of fugitive time in *Without a Name* and *We Need New Names*—the ways that these novels index on the body the alienation wrought by colonialism, patriarchy, and poverty, and the language with which Vera and Bulawayo articulate a proleptic inhabitation of disalienation. Using varied figurations of metaphor, narrative perspective, and narrative time, the two writers present interconnected societal allegories through their protagonists' yearning for wholeness in body and mind. But like the different versions of fugitive time in this book, what we find in these works is a continual deferral of that ultimate release and, in that deferral, a kind of ecstatic dwelling in the sociality and belonging shared by those envisioning the outside.

GENEALOGIES OF (DIS)ALIENATION

In their larger scope, Vera's and Bulawayo's novels are part of a sprawling body of African(ist) scholarly and literary work preoccupied with questions of alienation and disalienation. To fully engage the minutiae of these texts, a sense of this sprawl is useful. As it was at the start of this book, Frantz Fanon's *Black Skin, White Masks* is indispensable. For Fanon, black alienation is constructed through that entrenched Manichaean opposition of colonizer and colonized, subjector and subjected. And it's an alienation at once psychic and physical: "I took myself far off from my own presence, very far, constituting myself an object. What else could it be for me but a dismemberment, a wrenching, a hemorrhage that spattered my whole body with black blood?"[7] There's an internalization of nonbeing for Fanon that enacts a sense of corporeal excision, as if one were left with phantom limbs of a former wholeness. Crucially, Achille Mbembe brings a related framework to bear specifically on sub-Saharan Africa, wherein the state apparatus of early to mid-twentieth-century colonial power produces an ideology of the African as decidedly "other"—as less than human, a "bundle of drives," an objectified "body-thing" to be used for both colonial experimentation and forced labor.[8] Though more concerned with the structure that produces colonial alienation, Mbembe's framework does share that central Fanonian consequence of being evacuated from oneself, of occupying a body and consciousness that have effectively become occupied by another. These operations of colonial racialization and domination, of course, pervade modern African writing. In the Zimbabwean fiction that precedes Vera's and Bulawayo's work, it is, most prominently, the eating disorder that Nyasha develops in Tsitsi Dangarembga's *Nervous Conditions* (1988) and the psychic wreckage saturating Dambudzo Marechera's *The House of Hunger* (1978) that expose the workings and effects of colonial violence.

Moving into the postcolonial moment, a period that begins with the first rush of decolonization across the continent in the early 1960s, the forces of subjection that African writers respond to change guise. In various countries, Mbembe notes, newly independent states "reappropriated" many of the institutions and mechanisms that had been used to maintain colonial authority. In several, including independent Zimbabwe, the state maintained its power less through a reciprocal obligation between state authority and the people than through an amalgam of violent coercion, nativist ideology, and natural resource extractions that allowed the state to allocate privileges to secure its power. With these systems in place, the added effects of global structural adjustment and deregulation in the 1980s and 1990s were devastating throughout sub-Saharan Africa: unemployment and poverty soared, social welfare systems crumbled, migration to urban centers and other countries intensified.[9] Zimbabwe did experience an economic "boom" in the first few years after independence in 1980, largely caused by the termination of international sanctions that had been levied against the state during the war. But these "unsustainable" gains, as Alois Mlambo puts it, in access to health care and education collapsed by the end of the 1980s once structural adjustment measures were established, which in turn spurred a wave of deindustrialization, privatization, inflation, and unemployment across the country: "The result was 'permanent joblessness, hopelessness and economic insecurity' for the majority and the mortgaging of Zimbabwe's economy to foreign capital."[10] To be sure, societal alienation persisted in these conditions, but it no longer resembled that clear Fanonian oppositional structure of colonizer and colonized. In late twentieth- and early twenty-first-century Zimbabwe, the postcolonial state becomes a critical subjecting force in its effort to maintain power, but it subjugates in conjunction with the forces of global capital. The result, as we find in contemporary Zimbabwean fiction, is a kind of diffuse alienating structure of poverty, state-sponsored evictions and violence, alcoholism and the spread of infectious diseases, defunded schools and health care systems, and flight to Europe, North America, and nearby countries.[11]

As for Vera's and Bulawayo's novels, as well as those of many of their contemporaries, alienation resembles what Ato Quayson has characterized as a kind of societal and individual sublimation of the forces of subjection. If Fanon's alienation is based on that Manichaean structure of black and white relationality, then what we find in many African works of fiction, Quayson suggests, is a "skeptical interlocutor . . . structurally inextricable from the subjectivity of the alienated self." The forces of subjection—this "skeptical interlocutor"—come to reside in the "structural location of a matrix of anticipations that call up and yet persistently question the subject's identity," forming a kind of self-regulating, internalized structure of alienation.[12] Quayson's examples include the "communal ethos as expressed in the voice of Tradition" in Chinua Achebe's *Things Fall Apart* and, significant here, the "corporeal injunction of a traumatized body-politic" in Vera's *Without a Name*. Indeed, despite the presence of white settlers during the historical period of Vera's novel—set in 1977, three years before independence—Vera makes no explicit reference to any colonial figure. Instead, that colonial subjection is implied in Mazvita's perception of embodied pain, in her experience of trauma. By contrast, in Bulawayo's *We Need New Names*, set more than two decades after independence, alienation is derived not from colonial subjection but from the larger structural mechanisms that have impoverished, displaced, and infected the bodies of the novel's cast of characters.[13]

In the coming pages I want to trace the lineaments of alienation in these two novels, including their embodied temporalities of alienation. However, this focus is meant to deepen our understanding of the other side of the dialectic: *dis*alienation. Or rather, the desire for, the anticipation of, disalienation. For Fanon, we recall, disalienation is processual—a "quest," he says, leading to the point at which black life is freed of the "arsenal" of colonial complexes. This quest, this "authentic emergence," he says, is born in the "zone of nonbeing" that is paradoxically both the nadir of pathologized blackness and the site of radical refusal and inventive possibility.[14] It's also, as I suggested in the introduction, where fugitive time consciousness emerges, where one begins to imagine *in advance* that moment when the body and mind are at last freed of the trappings of colonial interpellation. What Ronald Judy observes as Fanon's "becoming consciousness" presumes a sense of affectively lunging beyond the reach of negation toward that moment of release.[15] This being-toward disalienation consumes Vera's account of Nehanda leaping beyond herself, "surpass[ing] the moment when they took her body."[16] And an analogous desire propels Mazvita in Vera's *Without a Name* and Darling in Bulawayo's *We Need New Names* to free themselves of the burdens of poverty, sexual violence, and state repression, daring to imagine that moment when their bodies feel lighter and entirely their own.

One of the central claims of this chapter is that this push toward disalienation that we encounter in Vera's and Bulawayo's protagonists cannot be severed from a larger societal desire for disalienation. Both novels, in other words, could be called national allegories—a term that opens up a host of debates in African and postcolonial studies. Aligned or not, critics have continued to return to Fredric Jameson's "Third-World Literatures in the Era of Multinational Capitalism" (1986) as a foundational essay on the relationship between literary form and the nation in the formerly colonized world.[17] Like Andrade's position on the novels she studies in *The Nation Writ Small*, much of Jameson's logic is upheld in the two novels considered in this chapter, despite his "romanticization" of the Third World as representing a "unitary critical perspective." But they do so by exposing Jameson's "critical blindness," as Andrade incisively suggests of her own archive, for "these novels by women from the Global South do not immediately demonstrate a national allegory, as Jameson insists all such novels do."[18] And yet, like Jameson's framing, in Vera's and Bulawayo's works the private and the public spheres are inseparable. The quotidian thoughts and experiences of their protagonists are inextricable from politics—from the violent conflicts, the diseases, the currency devaluations, the unspoken codes of patriarchy that saturate society. And like Jameson's flexible notion of allegory as "profoundly discontinuous, a matter of breaks and heterogeneities," Vera's and Bulawayo's novels are not just allegories of the Zimbabwean nation *tout court*. They instead reveal the contradictions and mutations of a sense of collective belonging in perpetual motion. They cut against monolithic conceptions of the nation that prescribe fixed roles for the land, ancestral belonging, and masculine authority. They show how nation can be forged in diaspora, how women can have a constitutive voice. In contrast to Benedict Anderson's strict sense of the nation as "limited" (encompassed by finite boundaries) and "sovereign" (organized around the symbol of the sovereign state), I read the "nation" in Vera's and Bulawayo's work in the more elastic Jamesonian sense of the "social" and the "political."[19] That is, as a larger, amorphous sense of heterogeneous collectivity, that, in the Zimbabwean case, refuses identification with a (repressive) sovereign state and refuses to fix that collectivity to a single geography of the world. As I chronicle the structures of desire and escape in Vera's and Bulawayo's fiction, I want to read them in and alongside a larger, polysemous sense of being-with, a category of the nation with its roots in the collectivity for which Nehanda took flight from her own body as she awaited her execution.

As I move into closer examinations of these two novels, I want to keep in mind the history that Nehanda initiates, which the figures in *Without a Name* and *We Need New Names* inherit, albeit in different forms and different moments of Zimbabwean history. Nehanda's body, I contend, connects to Mazvita's body, which in turn connects to the body of Darling and her youth counterparts. In Vera's and Bulawayo's novels we find particular descriptive and formal devices through which to view their own iterations of fugitive time that reflect the historical moment of their intervention in the evolution of the phenomenal desire to strip the body of trauma and imagine an elsewhere and an otherwise. Because "fugitivity morphs and changes according to the vicissitudes of power," what we witness in these novels are the continual mutations of that escapist desire as the forces of subjection themselves change shape over time.[20]

VERA'S DREAMING CYCLE

Vera's *Without a Name* is a novel very much preoccupied with the intimacy of violence. The third-person-limited voice that predominates gives us a "moment-by-moment" view into Mazvita's "mental world," as Vera has commented, showing how she processes the pain that courses throughout her mind and body, as well as how she imagines an end to that violence.[21] Throughout, the narrative perspective provides a singular view into Mazvita's journey. Having been raped by a freedom fighter in a field near her home village of Mubaira, Mazvita flees to Harare to escape her traumas. In the capital, though, she discovers that her rapist has impregnated her, and she falls into a precarious life unable to find work to support herself. Along the way, the narrative unfolds in two temporal registers—Mazvita's trajectory to Harare, told in flashbacks, and her course back to Mubaira, set in the present—which appear largely in alternating chapters and in fragmented pieces.

I want to begin by disentangling these layers of violence and trauma that weigh so heavily on Mazvita. As in many of the works examined in this book, desire and anticipation emerge from violation in this text. And deepening our sense of that violation, in turn, deepens our sense of the novel's iteration of fugitive time consciousness. In the broadest sense, violation in *Without a Name* begins with its narrative perspective, which engenders a unique interplay between Mazvita's body and consciousness, enabling Vera to use the body to "capture fractured consciousness" and to "allow its interiority to emerge on its surface."[22] The result is a sedimentation of subjection that accumulates throughout the novel, producing an internalized structure of alienation with a multitude of signs and symptoms, the foundation of which is Mazvita's rape. The narrator's interior access to Mazvita's thoughts tells us that her attacker had "claimed her, told her that she could not hide the things of her body. . . . *Hanzvadzi* . . . he said.

You are my sister...."[23] For the freedom fighter to call her his sister—in Shona, their common language—demonstrates his sense of entitlement, what he takes to be their prescribed roles in the larger struggle that authorize him to take her body and efface her identity, as Kizito Muchemwa suggests, in the name of the masculinist-nationalist project.[24] "Mazvita gathered the whispering he had spread between her legs, over her arms," the narration continues. "She ran far into the mist but the whispering, a frightful memory, encompassed her." Coursing throughout her body and mind, the memory of his words and touch cut into her experience of time throughout the novel, including this encounter's final and most detailed narrative appearance, when Mazvita recalls how "he removed her legs from her body, and she lay still, not recognizing her legs as her own." Here we find that Fanonian alienation as *décollement*, or dismemberment, as if she were standing outside of herself and witnessing herself, in pieces, as other. By the end of the novel we also find a very deliberate act of anamnesis, for "she was sure that if she remembered his face, she could free herself of remembering him."[25] But that face eludes Mazvita. She instead continues to "remember the mist and the whispers" like a knife repeatedly cutting into her, drawing her back to her violation.

In a larger scope, Mazvita's violation is a reminder of the ways that black women, whether on the continent or in diaspora, have been uniquely and historically targeted. In *Rape: A South African Nightmare* (2015), Pumla Dineo Gqola identifies black women in South Africa as those "longest burdened with assumptions of unrapability," assumptions that stem from seventeenth-century stereotypes of Africans as lascivious. Rape, Gqola maintains, has and continues to be a "powerful language with which to control women in South Africa."[26] Similarly, in her influential 1991 essay "Mapping the Margins," Kimberlé Crenshaw explains how a historical fixation on black male predation and white female victimhood in the United States has produced a kind of "sexual hierarchy . . . that holds certain female bodies in higher regard than others," specifically a "devaluation of Black women and the marginalization of their sexual victimizations."[27] Importantly, these issues have also played out in literary representation, as Lucy Graham's comparative study of the relationship between rape and narrative interiority in South African short fiction demonstrates. Whereas the privileging of the male rapist's interior perspective in Njabulo Ndebele's "Fools" reinforces tropes of masculine dominance, Graham finds that Gcina Mhlophe's "Nokulunga's Wedding" and Baleka Kgositsile's "In the Night" bring power and voice to women historically silenced after rape through their protagonists' internal processing of the burdens of complicity, shame, and societal expectations.[28] In *Without a Name* the interior voice is also a critical device through which we learn of Mazvita's processing, how she physically experiences her violation, how she perceives the structure of patriarchy around her.

A crucial additional layer of Mazvita's interior life is the question of land. In contrast to the view of her new partner in Mubaira, Nyenyedzi, who insists that "there is no prayer that reaches our ancestors without the blessing from the land," that their "ancient claim" must be restored, Mazvita comes to see the land itself as her violator: "She connected him only to the land. . . . The land had allowed the man to grow from itself into her body."[29] For Quayson, this indicates a displacement of the effects of trauma: the referential locus of the event—that image of her rapist's face—remains inaccessible. "The event-rape," Quayson says, "becomes a semiotic system which generates a series of signifiers . . . making the environment stand for the rape-event itself."[30] And indeed Mazvita's symbolic transference also illustrates the novel's contested conception of autochthony. Whereas her autochthony is registered as powerlessness, that she's somehow claimable like a piece of land, a natural object taken from a field to be used for the nationalist cause, the freedom fighter's autochthony—his emergence from the soil—is apparently constitutive of masculinity and power. As the novel progresses, this dissonance results in Mazvita's desire to escape the forms of knowledge and experience that encase her and prescribe her societal role, breaking with the "grand narratives" of the nationalist struggle, as Vera explains in an interview, to "redefine [her] consciousness toward the land."[31]

The most intimate optic into Mazvita's experience of subjection, however, comes in the chapters set on the bus in Harare, where she registers a growing embodied sense of alienation. In the first chapter, for instance, before we learn of her experienced violence, we read that "a lump was growing on the side of her neck," which "she had no doubt that all her body was moving slowly in that lump, that she would eventually turn to find her whole being had abandoned her, rushed into that space beside her neck."[32] There's a phenomenological movement of time in these lines, the lump "growing," her body "moving slowly" into that location of burden on her body. The lump causes her to take herself far off from her own presence, as Fanon would put it, signifying a kind of progressive alienation as it consumes her "being" and transforms her into an object other than herself. We encounter similarly moving and deepening pain in the novel's other bus passages, such as "mountains growing on her back," the way her skin "burns," how her toes "tighten and grow stiff." This is indeed reminiscent of Césaire's phenomenological language in the *Notebook* of festering wounds and growing pus, as if time itself were the instrument of violence slowly and continually wasting away at the body. What makes Mazvita's coursing pain so haunting, though, is the position of these bus chapters in narrative time. Halfway through, we discover that she has tied her infant son to her back in these bus scenes, but not until the final pages of the novel do we discover that this child is no longer living. So when we first encounter that growing "lump," for example, we cannot yet connect it to the dead child she carries on her back, the child drawing her back to that field and the soldier's whispering.

Indeed, this is the crux of the novel's narrative time. We repeatedly encounter these phenomenally deepening symptoms of trauma *in advance* of the narrative appearance of the principal violent events. In the final pages of the novel, we read that, prior to taking her seat on the bus, Mazvita had strangled the child in an effort to rid herself of her trauma, to "claim her dream and her freedom."[33] This narrative delay, as I've suggested of other works in previous chapters, constitutes a kind of formal mimicry of the temporality of trauma: the reader encounters the haunting repetition of the symptoms of some violent event without having access to the source of that trauma for most of the narrative. Built into the text's narrative architecture is a temporality that Cathy Caruth, reading Freud's work on neurosis and hysteria, describes as the "unassimilated nature" of an unexpected painful event: "the way it [is] precisely *not known* in the first instance . . . and returns to haunt the survivor later on." As in Caruth's formulation, there is a kind of "incomprehensibility" to Mazvita's rape. For her not to know the face of her rapist means that a certain structure of meaning is lost, and it is precisely this incomprehensibility that ensures she continually relives the event.[34] The delayed knowledge of the doubled trauma—of her rape and the killing of her child—retroactively recodes those deepening phenomenological wounds on Mazvita's body and mind that we initially encounter, augmenting the already intimate narrative voice that gives us access to her interior perceptions of pain.

The final component of Mazvita's alienation, beyond her seeming isolation, is the way that her experience is enmeshed in a larger societal structure. We find in an early chapter set in Harare, for instance, Mazvita's alienation stitched in and among a more expansive social alienation: "She breathed the poverty and the loneliness, the black walls tarnished and buried with the cries of abandoned dreams, of apparitions of laughter fueled with desperation, of voices pained." Here societal alienation is a kind of material vapor that Mazvita literally inhales, compounding the specificity of her own experienced subjection. Vera does a similar kind of work later on in one of the novel's many references to the civil war: "1977. Everyone was an accomplice to war. The war made them strangers to words. . . . The war changed everything, even the idea of their own humanity."[35] Here we get a kind of societal extension of Mazvita's symptoms of trauma: of her inability to articulate her rape fully to Nyenyedzi, her sense that her rape has dismembered her being. This third-person plural appears through the novel, as does the year 1977, constantly moving us between Mazvita's mind and the societal pulse of the moment, demanding that we put Mazvita in relation to a larger structure of alienation.

If the feeling of Mazvita's alienation accumulates throughout the novel, so too does her utopian anticipatory desire. On nearly every page, situated in Mazvita's consciousness we find language consistent with Vera's larger aesthetic examination of "how women feel in their own pursuit of their own freedom and their own desire to understand their own bodies."[36] Mazvita's sense of attunement to embodied desire manifests in swelling waves throughout *Without a Name*, propelling her mind outward toward disalienation. Like the novel's language of subjection, this language of utopian swelling emerges from the materiality of the body, corresponding to that Blochian notion of the body "fleeing from what damages it, searching for what preserves it."[37] Crucially, the searching wave-like structure of Mazvita's utopian consciousness is also consonant with Fred Moten's understanding of black fugitivity as a "swerve in and out of the confinements"—something akin, we might say, to the oscillation between diegesis and utopian nondiegesis in Black Audio's *Twilight City*.[38] There's a fugitive shuttling back and forth in the novel, in other words, between the world of subjection and Mazvita's proleptic inhabitation of absolute release in mind and body.

Among the many nodes of utopian swelling in Vera's novel, where Mazvita's mind races out in advance of her immediate moment and physical presence, is the protagonist's idea of Harare as a site of escape. "Do you see the people who come from the city," she tells Nyenyedzi ahead of her journey, "they have no fear in their eyes." "Mazvita had a profound belief in her own reality, in the transformation new geographies promised," seeing Harare as the "limitless place in which to dream, and to escape."[39] For her, moving across geographic space coincides with that Fanonian quest to "expel" her alienation, with the potential to engender a kind of bodily transcendence, stripping the fear from her eyes. But this utopian Harare recedes once she's finally arrived there, unable to find work, and, most of all, carrying the consequence of her sexual violation on her back, the baby literally generating the searing pain she feels throughout her body. The burden of the child in fact catalyzes a subsequent wave of fugitive anticipatory consciousness:

> It was the constant nearness of her head to the child that made her frenzied and perplexed. . . . If she could remove her head, and store it at a distance from the stillness on her back, then she could begin. She would be two people. She would be many. One of her would be free. . . . She wanted one other of her, that is how she conceived of escape. She attempted this enigmatic separation by drawing mightily forward. . . . Her neck rose upward and she felt a violent pain delve downward into her back. She looked up.[40]

Here we get a striking inversion of Fanonian alienation in which the imagined severing of her head paradoxically generates *dis*alienation, allowing her to steal away from her wounded self so that she might find "freedom." There's a Blochian structure of anticipation in Vera's prose, in the "drawing forward" so that she might quite literally live in excess of herself. But the passage is also in the conditional mood, with the speculative conjuring of "if," "could," and "would," as if Mazvita were beginning to see and even experience the pathway out to release before it's been properly lived. The "violent pain" shooting through her back is that signal that closes this moment of utopian anticipatory desire. The sentence "She looked up" is almost cinematic, as if cutting to the next scene, abruptly bringing Mazvita out of the imagined world of her release and back into the world that subjects her. It's the narrative cut that suspends her flight of proleptic consciousness, drawing her back into the confinements of her subjection.

Mazvita's larger desire for escape in the novel accrues with each of these waves of utopian anticipatory desire, creating a network in which they fuse and feed off one another, forming a larger structure of affective swelling in her. This phenomenon, I want to suggest, is akin to the quality that Baruch Spinoza attributes to the term "affection" (*affectio*), which Gilles Deleuze describes as the "state of a body insofar as it is subject to the action of another body," such as "the action of the sun or the effect of the sun on you."[41] In part three of his *Ethics*, Spinoza suggests that the body "retain[s] the impressions or traces of objects," that an affective *residue* of the sun's rays remains with the body after the initial contact.[42] This "impression," this "trace" of affection that remains with the body, is crucial to understanding the cumulative nature of utopian desire in *Without a Name*. In Mazvita's case, the "object" that touches her body and leaves a residual impression is that elusive object of fugitive time—that state in which violence and trauma have been definitively stripped from mind and body. That object, in her words, is her "freedom." So each time that freedom object seems to "touch" Mazvita—such as when she imagines severing her body to make "one other of her"—each of these advance tastes of freedom leaves a trace in her that subtly accumulates to constitute the larger, evolving affective architecture of her being-in-the-world. When the utopian swelling recedes each time, drawing Mazvita back into the world of her subjection, it doesn't disappear but instead resides in her as a dormant trace, waiting to fuse with the energy of other traces, using that connectivity to grow into an even more ecstatic anticipatory consciousness of utopian release.

So in the novel we have an affective structure that grows inside Mazvita and reaches its peak in the chapters when she's sitting on the bus in the narrative present, headed back to Mubaira with her deceased child tied to her back. The bus is where the specificity of Vera's articulation of fugitive time emerges most explicitly, where her utopian desire for release is most sustained and ecstatic. It's a structure of fugitive time generated by the sound of the *mbira*, a lamellophone that the Shona people of Southern Africa have historically used as a kind of medium, or technology, to commune with ancestral spirits. Sitting in the back of the bus, Mazvita listens to an elderly man play the instrument on his lap, which sits inside a dried calabash shell resonator, sending the sound coursing throughout the bus. In his influential study *The Soul of Mbira* (1978), Paul Berliner explains that among the Shona, "the mbira is believed to have the power of projecting its sound into the heavens and attracting the attention of the ancestors, who are the spiritual owners and keepers of the land and the benefactors of the people's welfare."[43] In *Without a Name*, Vera uses the mbira as a metonym for a kind of ancestral force that generates a *cyclical* version of fugitive time. Mazvita yearns for and anticipates release from the violence she experienced on her ancestral land, but that ancestral land—represented in the sonic register of the mbira—ultimately beckons her to return, to seek that release in body and mind through a restructured ancestral relationality.

It's Mazvita's *feeling* of the mbira's sound, her affective and physical perception of it, that generates the most utopian and fugitively proleptic sequence in the novel. Vera's evocative prose brings the instrument's sound and Mazvita's consciousness to life: "The sound reached her in generous waves of sustenance.... She turned her eyes from the window to the *mbira* and she cupped her fingers and held them forward. Her hands were still and seeking.... Her eyebrows softened into arches of wonder. Her lips softened. The tightness disappeared along her neck. . . . The *mbira* was a revelation, a necessary respite."[44] Phenomenological movement is central here: the coursing sound, how it moves throughout Mazvita's body. The sound "falls back" out of the resonator, "reaching" Mazvita in "waves," pouring into her ears, into her cupped hands, precipitating in her a sense of moving physically and affectively outward. She holds her hands "forward," we're told, "seeking" the sound's "sustenance." What Mazvita begins to anticipate, I contend, is a state of mind and body akin to what takes place during the Shona *bira* ceremony in which the meditative polyrhythms and repeating melodic cycles of the mbira call on ancestral spirits to take possession of a person physically and psychologically, that person becoming a medium through which an ancestor engages with the living directly. The language of "revelation" at the end of this passage indicates that initial moment of invocation, and the "softening" effect on her body evinces the beginning of something, or someone, coming to occupy her body. If the bira ceremony is an occasion in which "family members come together to call upon a common ancestor for help," then we might think of Mazvita's response to the mbira's sound as a call for ancestral intervention, a plea for help in escaping her trauma.[45]

The coursing of the music throughout Mazvita's body deepens in the next phase of this extended mbira sequence. The waves that were sonic in the previous paragraph become aquatic: "The sound came to her in subduing waves, in a growing pitch, in laps of clear water. Water. She felt the water slow and effortless and elegant. She breathed calmly, in the water." The sense of flow attributed to this water is registered in the flow of the prose itself—in an almost rhythmic oscillation between clipped, abbreviated sentences, and sprawling, additive sentences that grow with each clause. As she sits on the bus, the materiality of the sound allows Mazvita to sever herself from her immediate world, to seek out that calm. Also crucial to Mazvita's imagined escape here is a discrete grammatical device: "The people in the bus continued their chatter, they laughed loud, told their children to sit still, coughed from the dust that fell in through the open windows . . . Mazvita listened through that din of voices and received the *mbira* sound, guided it toward herself."[46] That ellipsis functions as a kind of threshold between the "din" of the world that subjects her and her proleptic consciousness of the world of her ancestors who have been called through the sound of this instrument. The sound ushers her into that fugitive interval "between the no longer and the not yet," between the devastations of alienation and the promise of disalienation.[47]

Mazvita's utopian longing for release soon peaks, anticipatory desire accruing as the sound courses and ushers her closer toward a transcendent state: "The sound looped in waves over her head, curled downward, sunk deep in her chest where she had been irrevocably wounded.... She heard the *mbira* grow loud, move nearer to her, nearer to her dream. She waited in waves of suspenseful wishing and longing, in rays of supple joy."[48] Blochian language of "wishing" and "longing" returns to prominence here, as it does in nearly every work examined in this book, animating how the music allows Mazvita to live fugitively in advance of the present moment, proleptically inhabiting that time when her body has been unburdened by her ancestors. This intersection of possession and sonic fugitivity is similar to the way that Nathaniel Mackey describes the fugitive impulse found in both John Coltrane's music and what he calls "African possession religions": a "surge, a runaway dilation, a quantum rush" when "something beyond your grasp of it grabs you."[49] The sound of the mbira initiates that "quantum rush" in Mazvita, that "something" from "beyond" that "grabs" her, driving her proleptic imagination, giving her an advance sense of otherworldly release even as she remains sitting in the bus. What makes this iteration of fugitive time distinctly Vera's are the "sympathetic vibrations" of the mbira, the object that effectively restructures Mazvita's relationship with her people and her land, allowing her to feel a kind of ecstasy in the sound's "glorious searching," in its easing of her "irrevocable wound," and its discovery of "parts of her which were still whole, which held some sweetness and longing."[50]

There's one brief sentence in this previous portion of the mbira sequence that bears subtle traces of a larger world for Mazvita: "There was forgiveness as she desired it, reconciliation and dream." Indeed, forgiveness reminds us of the baby tied to her back in the bus. The child encapsulates the paradoxical relation between trauma and utopian anticipatory desire at the core of Mazvita's embodied fugitive temporality: it serves as a persistent reminder of her rape and the traumatic events that followed, but its departure—in the Nehandan sense—also signals the child's own journey toward those ancestors from whom Mazvita seeks forgiveness and release. Mazvita's cyclical journey back to her people, in other words, cannot be severed from this trauma that rests literally on her back. The language of "forgiveness" and "reconciliation" also evokes Zimbabwe's emergence from settler colonialism in 1980, when Robert Mugabe, the then newly elected prime minister, initiated a discourse of "national reconciliation" that sought, in his words, to create a "new man ... and a new spirit that must unite and not divide." To a populace emerging from civil war, divided, in short, between a majority-black population that sought to reclaim dispossessed lands and a white population that feared losing their farmlands, Mugabe implored all to "become Zimbabweans with a single loyalty."[51] Vera's "reconciliation and dream" is a subtle nod to this postindependence discursive strategy, to a historical moment three years in advance of the novel's setting, when that "freedom" of independence was still feverishly anticipated.

At the end of this mbira sequence, we find, like her other fugitive anticipatory swellings, that Mazvita's sonic flight comes to a close, returning her to the world of the living: "She waited for a moment merciful with release, for the *mbira* held out a promise. She welcomed the *mbira* which brought to her a sky flaring with waves of white cloud. The *mbira* led her across a white sun. She waited for the sound to circle her with a new promise of freedom. . . . [The sound] died in slow undecided rhythms, as though someone hit hard at the instrument with a fist. The notes collapsed. She looked up."[52] We find here the anticipated "release" that's central to the different formations of fugitive time in this book. The mbira—that metonym for ancestrality—drives Mazvita's consciousness seemingly further away from the here and now, toward a new world that now takes on the image of a "flaring sky," a "white sun." The sound that was once water now lifts Mazvita up and out. And at last we have the word that's been constantly intimated in these three pages: "A new promise of *freedom*." But this freedom, the absolute outside of violence and traumatic memory, is one that Mazvita knows she may never entirely inhabit, even if her ancestors have allowed her to glimpse it. With its "new promise" saturating her anticipatory consciousness, the mbira brought her to freedom's edge, but it also brought her back with its silence, guiding Mazvita on a fugitive labyrinthine journey in and out of the confinements. That phrasing "she looked up" again cinematically cuts her back into the world of her subjection, ushering her back into the exclusionary frame so that she may once again take flight.

In the end, the sound-filled bus journeys on, moving toward Mubaira for Mazvita to bury her child. Between this extended mbira passage and Mazvita's return in the concluding pages, trauma and desire, past and present, continue to ebb and flow, moving her in and out of the world, with those ecstatically proleptic fragments gathering momentum, building toward the novel's final moments. Returning to a deserted and charred Mubaira, Mazvita's iteration of fugitive time appears to come full circle. "If she had no fears, she could begin here," the narrator suggests, "without a name." For Mazvita, having a name is "cumbersome," it evokes memory, "it recalls this place to her, which, earlier, she had chosen to forget." "She wishes . . . [that the] hills would name her afresh. She would have liked to begin without a name, soundlessly and without pain." The ancestors, speaking through the sound of the mbira, have called her back to the land, not to move back in time but for a "fresh" interpellation by the land itself: to escape the pain and whispering she hears and feels by reimagining her autochthony, effacing the claim made on her by Nyenyedzi and the man in the field. Mazvita, placing the baby on the burned grass, makes that reimagining material, allowing her to become open to the possibility of "forgiveness" and "reconciliation."[53] As Vera explains in an interview, "It might be an act of recovery for her if she can put the child in the land of her ancestors." Returning the child to her people might give her "redemption," a "lightness of being."[54]

The novel's final line, however, disrupts the closure of her cyclical time: "The silence is deep, hollow, and lonely." Clearly, Mazvita's redemption is not guaranteed. She may have come back to reconcile with her ancestors, but this "loneliness" gestures toward a necessary sociality. There's a sense, even after the mbira's ancestral sound has washed over her, even after she returns the child to her ancestors, that her imagined fugitive swellings must continue in pursuit of a collective that will help her find that lasting "lightness of being." In the same interview, Vera says that her interest in *Without a Name* was "to find out new directions which might offer us better possibilities for freeing ourselves." It is perhaps these collective possibilities of freedom that the novel's final resounding "lonely" pushes toward: a sociality that would allow Mazvita's fugitive time consciousness to become enmeshed among the multitude of different visions of freedom and desire that constituted that collective lunging toward liberation in 1977. A collective aspiration that would include the specificity of Mazvita's life experience and those of others like her, particularly those of women who, Vera suggests, were "left out in shaping the truth."[55]

If Mazvita's proleptic yearning for release is a kind of inheritance of Nehanda's late nineteenth-century yearning—as another stage in the evolution of a larger collective embodied longing that moves through Zimbabwean history—then Bulawayo's *We Need New Names* provides another historical iteration. Bulawayo's novel also puts pressure on the relation among embodied freedom, ancestrality, and collectivity, but during a historical moment several decades on, well after the elation of independence had worn off and the Zimbabwean state had collapsed. In Bulawayo's novel, fugitive time appears through the eyes of a girl who envisions the pathways of migration as her potential release from subjection.

BULAWAYO'S HAUNTOLOGICAL FLIGHT

From their vantage point in the Harare townships, Darling and her friends imagine the global North, and principally the United States, as a kind of promised land, a place that will relieve their pain and poverty, escaping the country collapsing around them. But as this coming-of-age novel moves along, with the teenage Darling eventually migrating to Michigan to live with relatives, the protagonist comes to think otherwise. Along the way, she ushers us into her meticulous quotidian thoughts and observations—her fears, memories, and desires, as well as those of others around her. And Darling's micro-lens is complemented by three interlude chapters that divide her narrative into quarters, each told in an omniscient voice that pans out like a camera to take a macro-view of a larger national collective seeking flight.

Darling's journey doesn't begin with her fugitive anticipations of America, but with the conditions that propel those anticipations. By the time that we enter the novel's early-2000s setting, independent Zimbabwe has experienced two decades of state corruption, violence, and mismanagement that, in conjunction with the afterlives of structural adjustment in the 1980s, has produced a deepening societal collapse, manifest in pervasive unemployment, public health crises, widespread poverty, and mass emigration. Alienation in this novel is wrought not through a Fanonian Manichaean structure of colonizer and colonized but largely through the postcolonial state's subjection of the majority—through mass evictions, sanctioned violence, and vanishing public services. If, as Mbembe argues, many postcolonial states on the continent inherited critical mechanisms of colonial power, such that "we find the same theater, the same mimetic acting, with different actors and spectators, but with the same convulsions and the same insult," then we might say that *We Need New Names* exhibits traces in the postcolonial moment of what Mbembe refers to as colonialism's "phenomenology of violence," in which "violence insinuates itself into the economy, domestic life, language, consciousness." It's a structure that operates externally as an imposition of subjection on the formerly colonized but also internally in the way that Quayson characterizes the sublimation of those forces of subjection. An omnipresence of violence produces what Mbembe calls, with characteristic hyperbole, the postcolonial African subject's condition of "half-death," where "life and death are so entangled that it is no longer possible to distinguish them." Consequently, a "metaphysics of sorrow" envelops the formerly colonized society, caused in part by the "excessive burden of mass suffering and the omnipresence of death."[56] In Bulawayo's novel, this insinuated violence and even this precarious "half-death" ontology are brought to the fore, ultimately propelling Darling on her fugitive course.

Similar to the temporality of alienation in Vera's *Without a Name*, the body registers a kind of wounding in Bulawayo's novel as an index of these different structures of alienation. One of the more prominent instances comes from Darling's observations of her father's HIV-ravaged body following his return from South Africa, where he had spent years seeking work: "We just peer in the tired light at the long bundle of bones, at the shrunken head, at the wavy hair, most of it fallen off, at the face that is all points and edges from bones jutting out, the pinkish-reddish lips, the ugly sores, the skin sticking to the bone like somebody ironed it on, the hands and feet like claws."[57] Here we get a certain "phenomenology of violence," as Mbembe would put it, even a phenomenology of that "half-death" ontology as Darling notes how the disease has withered her father, transforming his hands into claws, melting the skin from his face. Adjectives and similes establish a temporality of decay, a phenomenal structure of time that chronicles the interstitial passage from life to death. This phenomenological reading provides another layer to Anna Chitando's claim that the male figures in *We Need New Names* have "lost their status," becoming disempowered by an "economy that forces them to leave home and come back to die."[58] As such, we might read this passage's temporality of emaciation as a temporality of emasculation, of the slow decay of the man's status as patriarch. Crucial in this passage, too, is Darling's point of view as a child, evident as she "peers in" at her father, likening him to a monster. It's an optic, as Bulawayo herself has noted, more concerned with "the business of the everyday, of living, of play," and less with the politics and histories that engender the immediate phenomena around her.[59] But the space of childhood in contemporary African literature, as Christopher Ouma points out, is richly layered, "presenting a discursive field of memories, times, places, spaces, heritages, legacies and traditions that are motific of evolving contemporary experiences and constructions of identities."[60] And indeed Darling's perspective affords a sprawling view of the world around her. Most immediately, the same perspective that doesn't note (yet nonetheless absorbs) the structural reasons for her father's arrival and departure is also the perspective that reveals these detailed, almost telescopic descriptions of how the disease has moved through his body, breaking it down moment by moment. As in Vera's novel, establishing a sense of the coursing temporal layers of subjection in

We Need New Names is crucial to fully apprehending the text's architecture of anticipatory desire.

The novel's first interlude chapter provides an important societal extension of this phenomenal wounding. Bulawayo charts the formation of Darling's ironically named township, Paradise, and the other townships that developed in the wake of "Operation Murambatsvina" ("Move the Rubbish"), in which the Mugabe government, under the guise of cracking down on illegal housing and commerce, demolished entire townships and displaced hundreds of thousands in order to disrupt growing opposition to the government.[61] The body in this chapter registers the physical and emotional effects of the Operation: "They appeared with the dust from their crushed houses clinging to their hair and skin and clothes. . . . Swollen ankles and blisters under their feet."[62] The "dust" of their former homes "clinging" to their bodies is a kind of literal residue of the trauma of their forced relocation. Their "swollen" ankles and "blisters" index how their wounding continues to deepen, expand, and inflame, entrenching their alienation. This chapter, and the other two like it, are nation chapters. The indefinite plural subjects—*we, they, women*—serve as a counterpoint to the child's vantage point, giving us access to the social histories that move beneath immediate observations, galvanizing a sense of collectivity in the face of crisis.

Throughout the novel, Bulawayo uses a telling expression to refer to the various manifestations of societal crisis that exceed Darling's limited vantage point. The phrase "things falling apart" appears more than a dozen times as a kind of elastic, all-encompassing expression for civil society's postindependence unraveling, signifying the devastating accumulation of currency devaluations, unemployment, forced relocations, food insecurity, and collapsing education and health care systems. "Look at how things are falling apart," Darling's father says before leaving for South Africa. "Is this what I went to university for?"[63] Each appearance of the phrase evokes a kind of apocalyptic image, a world literally and figuratively breaking. Indeed, there is an important consonance between *We Need New Names* and Chinua Achebe's celebrated first novel, which Bulawayo clearly evokes with each appearance of the expression. In *Things Fall Apart* (1958) the phrase signals the collapse of a cosmology and a way of life, the beginning of colonialism's uprooting of a distinctly Igbo being-in-the-world. The phrase marks, for example, the moment when Okonkwo "felt a cold shudder run through him" at the thought of his sons joining the missionaries, "like the prospect of annihilation."[64] In both novels, the phrase suggests a simultaneous infrastructural and metaphysical rupture: in Achebe, it's the Igbo laws, institutions, and beliefs usurped by British ones; in Bulawayo, it's the collapse of the promise of those same British laws and institutions that ruptured the nineteenth-century Igbo worldview of Achebe's novel. Like many former British colonies across the continent, Zimbabwean postindependence law remained largely British. These novels are, in other words, of the same historical cloth, with each in its own way wrestling with how to (re)build a world in the wake of apocalypse. And just as the collapsing world engenders contingency in *Things Fall Apart*, it brings radical uncertainty for those in Bulawayo's Zimbabwe willing to risk their lives for a chance at a better life abroad.

Emerging from these layers of devastation in *We Need New Names* is a persistent fugitive time consciousness, driven by the desire to take flight from those wounds, to flee the confines of all that's decaying and crumbling. Similar to how the body indexes these formations of alienation, it also registers what Bulawayo has referred to as the novel's search for "new ways of being."[65] We encounter this search throughout the novel as prolepsis, specifically through Darling's subtle perceptions of her own body, and in the way she identifies certain sensations with a remade self abroad. Consider the moment early on when Darling and her friends see a woman with "clean and pretty feet" eating behind the iron gates of a compound in the wealthy neighborhood of Budapest, which Darling likens to "a nice country where people who are not like us live." Despite her unfamiliarity with the decadent treat, Darling recognizes from "the way she smacks her lips that whatever she is eating tastes really good." As the woman finishes, Darling "swallow[s] with her, my throat tingling."[66] A metonym for an idealized country, the treat enables Darling to live in advance of herself, however fleetingly, outside of her immediate moment and location, beyond the confines of her alienation. She imagines the moment when she has escaped the poverty and violence of Paradise and assumed those "clean and pretty feet" for herself, taking on a new body and being-in-the-world. That "tingling" feeling in her throat, we might say, marks that trace of utopia that she can almost literally taste, as if the food is already in her mouth, allowing her for one brief moment to escape her world in her mind.[67] The geopolitical imaginary engendered by this "tingling" also marks Bulawayo's novel as a kind of historical extension of Mazvita's geographically structured longing for release in Vera's *Without a Name*. If in Vera's late-1970s Zimbabwe, Harare is the imagined site of escape from rural violence, in Bulawayo's version, anywhere beyond Zimbabwe's borders is seen as the escape from a country falling apart.

Most of these subtle physical sensations correspond to these youths' desire to "blaze out of this kaka country," specifically to America. Ahead of her eventual migration to live with her aunt, Darling boasts to her friends that in the United States she will eat "real food," as if her poverty in Zimbabwe has somehow tainted the food, the world around her, and in turn, herself, with inauthenticity and inadequacy. She also reveals her intention to own a Lamborghini like the one they see in Budapest. "I just know," she says, "because of this feeling in my bones, that the car is waiting for me in America."[68] For Darling, the United States is not just a place of satiation. It's also a site of self-fashioning, of adorning the body so that she can announce her escape from the world. This "feeling in my bones" functions like the "tingling" in her throat. It's the understated way that Darling lives in advance of herself in time and space, as if she's already there and then.

Of all the works I've studied to this point, the ones that feature some experience of migration, however subtly—*Handsworth Songs, Beloved, Without a Name*—are where fugitive time is most prominently spatialized. *We Need New Names*, though, is by far the most chronotopic of these works: at every turn, Darling and her fellow dreaming migrants situate their desires for self-transformation in a specific, mappable geography. In *The Dialogic Imagination*, Mikhail Bakhtin defines the artistic chronotope as the way that an aesthetic work's "spatial and temporal indicators are fused into one carefully thought-out, concrete whole." The novel as a form is central to his analysis, noting that "in literature the primary category in the chronotope is time."[69] Although fugitive anticipation is often spatialized and geographically mappable in Bulawayo's novel, the temporal, as in Bakhtin's view, is always conspicuously at the fore. If we were to name this novel's specific chronotopic genre, it would be something like a "proleptic chronotope," for its temporal valence is decidedly one of anticipation, of living in advance of the self, such as the language of "blazing out of this kaka country" or the way Bulawayo locates this fugitively proleptic sense in the body. If, for Bakhtin, time "thickens, takes on flesh" in literature, in *We Need New Names*, anticipatory consciousness "tingles" in the throat; it's "felt in the bones." Indeed, what we find in this novel is a distinct version of fugitive time, one that takes on a clear spatialization even as fugitive anticipatory consciousness animates its language on nearly every page.

One distinct form of the fugitive anticipation of a remade self in Bulawayo's novel—one certainly with chronotopic implications—is the role of divination, practices in which a diviner figure is called on to intervene in, or foresee an end to, a personal crisis. In his classic *African Religions and Philosophy* (1969), John Mbiti describes the role of diviners as "suppliers of assurance and confidence during people's crises . . . fortune-tellers and solvers of problems." "The diviner fulfills an intermediary function," Mbiti suggests, "between the physical and the psychical, between the human and the spiritual, for the sake of his own community."[70] Indeed, there's a way we might think of divination on the continent as an indigenous form of fugitive time consciousness, specifically in its threefold potential to relieve people in crisis, to enable people to live in excess of the present moment, and to shape community. Although divination of course precedes (and exceeds) the violence of formal colonialism, in the context of the novel's postcolonial crisis we might understand it as a kind of fugitive science: the science of generating the imagined idea of an end to one's physical and affective burdens, the science of taking imaginative flight from myriad forms of personal and shared subjection.[71]

The two appearances of the novel's diviner, Vodloza, demonstrate this role. The first comes when Darling encounters the sign detailing his services: "Vodloza, the BESTEST healer in all of this Paradise and beyond will proper fix these problemsome things that you may encounter in your life: bewitchedness, curses . . . poverty, joblessness, AIDS, madness, small penises, epilepsy, bad dreams, bad marriage/marriagelessness . . . bad luck with getting visa especially to USA and Britain." We're given a sprawling list of the problems of a nation in crisis, some social, some emotional, some physical, all of which Vodloza promises to lift from people's bodies and minds. Facilitating dreams of fleeing to the US and the UK takes on a special role in Vodloza's practice, including when he spreads tobacco leaves and invokes the ancestors to ensure Darling's safe Atlantic crossing: "Open the way for your wandering calf, you, Vusamazulu, pave the skies, summon your fathers, Mpabanga and Nqabayezwe and Mahlathini, and draw your mighty spears to clear the paths and protect the child from dark spirits on her journey."[72] Here, chronotopically, divinatory objects and invocations clear what Barnor Hesse calls the "escapist pathways" of fugitive experience, setting Darling out ahead of herself, her mind advancing even as she sits in front of the healer.[73] The fetish object that Vodloza gives her is also crucial to this sense of fugitive anticipation. "He tied a bone attached to a rainbow-colored string around my wrist and said, This is your weapon, it will fight off all evil in that America."[74] The proximity of this bone to Darling's body—and certainly the force of the speech act ("it will fight")—enhances her anticipation of transcendence in the United States, assuring her protection as she moves outward. It's an object, as William Pietz argues in his influential series of essays on the fetish, that is "established in an intense relation to and with power over the desires, actions, health, and self-identity of individuals."[75] The diviner sutures this fetish object into Darling's structure of desire, into her belief that her arrival will bring a new self, a new being-in-the-world.

All of these components of Darling's escape—from the feeling in her bones to Vodloza's divined pathway—culminate in the second interlude chapter. There we find a dispersal that transforms the sociality of the nation into diaspora: "Look at them leaving in droves . . . the children of the land scurry and scatter like birds escaping a burning sky. They flee their own wretched land so their hunger may be pacified in foreign lands, their tears wiped away in strange lands, the wounds of their despair bandaged in faraway lands."[76] In this language we get a kind of collective wounded body stealing away from a traumatic world, searching for that outside. The spatial is clear here in the repeated mention of the "land" from which they're fleeing and the "lands" they long for, but what drives this passage is the temporality of the fugitive, anticipatory verbs: *leaving, fleeing, scurrying, scattering*. These terms imply a physical movement of the body but also a proleptic sensibility: a desired imagined object, some kind of mental map of a pathway out, maybe even the imagined idea of what it might *feel* like in that very moment when hunger is sated and wounds are bandaged. Their exodus is an insurgent refusal of that world left behind, and—to extend Damien Sojoyner's framing of fugitivity to an autocratic postcolonial context—a "singular exposure of the state as a tenuous system of unstable structures constantly teetering on the brink of illegitimacy."[77] But to flee their land marks a critical distancing from their autochthony, indicating that their sense of being together, their sense of nation, can no longer be derived solely from that land, that it must come in greater parts from what Brent Edwards calls the "prosthetic" linkages of diaspora. In Edwards's formulation, as I've discussed in various parts of this book, what constitutes the African diaspora are the "practices" of strategy, rhetoric, and affinity that together engender a sense of belonging across difference—across those "uneasy encounters," "misrecognitions," and "mistranslations" generated when the disparate global cultures, languages, and histories of people of African descent intersect.[78] Even in Zimbabwe, certainly, Bulawayo's droves were an integral part of this prosthetic global collectivity, given how the continent has become a nexus of "passage, circulation, and opening" in the twenty-first century. But the transnational movement of Bulawayo's droves signals a new positioning within this global diasporic structure. Their movement is part of what Mbembe calls the "new African diasporas" of our century, the *plurality* of circulations of people of African descent across disparate nodes of the globe that require different prosthetic configurations to shape belonging.[79]

The global circulation of Bulawayo's escaping droves, though, requires a kind of stealth negotiation, a necessary fugitive sensibility to pass through what Sandro Mezzadra and Brett Neilson call the "temporal thickness" of state borders—those "technologies of temporal management, whether they seek to speed border-crossing processes by using biometrics and chipped passports or to slow and even block border passages through such technologies as detention, interceptions, or 'preemptive *refoulement.*'" The fugitive time consciousness of these droves is one that must anticipate how they will navigate this "thickness," how they will move through the unpredictable barrage of interrogations, verifications, searches, and technologies, including the biometrics that "[inscribe] the border onto migrants' bodies."[80] Their border fugitivity also requires what Stefano Harney and Fred Moten call a "constant economy of misrecognition," which, in contrast to Edwards's diasporic "misrecognition" that shapes belonging across cultural difference, entails an insistence, however feigned, that these droves are willing and capable of "providing 'human capital' according to the changing and elusive needs of flexible economic systems and labor markets."[81] In order to realize their escape, in other words, they must insist that they will be useful bodies, adaptable to the labor market, capable of any kind of work, even if these are just words to get them to the other side. With this sense of anticipatory pragmatism, Darling and her fellow droves dream of making it through the crossing's thickness, seeping into the other side in search of release.

Perhaps expectedly, as soon as Darling has made it through this thickness, arriving in Destroyedmichygan, as she calls it, she realizes that she hasn't escaped the frame of her confinement after all. Experience doesn't match the dream, and the much-anticipated utopian "realness" of America is nowhere to be found. She reasons that the cold and dreary place she has come to "doesn't look like my America, it doesn't even look real"; even a glass of Coke "doesn't even taste real." Indeed, this nonmaterialization marks a crucial threshold in the *Bildung* structure of her narrative. The crumbling of the utopian ideal upon arrival advances her maturation, her cognizance of the world's inequities and hypocrisies. There is perhaps no more telling a scene than when Darling glimpses the Lamborghini that drove her earlier fugitive visions in Zimbabwe. Shocked when she's told the car's multimillion-dollar value, Darling thinks, "What is America for, then?" The car then seems to disappear from view, "just like a dream that you dream and you know you dreamed it but you can't even remember what it was."[82]

With the collapse of her fugitive desire comes the collapse of her memory of what constituted that image of desire in the first place.

In that vanishing moment, however, Darling's utopian anticipatory consciousness redirects, recommencing the fugitive search for that elusive otherwise life. Her mind now takes aim at an indefinite desire for the pieces of home that she loved, memories of experienced relief and pleasure that allow her, briefly, to feel that pleasure as an escape from the present. What distinguishes this fugitive desire from mere homesickness is Darling's ultimate inability to return to Zimbabwe, transforming these escapist memories into a new utopian horizon. Above all, it is embodied sensorial experience that precipitates this recalibrated fugitive time consciousness. Take the scene in which Darling eats a guava for the first time since leaving Zimbabwe. With each smell and bite, she thinks, "I leave the house, Kalamazoo, and Michigan, leave the country altogether and find myself back in my Paradise, in Budapest." If in Zimbabwe an excess of guavas disrupted her digestion, enacting a kind of violence on her body, here the taste of one instead enacts a feeling of nostalgia for the trauma-less fragments of that prior world. We find a similar moment of sensory-generated imagined flight when Darling finds a piece of fabric painted with a familiar marketplace scene: "Looking at the cloth I'm remembering how beautiful it felt to be in a real scene like that, everybody just there together, mingling together, living together, before things fell apart." The sight of this image evokes memories of her life before the government razed her family's home, before her father's departure and illness. That same utopian "real" reappears in this market memory, now redirected toward a new image of release in the wake of the prior's collapse. In the final interlude chapter we find a related collective longing for return also precipitated by sensory experience, when Darling describes how other diasporans, after years abroad, would ask the newly arrived "to describe how the earth smelled right before it rained."[83] In all three of these scenes the immediacy of sensory experience draws the mind back to the land and the sociality begat by that land, taking momentary flight from the suffocations of the present. Although only the guava would fit the definition of "home-food" that Oliver Nyambi, Rodwell Makombe, and Nonki Motahane present in their reading of the novel, each of the above examples is similarly a "symbolic performance of home," a "site for archiving and recovering certain essential elements of the old home and identity."[84]

Crucially, because returning to that time before "things fell apart" appears to be yet another ever-receding horizon, diasporic life becomes a kind of exile. Their dreams of return take on a melancholic structure, a kind of unassimilable loss that simultaneously serves as the utopian object toward which they are proleptically drawn. More precisely, we find a kind of *refusal* to assimilate loss, a deliberate act of anamnesis which allows that loss to become generative in their fugitive anticipation of release. But crisis, we learn, ensues in Zimbabwe as Darling looks on from afar, a reality further magnified when the tourist visas that Darling and many of her fellow diasporans traveled with expire, leaving them without papers to reenter the United States if they were to leave. "We stayed, like prisoners," the third interlude tells us, "only we chose to be prisoners and we loved our prison. . . . And when things got worse in our country, we pulled our shackles even tighter and said, We are not leaving America, no, we are not leaving."[85] America, once their object of desire, has become for them the place of least precarity. Just as the proleptic chronotopic structure of the narrative has shifted its spatial orientation, fugitive time takes on a valence of something like *refugee* time. The latter retains fugitivity's root—*fug*, to flee—but the normative notion of the figure of the refugee and its corresponding temporality is of a person, over a temporary period of time, seeking refuge from a nation in crisis. However, as Vinh Nguyen usefully counters, "Most refugees experience their condition as refugees indefinitely, sometimes for an entire lifetime." Indeed, we come to learn that Darling's experience confirms that "refuge is a fiction for many refugees who are resettled in neoliberal, late-capitalist Western nations" and that, for many, that longed-for refuge remains "elusive."[86] Fugitive time recalibrates in the novel to fit a new genre of indefiniteness and precariousness.

Through all of this, the idealized Zimbabwe remains the object of utopian desire once in the United States. However, the foreclosure of return is central to the *hauntological* structure of their fugitive time consciousness in the US. The ideal Zimbabwe, which is at once remembered and desired, takes on a kind of spectral quality as, on the one hand, something that once was, that comes from the past, residing in the present as a residue, and on the other, something yet to come, something anticipated, something proleptically felt in the present although it hasn't yet been properly lived. Like Jacques Derrida's influential formulation of the specter as "always to come and to come-back," the spectral object for these diasporans—the ideal Zimbabwe of sociality, of intimacy with the ancestors, of life without violence and poverty, of feeling at peace in mind and body—is marked by "frequentation," as Derrida puts it, by repeated visitations from this simultaneous once-was and to-come.[87] Nostalgia and utopia converge to constitute that reshaped object of desire in which the body and mind are finally at ease. When Darling tastes those traces of her ideal homeland in the guava, she's simultaneously remembering and imaginatively leaping toward wholeness. "How will these ones ever be whole in that 'Melika,'" the final interlude asks, "as far away from the graves of the ancestors as it is?"[88] To be "whole" is this novel's language for that state of release in mind and body so fervently sought in diaspora.

Haunting, of course, manifests in many of the works I've examined to this point, whether it's Sethe being called back to the violence of Sweet Home in *Beloved* or the sonic traces of the subjecting world that seep into *Twilight City*'s queer nondiegetic refuge. I use the term *hauntological* here in part to distinguish the dual temporal operation of haunting in Bulawayo's novel—the way the specter of the ideal Zimbabwe is simultaneously remembered and desired, at once coming from the past and proleptically inhabited. There are certainly other conceptualizations of the hauntological that are relevant here, though, even if Derrida's is the most proximate to Bulawayo's dual operation. I'm thinking in particular of Ayo Coly's framing of African postcolonial hauntology as "a manifestation of the lingering violence of colonialism, the subjection of formerly colonized communities to new forms of colonialism and the apprehensive alertness of these communities to future forms of colonialism."[89] If we think of *We Need New Names* within this logic, and perhaps expand the idea of colonialism to include the diffuse forms of subjection in the postcolonial moment that are in many ways residual of formal colonialism, then we can see Darling's continual navigation of a "falling apart" world, before and even after migration, as a navigation of the vestiges of colonialism and the unpredictable forms of colonialism she'll invariably encounter. Such a framing of hauntology is clearly fundamental to the persistence of fugitive time and desire in the novel. What I want to keep at the fore of my analysis, though, is that spectral idea of "wholeness" articulated by Bulawayo's diasporans: at once a structure of loss and a structure of desire.[90]

This hauntology of wholeness is pivotal to the time consciousness that shapes Bulawayo's characters in the United States as they navigate a renewed alienation. With expired visas, "we were now illegals," Darling tells us, forced into a refigured fugitive life of constantly anticipating and avoiding the detection of authorities. "We did not meet stares and we avoided gazes. . . . We built mountains between us and them, we dug rivers, we planted thorns—we had paid so much to be in America and we did not want to lose it all. . . . And when at work they asked us for our papers, we scurried like startled hens and flocked to unwanted jobs."[91] These images of growing mountains and fleeing hens evince a literal escapist movement, a kind of insurgent stealth away from predation. Here, we might say, the indefiniteness and precariousness of refugee time modulate again, deepening into a time consciousness distinct to the undocumented—adding to the layers and contours of what fugitive time has become by the end of the novel. We know from recent research into the experiences of the undocumented that the position of Bulawayo's diasporans is "marked by and negotiated through the condition of deportability."[92] In the United States in particular, they are "constructed as criminal anti-citizens," targeted in practices that seek "to securitize the nation through the abjection and exclusion of individuals and populations deemed threatening to the social body."[93] America's post-9/11 security apparatus keeps Bulawayo's figures constantly on the run, circulating at the periphery of American society, resulting in a simultaneous sense of confinement and stealth improvisatory movement that's always anticipating the next refuge. An imminently deportable life festers beneath that hauntological superstructure oriented toward release in a utopian Zimbabwe. Their precarious prospects in the United States and at home necessitate that they live in the imagination even as they engage in quotidian practices of avoidance, for imagining "the creation of new possibilities for living lives that refuse the regulatory regime from which they could not be removed" is what drives them, what keeps them on their fugitive course.[94]

In the United States the novel's diasporans do establish new critical solidarities in their flux and flight. They create alliances with their fellow undocumented immigrants, who have also left behind their homelands all over the world, but Bulawayo seems to take particular care in connecting these newly arrived Zimbabweans with those who, centuries ago, were captured and enslaved in America. Appearing as a kind of collective memory in the final interlude chapter, we find the elders back home cautioning those who envision the US as utopia: "Is not 'Melika also that wretched place where they took looted black sons and daughters those many, many years ago?" To which the hopeful respond, "In the footsteps of those looted black sons and daughters, we were going, yes, we were going."[95] Evoking this history allows Bulawayo to juxtapose two mass population movements centuries removed, implicitly likening the cargo of a plane with that of a slave ship. Within the purview of this book and the genealogy I gesture to in the introduction, it's as if Olaudah Equiano has suddenly irrupted to the surface more than two centuries later, the novel positioning him among the ancestors who originally and involuntarily carved out Darling's transatlantic pathway.[96] To say that these droves follow in those footsteps is to question these contemporary crossings, to ask indeed if we might perhaps call their migration *involuntary*, given the structural collapse that engendered their flight, despite their steadfast refusal of that fallen-apart world. And it places these droves in an important relation to the contemporary descendants of those looted ones, as if implicitly to insist on Edwards's prosthetic framework of diasporic belonging.

Darling's structure of solidarity in the United States with her black American and Nigerian peers is just that: a set of practices, as Edwards frames it, that reaches across uneasy encounters and mistranslations. Their sense of mutual belonging far from assumes cultural sameness. This is perhaps best exemplified in a conversation the three friends have about language during a drive to the mall: Darling accuses her black American friend, Kristal, of not knowing how to speak proper English, to which Kristal retorts, "It's called Ebonics, and it be a language system"; Kristal then accuses their Nigerian friend, Marina, of the same inability, based on the seemingly indecipherable English of Nigerian video films; and finally, Kristal calls out Darling for just "trynna sound like stupid white folk." But any difference they establish in this brief exchange is quickly sidestepped when it appears a police car is pulling them over, and Darling considers running: "but then I remember," she thinks, "that the police will shoot you for doing a little thing like that if you are black."[97] Their common blackness, their common racialized marking in the eyes of the world, implicitly jolts them back to shared life experiences and the necessity of working through any sort of "uneasy encounters." Darling's perception of the relation between blackness and the state also gestures to what Saidiya Hartman calls "the commons created by fugitives": that shared desire, despite apparent cultural difference, to flee that which subjugates blackness, to seek a better life.[98]

Within the novel's various practiced solidarities, however, remains the singularity of each group. Bulawayo's Zimbabweans may share structures of feeling with diverse peoples, but they still feel the pull of their homeland and the particularity of their own trajectory toward release and freedom. The minds of Darling and her people, in other words, continue to be animated by that fugitive hauntological structure. At the end of the final interlude chapter, we get one last reprise of their collective searching voice: "Here our own parents come to us in dreams. They do not touch us, they do not speak to us; they only behold us with looks we cannot remember. We approach them, we find ourselves surrounded by oceans we cannot cross. . . . Always, we wake from these dreams groping for mirrors, wounds in our eyes; we see ourselves through searing pain."[99] This dream bears the hallmark of that simultaneous coming back and proleptic towardness of Derrida's specter, the sense that their parents are emerging at once from memory and anticipatory consciousness. To be with them, to touch them, to reach across that ocean would mean to at last find the release of wholeness, to escape the "searing pain" that first cut them in their homeland, a wounding engendered by their poverty and powerlessness, later deepened by the vanishing of their initial utopian dream. In the end, the fugitive time of Bulawayo's droves runs its own circuitous, stealthy course. As they hold out for that spectral image to come to life, they will dwell in the not-yet-ness of their anticipatory consciousness. They will remember the smell of the soil at home just before it's rained. In their minds they will inhabit the ecstasy of the chase and its sociality as if they're already there and then.

....

Ultimately, for Mazvita and Darling's droves in diaspora, home beckons. Their autochthony leads their minds back to the land, no matter how far or how long they've strayed. In advance of time, they imagine themselves inhabiting the sociality of that land, among the living and the departed, finding release from the subjections that have burdened their people since the British South Africa Company first seized their lands and resources, imposed taxes on them, and conscripted their labor. From Nehanda to Mazvita to Darling, we find a history of Zimbabwean women who have stolen away from a world that has crushed them and their people for more than a century. Mazvita and Darling are inheritors of Nehanda's "hope for the nation," of her refusal to live in negation and "not rest in bondage." Mazvita and Darling, we might say, are extensions of that collective of women that Vera presents at the end of her first novel, waiting for what will follow Nehanda's capture: "In cheerful voices the women . . . see new existences come out of the dreaming air. They too are in a state of birth, and growth, and unstoppable exultation. . . . They clap their hands and create new songs to clear the path into new lives. . . . The air waits to be transformed into the ecstasy of their release."[100] Like Mazvita and Darling, Nehanda's anticipated release is the nation's anticipated release. The music of these women clears the path to that ecstatic moment, much like the mbira clears the path for Mazvita and the fetish does for Darling. It's an inheritance of fugitive time consciousness, of dreaming air: a yearning passed down through the generations to escape the "dismemberment," as Fanon would put it, of dispossession. A transgenerational flight of the mind that exceeds the limits of the present. Together this sprawling collective, this nation, wherever and whenever they may be in the world, leans toward that world beyond, planning its escape from the interpellators' gaze so that they may find new lives, new bodies, and new existences. It's a fugitive desire very much kindred to Sethe's desire to flee to the other side of the veil with her children. It's an impulse not unlike Césaire's dove rising further and further into the cosmos. Like Morrison and Césaire, Vera and Bulawayo are the mediums through which we trace and witness a fugitive time that's simultaneously their own and not their own. Their manipulations of language and form reveal a culturally and historically distinct formation of the time consciousness that itself is constantly on the run, migrating throughout the geographies, histories, and aesthetic forms of diaspora, changing guise at each turn as it gravitates toward that ever-deferred release.

CODA
FUGITIVE
ETHER

>   the breath we took ... It was only
>   there we wanted to be, the everywhere
>   we'd always wanted,   ours,
>   albeit
>   only an instant, forever, never to be
>   heard
> from again
>
> **Nathaniel Mackey, *Splay Anthem***

There's a larger view of Shikeith's *The Moment You Doubt Whether You Can Fly*—a view beyond the single image I began with in the introduction—that somehow feels necessary at this book's closing. If it's not two young men in that image, but a single one occupying discrete moments in time—the one figure a representation of the other's anticipatory desire to flee into the sky, away from this devastating world—there's another piece to consider in the larger installation. It's the life-sized sculpture of a young black man lying in the middle of the gallery floor, mere steps from the 6 × 8-inch stencil of the balloon fliers mounted on the adjacent wall. In the rising figure's downward, surveying gaze on the wall, it's hard not to imagine him looking back to the man lying on the floor, the sculpted figure resting on a bed of soil, nude except for the white cloth that shrouds parts of his legs. With his head slightly turned, eyes closed, one hand resting on his chest, the other holding a literal floating black balloon, is he sleeping? Is he dreaming? Could he be dead? What if this figure is yet another representation of the young man in the mounted image rising with the balloon, yet another moment earlier in time, the prostrate and motionless man dreaming of ascending into another world, picturing himself leaping from the wall in flight? The voice singing "somewhere over the rainbow, skies are blue" seems to suggest this dreaming, this proleptic reach toward something beyond. But there's a decided ambiguity. The soil intimates his passing, the return of his body to the earth, a closure of his material existence. If this is so, then that dream extension of the balloon lifting him away might be his fugitive spirit taking flight from the heaviness of the body as it sinks into the soil, like Nehanda fleeing the flesh altogether, in search of otherwise existences.

I return to Shikeith's stunning work to reprise perhaps the most elemental dialectic that structures *Fugitive Time*. Each work I've examined bespeaks a constant interplay between the material and the immaterial, captivity and prolepsis. Between, on the one hand, the weight and immediacy of the physical body, and, on the other, what Nel at the end of *Sula* calls "wishes, longings." This interplay in *The Moment You Doubt Whether You Can Fly* is in the literal, sculpted body on the floor, perhaps without breath, and what we might read as this figure's phenomenal anticipation of an out-of-body experience, imagining riding that balloon up, out, and away to a freedom in excess of this world. Each of the works in these chapters evinces a similar simultaneity of devastating everyday sentience, of living and perceiving as a pained body in the world, but also this ecstatic energy of dreaming of an outside, anticipating, no matter how seemingly futile, an end to the centuries of violence that course through black flesh. This doubled formation appears in the embodied valence of Equiano's account of the hold's "pestilential conditions" alongside what he imagines to be the freedom among the "inhabitants of the deep." It's in Césaire's language of "festering" flesh that ultimately rises *debout* and takes to the sky in anticipation of new life. It's in Issa Samb's provocative characterization of slaves as "human wood," set against the world-building opacity of "this desire to walk, to dream," to "escape by refusal." The works studied in this book constitute a kind of historical archive of this dialectic: indexings, documentations, and excavations, over centuries and across diaspora, of the fundamental inseparability of the violence that haunts black life and the persistent imaginings of seemingly unfathomable freedoms.

Fugitivity is the frame I've chosen to name, gather, and assemble the disparate threads of this dialectic. It's where the myriad objects, histories, and cultural geographies of this project touch. Where they breathe together, in solidarity, in difference, in unexpected intersections, in imagined transcendence. From the start it's been my contention that the experience and imagination of fugitivity can be phenomenalized. I draw on common terms in the discourse of fugitivity, like movement and escape, that imply phenomenological movement, but I try to show how aesthetic works reveal—both descriptively and formally—the minutiae of that phenomenal movement, how aesthetics can open up that gesture of implication. Showing how stealing away toward a certain idea of freedom operates as a continuous motion of the body and mind from moment to moment, from breath to breath. A phenomenological approach opens up the structure of time inherent in the movement of fugitive escape, which is to say, the phenomenological temporality of one's body literally moving through space, but also a phenomenological temporality built into the mind of the fugitive in flight. The latter, I've suggested, is animated by an anticipatory consciousness, a surging outward toward the elusive promise of release in mind and body located in the coming phenomenal moment. It's a release moment that corresponds to the instant in which one escapes the objectifying encounter, untethering blackness from the historical imposition of nonbeing and that imposition's attendant corporeal and psychological wreckage. But this is a utopian consciousness. Its operations are ceaseless. Because as long as black life remains in the hold, as long as we continue to lose Daniel Prudes, Atatiana Jeffersons, Emmanuel Sitholes, and Ibrahima Barries, as long as the state continues to kill unarmed black folks throughout the world, spectacularly or unspectacularly, filmed or unfilmed, there will always be a desire for the outside.

Perhaps the persistent yearning that saturates the aesthetics in this study comes from a seemingly undetectable trace of that outside world, one that insistently seeps into present consciousness. A signal on what Ralph Ellison once called the "lower frequencies," ensuring the ceaselessness of utopian desire. Some kind of fugitive ether that stretches from the horizon, beckoning followers toward absolution in a world beyond. In medieval Europe, the Latin *aether* referred to the purest possible air, found only in heaven and breathed in by the gods. Plato and Aristotle thought of it as the fifth element—quintessence, the lightest and most sublime of airs in the upper sky. What if this were the evidence, however impalpable and impossible, of another world, driving the promise, the anticipations, impelling those fugitive figures up and away? Nehanda's "dreaming air," from which she sees coming "new existences," could be sublime air. It could be ether that drives Shikeith's balloon-riding figure. Sethe does "hear wings," after all, hummingbirds, seemingly out of nowhere, that would guide her and her children "through the veil, out, away, over there," "where they would be safe." And Mazvita hears the sound of the mbira coursing throughout the bus, reaching her "in generous waves of sustenance," "sink[ing] deep in her chest where she had been irrevocably wounded," "circl[ing] her with a new promise of freedom." Perhaps those hummingbird and mbira sounds are phenomenal traces of that sublime air, a residue of the immanently breathable air that might lead Mazvita and Sethe beyond this world, to a place where blackness might at last breathe the breaths that Eric Garner, George Floyd, and Harriet Jacobs have gasped and sought for centuries. "The breath we took . . . It was only / there we wanted to be," Mackey suggests, "the everywhere / we'd always wanted."[1] That fugitive sonic ether sustains Mazvita and Sethe's dreams that one day, one moment, any moment, their pain might vanish. That sound, that breath, just might take them where and when they want to be. It seeps into their minds as a promise too immense to abandon, too devastatingly utopian to forget. And although it may never come true, although wounding may never be lifted unequivocally from blackness, that ether is there to assure them that there's a way out, that there *must* be a way out. So they inhabit that drive toward the outside, ecstatically believing in the possibility of a time and place where blackness is no longer disposable. Where black life can at last *be*.

NOTES

INTRODUCTION. BLACK BEYONDNESS

1. Shikeith, *The Moment You Doubt Whether You Can Fly*.
2. Hesse and Hooker, "Introduction," 448.
3. Sharpe, *In the Wake*, 7.
4. Spillers, "Idea of Black Culture," 25.
5. Gilroy, *Black Atlantic*, 38.
6. Levine, *Forms*, 6–10.
7. Soldi, "Q&A: Shikeith."
8. Wilderson, "Grammar & Ghosts," 122.
9. Patterson, *Slavery and Social Death*, 5.
10. Hartman, *Lose Your Mother*, 234.
11. Mbembe, *Critique of Black Reason*, 26.
12. Edwards, *Practice of Diaspora*, 5.
13. Jaji, *Africa in Stereo*, 12–14.
14. Macharia, *Frottage*, 53, 5, 7. Carole Boyce Davies's conception of diaspora in *Black Women, Writing and Identity*, which "assumes expansiveness and elsewhereness," has also been formative in assembling *Fugitive Time*, as has the global diasporic frame that Samantha Pinto devises in her examination of black women writers and formal innovation in *Difficult Diasporas*. Another is Xavier Livermon's conception of diaspora in *Kwaito Bodies* as shaped by spaces of "(mis)recognition . . . [and] friction that may exist between Black people in Afrodiasporic spaces while also insisting that such friction can be productive spaces of affinity" (31–32). However, I should mention that the notion of diaspora I cultivate in this project doesn't align with all. Whereas I find much of Neil Roberts's *Freedom as Marronage* insightful, for instance, especially the conceptual kinship he sees between fugitivity and marronage, I find less productive his understanding of diaspora as only "able to describe flight either unidirectionally or . . . flight and return over time in a boomerang trajectory" (11). Instead, for me and a range of thinkers, diaspora is a constellation of connective nodes that are always shifting and contingent; it's a network that spans the globe, with movements, desires, and

vectors that move in any which way, creating belonging anywhere and everywhere, practicing solidarity across difference. It's less a movement from a single natal site than a constellation of ongoing extensions, additions, and adaptations, where all cultural geographies are coeval.

15 Brand, *In Another Place*, 126, 169, 243, 246, 247.
16 Moten, *Universal Machine*, 180.
17 The approaches I have in mind here include the founding generation of thinkers in postcolonial theory, a field that emerged in the 1980s and concentrated on identifying subaltern opposition. As Timothy Brennan puts it, "With unfeigned militancy, [postcolonial] theory set about codifying forms of resistance that explicitly precluded Marxist contributions to anti-colonial independence, not simply as the by-product of its search for fresh paradigms, but as a central and self-defining *telos*" ("Subaltern Stakes"). In a similar vein is Walter Johnson's critique of the New Social History, which in part was built on a rigid notion of "agency" as opposition in studies of slavery, effectively evacuating any consideration of the everyday, of the "longing and hope and sadness and anger" that shaped an enslaved community's perception and experience of the world ("On Agency," 116, 188). And related to this is the distinct way in which black life in America has exclusively come to be seen as publicly expressive, resistant, and oppositional. This is a larger claim that Kevin Quashie pursues in *The Sovereignty of Quiet*, where he argues that "resistance . . . is the dominant framework for reading black culture" (11). Such a view, he suggests, occludes readings and apprehensions of black interiority, the "inner reservoir of thoughts, feelings, desires, fears, ambitions that shape a human self" (21).
18 Samb, "Life Has Long Legs."
19 Walcott et al., "Diaspora, Humanism and the Global Project of Black Freedom."
20 Scott, *Extravagant Abjection*, 24.
21 Sexton, "Social Life of Social Death," 9–10.
22 Hartman, *Lose Your Mother*, 234.
23 Roberts, *Freedom as Marronage*, 4.
24 Husserl, *On the Phenomenology of the Consciousness of Internal Time*, 11–14.
25 Wynter, "Unsettling the Coloniality of Being/Power/Truth/Freedom," 313.
26 Bloch, *Principle of Hope*, 287–89.
27 Bloch, *Principle of Hope*, 40, 144, 49.
28 Brooks, *Bodies in Dissent*, 67.
29 Spillers, "Mama's Baby, Papa's Maybe," 206.
30 Sexton, "Unbearable Blackness," 168.
31 I should note from the outset that I don't maintain throughout *Fugitive Time* Spillers's distinction between the "flesh" and the "body" as "captive and liberated subject-positions." In many cases, the works I study in

this book refer to the "body" with a similar valence as Spillers's "flesh," so I've chosen to do the same. When I evoke the body in these chapters, I'm evoking that woundedness that Spillers ascribes to black flesh, although where "flesh" does manifest in a work, I try to make that Spillersian valence evident.

32 Brand, *In Another Place*, 215.
33 Moten, *Universal Machine*, 197.
34 Marriott, "The X of Sacrifice"; Sharpe, *In the Wake*, 21.
35 Wilderson, *Red, White & Black*, xi, 141.
36 Sexton, "'The Curtain of the Sky,'" 16.
37 Jameson, *Archaeologies of the Future*, 171, 175.
38 Nyong'o, *Afro-fabulations*, 101.
39 Brown, *Black Utopias*, 158.
40 Baucom, *Specters of the Atlantic*, 30–31.
41 Mbembe, *On the Postcolony*, 14–16. Though far from a comprehensive list, other nonlinear accounts of historical time in black studies, many of which appear as a component of a monograph rather than the focus of an entire study, include the following: Keguro Macharia's diasporic "wrinkled time . . . calibrated by the whip" (*Frottage*, 92); the subjecting forces and the emancipatory potentialities of what Habiba Ibrahim calls "black age" (*Black Age*, 3–4, 29–30); M. Jacqui Alexander's "palimpsestic" time (*Pedagogies of Crossing*, 190–92); Tejumola Olaniyan's "atavistic time" of the "postcolonial African condition," largely an effect of the perpetual crisis of the postcolonial state (*Arrest the Music!*, 67, 70); Darieck Scott's Fanonian notion of "interarticulated temporality" (*Extravagant Abjection*, 71–77); Kara Keeling's queer, errant, and unpredictable "black futures" (*Queer Times, Black Futures*, 19, 32); Tavia Nyong'o's "tenseless time," which is built into his larger theory of "Afro-fabulation" (*Afro-fabulations*, 5–11, 21–24); the notion of "penal time" that Nicole Fleetwood isolates in the experiences and art practices of incarcerated people (*Marking Time*, 37–42); Jennifer Wenzel's "prophetic memory" in the South African context and beyond (*Bulletproof*, 125–29); Alexander Weheliye's historical time "as a series of cross-currents and discontinuities" (*Phonographies*, 80–82); Ayo Coly's "postcolonial hauntology," which appears "in the form of the hold of the colonial past on postcolonial discourses of the African female body" (*Postcolonial Hauntologies*, 2); Rinaldo Walcott's "time of long emancipation," where black life and potential freedoms "erupt" through the linearity of modernity (*Long Emancipation*, 3); and Amber Musser's discussion of Fanon, Freud, and the "atemporality of the becoming-biological of black bodies" (*Sensational Flesh*, 103–7).
42 See Scott, *Omens of Adversity*, 1–29. La Marr Bruce's notion of "madtime" as a "feeling [of] time [that] coincides with the spasms of and rhythms of madness," especially as it relates to music, is another generative

framework of black time that moves between the experiential and the historical. See Bruce, *How to Go Mad*, 204–7.
43 Wright, *Physics of Blackness*, 16, 41–44.
44 Brown, *Black Utopias*, 12–16.
45 Reed, *Freedom Time*, 170–77.
46 Hartman, *Wayward Lives, Beautiful Experiments*, 33.
47 Reed makes clear that *Freedom Time* "does not offer a new conception of time." His assiduous attention to the otherwise as it's registered in poetic form, however, has deeply influenced my own reading practice. Beyond the recent work of Brown, Reed, and Hartman, other studies of black utopian thought and otherwise desire have shaped this book. Among them is Ashon Crawley's study of the aesthetics of Blackpentacostalism, such as shouting, whooping, and speaking in tongues, and how they're subtended by a desire to disrupt post-Enlightenment epistemologies and to create otherwise possibility (*Blackpentacostal Breath*, 8–9). And though firmly within the frame of what Paul Gilroy would call the "politics of fulfillment," despite his invocation of utopia, Felwine Sarr's vision of African futures in *Afrotopia*, calling for a "civilizational shift" in refusing the temporal, cultural, and economic models of the global North, serves as critical ground that *Fugitive Time* stands on as it seeks to place utopian desire in relation across African, European, Caribbean, and North American cultural geographies. And there are, of course, the earlier articulations of black utopian desire that this project is no less shaped by. Gilroy's notion of the "politics of transfiguration" in *The Black Atlantic*, which I gesture to at the opening of this introduction and unpack further in chapter 4, is foundational, as is Saidiya Hartman's study in *Scenes of Subjection* of the "desires and longings that exceed the frame of civil rights and political emancipation" in nineteenth-century black America (13).
48 Bakhtin, *Dialogic Imagination*, 84.
49 Bulawayo, *We Need New Names*, 17.
50 Bakhtin, *Dialogic Imagination*, 84.
51 See Jameson, *Archaeologies of the Future*.
52 Stephens and Stephens, "Embodied/Disembodied," 262.
53 Samatar, "Account of the Land of Witches," 148, 149, 152, 159, 161–63.
54 As with many studies, I could have taken up innumerable directions in this book in terms of the curation of aesthetic objects. One of the more obvious of these is speculative aesthetics—artists such as Samatar, Octavia Butler, Nalo Hopkinson, and Wangechi Mutu. However, I would argue that the speculative mode saturates the vast majority of the works I examine in the coming chapters, even if most don't fit the normative definitions of science fiction and fantasy. Sun Ra—with his interstellar ambitions and his standing as an early forerunner of Afrofuturism—

as well as Morrison's *Beloved*—indisputably a work of supernatural horror—are the most "speculative" artists and works taken up here. But Ra's vision of escape into the cosmos isn't far removed from Issa Samb's visions of other worlds in stones, or Plum's anticipation of the "bright hole of sleep" in *Sula*. These are improbable visions, searchings for otherwise worlds and existences. Another way of framing this project is that it traces the speculative in what most would consider the nonspeculative. This book troubles that distinction, showing how a desire for reimagined worlds and bodies doesn't just lie in works set on distant planets or in alternative pasts.

55 See Higgs, *Chocolate Islands*; and Rodney, *How Europe Underdeveloped Africa*.

56 Smith, *Senegal Abroad*, 20.

57 Pinto, *Difficult Diasporas*, 166.

58 The now well-known correction of Equiano's nativity arose from Vincent Carretta's late-1990s discovery of a baptismal record and a ship muster list that indicate Equiano may have been born in South Carolina—which, if true, would render his accounts of West Africa and the middle passage fabrications, effectively falsifying a voice that served at the time to "validate much of the evidence conventionally cited in abolitionist discourse" ("Olaudah Equiano or Gustavus Vassa?," 98). Although rigorous defenses by Catherine Acholonu, Paul Lovejoy, and others have been mounted in favor of his African nativity, my interest has less to do with the text's veracity and more in what its early sections engender. See Acholonu, "The Home of Olaudah Equiano"; and Lovejoy, "Autobiography and Memory."

59 Equiano, *Interesting Narrative*, 40–41.

60 Howard, "Swim Your Ground," 17.

61 Spillers, "Mama's Baby, Papa's Maybe," 215. In addition to antecedent representations of fugitive time, I want to note the actual forms of time consciousness that likely came before. If fugitive time—whether represented in creative expression or present in one's consciousness—was inaugurated by the fifteenth-century conjuncture of capitalism, captivity, and passage that brought millions to the Americas and buried millions at sea, then the time consciousness that came before (we can of course only speculate) was not one, but many: a multitude of ways of conceiving of the movement of time itself, corresponding to the myriad cosmologies—systems of belief and knowledge production—among the ethnic groups living on the continent prior to Portuguese sub-Saharan arrival. One of the more influential of these indigenous modalities is the cyclical concept of time in Yoruba metaphysics brought to prominence most notably by Wole Soyinka in *Death and the King's Horseman* (1975) and *Myth, Literature and the African World* (1976). In the latter

he explains how the Yoruba conception of "life, present life, contains within it manifestations of the ancestral, the living and the unborn": "All are vitally within the intimations and affectiveness of life" (144). Although we can't be certain precisely what constituted this particular cosmological structure in, say, the ninth century, time consciousness was likely radically altered for the uncountable Yoruba who for more than a month were chained to the holds of ships and taken across the sea, even if those individuals and their descendants retained a certain belief in that expansive cyclical structure. What's more, this ruptured consciousness likely had a rippling effect of profound psychic loss on those left behind in West Africa and their descendants. And the same logic stands, I would argue, for those groups whose cosmologies were disrupted not by the slave trade but by the violence and ideologies of European (settler) colonialism, like those of the Kamba and the Kikuyu of East Africa that John Mbiti examines in *African Religions and Philosophy* (1969), which, like Yoruba metaphysics, are so clearly distinct from European chronological accountings and Judeo-Christian eschatology.

62 Drexciya, *The Quest*, Submerge (3), 1997, compact disc, liner notes.

63 In the last two decades, but especially the most recent, Drexciya's aquatic myth has been taken up by a host of black artists, scholars, and creative intellectuals, providing their own extensions and samplings of this submarine utopian sociality. A few include Ellen Gallagher's "Watery Ecstatic" series (2001–); clipping's "The Deep" (2017); the Otolith Group's "Hydra Decapita" (2010); Kevin Young's *The Grey Album* (2012); Katherine McKittrick's *Dear Science and Other Stories* (2021); Akosua Adoma Owusu's *Drexciya* (2010); Nettrice Gaskins's "Deep Sea Dwellers: Drexciya and the Sonic Third Space" (2016); and Sherwin Ovid's "Breath between Ledgers Measured" (2020). See the Broad, "Watery Ecstatic Series: Ellen Gallagher," accessed October 18, 2022; clipping, "The Deep," accessed October 18, 2022; the Otolith Group, "Hydra Decapita," accessed October 18, 2022; Young, *Grey Album*; McKittrick, *Dear Science and Other Stories*; Owusu, *Drexciya*, accessed October 18, 2022; Gaskins, "Deep Sea Dwellers"; and Goldfinch Gallery, "Sherwin Ovid," accessed October 18, 2022.

64 Sharpe, *In the Wake*, 40–41.

65 See, for instance, Sylvia Wynter's framing of the "alternative thrust" of marronage in her essays "One Love" (1972) and "Beyond the Word of Man" (1989). In *Black Marxism* (1983), Cedric Robinson also gives voice to various formations of fugitivity and fugitive consciousness, including prophecy. See Robinson's reading of Nongqawuse's 1856 prophecy on southern Africa's eastern Cape that, as he puts it, "continues to evade Western comprehension" (166, 168). As for Nathaniel Mackey, fugitivity as a kind of ecstatically (and often musically) lived experience appears

throughout his poetry, prose, and critical theory. See, for example, "Cante Moro" and "Bedouin Hornbook."

66 Fanon, *Peau noire, masques blancs*, 88, 112. Although I consult Markmann's English translation of *Black Skin, White Masks* as a reference throughout this book, citations refer to the original French of Fanon's *Peau noire, masques blancs*. The portions of the text excerpted are my own translations, which in many cases are similar to Markmann's. I use my own to take advantage of the plasticity of the French so that we might consider the array of possible meanings of a given term that might alter, or add layers to, how one reads a certain passage. For the reference translation, see Fanon, *Black Skin, White Masks*.

67 Fanon, *Peau noire*, 91.

68 Fanon, 6, 24, 42.

69 Roberts, *Freedom as Marronage*, 118–19.

70 Fanon, *Peau noire*, 186.

71 Mudimbe, *The Invention of Africa*, 107, 4, 20. See also Johannes Fabian's influential and related "denial of coevalness" in *Time and the Other*, 31–32. For more on the historicist framing of historical time, see Reinhart Koselleck's *Futures Past* (2004). For a more broadly postcolonial analysis of this temporality and its countercurrents, see Simon Gikandi, "Globalization and the Claims of Postcoloniality."

72 Fanon, *Peau noire*, 187.

73 Fanon, 182, 186; Marriott, "Inventions of Existence," 46.

74 Critically, though, this refusal doesn't eclipse the possibility of the traumatic past shaping that temporal movement in a constitutive way. Fanon's disavowal of the past speaks to the *conscious* effort to distance oneself from past events, not necessarily those *unconscious* hauntings of past violence, shame, and abjection that unevenly seep into the everyday, as Françoise Vergès suggests, constituting the ways in which time is lived as anticipation (*Monsters and Revolutionaries*, 4–15).

75 Hartman, *Scenes of Subjection*, 6; Sharpe, *In the Wake*, 12.

76 Lightfoot, *Troubling Freedom*, 3–8, 230–31.

77 Mbembe, *On the Postcolony*, 237.

78 Lightfoot, *Troubling Freedom*, 8. In addition to these thinkers, the idea of the nonevent of emancipation and decolonization bears out across a wide range of recent work in global black studies: Walcott explicitly frames this globally in the first lines of *The Long Emancipation* (1); Livermon addresses the "political compromise" that "fosters and perpetuates" inequality specifically in post-apartheid South Africa (*Kwaito Bodies*, 3); concurring with Hartman, Jackson refers to this nonevent in the United States as "a reorganization of a structure of violence" (*Becoming Human*, 28); and this idea is at the heart of Coly's centering of the African female body in her notion of "postcolonial hauntology," where "a

postcolonial African present [is] haunted by colonial specters" (*Postcolonial Hauntologies*, 28).
79   Brown, *Black Utopias*, 16.
80   Keeling, *Witch's Flight*, 37.
81   Brand, *Map to the Door of No Return*, 4, 5.
82   Macharia, *Frottage*, 51–52.
83   The Greene Space at WNYC & WQXR, "Black Icons of Art," accessed October 7, 2019.
84   Buck-Morss, *Dreamworld and Catastrophe*, 97.
85   Bloch, *Utopian Function of Art and Literature*, 73.

CHAPTER 1. TONI MORRISON'S ANACHRONIC EASE

1   Morrison, *Beloved*, 103.
2   Morrison, *Bluest Eye*, 124, 139.
3   Morrison, *Beloved*, 66.
4   Lorde, "Uses of the Erotic," 55–58.
5   Morrison, *Beloved*, 4, 101.
6   Hartman, *Wayward Lives*, xv, 242.
7   McKay, "An Interview with Toni Morrison," 145.
8   Hartman, *Scenes of Subjection*, 63, 77.
9   The majority of instances in which I use the term *prolepsis* in this chapter pertain to the particular operations of *narrative* prolepsis that Genette lays out and that appear in Morrison's fiction.
10 Morrison, *Beloved*, 101 (my emphasis).
11 I should note that Morrison is not the only black American writer to express such a desire in her work. We might think of the moment in James Baldwin's 1953 novel *Go Tell It on the Mountain* when a young John Grimes looks out over the New York skyline, proclaiming, "To hurl away, for a moment of ease, the glories of eternity!" (32). Or, perhaps even more resonant with the utopian valence in Morrison's fiction, the visionary healer figure Minnie Ransom in Toni Cade Bambara's *The Salt Eaters* (1980): "Eyes wide open to the swing from expand to contract, dissolve congeal, release restrict, foot tapping, throat throbbing in song to the ebb and flow of renewal, she would welcome them healed into her arms" (48). In Ransom we find a kindred figure to Baby Suggs, in her capacity to initiate an ecstatically excessive physiological and affective renewal in another that courses throughout the body.
12 Alexander, *Black Interior*, 5.
13 On this question of the interior, my selection of *Sula* and *Beloved* has to do with the degree of interiority we find in Morrison's novels. Works like

Love, *Song of Solomon*, and *Paradise* have an omniscience, certainly, but one with far less phenomenological detail than *Sula* and *Beloved*. In these latter two, omniscience takes on a closeness to character consciousness, giving us an intimate view of how a given character perceives the subtle phenomenological changes and movements of her body, time consciousness, and being-in-the-world. "In *Beloved*," Ato Quayson concurs, "the third-person narration unfolds in close proximity to the consciousness of the characters themselves." Noting the specter of slavery that haunts, he suggests that "the narrative is concomitantly fragmentary and shifts constantly between the immediate represented foreground and the events that lie in the past but which constantly intrude into the consciousness of the present" (*Aesthetic Nervousness*, 109).

14 Ricoeur, *Time and Narrative*, vol. 2, p. 106.
15 Hartman, *Scenes of Subjection*, 42.
16 Spillers, "Mama's Baby, Papa's Maybe," 207.
17 Hartman, *Scenes of Subjection*, 51.
18 Beavers, *Geography and the Political*, 6.
19 Dennis Childs has an insightful way of thinking about the temporality of subjection in *Beloved* through what he calls the "time-bending capacities of racialized imprisonment" enacted particularly through the novel's references to the hold of the slave ship and the mobile chain-gang prison cage. See Childs, "'You Ain't Seen Nothin' Yet.'" I should note, too, that beyond the specificity of Morrison's fiction, scholars have recently done important work to theorize something akin to this black subjection time. See, for instance, John Murillo's notion of black "untime" in *Impossible Stories: On the Space and Time of Black Destructive Creation* (2021); Julius Fleming's "black patience" in *Black Patience: Performance, Civil Rights, and the Unfinished Project Emancipation* (2022); and Habiba Ibrahim's concept of "black age" in *Black Age: Oceanic Lifespans and the Time of Black Life* (2021). In addition to providing tools to describe mechanisms of temporal violence, Ibrahim and Fleming importantly also present their respective formulations as conditions of possibility and reclamation.
20 Christian, "Layered Rhythms," 489.
21 Morrison, *Beloved*, 63.
22 Morrison, *Beloved*, 111, 28, 21.
23 Morrison, *Beloved*, 303.
24 Sharpe, *In the Wake*, 104, 106.
25 Morrison, "Unspeakable Things Unspoken," 33.
26 Morrison, *Sula*, 32–33, 152.
27 Murillo, *Impossible Stories*, 58.
28 Caruth, *Unclaimed Experience*, 5.

29 Best, *None like Us*, 73.
30 Glissant, *Poetics of Relation*, 7.
31 Jones and Vinson, "An Interview with Toni Morrison," 175.
32 Sexton, "Social Life of Social Death," 28.
33 Genette, *Narrative Discourse*, 35–36.
34 Genette, 40.
35 Christian, "Contemporary Fables of Toni Morrison," 76.
36 Morrison, *Sula*, 37, 47, 48.
37 Morrison, *Sula*, 70–71.
38 Morrison, *Sula*, 71–72.
39 Morrison, *Sula*, 148–49.
40 Spillers, "Mama's Baby, Papa's Maybe," 67.
41 Hartman, *Scenes of Subjection*, 77.
42 Spillers, "A Hateful Passion, a Lost Love," 118. See also McDowell, "'Self and the Other,'" 81.
43 Morrison, *Sula*, 171–72.
44 Genette, *Narrative Discourse*, 73.
45 hooks and West, *Breaking Bread*, 84.
46 Morrison, *Beloved*, 5.
47 Morrison, *Beloved*, 60, 68, 62, 116.
48 Morrison, *Beloved*, 112, 163.
49 Morrison, *Beloved*, 175–76, 185.
50 Morrison, *Beloved*, 192–93.
51 Henderson, "Toni Morrison's *Beloved*," 80.
52 Morrison, *Beloved*, 240.
53 Miller, "Boundaries in *Beloved*," 28, 35.
54 Brooks, *Bodies in Dissent*, 108; Cobb, *Picturing Freedom*, 32.
55 Bruce, *How to Go Mad*, 19.
56 Ricoeur, *Time and Narrative*, vol. 2, p. 103.
57 Morrison, *Beloved*, 6–7.
58 Morrison, *Beloved*, 19–20.
59 Henderson, "Toni Morrison's *Beloved*," 68–69.
60 Morrison, *Beloved*, 33, 111, 160.
61 Morrison, *Beloved*, 24.
62 Morrison, *Beloved*, 25, 24, 30.
63 Griffin, "Textual Healing," 528.
64 Morrison, *Beloved*, 308–9.
65 Glissant, *Poetics of Relation*, 82–83.
66 Bey, "Trans*-ness of Blackness," 279.
67 Moten, "Blackness and Nothingness," 742.

CHAPTER 2. AIMÉ CÉSAIRE, WIFREDO LAM, AND THE AESTHETICS OF SURGING LIFE

1. Cernuschi, "Art of Wifredo Lam," 62. The handwritten inscription in the copy of the *Notebook* that Césaire gave Lam, dated May 1941, is an intimate confirmation of this: "to Wifredo Lam / a testimony of friendship / and admiration / this poem of our revolts / of our hopes / of our fervor." Reproduced in Maximin, *Césaire et Lam*, 15.
2. Césaire, "Poésie et connaissance," 166–67, 169.
3. Mosquera, "'My Painting Is an Act of Decolonization,'" 3.
4. English, *To Describe a Life*, 5.
5. Ades, "Wifredo Lam and Surrealism," 38–39; Hale, "Two Decades, Four Versions," 189.
6. Arnold, "'À l'Afrique' avec Césaire et Lam," 1617–18.
7. Breton, "Second Manifesto of Surrealism," 162–63.
8. Depestre, "Itinéraire d'un langage," 10.
9. Rowell, "It Is through Poetry," 996. For more on Césaire's coining of the term in *L'Etudiant noir* four years before the publication of the *Notebook*, see Miller, "The (Revised) Birth of Négritude," 743–44.
10. Depestre, "Itinéraire d'un langage," 10.
11. Césaire, "Cahier d'un retour au pays natal (Présence Africaine 1956)," 194–95. All translations of the *Notebook* from the French are my own, although I have consulted various translations in most instances, particularly Arnold and Eshleman's 2013 translation of the original 1939 poem (Césaire, *Original 1939 Notebook*) and Eshleman and Smith's 2001 translation of the final 1956 poem (Césaire, *Notebook of a Return to the Native Land*).
12. Depestre, "Itinéraire d'un langage," 9.
13. Sartre, "Orphée Noir," xx–xxi.
14. Hénane, *Glossaire*, 8.
15. Césaire, *Collected Poetry*, 106 (my emphasis).
16. Reed, *Freedom Time*, 39; Hénane, *Glossaire*, 61.
17. Depestre, "Itinéraire d'un langage," 15.
18. Edwards, *Practice of Diaspora*, 26, 33.
19. Césaire, "Cahier d'un retour au pays natal (Volontés 1939)," 91–92. For my purposes in this chapter, I retain the word *nègre* as a cognate in my translations of Césaire's work. When I do use the terms *black* and *blackness* in the Césairean context, I'm invoking the same lexical history and register as Césaire's *nègre*. It's important to note that the translation of *nègre* into English has been disputed. Clayton Eshleman and Annette Smith, the translators of Césaire's collected poetry, opted to translate it as "nigger," since, in their view, the latter term best reflected the poet's "process of self-irony and self-denigration . . . [as a] necessary step

on the path to a new self image" (Césaire, *Collected Poetry*, 27). Brent Edwards, on the other hand, suggests that "in the interwar period . . . the function of *nègre* in French . . . may be closest to the word *black*, a derogatory appellation in the 1920s (both are terms that populist radicals such as Lamine Senghor in French and Marcus Garvey in English were keen to rehabilitate in the service of a certain nationalism)" (*Practice of Diaspora*, 34–35). Given the term's fraught translation, I want to remain as close to Césaire's use of it as possible, allowing us as readers the possibility to learn to hear the nuance of the term as the poet himself intended.

20 Sartre, "Orphée Noir," 33, 47–48.
21 Mosquera, "'My Painting Is an Act of Decolonization,'" 4.
22 Linsley, "Wifredo Lam," 531.
23 Stokes Sims, *Wifredo Lam*, 30.
24 Linsley, "Wifredo Lam," 531.
25 Mosquera, "'My Painting Is an Act of Decolonization,'" 3.
26 Mercer, "Wifredo Lam's Afro-Atlantic Routes," 26–27.
27 Arnold, "À 'l'Afrique' avec Césaire et Lam," 1618–19.
28 Stokes Sims, *Wifredo Lam*, 69.
29 Césaire, "Cahier d'un retour au pays natal (Volontés 1939)," 83.
30 Spillers, "Mama's Baby, Papa's Maybe," 206, 207.
31 Moten, "Case of Blackness," 186. See also Nahum Chandler's related category of the "paraontological" in *"Beyond This Narrow Now"* (224) and Ronald Judy's extensive engagement with Chandler's term in *Sentient Flesh* (322–76).
32 Moten, "Case of Blackness," 187.
33 Weheliye, *Habeas Viscus*, 44–45.
34 On the dominant critical approaches to the *Notebook*'s structure, see Hale, "Structural Dynamics in a Third World Classic"; and Pestre de Almeida, *Aimé Césaire*.
35 As I've already noted for the range of works studied in this book, Spillers's theoretical language of the body and flesh does not fit neatly into Césaire's aesthetics of metaphorical and linguistic contortion. He clearly does not distinguish between the "body" as liberated and the "flesh" as captive. Instead, Césaire's reference and allusion to both "body" (*corps*) and "flesh" (*chair*) broadly aligns with the way that Spillers theorizes the "flesh" as that surface which bears the "lacerations" and "woundings" that together instantiate the "hieroglyphics" of black vestibularity.
36 Césaire, "Cahier d'un retour au pays natal (Volontés 1939)," 74.
37 Césaire, "Cahier d'un retour au pays natal (Volontés 1939)," 75.
38 Césaire, "Cahier d'un retour au pays natal (Volontés 1939)," 75.
39 Césaire, "Cahier d'un retour au pays natal (Volontés 1939)," 80.
40 Césaire, "Cahier d'un retour au pays natal (Volontés 1939)," 83, ellipses in the original.

41 Spillers, "Mama's Baby, Papa's Maybe," 207.
42 Davis, *Aimé Césaire*, 45.
43 Césaire, "Cahier d'un retour au pays natal (Volontés 1939)," 83–84.
44 Césaire, "Cahier d'un retour au pays natal (Volontés 1939)," 82, 88, ellipses in the original.
45 Césaire, "Cahier d'un retour au pays natal (Volontés 1939)," 86, 88.
46 Irele, "Commentary and Notes," 260–61.
47 Césaire, *Une Saison au Congo*, 1126.
48 Royster, *Sounding like a No-No*, 9.
49 Bloch, *Principle of Hope*, 67, 69, 49.
50 Césaire, "Cahier d'un retour au pays natal (Volontés 1939)," 76.
51 Césaire, "Cahier d'un retour au pays natal (Volontés 1939)," 77.
52 Sojoyner, "Another Life Is Possible," 531.
53 Césaire, "Cahier d'un retour au pays natal (Volontés 1939)," 87–88.
54 Césaire, "Cahier d'un retour au pays natal (Volontés 1939)," 86.
55 Césaire, "Cahier d'un retour au pays natal (Volontés 1939)," 88.
56 It's often overlooked, perhaps, because the chapter was not translated and included in the English version of the text. My page citations here refer to the original *Le Discours antillais*.
57 Glissant, *Le Discours antillais*, 505.
58 Tinsley, *Thiefing Sugar*, 178–79, 180.
59 Césaire, "Cahier d'un retour au pays natal (Volontés 1939)," 87.
60 Césaire, "Cahier d'un retour au pays natal (Brentano's 1947)," 114.
61 Quintata, "Aimé Césaire y Wifredo Lam," 240.
62 Césaire, "Poésie et connaissance," 166–67, 169.
63 Césaire, "Cahier d'un retour au pays natal (Brentano's 1947)," 123. For more on the likely timing of when Césaire completed the Brentano's manuscript, see James Arnold's notes in Césaire, "Cahier d'un retour au pays natal (Brentano's 1947)," 101–5.
64 Irele, "Commentary and Notes," 221–22.
65 Campt, "Black Feminist Futures and the Practice of Fugitivity."
66 Césaire, "Cahier d'un retour au pays natal (Brentano's 1947)," 114.
67 Pestre de Almeida, *Aimé Césaire*, 97.
68 Muñoz, *Cruising Utopia*, 1, 27, 22.
69 Spillers, "Mama's Baby, Papa's Maybe," 207.
70 Edelman, *No Future*, 17, 31, 25.
71 Muñoz, *Cruising Utopia*, 92–95.
72 Tinsley, "Black Atlantic, Queer Atlantic," 199, 203.
73 Tinsley, *Ezili's Mirrors*, 34, 43.
74 Césaire, "Cahier d'un retour au pays natal (Volontés 1939)," 91. The final two ellipses in this passage appear in the original.
75 Césaire, "Cahier d'un retour au pays natal (Volontés 1939)," 92.
76 Césaire, "Cahier d'un retour au pays natal (Volontés 1939)," 93.

77 Césaire, "Cahier d'un retour au pays natal (Volontés 1939)," 93.
78 Suzanne Césaire, "Léo Frobenius et la problem des civilisations," 30.
79 Ra, *The Immeasurable Equation*, 343.
80 Wilder, *Freedom Time*, 21, 121, 131.
81 Marx, "Eighteenth Brumaire of Napoleon Bonaparte," 595.
82 Sexton, "Social Life of Social Death," 28.
83 *Annonciation*, published in 1982, the year of Lam's death, consisted of ten poems by Césaire and seven etching and aquatint prints produced by Lam between 1969 and 1971. Césaire would go on to include his ten *Annonciation* poems in his own collection *Moi, Laminaire* (1982).
84 Césaire, "Moi, Laminaire," 782.
85 Jackson, *Becoming Human*, 157–58.
86 Derrida, *Specters of Marx*, 25, 74, 210.
87 Bloch, *Spirit of Utopia*, 171.

CHAPTER 3. BLACK AUDIO'S ARCHIVAL FLIGHT

1 Akomfrah, "On the Borderline," 198–99; Fani-Kayode, "Traces of Ecstasy," 6.
2 Mercer, "Becoming Black Audio," 87–89.
3 Alter, *Essay Film after Fact and Fiction*, 5–7.
4 Auguiste and Black Audio Film Collective, "Black Independents and Third World Cinema," 165.
5 Eshun, "Absence of Ruins," 137.
6 Although John Akomfrah and Reece Auguiste are listed as the respective directors of *Handsworth Songs* and *Twilight City*, I refer to the collective as the creator of the works discussed in this chapter as a gesture to Black Audio's deliberately cultivated collective practice. Where possible I credit individual members identified in the production notes as responsible for particular filmic aspects.
7 Jaji, *Africa in Stereo*, 214.
8 Heidegger, *Being and Time*, 131–32, 310.
9 Hall et al., *Policing the Crisis*, 342.
10 Hall, "Preface," 7.
11 Fryer, *Staying Power*, 372.
12 Deleuze, *Cinema 2*, 250–51.
13 Akomfrah's more recent work extends this focus on migration and British identity. *The Nine Muses* (2010) revisits the archive of twentieth-century black migration to Britain through the optic of Homer's *Odyssey*, taking after *Handsworth Songs* in its strategies of historical, cultural, and visual juxtaposition.
14 Alter, *Essay Film after Fact and Fiction*, 273.

15 Deleuze, *Cinema 1*, 29.
16 Hartman, *Wayward Lives, Beautiful Experiments*, 24.
17 Hall et al., *Policing the Crisis*, 223–29.
18 Hall et al., *Policing the Crisis*, 241.
19 Hall, "Racism and Reaction," 27–29; Fryer, *Staying Power*, 376–81.
20 Hall, "Racism and Reaction," 29–30.
21 Auguiste, "Outline for *Twilight City*," 165.
22 Fanon, *Peau noire, masques blancs*, 88.
23 Carby, "Becoming Modern Racialized Subjects," 641–50.
24 Hall, *Hard Road to Renewal*, 47.
25 Hall et al., *Policing the Crisis*, 244; Sivanandan, *Different Hunger*, 25–37.
26 Hall et al., *Policing the Crisis*, 325. Stuart Hall's work is essential to understanding both the deep-seated nature of this economic crisis, which commenced in full in the late 1960s, as well as the ways that blackness came to symbolize the larger social and economic crisis in the 1970s. On the historical formation of the recession, see "The Great Moving Show" in *The Hard Road to Renewal* (1988). On the symbolics of blackness and crisis, see "Racism and Reaction" in *Five Views on Multi-racial Britain* (1978).
27 Mercer, *Welcome to the Jungle*, 7.
28 Fryer, *Staying Power*, 387–99; Hall, "From Scarman to Stephen Lawrence," 190. This climate is further examined in Black Audio's 1991 film *Mysteries of July*, which focuses on the 1989 deaths of four black youths in police custody in London.
29 Sivanandan, *Different Hunger*, 62, 23; Hall, "Question of Cultural Identity," 308–9.
30 Hall, "Whose Heritage?," 9–10. For more on the diversity and historical differentiation within this coalitional blackness, see Hall et al., *Policing the Crisis*, 341. I should note that this coalitional blackness effectively collapsed with the breakdown of the ethnic minority versus British majority binary in the 1990s. On this collapse, see Hall, "Frontlines and Backyards"; and Owusu, "The Struggle for a Radical Black Political Culture," 423.
31 Auguiste, "Black Cinema," 153. Importantly, this pluralist black identity was not embraced by all of Black Audio's artistic contemporaries. Indicating just how emergent it was, Eddie Chambers, a founding member of BLK Art Group, explained in an interview how he felt "steamrollered by this other view that 'black' should include all sorts of other people beyond the African diaspora" (Archer-Straw, "Eddie Chambers," 30).
32 Mercer, "Post-colonial Trauerspiel," 46.
33 Ross, "Camping the Dirty Dozens," 291. See also Harper, *Are We Not Men?*, 39–53.
34 Walcott, "Somewhere out There," 33.

35   Although the footage we find in *Handsworth Songs* concentrates on the aftermath of the 1985 uprisings in Handsworth, other black independent films of the time, notably by Sankofa Film and Video, incorporated actual uprising footage. In Isaac Julien's *Territories* (1984) and Julien and Maureen Blackwood's *Passion of Remembrance* (1986), footage of uprisings in 1976 and 1981 is central to their articulation of black Britishness—particularly police-community relations as well as intersectional differences of class, gender, and sexuality.

36   Wilderson, *Red, White & Black*, 128.

37   This repeated footage and its slowing down calls to mind important work that helps conceptualize the fraught relation between black life and the police. I'm thinking, for instance, of Jeffrey McCune's reading of the 2015 video of the assassination of Walter Scott, the South Carolina man running away only to be shot in the back by police, as symbolic of "the queer position of black people in Ferguson and beyond: as runners from violent authority and institutions; seemingly eternal sojourners of freedom" ("Queerness of Blackness," 175). Pertinent, too, is André Lepecki's conceptualization of the way that police in urban spaces seek to "de-mobilize political action by means of implementing a certain kind of movement that prevents any formation and expression of the political." The consequence of such control—evinced in the improvisatory and evasive movement of the youth in the *Handsworth* sequence—is what Lepecki calls "choreopolitics": the "redistribution and reinvention of bodies, affects, and senses through which one may learn how to move politically, how to invent, activate, seek, or experiment with a movement whose only sense (meaning and direction) is the experimental exercise of freedom" (Lepecki, "Choreopolice and Choreopolitics," 20).

38   Glissant, *Poetics of Relation*, 18–20.
39   Cervenak, *Wandering*, 6, 172.
40   Copeland, *Bound to Appear*, 150.
41   "John Akomfrah—Why History Matters | TateShots."
42   Eisenstein, "Dialectic Approach to Film Form," 49.
43   Deleuze, *Cinema 1*, 36.
44   Akomfrah, "On the Borderline," 198.
45   Lyotard, "Acinema," 355.
46   Spillers, "Mama's Baby, Papa's Maybe," 207, 220.
47   Caruth, *Unclaimed Experience*, 92.
48   Aumont, "Veritable Eye," 245.
49   Power, "Counter-media, Migration, Poetry," 60.
50   Wahlberg, *Documentary Time*, 44, 68, 53.
51   Fusco, *Young, British & Black*, 18.
52   Mercer, *Welcome to the Jungle*, 60.

53 Sessolo, "Epic of Riots," 749.
54 Mroz, *Temporality and Film Analysis*, 34.
55 Bey, "Trans*-ness of Blackness," 282.
56 Genette, *Narrative Discourse Revisited*, 17.
57 Branigan, *Narrative Comprehension and Film*, 35, 49.
58 Walcott, *Long Emancipation*, 12–13; for extended discussion, see 69–80.
59 Moten, "Case of Blackness," 179.
60 Eshun, "Untimely Meditations," 42.
61 Nash, *Black Body in Ecstasy*, 148; Brown, *Black Utopias*, 25.
62 Fani-Kayode, "Traces of Ecstasy," 6.
63 Mercer, *Welcome to the Jungle*, 227.
64 Nelson, "Transgressive Transcendence," 18.
65 Muñoz, *Cruising Utopia*, 1, 27, 25.
66 Bourland, *Bloodflowers*, 147.
67 Mercer, *Travel & See*, 115–16.
68 Jagose, *Orgasmology*, 208–9.
69 Keeling, *Queer Times, Black Futures*, 32.
70 Gumbs and Wallace, "Something Else to Be," 391.
71 There's an array of work in black queer studies that speaks to the desire these nondiegetic spaces evoke. Because they intersect so well, and, alongside the black British context assemble a kind of African diasporic queer resonance, there's a special pertinence in Xavier Livermon's *Kwaito Bodies* (2020) and Jeffrey McCune's *Sexual Discretion* (2014). I have in mind the nightclub chapters in these books: the former, in Johannesburg, exploring how "practices of leisure and partying" help to create an "alternative geography of the city" (Livermon, 60); the latter, in Chicago, revealing the ways that publicly straight black men practicing queerness on the "down low" explore the often "unavailable, or inconvenient, possibilities" of living queerly (McCune, *Discretion*, 99).
72 Chion, *Audio-vision*, 13–16.
73 Hartman, *Lose Your Mother*, 234.
74 Cervenak, *Wandering*, 172.
75 Chion, *Audio-vision*, 47.
76 Green-Simms, *Queer African Cinemas*, 26.
77 Macharia, *Frottage*, 126.
78 Hall, "From Scarman to Stephen Lawrence," 188.
79 See Sam Francis, Tarah Welsh, and Zack Adesina, "Met Police 'Four Times More Likely' to Use Force on Black People," BBC, July 30, 2020; Vikram Dodd, "Young Black Males in London '19 Times More Likely' to Be Stopped and Searched," *Guardian*, December 3, 2020; Siana Bangura, "We Need to Talk about Police Brutality in the U.K.," *Fader*, March 29, 2016.

CHAPTER 4. SUN RA, ISSA SAMB, AND THE DRAPETOMANIACAL AVANT-GARDE

1. Cartwright, "Diseases and Peculiarities of the Negro Race," 27–36.
2. Warren, *Ontological Terror*, 126.
3. Quashie, *Black Aliveness*, 1.
4. Glissant, *Poetics of Relation*, 190.
5. Rotenstein, "Jazz Pianist Sun Ra"; Harbaoui, "Joe Ouakam."
6. Bruce, *How to Go Mad*, 8, 162, 195.
7. Marriott, *Whither Fanon*, 45–52.
8. Glissant, *Caribbean Discourse*, 123–24.
9. Harney and Moten, *Undercommons*, 133–38. My conception of madness in this chapter is also indebted to Therí Pickens's theorizations of black madness, and more broadly the intersection of blackness, disability studies, and speculative fiction. Useful in the context of the work studied in this chapter is Pickens's assertion that madness, in black literature, "surfaces not solely as pathology or as part of a holy fool tradition, but also as a viable alternative to engagement with white racism even if it does not result in increased agency. Madness becomes a place to engage because racism adheres to a peculiar kind of rationality, predicated on the long history of the Enlightenment and its material effects" (*Black Madness*, 14). I also appreciate Pickens's caution against blindly seeing black madness as agentially recuperative, or resistant: "We must be wary of projects that locate resistance on Black mad bodies," she writes, "solely in the service of white bodies (regardless of ability status), avoiding the seduction of ascribing agency at the cost of ignoring material reality" (35).
10. Chandler, *X—The Problem of the Negro*, 23.
11. Glissant, *Poetics of Relation*, 190.
12. Du Bois, *Souls of Black Folk*, 15.
13. Njami, "Issa Samb," 43.
14. Thomas, *Sufism, Mahdism and Nationalism*, 58.
15. Thomas, 65.
16. Kouoh, "In His Own Words," 19–20.
17. Brown, *Black Utopias*, 25, 34.
18. Guèye, "May 1968 in Senegal."
19. On the larger wave of "Marxist Africanism" that unfolded across the continent, of which Diop, Samb, and Senghor were differential players, see Mudimbe, *Idea of Africa*, 42–46.
20. Bianchini, "1968 Years," 191.
21. Quoted in Harney, *In Senghor's Shadow*, 54–63, 120.
22. Enwezor, "Where, What, Who, When," 111–12. See also Enwezor and Okeke-Agulu, *Contemporary African Art since 1980*, 31–32.

23 Harney, *Senghor's Shadow*, 111.
24 Agulu-Okeke, *Postcolonial Modernism*, 89–91.
25 Hassan and Oguibe, "'Authentic/ex-centric' at the Venice Biennale," 73.
26 One of the difficulties of this written work is that much of it was not published at the time Samb wrote it. Whereas Samb did publish a number of pieces in various venues, including Senegalese newspapers and art magazines, such as *Metronome*, many went unpublished until Koyo Kouoh's edited volume, *Word! Word? Word! Issa Samb and the Indecipherable Form* (2013). Even in this text it's difficult in some cases to tell when certain pieces were written.
27 Samb, *On the Art of Recording Trivial Ideas*, 26, 15; Samb, "Poto-Poto Blues," 144.
28 Szwed, *Space Is the Place*, 28. Ra changed his name legally from Herman Blount to Le Sony'r Ra in 1952, although most referred to him by his longtime nickname, Sonny, or what he called his "vibrational name," Sun Ra. For more on Ra's names and naming, see Youngquist, *Pure Solar World* (41); Locke, *Blutopia* (50–51); and especially Szwed, *Space Is the Place* (79–87). One interesting point of convergence is that Samb was also known to many by the stage name "Joe Ouakam," after the neighborhood of Ouakam, where he grew up.
29 Brown, *Black Utopias*, 166.
30 Szwed, *Space Is the Place*, 75–76, 109.
31 Quoted in Szwed, 88.
32 Ra, *Immeasurable Equation*, 447, 255. The first of the two ellipses is in the original.
33 Szwed, *Space Is the Place*, 29–30.
34 Ra, "Why Don't You Turn Again!," 110.
35 Edwards, *Epistrophies*, 144.
36 Sinclair, "Collision of the Suns."
37 Ra, "Your Only Hope Now is a Lie," 98, 107.
38 Ra, "My Music Is Words," 4.
39 Ra, "I Have Set before You Life and Death," 132.
40 Ra, "I Don't Give a Hoot," 96; "The Poor Little Rich One," 101.
41 Ra, "My Music Is Words," 4–5.
42 A single full lecture from Ra's 1971 UC Berkeley course, "The Black Man in the Cosmos," was recorded and has been made available in four parts on YouTube. For more on the course, see Szwed, *Space Is the Place* (294–95); Locke, *Blutopia* (19); and Youngquist, *Pure Solar World* (206–7).
43 Ra, "Berkeley Lecture Part 3."
44 Gill, "Sun Ra," 26.
45 Ra, *Immeasurable Equation*, 93.
46 Ra, "My Music Is Words," 5; "Detroit Black Journal—Sun Ra."
47 Walcott, *Long Emancipation*, 76–77.

48 Kouoh, "In His Own Words," 23–24.
49 For more on this debate, see the preface to Jemima Pierre's *Predicament of Blackness*, xi–xv.
50 Pierre, *Predicament of Blackness*, 38.
51 Quoted in Smith, *Senegal Abroad*, 20.
52 Sarr, *Afrotopia*, 94–95.
53 Moten, "Notes on Passage," 54.
54 Johnson, *Panthers Can't Save Us Now*, 14.
55 Edwards, *Practice of Diaspora*, 14.
56 In March 2019 I found this document, written in French, in Issa Samb's dossier at the Robbins Library at the National Museum of African Art in Washington, DC. The beginning of the two-page essay has no title and only a printed label that reads, "Samb, Issa / 1995." The following is included in the original typewriter text at the end of the document: "Dakar / juillet 95 / Joe Ramanguelissa Ouakam / La Vie a de Longues Jambes." In the absence of clearer identifying material in this document or even online, I take this information to mean that Samb is the author of the text, and that "La Via a de Longues Jambes" is likely the title. However, I should note that Oumou Sy, the Senegalese fashion designer and former member of Laboratoire Agit-Art, premiered her first theater show, titled "La Vie a de Longues Jambes," in 1995. Samb may very well have been a collaborator, and this manifesto could have come from that project. But because the Smithsonian document is unequivocally attributed to Samb and because its style and subject matter closely resemble his politics and prose style, I've chosen to present the essay as if it is Samb's ideas and voice. All translations of this document from the French are my own.
57 Moten, "Case of Blackness," 211; Hartman, *Lose Your Mother*, 234.
58 Cartwright, "Diseases and Peculiarities of the Negro Race," 34.
59 Benjamin, *Arcades Project*, 461n2, 461n6.
60 Eiland and McLaughlin, "Translator's Foreword," xi.
61 Samb, "Deconstructing Time," 244/245. The texts of "Deconstructing Time" and "Poto-Poto Blues" that I consult here are the bilingual versions included in Kouoh's edited volume *Word! Word? Word!* Pagination for "Deconstructing Time" indicates the English on the left page and the French on the right, whereas in "Poto-Poto" the English and French are laid out in two narrow columns side by side on the same page. I'm reading both the French and the English in my analysis, and at times making slight modifications to the English translation to better capture the original.
62 Samb, "Deconstructing Time," 252/253, 258/259.
63 Samb, "Deconstructing Time," 260/261.
64 Samb, "Deconstructing Time," 264/265.

65 Samb, "Deconstructing Time," 268/269.
66 Olaniyan, *Arrest the Music!*, 97, 98.
67 Schmidt-Linsenhoff, "Court in Dakar," 271.
68 For more on the history and evolution of Samb's courtyard, see Harney, *In Senghor's Shadow* (120–21); Grabski, *Art World City* (21–24); and Deliss, "Brother in Arms" (189–91).
69 Diabate, *Naked Agency*, 55.
70 "Un Samedi Apres Midi Chez Joe Ouakam."
71 Hartman, *Wayward Lives, Beautiful Experiments*, 227.
72 Thomas, *Sufism, Mahdism and Nationalism*, 63.
73 Deliss, "Brother in Arms," 193; Thomas, *Sufism, Mahdism and Nationalism*, 63.
74 Samb, "Poto-Poto Blues," 139.
75 "La Cour de Joe Ouakam."
76 Samb, "Poto-Poto Blues," 143.
77 Many of Samb's approaches, I should note, figure in the work of his Agit-Art collaborators. Painter El Hadji Sy, for one, particularly early in his career, imbued his work with a sense of embodied movement by literally placing his own paint-covered feet on his canvases in choreographic configurations. In "La Marche" (1978) white footprints walk off the edge of the canvas, fading as they move away from the initial point of contact, "in search of an alternative universe," as Mamadou Diouf has put it ("El Hadji Sy and the Quest," 138). Movement and escape also figure in the films of Djibril Diop Mambéty, but so does an opacity-generating montage form. His iconic *Touki Bouki* (1973) is filled with Sambian disparate juxtapositions that vector out toward innumerable lines of thought. In one sequence the frame oscillates between footage of, on the one hand, the protagonist standing nude in the back of a convertible as it drives past an abandoned semi-urban landscape, and on the other, dozens of young children running, the camera peering out of a moving car as if the children were chasing this nude figure with his fist raised in a black power salute. But it's the overlaid audio that bridges these disparate montage cells, sounds of a traditional Senegalese wrestling announcer screaming to a cheering crowd, that gives this entire sequence a kind of deliberate, otherworldly opacity reminiscent of the seemingly impenetrable combinations of fragments that constitute any one of Samb's texts.
78 Samb, "Poto-Poto Blues," 137, 141, 137–38.
79 Deliss, "Brother in Arms," 194.
80 Only an English version of this text has been published, as part of dOCUMENTA (13).
81 Samb, *On the Art of Recording Trivial Ideas*, 14.
82 Samb, *On the Art of Recording Trivial Ideas*, 18, 20, 32.

83 Bruce, *How to Go Mad*, 22.
84 Ra, *Immeasurable Equation*, 420.
85 Ra, *Immeasurable Equation*, 426.
86 In her study of Ra's philosophy, Brown notes a fundamental distinction between the "unknown" and the "unknowable": "I use the term *unknowable* instead of *unknown*, for there is no hope that humans could master or conquer or classify this universe in their current epistemological condition" (*Black Utopias*, 160). Although I appreciate this incisive distinction, "unknown" saturates Ra's work. To stay within the philosophical and lexical frame of the work itself, I do retain the term in my own prose in this chapter, but I also use "unknowable," using both interchangeably to evoke Brown's sentiment of the uncolonizability and radical inaccessibility of Ra's visions.
87 Reed, "After the End of the World," 123.
88 Ra, "Your Only Hope Now Is a Lie," 102.
89 Gilroy, *Black Atlantic*, 37.
90 "Sun Ra Interview (Helsinki, 1971)."
91 Corbett, *Extended Play*, 313.
92 Mugge, *Joyful Noise*; "Detroit Black Journal—Sun Ra."
93 For more on how this melding of ancient Egypt and the cosmos figures into Ra's conception of myth, see Graham Locke's chapter in *Blutopia*, "Astro Black: Mythic Future, Mythic Pasts," where he argues that one of the Arkestra's musical subgenres, known as "space chants," are fundamentally similar to the "mythic world" of black spirituals.
94 Walcott, *Long Emancipation*, 76.
95 Cartwright, "Diseases and Peculiarities of the Negro Race," 35.
96 Edwards, *Epistrophies*, 127.
97 Ra, "Your Only Hope Now Is a Lie," 111.
98 Ra, *Immeasurable Equation*, 387.
99 Ra, *Immeasurable Equation*, 181.
100 Olaniyan, *Arrest the Music!*, 98.
101 Dery, "After 50 Years in Jazz."
102 Moten, *In the Break*, 63. The year 1965 was a watershed for "The New Thing," as free jazz came to be known, not just because of Ra's record but because it was also the year John Coltrane recorded *Ascension*. Like "Magic City," Coltrane's title track is a long-form collective improvisation, sharing that free, open, "ocean of sound" feel, with individual voices—including two acoustic bass players—weaving in and out of one another to form a swelling, heaving mass. That year also saw kindred spirits to Ra's *Magic City* in Albert Ayler's influential album *Spiritual Unity* and the formation of the renowned Chicago-based experimental group the Association for the Advancement of Creative Musicians (AACM). However, the free-form influences on Ra likely go back at least to the

late 1950s and early 1960s, with innovative releases such as Cecil Taylor's *Looking Ahead!* (1959) and perhaps especially Ornette Coleman's landmark *Free Jazz: A Collective Improvisation* (1961), a single thirty-seven-minute minimally structured improvisation featuring what Coleman called his "double quartet."

103 Ra, *Immeasurable Equation*, 82, 289.

104 This is clear in the *Immeasurable Equation* volume of collected poetry, where the editors have Ra's originals and revisions of dozens of poems placed side by side, with most revised versions dated in the early 1980s, often a full decade later than the earlier (noticeably less ellipsis-heavy) versions. Interestingly, ellipses also saturate Ra's Chicago broadsides, some of his first writings. See, for example, ". . . . . solution to the negro problem . . . ." and "spo de o de . . . . hoc way . . . . ," collected in Elms and Corbett's edited volume *The Wisdom of Sun Ra*.

105 Ra, *Immeasurable Equation*, 225.

106 Numerology could be an entire subfield in the study of Sun Ra's work. We get some sense of Ra's interest in numbers in his Chicago broadsides, for instance, many of which are collected in *The Wisdom of Sun Ra*, edited by Elms and Corbett. The collection's titular leaflet is a short opaque study on the numbers 1, 2, and 9, making reference to Greek and Hebrew and to how certain numbers and combinations reveal "truth," "semi-truth," and "non-truth." The critical point of entry into Ra's numerology, however, is probably the list of texts from Ra's personal library compiled by John Szwed and included in *Immeasurable Equation*. The stunningly diverse list includes an array of esoteric works that likely would have dealt with numerology in some way, including A. E. Abbot's *Encyclopedia of Numbers*, issues of the nineteenth-century astrology journal *Radix*, and theosophical works by Helena Blavatsky.

107 As with his music, Ra's poetry has drawn comparisons to a host of twentieth-century black writers, including the confluence of science fiction and Egyptology in Ishmael Reed's 1972 novel *Mumbo Jumbo*, and the radical poetics of the Umbra Collective. For more on the relation to Reed, see Szwed, *Space Is the Place* (222), and Locke, *Blutopia* (50). For a more sustained discussion of Ra's relation to other writers, such as the Umbra Collective, Amiri Baraka, Kamau Brathwaite, and Wilson Harris, see chapter 4, "The Race for Space: Sun Ra's Poetry," in Brent Edwards's *Epistrophies*.

108 Ra, *Immeasurable Equation*, 163.

109 Reed, *Freedom Time*, 38, 43.

110 Walcott, *Long Emancipation*, 77.

111 Mackey, *Blue Fasa*, 93.

112 Szwed, *Space Is the Place*, 248.
113 Corbett, *Extended Play*, 309.
114 Bruce, *How to Go Mad*, 170–71.
115 Glissant, *Poetics of Relation*, 190–94.
116 Weheliye, *Phonographies*, 207.
117 "Ibaaku—Djula Dance."
118 Macharia, *Frottage*, 6.

CHAPTER 5. YVONNE VERA, NOVIOLET BULAWAYO, AND THE IMMINENCE OF DREAMING AIR

1 Hunter, "'Shaping the Truth of the Struggle,'" 77.
2 Bryce, "Interview with Yvonne Vera," 221.
3 Vera, *Nehanda*, 92–93.
4 Moten, "Case of Blackness," 211.
5 This chapter focuses on the afterlives of Nehanda's flight, but I do want to point out a wonderful trans-diasporic resonance between the way Vera articulates Nehanda's ecstatic flight from her own body and the various black women mystic figures that Jayna Brown centers in *Black Utopias*. Brown frames the nineteenth-century American itinerant preacher Zilpha Elaw, for example, as inhabiting a "state of ecstasy . . . as self-annihilation, a condition when a centered sense of subjectivity explodes or melts away" (48). Or, a century later, the "ascetic practices" of mystic and jazz harpist Alice Coltrane, who understood "the body [as] a burden and the result of true devotion was the ability to escape the flesh, to be transmuted into formless matter latticed with thought and thought's manifestation as various selves in different dimensions" (62). Although the structures that propelled and animated their ecstatic flights may have been quite disparate, there's a kindred utopian anticipatory desire to flee from the body that connects Vera's account of Nehanda and Brown's characterization of Elaw and Coltrane. A certain diasporic will toward ecstasy and a flight from corporeal devastation links these influential women.
6 Andrade, *Nation Writ Small*, 36, 30.
7 Fanon, *Peau noire, masques blancs*, 91.
8 Mbembe, *On the Postcolony*, 26–27.
9 Mbembe, 40–58. For more on the differential effects of structural adjustment across the continent, see Frederick Cooper, "Development and Disappointment" in *Africa since 1940*. For Zimbabwe specifically, see Clever Mumbengegwi's edited volume *Macroeconomic and Structural Adjustment Policies in Zimbabwe*.
10 Mlambo, *History of Zimbabwe*, 206–23, 215.

11 Mlambo provides a useful overview of the escalations of the crisis in the 2000s and the effects on the vast majority of Zimbabweans in "The Crisis Years, 2000–2008" in *History of Zimbabwe*.
12 Quayson, "Self-Writing," 34–35.
13 *We Need New Names* is part of a twenty-first-century cohort of Zimbabwean fiction that chronicles these sublimated structures of alienation, both on the continent and in diaspora. I'm thinking of Petina Gappah's story "The Cracked, Pink Lips of Rosie's Bridegroom" in the collection *An Elegy for Easterly* (2009), for instance, which revolves around wedding guests' observations of the body of a groom standing at the altar: they see the "sickness [that] screams out its presence from every pore" and the broad smile on his face when he's told about a gift of two hundred million Zimbabwean dollars (161–62). Brian Chikwava's novel *Harare North* (2009) also demonstrates this sublimated alienation, specifically in the hallucinations of the unnamed protagonist, whose traumatic memories of being a member of a pro-Mugabe youth militia catch up to him in London.
14 Fanon, *Peau noire, masques blancs*, 24, 6.
15 Judy, "Fanon's Body of Black Experience," 70.
16 Bryce, "Interview with Yvonne Vera," 221.
17 See, for instance, Imre Szeman's "Who's Afraid of National Allegory?" (2001); Joseph Slaughter's "Master Plans" (2004); and Elleke Boehmer's *Stories of Women* (2005).
18 Andrade, *Nation Writ Small*, 24–25, 36.
19 Anderson, *Imagined Communities*, 7; Jameson, "Third-World Literatures in the Era of Multinational Capitalism," 72.
20 King, *Black Shoals*, 26.
21 Primorac, "The Place of the Woman," 385.
22 Nuttall, "Reading, Recognition and the Postcolonial," 398–99.
23 Vera, *Without a Name*, 34–35. The final two ellipses in this passage are in the original.
24 Muchemwa, "Language, Voice and Presence," 13.
25 Vera, *Without a Name*, 34, 97, 96.
26 Gqola, *Rape*, 43–53.
27 Crenshaw, "Mapping the Margins," 1268–69.
28 Graham, *State of Peril*, 123, 128.
29 Vera, *Without a Name*, 39–40, 37.
30 Quayson, *Calibrations*, 90.
31 Hunter, "'Shaping the Truth of the Struggle,'" 80.
32 Vera, *Without a Name*, 8.
33 Vera, 109.
34 Caruth, *Unclaimed Experience*, 4–6.
35 Vera, *Without a Name*, 25, 88.

36 Hunter, "'Shaping the Truth of the Struggle,'" 80.
37 Bloch, *Principle of Hope*, 49.
38 Moten, *Black and Blur*, 67.
39 Vera, *Without a Name*, 30, 64.
40 Vera, 25–26.
41 Deleuze, "On Spinoza's Concept of Affect."
42 Spinoza, *Ethics*, 165.
43 Berliner, *Soul of Mbira*, 43.
44 Vera, *Without a Name*, 78.
45 Berliner, *Soul of Mbira*, 87.
46 Vera, *Without a Name*, 78, ellipsis in the original.
47 Hartman and Best, "Fugitive Justice," 3.
48 Vera, *Without a Name*, 78.
49 Mackey, "Cante Moro," 191.
50 Fretwell, *Sensory Experiments*, 116; Vera, *Without a Name*, 78. I borrow the term "sympathetic vibrations" from Erica Fretwell, specifically where she describes it phenomenologically—psychoacoustically—in Pauline Hopkins's *Of One Blood*. Although Vera's novel is removed historically, culturally, and politically from Hopkins's, they do share the idea that music can evoke affective vibrations that connect generations and galvanize ancestrality. Fretwell also makes clear the value of examining the sonic and musical dimensions of fiction: "Attending to the sensory dimensions of literary tone helps us engage the materiality of a most diffuse and disembodied affect." Indeed, *Without a Name* similarly renders legible these seemingly invisible affective registers, perhaps allowing us, as readers, to see, as Fretwell speculates of Hopkins's novel, "contained within a psychophysical account of tone . . . the dream of a vibratory subjectivity organized around inflection rather than intentionality, amorphousness rather than agency" (123). See Fretwell, *Sensory Experiments*, 108–23.
51 De Waal, *Politics of Reconciliation*, 47.
52 Vera, *Without a Name*, 78.
53 Vera, 115–16.
54 Hunter, "'Shaping the Truth of the Struggle,'" 83.
55 Hunter, 80.
56 Mbembe, *On the Postcolony*, 197, 199.
57 Bulawayo, *We Need New Names*, 103.
58 Chitando, "Girl Child's Resilience," 117.
59 Cameron, "Finding Her Voice."
60 Ouma, *Childhood in Contemporary Diasporic African Literature*, 7.
61 For a detailed sociological and historical account of the operation, see Maurice Vambe's *The Hidden Dimensions of Operation Murambatsvina*

in Zimbabwe. Anna Chitando ("Girl Child's Resilience") and Polo Moji ("New Names, Translational Subjectivities") also identify the dislocations in Bulawayo's novel with "Operation Murambatsvina," given its historical setting.

62   Bulawayo, *We Need New Names*, 75–76.
63   Bulawayo, 93–94.
64   Achebe, *Things Fall Apart*, 153.
65   Driver, "Writing about Women at the Margins."
66   Bulawayo, *We Need New Names*, 6, 8–9.
67   Bulawayo's novel is part of a cohort of contemporary African transnational migration novels that articulate related formations of fugitive time, in the fundamental sense of associating the end of one's subjection in mind and body with escape to the seeming promised lands of Europe and North America, and inhabiting that release in advance of migration. Such a structure of desire can be found, for example, in the impersonation of Elvis Presley by the protagonist in Chris Abani's *GraceLand* and in the way that Spain can be "smelled" from the Moroccan side of the Strait of Gibraltar by the youth figures in Tahar Ben Jelloun's *Partir*, as well as in the way that the youths in Fatou Diome's *Le Ventre de l'Atlantique* imagine themselves playing professional football in the biggest stadiums of Europe as they play on the beaches of Senegal. For a sense of this in *GraceLand*, see Omelsky, "Chris Abani and the Politics of Ambivalence."
68   Bulawayo, *We Need New Names*, 113.
69   Bakhtin, *The Dialogic Imagination*, 84–85.
70   Mbiti, *African Religions and Philosophy*, 232–33.
71   The term "fugitive science" comes from the work of Britt Rusert, although it takes on a very different constellation of meanings in the context of Zimbabwean divination. Rusert's analysis centers on how nineteenth-century African American scientists, writers, and artists pressed the limits of what constituted scientific inquiry, challenged scientific conceptions of race, and used science to devise novel conceptions of freedom and the human. In the context of Bulawayo's novel, I'm using the term "science" to denote the systematicity of divination to achieve certain ends, to engage with the physical, natural, and spiritual worlds in order to change the way people conceive of the world around them and, in turn, alter personal and communal circumstances. My formulation does overlap with Rusert's in the broad sense of the use of systematic practices in the service of a certain idea of freedom, even if what constitutes freedom, and what constitutes the structures of subjection from which one strives to escape, are very much distinct in their respective American and Zimbabwean contexts. See Rusert, *Fugitive Science* (2017).

72 Bulawayo, *We Need New Names*, 29, 152.
73 Hesse, "Escaping Liberty," 308.
74 Bulawayo, *We Need New Names*, 152.
75 Pietz, "Problem of the Fetish," 10.
76 Bulawayo, *We Need New Names*, 147–48.
77 Sojoyner, "Another Life Is Possible," 526.
78 Edwards, *Practice of Diaspora*, 14, 118.
79 Mbembe, *Sortir*, 224.
80 Mezzadra and Neilson, *Border as Method*, 133, 173.
81 Harney and Moten, *Undercommons*, 51; Mezzadra and Neilson, *Border as Method*, 174.
82 Bulawayo, *We Need New Names*, 152, 186, 227.
83 Bulawayo, 188, 285, 248.
84 Nyambi, Makombe, and Motahane, "Some Kinds of Home," 91.
85 Bulawayo, *We Need New Names*, 249.
86 Nguyen, "Refugeetude," 113–14.
87 Derrida, *Specters of Marx*, 123, 126, 243.
88 Bulawayo, *We Need New Names*, 243.
89 Coly, *Postcolonial Hauntologies*, 15.
90 Coly's analysis more specifically focuses on how discourses of the African female body are shaped by this haunting of colonialism in the postcolonial moment. See, for instance, her examination of the historical figure Sarah Baartman in "Haunted Silences: African Feminist Criticism and the Specter of Sarah Baartman" (*Postcolonial Hauntologies*, 49–86). See also Yogita Goyal's brief allusion to a related hauntological structure in her reading of *We Need New Names*, where she suggests, "Darling keeps finding her friends appear in her imagination in the American mall, thus interrupting her present in spectral fashion" (*Runaway Genres*, 186).
91 Bulawayo, *We Need New Names*, 244.
92 Mezzadra and Neilson, *Border as Method*, 146.
93 Dowling and Inda, "Introduction: Governing Migrant Illegality," 6, 11.
94 Campt, "Black Feminist Futures and the Practice of Fugitivity."
95 Bulawayo, *We Need New Names*, 243.
96 Goyal rightly situates *We Need New Names* among the recent African novels that chart migrations to the United States beyond "those occasioned by the Middle Passage," noting, in the specific case of Bulawayo's novel, that "notions of an afterlife of slavery . . . [as] representing 'living memory'" don't "seem appropriate." I do think there's an explicit and crucial linkage that Bulawayo makes to these histories, however, even if it's not the dominant "afterlife" that structures the novel (*Runaway Genres*, 173, 189).

97   Bulawayo, *We Need New Names*, 223–24, 221.
98   Hartman, *Lose Your Mother*, 234.
99   Bulawayo, *We Need New Names*, 252.
100 Vera, *Nehanda*, 92, 97, 93–94.

CODA. FUGITIVE ETHER

1   Mackey, *Splay Anthem*, 35.

BIBLIOG-
RAPHY

Abani, Chris. *GraceLand*. New York: Farrar, Straus and Giroux, 2004.
Achebe, Chinua. *Things Fall Apart*. New York: Anchor, 1994.
Acholonu, Catherine. "The Home of Olaudah Equiano—A Linguistic and Anthropological Search." *Journal of Commonwealth Literature* 22, no. 1 (1987): 5–16.
Ades, Dawn. "Wifredo Lam and Surrealism." In *Wifredo Lam in North America*, edited by Paula Schulze, 37–48. Milwaukee: Haggerty Museum of Art and Marquette University, 2007.
Agulu-Okeke, Chika. *Postcolonial Modernism: Art and Decolonization in Twentieth-Century Nigeria*. Durham, NC: Duke University Press, 2015.
Akomfrah, John, dir. *Handsworth Songs*. London: Black Audio Film Collective, 1986.
Akomfrah, John, dir. *The Nine Muses*. London: Smoking Dogs Films, 2010.
Akomfrah, John. "On the Borderline." In *The Ghosts of Songs: The Film Art of the Black Audio Film Collective 1982–1998*, edited by Kodwo Eshun and Anjalika Sagar, 198–99. Liverpool: Liverpool University Press, 2007.
Alexander, Elizabeth. *The Black Interior*. Minneapolis: Graywolf, 2004.
Alexander, M. Jacqui. *Pedagogies of Crossing: Meditations on Feminism, Sexual Politics, Memory, and the Sacred*. Durham, NC: Duke University Press, 2006.
Alter, Nora. *The Essay Film after Fact and Fiction*. New York: Columbia University Press, 2018.
Anderson, Benedict. *Imagined Communities: Reflections on the Origin and Spread of Nationalism*. London: Verso, 2006. First published 1983 by Verso (London).
Andrade, Susan. *The Nation Writ Small: African Fictions and Feminisms, 1958–1988*. Durham, NC: Duke University Press, 2011.
Archer-Straw, Petrine. "Eddie Chambers: Interview with Petrine Archer-Straw." In *Run through the Jungle: Selected Writings by Eddie Chambers (Annotations 5)*, 21–31. London: Iniva, 1999.
Arnold, James. "'À l'Afrique' avec Césaire et Lam." In *Aimé Césaire: Poésie, Théâtre, Essais et Discours*, edited by A. James Arnold, 1615–24. Paris: CNRS Éditions and Présence Africaine, 2013.

Auguiste, Reece. "Black Cinema, Poetics and New World Aesthetics." In *The Ghosts of Songs: The Film Art of the Black Audio Film Collective 1982–1998*, edited by Kodwo Eshun and Anjalika Sagar, 152–55. Liverpool: Liverpool University Press, 2007.

Auguiste, Reece, dir. *Mysteries of July*. London: Black Audio Film Collective and Channel Four, 1991.

Auguiste, Reece. "Outline for *Twilight City*." In *The Ghosts of Songs: The Film Art of the Black Audio Film Collective 1982–1998*, edited by Kodwo Eshun and Anjalika Sagar, 165. Liverpool: Liverpool University Press, 2007.

Auguiste, Reece, dir. *Twilight City*. London: Black Audio Film Collective and Channel Four, 1989.

Auguiste, Reece, and Black Audio Film Collective. "Black Independents and Third World Cinema: The British Context." In *The Ghosts of Songs: The Film Art of the Black Audio Film Collective 1982–1998*, edited by Kodwo Eshun and Anjalika Sagar, 162–69. Liverpool: Liverpool University Press, 2007.

Aumont, Jacques. "The Veritable Eye, or the Mobilization of the Gaze." In *The Image in Dispute: Art and Cinema in the Age of Photography*, edited by Dudley Andrew, 231–58. Austin: University of Texas Press, 1999.

Ayler, Albert. *Spiritual Unity*. New York: ESP-Disk', 2009.

Bakhtin, Mikhail. *The Dialogic Imagination: Four Essays*. Edited by Michael Holmquist and translated by Caryl Emerson and Michael Holmquist. Austin: University of Texas Press, 1981.

Baldwin, James. *Go Tell It on the Mountain*. New York: Vintage, 2013. First published 1953 by Knopf (New York).

Bambara, Toni Cade. *The Salt Eaters*. New York: Vintage, 1981. First published 1980 by Random House (New York).

Baucom, Ian. *Specters of the Atlantic: Finance Capital, Slavery, and the Philosophy of History*. Durham, NC: Duke University Press, 2005.

Beavers, Herman. *Geography and the Political Imaginary in the Novels of Toni Morrison*. London: Palgrave, 2018.

Benjamin, Walter. *The Arcades Project*. Edited by Rolf Tiedemann and translated by Howard Eiland and Kevin McLaughlin. Cambridge, MA: Harvard University Press, 1999.

Ben Jelloun, Tahar. *Partir*. Paris: Gallimard, 2006.

Berliner, Paul. *The Soul of Mbira*. Chicago: University of Chicago Press, 1993.

Best, Stephen. *None like Us: Blackness, Belonging, Aesthetic Life*. Durham, NC: Duke University Press, 2018.

Bey, Marquis. "The Trans*-ness of Blackness, the Blackness of Trans*-ness." *TSQ: Transgender Studies Quarterly* 4, no. 2 (2017): 275–95.

Bianchini, Pascal. "The 1968 Years: Revolutionary Politics in Senegal." *Review of African Political Economy* 46, no. 160 (2019): 184–203.

Bloch, Ernst. *The Principle of Hope*, vol. 1. Cambridge, MA: MIT Press, 1986.

Bloch, Ernst. *The Spirit of Utopia*. Translated by Anthony Nassar. Stanford, CA: Stanford University Press, 2000.

Bloch, Ernst. *The Utopian Function of Art and Literature*. Translated by Jack Zipes and Frank Mecklenburg. Cambridge, MA: MIT Press, 1988.

Boehmer, Elleke. *Stories of Women: Gender and Narrative in the Postcolonial Nation*. Manchester: Manchester University Press, 2005.

Bourland, Ian. *Bloodflowers: Rotimi Fani-Kayode, Photography, and the 1980s*. Durham, NC: Duke University Press, 2019.

Boyce Davies, Carole. *Black Women, Writing and Identity: Migrations of the Subject*. London: Routledge, 1994.

Brand, Dionne. *In Another Place, Not Here*. New York: Vintage, 1997.

Brand, Dionne. *A Map to the Door of No Return: Notes to Belonging*. New York: Vintage, 2002.

Branigan, Edward. *Narrative Comprehension and Film*. London: Routledge, 1992.

Brennan, Timothy. "Subaltern Stakes." *New Left Review* 89 (September/October 2014). https://newleftreview.org/issues/ii89/articles/timothy-brennan-subaltern-stakes.

Breton, André. *Fata Morgana*. Buenos Aires: Éditions des Lettres Françaises, 1942.

Breton, André. "Second Manifesto of Surrealism." In *Manifestos of Surrealism*, translated by Richard Seaver and Helen Lane, 117–94. Ann Arbor: University of Michigan Press, 1969.

Broad, the. "Watery Ecstatic Series: Ellen Gallagher." Accessed October 18, 2022. www.thebroad.org/art/ellen-gallagher/watery-ecstatic-series.

Brooks, Daphne. *Bodies in Dissent: Spectacular Performance of Race and Freedom, 1850–1910*. Durham, NC: Duke University Press, 2006.

Brown, Jayna. *Black Utopias: Speculative Life and the Music of Other Worlds*. Durham, NC: Duke University Press, 2021.

Bruce, La Marr Jurelle. *How to Go Mad without Losing Your Mind*. Durham, NC: Duke University Press, 2021.

Bryce, Jane. "Interview with Yvonne Vera." In *Sign and Taboo: Perspectives on the Poetic Fiction of Yvonne Vera*, edited by Robert Muponde and Mandivavarira Maodzwa Taruvinga, 217–26. Harare, Zimbabwe: Weaver, 2002.

Buck-Morss, Susan. *Dreamworld and Catastrophe: The Passing of Mass Utopia in East and West*. Cambridge, MA: MIT Press, 2002.

Bulawayo, NoViolet. *We Need New Names*. New York: Reagan Arthur, 2013.

Cameron, Claire. "Finding Her Voice: An Interview with NoViolet Bulawayo." *Los Angeles Review of Books*. Accessed August 7, 2013. https://lareviewofbooks.org/article/finding-her-voice-an-interview-with-noviolet-bulawayo.

Campt, Tina. "Black Feminist Futures and the Practice of Fugitivity." YouTube. Accessed October 21, 2014. www.youtube.com/watch?v=2ozhqw840PU.

Carby, Hazel. "Becoming Modern Racialized Subjects." *Cultural Studies* 23, no. 4 (2009): 624–57.

Carretta, Vincent. "Olaudah Equiano or Gustavus Vassa? New Light on an Eighteenth-Century Question of Identity." *Slavery and Abolition* 20, no. 3 (1999): 96–105.

Cartwright, Samuel. "Diseases and Peculiarities of the Negro Race." In *The Cause of the South: Selections from* De Bow's Review 1846–1867, edited by Paul Paskoff and Daniel Wilson, 26–43. Baton Rouge: Louisiana State University Press, 1982.

Caruth, Cathy. *Unclaimed Experience: Trauma, Narrative, and History*. Baltimore: Johns Hopkins University Press, 1996.

Cernuschi, Claude. "The Art of Wifredo Lam and the Anthropology of Lucien Lévy-Bruhl and Claude Lévi-Strauss." In *Wifredo Lam: Imagining New Worlds*, edited by Elizabeth Goizueta, 25–68. Chestnut Hill, MA: McMullen Museum of Art and Boston College, 2014.

Cervenak, Sarah. *Wandering: Philosophical Performances of Racial and Sexual Freedom*. Durham, NC: Duke University Press, 2014.

Césaire, Aimé. *Annonciation: Dix Poèmes d'Aimé Césaire et sept eaux-fortes et aquatintes de Wifredo Lam*. Milan: Grafica Uno, 1982.

Césaire, Aimé. "Cahier d'un retour au pays natal (Brentano's 1947)." In *Aimé Césaire: Poésie, Théâtre, Essais et Discours*, edited by A. James Arnold, 101–35. Paris: CNRS Éditions and Présence Africaine, 2013.

Césaire, Aimé. "Cahier d'un retour au pays natal (Présence Africaine 1956)." In *Aimé Césaire: Poésie, Théâtre, Essais et Discours*, edited by A. James Arnold, 186–219. Paris: CNRS Éditions and Présence Africaine, 2013.

Césaire, Aimé. "Cahier d'un retour au pays natal (Volontés 1939)." In *Aimé Césaire: Poésie, Théâtre, Essais et Discours*, edited by A. James Arnold, 74–99. Paris: CNRS Éditions and Présence Africaine, 2013.

Césaire, Aimé. *The Collected Poetry*, bilingual ed. Edited and translated by Clayton Eshleman and Annette Smith. Berkeley: University of California Press, 1993.

Césaire, Aimé. *Moi, laminaire*. Paris: Éditions du Seuil, 1982.

Césaire, Aimé. "Moi, Laminaire." In *The Complete Poetry of Aimé Césaire*, edited by A. James Arnold and Clayton Eshleman. Middletown, CT: Wesleyan University Press, 2017.

Césaire, Aimé. *Notebook of a Return to the Native Land*. Translated by Clayton Eshleman and Annette Smith. Middletown, CT: Wesleyan University Press, 2001.

Césaire, Aimé. *The Original 1939 Notebook of a Return to the Native Land*. Edited by A. James Arnold and Clayton Eshleman. Middletown, CT: Wesleyan University Press, 2013.

Césaire, Aimé. *Retorno al país natal*. Translated by Lydia Cabrera. Preface by Benjamin Péret. Havana, Cuba: Molina y Cía, 1943.

Césaire, Aimé. "Poésie et connaissance." *Tropiques* 12 (1945): 157–70.

Césaire, Aimé. *Une Saison au Congo*. In *Aimé Césaire: Poésie, Théâtre, Essais et Discours*, edited by A. James Arnold, 1112–82. Paris: CNRS Éditions and Présence Africaine, 2013.

Césaire, Suzanne. "Léo Frobenius et le problème des civilisations." *Tropiques* 1 (1941): 27–36.

Chandler, Nahum. *"Beyond This Narrow Now": Or, Delimitations, of W. E. B. Du Bois*. Durham, NC: Duke University Press, 2021.

Chandler, Nahum. *X—The Problem of the Negro as a Problem for Thought*. New York: Fordham University Press, 2014.

Chikwava, Brian. *Harare North*. New York: Vintage, 2009.

Childs, Dennis. "'You Ain't Seen Nothin' Yet': *Beloved*, the American Chain Gang, and the Middle Passage Remix." *American Quarterly* 61, no. 2 (2009): 271–97.

Chion, Michel. *Audio-vision: Sound on Screen*. Translated and edited by Claudia Gorbman. New York: Columbia University Press, 1994.

Chitando, Anna. "The Girl Child's Resilience and Agency in NoViolet Bulawayo's *We Need New Names*." *Journal of Literary Studies* 32, no. 1 (2016): 114–26.

Christian, Barbara. "The Contemporary Fables of Toni Morrison." In *Toni Morrison: Critical Perspectives Past and Present*, edited by Henry Louis Gates and Kwame Anthony Appiah, 59–99. New York: Amistad, 1993.

Christian, Barbara. "Layered Rhythms: Virginia Woolf and Toni Morrison." *Modern Fiction Studies* 39, nos. 3/4 (1993): 483–500.

clipping. "The Deep." 2017. Accessed October 18, 2022. https://clppng.bandcamp.com/album/the-deep-3.

Cobb, Jasmine. *Picturing Freedom: Remaking Black Visuality in the Early Nineteenth Century*. New York: New York University Press, 2015.

Coleman, Ornette. *Free Jazz: A Collective Improvisation*. New York: Atlantic Jazz, 1987.

Coltrane, John. *Ascension*. New York: Impulse, 2000.

Coly, Ayo. *Postcolonial Hauntologies: African Women's Discourses of the Female Body*. Lincoln: University of Nebraska Press, 2019.

Cooper, Frederick. *Africa since 1940: The Past of the Present*. New York: Cambridge University Press, 2002.

Copeland, Huey. *Bound to Appear: Art, Slavery, and the Site of Blackness in Multicultural America*. Chicago: University of Chicago Press, 2013.

Corbett, John. *Extended Play: Sounding off from John Cage to Dr. Funkenstein*. Durham, NC: Duke University Press, 2012.

"La Cour de Joe Ouakam." Vimeo. Uploaded by Sara Maurin Kane. May 19, 2017. https://vimeo.com/218153567.

Crawley, Ashon. *Blackpentecostal Breath: The Aesthetics of Possibility*. New York: Fordham University Press, 2017.

Crenshaw, Kimberlé. "Mapping the Margins: Intersectionality, Identity Politics, and Violence against Women of Color." *Stanford Law Review* 43, no. 6 (1991): 1241–99.

Dangarembga, Tsitsi. *Nervous Conditions*. Cypress: Seal, 1998.

Davis, Gregson. *Aimé Césaire*. New York: Cambridge University Press. 1997.

Deleuze, Gilles. *Cinema 1: The Movement-Image*. Translated by Hugh Tomlinson and Barbara Habberjam. Minneapolis: University of Minnesota Press, 1986.

Deleuze, Gilles. *Cinema 2: The Time-Image*. Translated by Hugh Tomlinson and Robert Galeta. Minneapolis: University of Minnesota Press, 1989.

Deleuze, Gilles. "On Spinoza's Concept of Affect: Cours Vincennes 24/01/1978." Translated by Emilie and Julien Deleuze. Academia. Accessed March 19, 2015. www.academia.edu/15948754/gilles_deleuze_lecture_transcripts_on_spinozas_concept_of_affect.

Deliss, Clémentine. "Brother in Arms: Laboratoire Agit-Art and Tenq in the 1980s." In *El Hadji Sy: Painting, Performance, Politics*, edited by Clémentine Deliss and Yvette Mutumba, 188–225. Berlin: Diaphanes, 2015.

Depestre, René. "Itinéraire d'un langage, de L'Afrique à la Caraïbe: Entretien avec Aimé Césaire." *Europe* 612 (1980): 8–19.

Derrida, Jacques. *Specters of Marx: The State of the Debt, the Work of Mourning and the New International*. Translated by Peggy Kamuf. London: Routledge, 2006.

Dery, Mark. "After 50 Years in Jazz the Bandleader from Saturn Finally Lands a Major Record Deal." *Keyboard*, March 1991, 39–46.

"Detroit Black Journal—Sun Ra." YouTube. Uploaded by ukvibeorg. March 21, 2011. www.youtube.com/watch?v=mNgwzYoKzlM.

De Waal, Victor. *The Politics of Reconciliation: Zimbabwe's First Decade*. Trenton, NJ: Africa World, 1990.

Diabate, Naminata. *Naked Agency: Genital Cursing and Biopolitics in Africa*. Durham, NC: Duke University Press, 2020.

Diome, Fatou. *Le Ventre de l'Atlantique*. Paris: Anne Carrière, 2003.

Diouf, Mamadou. "El Hadji Sy and the Quest for a Post-négritude Aesthetics." In *El Hadji Sy: Painting, Performance, Politics*, edited by Clémentine Deliss and Yvette Mutumba, 134–40. Berlin: Diaphanes, 2015.

Dowling, Julie, and Jonathan Inda. "Introduction: Governing Migrant Illegality." In *Governing Immigration through Crime: A Reader*, edited by Julie Dowling and Jonathan Inda, 1–36. Stanford, CA: Stanford University Press, 2013.

Drexciya. *The Quest*. Detroit: Submerge Records, 1997.

Driver, Alice. "Writing about Women at the Margins: An Interview with NoViolet Bulawayo." *Vela: Written by Women*. Accessed February 19, 2017. http://velamag.com/writing-about-women-at-the-margins-an-interview-with-noviolet-bulawayo.

Du Bois, W. E. B. *The Souls of Black Folk*. Oxford: Oxford University Press, 2007.

Edelman, Lee. *No Future: Queer Theory and the Death Drive*. Durham, NC: Duke University Press, 2004.

Edwards, Brent Hayes. *Epistrophies: Jazz and the Literary Imagination*. Cambridge, MA: Harvard University Press, 2017.

Edwards, Brent Hayes. *The Practice of Diaspora: Literature, Translation, and the Rise of Black Internationalism*. Cambridge, MA: Harvard University Press, 2003.

Eiland, Howard, and Kevin McLaughlin. "Translators' Foreword." In *The Arcades Project* by Walter Benjamin, edited by Rolf Tiedemann, ix–xiv. Cambridge, MA: Harvard University Press, 1999.

Eisenstein, Sergei. "A Dialectic Approach to Film Form." In *Film Form: Essays in Film Theory*, edited and translated by Jay Leyda, 45–63. San Diego: Harcourt, 1977.

English, Darby. *To Describe a Life: Notes from the Intersection of Art and Race Terror*. New Haven, CT: Yale University Press, 2019.

Enwezor, Okwui. "Where, What, Who, When: A Few Notes on 'African' Conceptualism." In *Global Conceptualism: Points of Origin, 1950s–1980s*, edited by Luis Camnitzer and László Beke, 109–17. New York: Queens Museum of Art, 1999.

Enwezor, Okwui, and Chika Okeke-Agulu. *Contemporary African Art since 1980*. Bologna: Damiani, 2009.

Equiano, Olaudah. *The Interesting Narrative of the Life of Olaudah Equiano, or Gustavus Vassa, the African*. New York: Norton, 2001.

Eshun, Kodwo. "An Absence of Ruins: John Akomfrah in Conversation with Kodwo Eshun." In *The Ghosts of Songs: The Film Art of the Black Audio Film Collective 1982–1998*, edited by Kodwo Eshun and Anjalika Sagar, 130–39. Liverpool: Liverpool University Press, 2007.

Eshun, Kodwo. "Untimely Meditations: Reflections on the Black Audio Film Collective." *Nka: Journal of Contemporary African Art* 19 (2004): 38–45.

Eshun, Kodwo, and Anjalika Sagar, eds. *The Ghosts of Songs: The Film Art of the Black Audio Film Collective 1982–1998*. Liverpool: Liverpool University Press, 2007.

Fabian, Johannes. *Time and the Other: How Anthropology Makes Its Object*. New York: Columbia University Press, 1983.

Fani-Kayode, Rotimi. "Traces of Ecstasy." In *Rotimi Fani-Kayode & Alex Hirst*, edited by Mark Sealy and Jean Loup Pivin, 4–11. London and Paris: Autograph and Éditions Revue Noire, 1996.

Fanon, Frantz. *Black Skin, White Masks*. Translated by Charles Markmann. New York: Grove, 1967.

Fanon, Frantz. *Peau noire, masques blancs*. Paris: Points, 1971.

Fleetwood, Nicole. *Marking Time: Art in the Age of Mass Incarceration*. Cambridge, MA: Harvard University Press, 2020.

Fleming, Julius. *Black Patience: Performance, Civil Rights, and the Unfinished Project Emancipation*. New York: New York University Press, 2022.

Fretwell, Erica. *Sensory Experiments: Psychophysics, Race, and the Aesthetics of Feeling*. Durham, NC: Duke University Press, 2020.

Fryer, Peter. *Staying Power: The History of Black People in Britain*. London: Pluto, 2010.

Fusco, Coco. *Young, British & Black: The Work of Sankofa and Black Audio Film Collective*. London: Hallwalls, 1988.

Gappah, Petina. *An Elegy for Easterly*. London: Faber and Faber, 2009.

Gaskins, Nettrice. "Deep Sea Dwellers: Drexciya and the Sonic Third Space." *Shima* 10, no. 2 (2016): 68–80.

Genette, Gérard. *Narrative Discourse: An Essay in Method*. Translated by Jane Lewin. Ithaca, NY: Cornell University Press, 1980.

Genette, Gérard. *Narrative Discourse Revisited*. Translated by Jane Lewin. Ithaca, NY: Cornell University Press, 1988.

Gikandi, Simon. "Globalization and the Claims of Postcoloniality." *South Atlantic Quarterly* 100, no. 3 (2002): 627–58.

Gill, Andy. "Sun Ra: Space Is the Place." *New Musical Express*, August 7, 1982, 24–26.

Gilroy, Paul. *The Black Atlantic: Modernity and Double Consciousness*. Cambridge, MA: Harvard University Press, 1993.

Glissant, Édouard. *Caribbean Discourse: Selected Essays*. Translated by J. Michael Dash. Charlottesville: University of Virginia Press, 1989.

Glissant, Édouard. *Le Discours antillais*. Paris: Gallimard, 1997.

Glissant, Édouard. *Poetics of Relation*. Translated by Betsy Wing. Ann Arbor: University of Michigan Press, 1997.

Goldfinch Gallery. "Sherwin Ovid: Breath between Ledgers Measured." Accessed October 18, 2022. https://goldfinch-gallery.com/publications/9-sherwin-ovid-breath-between-ledgers-measured.

Goyal, Yogita. *Runaway Genres: The Global Afterlives of Slavery*. New York: New York University Press, 2019.

Gqola, Pumla Dineo. *Rape: A South African Nightmare*. Johannesburg: MFBooks, 2015.

Grabski, Joanna. *Art World City: The Creative Economy of Artists and Urban Life in Dakar*. Bloomington: Indiana University Press, 2017.

Graham, Lucy. *State of Peril: Race and Rape in South African Literature*. Oxford: Oxford University Press, 2012.

Greene Space at WNYC & WQXR, the. "Black Icons of Art: Thelma Golden and Rujeko Hockley." YouTube. Accessed October 7, 2019. www.youtube.com/watch?v=kq3cWtSymdo.

Green-Simms, Lindsey. *Queer African Cinemas*. Durham, NC: Duke University Press, 2022.

Griffin, Farah Jasmine. "Textual Healing: Claiming Black Women's Bodies, the Erotic and Resistance in Contemporary Novels of Slavery." *Callaloo* 19, no. 2 (1996): 519–36.

Guèye, Omar. "May 1968 in Senegal." Verso. Accessed June 14, 2018. www.versobooks.com/blogs/3880-may-1968-in-senegal.

Gumbs, Alexis Pauline, and Julia Roxanne Wallace. "Something Else to Be." In *No Tea, No Shade*, edited by E. Patrick Johnson, 380–94. Durham, NC: Duke University Press, 2016.

Hale, Thomas. "Structural Dynamics in a Third World Classic: Aimé Césaire's *Cahier d'un retour au pays natal*." *Yale French Studies* 53 (1976): 163–74.

Hale, Thomas. "Two Decades, Four Versions: The Evolution of Aimé Césaire's *Cahier d'un retour au pays natal*." In *When the Drumbeat Changes*, edited by Carolyn Parker and Stephen Arnold, 186–95. Washington, DC: Three Continents, 1981.

Hall, Stuart. "From Scarman to Stephen Lawrence." *History Workshop Journal* 48 (1999): 187–97.

Hall, Stuart. "Frontlines and Backyards: The Terms of Change." In *Black British Culture and Society: A Reader*, edited by Kwame Owusu, 135–39. London: Routledge, 2000.

Hall, Stuart. *The Hard Road to Renewal: Thatcherism and the Crisis of the Left*. London: Verso, 1988.

Hall, Stuart. "Preface." In *Black Britain: A Photographic History*, edited by Paul Gilroy, 5–10. London: SAQI, 2007.

Hall, Stuart. "The Question of Cultural Identity." In *Modernity and Its Futures*, edited by Stuart Hall, David Held, and Anthony McGrew, 273–326. Cambridge: Polity, 1992.

Hall, Stuart. "Racism and Reaction." *Five Views of Multi-racial Britain*. BBC TV, 1978.

Hall, Stuart. "Whose Heritage? Un-settling 'The Heritage,' Re-imagining the Post-nation." *Third Text* 49 (2000): 3–13.

Hall, Stuart, Chas Critcher, Tony Jefferson, John Clarke, and Brian Roberts. *Policing the Crisis: Mugging, the State, and Law and Order*. London: Palgrave Macmillan, 1978.

Harbaoui, Zouhour. "Joe Ouakam: L'Intelligence artistic à la vie à la mort." *Leral*, 2010. www.leral.net/JOE-OUAKAM-L-intelligence-artistique-a-la-vie-a-la-mort_a8973.html.

Harney, Elizabeth. *In Senghor's Shadow: Art, Politics, and the Avant-Garde in Senegal, 1960–1995*. Durham, NC: Duke University Press, 2004.

Harney, Stefano, and Fred Moten. *The Undercommons: Fugitive Planning & Black Study*. New York: Minor Compositions, 2013.

Harper, Phillip Brian. *Are We Not Men? Masculine Anxiety and the Problem of African-American Identity*. Oxford: Oxford University Press, 1996.

Hartman, Saidiya. *Lose Your Mother: A Journey along the Atlantic Slave Route*. New York: Farrar, Straus and Giroux, 2007.

Hartman, Saidiya. *Scenes of Subjection: Terror, Slavery, and Self-Making in Nineteenth-Century America*. Oxford: Oxford University Press, 1997.

Hartman, Saidiya. *Wayward Lives, Beautiful Experiments: Intimate Histories of Social Upheaval*. New York: Norton, 2019.

Hartman, Saidiya, and Stephen Best. "Fugitive Justice." *Representations* 92, no. 1 (2005): 1–15.

Hassan, Salah M., and Olu Oguibe. "'Authentic/ex-centric' at the Venice Biennale: African Conceptualism in Global Contexts." *African Arts* 34, no. 4 (2001): 64–96.

Heidegger, Martin. *Being and Time*. Translated by Joan Stambaugh. New York: State University of New York Press, 2010.

Hénane, René. *Glossaire des termes rares dans l'oeuvre d'Aimé Césaire*. Paris: Jean Michel Place, 2004.

Henderson, Mae. "Toni Morrison's *Beloved*: Re-membering the Body as Historical Text." In *Comparative American Identities: Race, Sex, and Nationality in the Modern Text*, edited by Hortense Spillers, 62–86. London: Routledge, 1991.

Hesse, Barnor. "Escaping Liberty: Western Hegemony, Black Fugitivity." *Political Theory* 42 (2014): 288–313.

Hesse, Barnor, and Juliet Hooker. "Introduction: On Black Political Thought inside Global Black Protest." *South Atlantic Quarterly* 116, no. 3 (2017): 443–56.

Higgs, Catherine. *Chocolate Islands: Cocoa, Slavery, and Colonial Africa*. Athens: Ohio University Press, 2012.

hooks, bell, and Cornel West. *Breaking Bread: Insurgent Black Intellectual Life*. Boston: South End, 1991.

Hopkins, Pauline. *Of One Blood*. New York: Washington Square, 2004.

Howard, Jonathan. "Swim Your Ground: Towards a Black and Blue Humanities." *Atlantic Studies* (June 27, 2022): 1–23. https://doi.org/10.1080/14788810.2021.2015944.

Hunter, Eva. "'Shaping the Truth of the Struggle': An Interview with Yvonne Vera." *Current Writing* 10, no. 1 (1998): 75–86.

Husserl, Edmund. *On the Phenomenology of the Consciousness of Internal Time (1893–1917)*. Translated by John Brough. Dordrecht: Kluwer, 1991.

"Ibaaku—Djula Dance." YouTube. Uploaded by Ibaaku. November 19, 2015. www.youtube.com/watch?v=XBdBPiRywIA.

Ibrahim, Habiba. *Black Age: Oceanic Lifespans and the Time of Black Life*. New York: New York University Press, 2021.

Irele, Abiola. "Commentary and Notes." In *Journal of a Homecoming / Cahier d'un retour au pays natal*, edited by Abiola Irele and translated by Gregson Davis, 151–294. Durham, NC: Duke University Press, 2017.

Jackson, Zakiyyah Iman. *Becoming Human: Matter and Meaning in an Antiblack World*. New York: New York University Press, 2020.

Jagose, Annamarie. *Orgasmology*. Durham, NC: Duke University Press, 2012.

Jaji, Tsitsi. *Africa in Stereo: Modernism, Music, and Pan-African Solidarity*. Oxford: Oxford University Press, 2014.

Jameson, Fredric. *Archaeologies of the Future: The Desire Called Utopia and Other Science Fictions*. London: Verso, 2005.

Jameson, Fredric. "Third-World Literatures in the Era of Multinational Capitalism." *Social Text* 15 (1986): 65–88.

"John Akomfrah—Why History Matters | TateShots." YouTube. Uploaded by Tate. July 2, 2015. www.youtube.com/watch?v=jDJYyG7jKV0.

Johnson, Cedric. *The Panthers Can't Save Us Now: Debating Left Politics and Black Lives Matter*. London: Verso, 2022.

Johnson, Walter. "On Agency." *Journal of Social History* 37, no. 1 (2003): 113–24.

Jones, Bessie, and Audrey Vinson. "An Interview with Toni Morrison." In *Conversations with Toni Morrison*, edited by Danille Taylor-Guthrie, 171–87. Jackson: University Press of Mississippi, 1994.

Judy, Ronald. "Fanon's Body of Black Experience." In *Fanon: A Critical Reader*, edited by Lewis Gordon, T. Deanan Sharpley-Whiting, and Renée White, 53–73. New York: Wiley-Blackwell, 1996.

Judy, Ronald. *Sentient Flesh: Thinking in Disorder, Poiesis in Black*. Durham, NC: Duke University Press, 2020.

Julien, Isaac, dir. *Territories*. London: Sankofa Film and Video, 1984.

Julien, Isaac, and Maureen Blackwood, dirs. *The Passion of Remembrance*. London: Sankofa Film and Video, 1986.

Keeling, Kara. *Queer Times, Black Futures*. New York: New York University Press, 2019.

Keeling, Kara. *The Witch's Flight: The Cinematic, the Black Femme, and the Image of Common Sense*. Durham, NC: Duke University Press, 2007.

King, Tiffany Lethabo. *The Black Shoals: Offshore Formations of Black and Native Studies*. Durham, NC: Duke University Press, 2019.

Koselleck, Reinhart. *Futures Past: On the Semantics of Historical Time*. New York: Columbia University Press, 2004.

Kouoh, Koyo. "In His Own Words: Issa Samb's Ultimately Decipherable Form." In *Word! Word? Word! Issa Samb and the Undecipherable Form*, edited by Koyo Kouoh, 7–34. London: Sternberg, 2013.

Lepecki, André. "Choreopolice and Choreopolitics: or, the Task of the Dancer." *Drama Review* 57, no. 4 (2013): 13–27.

Levine, Caroline. *Forms: Whole, Rhythm, Hierarchy, Network*. Princeton, NJ: Princeton University Press, 2015.

Lightfoot, Natasha. *Troubling Freedom: Antigua and the Aftermath of British Emancipation*. Durham, NC: Duke University Press, 2015.

Linsley, Robert. "Wifredo Lam: Painter of Négritude." *Art History* 11, no. 4 (1988): 527–44.

Livermon, Xavier. *Kwaito Bodies: Remastering Space and Subjectivity in Post-apartheid South Africa*. Durham, NC: Duke University Press, 2020.

Locke, Graham. *Blutopia: Visions of the Future and Revisions of the Past in the Work of Sun Ra, Duke Ellington, and Anthony Braxton*. Durham, NC: Duke University Press, 1999.

Lorde, Audre. "Uses of the Erotic: The Erotic as Power." In *Sister Outsider*, 53–59. Trumansburg, NY: Crossing, 2007.

Lovejoy, Paul. "Autobiography and Memory: Gustavus Vassa, Alias Olaudah Equiano, the African." *Slavery and Abolition* 27, no. 3 (2006): 317–47.

Lyotard, Jean-François. "Acinema." In *Narrative, Apparatus, Ideology: A Film Studies Reader*, edited by Philip Rosen, 349–60. New York: Columbia University Press, 1986.

Macharia, Keguro. *Frottage: Frictions of Intimacy across the Black Diaspora*. New York: New York University Press, 2019,

Mackey, Nathaniel. "Bedouin Hornbook." In *From a Broken Bottle Traces of Perfume Still Emanate*, 191–94. New York: New Directions, 2010.

Mackey, Nathaniel. *Blue Fasa*. New York: New Directions, 2015.

Mackey, Nathaniel. "Cante Moro." In *Paracritical Hinge: Essays, Talks, Notes, Interviews*, 181–98. Madison: University of Wisconsin Press, 2005.

Mackey, Nathaniel. *Splay Anthem*. New York: New Directions, 2006.

Mambéty, Djibril Diop. *Touki Bouki*. New York: Kino Video, 1973.

Marechera, Dambudzo. *The House of Hunger*. Long Grove, IL: Waveland, 2013.

Marriott, David. "Inventions of Existence: Sylvia Wynter, Frantz Fanon, Sociogeny, and 'The Damned.'" CR: *The New Centennial Review* 11, no. 3 (2012): 45–90.

Marriott, David. *Whither Fanon: Studies in the Blackness of Being*. Stanford, CA: Stanford University Press, 2018.

Marriott, David. "The X of Sacrifice: Fanon, Shariati, Bataille." Public lecture, Pennsylvania State University, State College, PA, October 30, 2018.

Marx, Karl. "The Eighteenth Brumaire of Napoleon Bonaparte." In *The Marx-Engels Reader*, edited by Robert Tucker, 594–617. New York: Norton, 1978.

Maximin, Daniel. *Césaire et Lam: Insolites bâtisseurs*. Bordeaux: HC Éditions, 2011.

Mbembe, Achille. *Critique of Black Reason*. Translated by Laurent Dubois. Durham, NC: Duke University Press, 2017.

Mbembe, Achille. *On the Postcolony*. Berkeley: University of California Press, 2001.

Mbembe, Achille. *Sortir de la grande nuit*. Paris: Éditions la Découverte, 2010.

Mbiti, John. *African Religions and Philosophy*. New York: Anchor, 1969.

McCune, Jeffrey. "The Queerness of Blackness." QED 2, no. 2 (2015): 173–76.

McCune, Jeffrey. *Sexual Discretion: Black Masculinity and the Politics of Passing*. Chicago: University of Chicago Press, 2014.

McDowell, Deborah. "'The Self and the Other': Reading Toni Morrison's *Sula* and the Black Female Text." In *Critical Essays on Toni Morrison*, edited by Nellie McKay, 77–89. Boston: G.K. Hall, 1988.

McKay, Nellie. "An Interview with Toni Morrison." In *Conversations with Toni Morrison*, edited by Danille Taylor-Guthrie, 138–55. Jackson: University Press of Mississippi, 1994.

Mercer, Kobena. "Becoming Black Audio: An Interview with John Akomfrah and Trevor Mathison." *Black Camera* 6, no. 2 (2015): 79–93.

Mercer, Kobena. "Post-colonial Trauerspiel." In *The Ghosts of Songs: The Film Art of the Black Audio Film Collective 1982–1998*, edited by Kodwo Eshun and Anjalika Sagar, 43–73. Liverpool: Liverpool University Press, 2007.

Mercer, Kobena. *Travel & See: Black Diaspora Art Practices since the 1980s*. Durham, NC: Duke University Press, 2016.

Mercer, Kobena. *Welcome to the Jungle*. London: Routledge, 1994.
Mercer, Kobena. "Wifredo Lam's Afro-Atlantic Routes." In *Wifredo Lam: The Ey Exhibition*, edited by Catherine David, 22–35. London: Tate, 2016.
Mezzadra, Sandro, and Brett Neilson. *Border as Method, or, the Multiplication of Labor*. Durham, NC: Duke University Press, 2013.
Miller, Christopher. "The (Revised) Birth of Négritude: Communist Revolution and 'the Immanent Negro' in 1935." PMLA 125, no. 3 (2010): 743–49.
Miller, J. Hillis. "Boundaries in *Beloved*." *symploke* 15, nos. 1/2 (2007): 24–39.
Mlambo, Alois. *A History of Zimbabwe*. Cambridge: Cambridge University Press, 2014.
Moji, Polo Belina. "New Names, Translational Subjectivities: (Dis)location and (Re)naming in NoViolet Bulawayo's *We Need New Names*." *Journal of African Cultural Studies* 27, no. 2 (2015): 181–90.
Morrison, Toni. *Beloved*. New York: Vintage, 2004.
Morrison, Toni. *The Bluest Eye*. New York: Plume, 1994.
Morrison, Toni. *Love*. New York: Knopf, 2003.
Morrison, Toni. *Paradise*. New York: Vintage, 2014.
Morrison, Toni. *Song of Solomon*. New York: Knopf, 1995.
Morrison, Toni. *Sula*. New York: Plume, 1982.
Morrison, Toni. "Unspeakable Things Unspoken: The Afro-American Presence in American Literature." *Michigan Quarterly Review* 28, no. 1 (1989): 1–34.
Mosquera, Gerardo. "'My Painting Is an Act of Decolonization': An Interview with Wifredo Lam by Gerardo Mosquera (1980)." *Journal of Surrealism and the Americas* 3, nos. 1–2 (2009): 1–8.
Moten, Fred. *Black and Blur*. Durham, NC: Duke University Press, 2017.
Moten, Fred. "Blackness and Nothingness (Mysticism in the Flesh)." *South Atlantic Quarterly* 112, no. 4 (2013): 737–80.
Moten, Fred. "The Case of Blackness." *Criticism* 50, no. 2 (2008): 177–218.
Moten, Fred. *In the Break: The Aesthetics of the Black Radical Tradition*. Minneapolis: University of Minnesota Press, 2003.
Moten, Fred. "Notes on Passage (The New International of Sovereign Feelings)." *Palimpsest: A Journal on Women, Gender, and the Black International* 3, no. 1 (2014): 51–74.
Moten, Fred. *The Universal Machine*. Durham, NC: Duke University Press, 2018.
Mroz, Matila. *Temporality and Film Analysis*. Edinburgh: Edinburgh University Press, 2012.
Muchemwa, Kizito. "Language, Voice and Presence in *Under the Tongue* and *Without a Name*." In *Sign and Taboo: Perspectives on the Poetic Fiction of Yvonne Vera*, edited by Robert Muponde and Mandivavarira Maodzwa Taruvinga, 3–14. Harare, Zimbabwe: Weaver, 2002.
Mudimbe, V. Y. *The Idea of Africa*. Bloomington: Indiana University Press, 1994.
Mudimbe, V. Y. *The Invention of Africa*. Bloomington: Indiana University Press, 1988.
Mugge, Robert, dir. *A Joyful Noise*. Pottstown: MVD Visual, 2015.

Mumbengegwi, Clever, ed. *Macroeconomic and Structural Adjustment Policies in Zimbabwe*. London: Palgrave, 2002.

Muñoz, José Esteban. *Cruising Utopia: The Then and There of Queer Futurity*. New York: New York University Press, 2009.

Murillo, John, III. *Impossible Stories: On the Space and Time of Black Destructive Creation*. Columbus: Ohio State University Press, 2021.

Musser, Amber. *Sensational Flesh: Race, Power and Masochism*. New York: New York University Press, 2014.

Nash, Jennifer. *The Black Body in Ecstasy: Reading Race, Reading Pornography*. Durham, NC: Duke University Press, 2014.

Nelson, Steven. "Transgressive Transcendence in the Photographs of Rotimi Fani-Kayode." *Art Journal* 64, no. 1 (2005): 4–19.

Nguyen, Vinh. "Refugeetude: When Does a Refugee Stop Being a Refugee?" *Social Text* 37, no. 2 (2019): 109–31.

Njami, Simon. "Issa Samb: The Stranger." In *Word! Word? Word! Issa Samb and the Undecipherable Form*, edited by Koyo Kouoh, 35–50. London: Sternberg, 2013.

Nuttall, Sarah. "Reading, Recognition and the Postcolonial." *Interventions* 3, no. 3 (2011): 391–404.

Nyambi, Oliver, Rodwell Makombe, and Nonki Motahane. "Some Kinds of Home: Home, Transnationality and Belonging in NoViolet Bulawayo's *We Need New Names*." *Forum for Modern Language Studies* 56, no. 1 (2020): 78–95.

Nyong'o, Tavia. *Afro-fabulations: The Queer Drama of Black Life*. New York: New York University Press, 2018.

Olaniyan, Tejumola. *Arrest the Music! Fela and His Rebel Art and Politics*. Bloomington: Indiana University Press, 2004.

Omelsky, Matthew. "Chris Abani and the Politics of Ambivalence." *Research in African Literatures* 42, no. 4 (2011): 84–96.

Otolith Group, the. "Hydra Decapita." 2010. Accessed October 18, 2022. https://otolithgroup.org/index.php?m=project&id=3.

Ouma, Christopher. *Childhood in Contemporary Diasporic African Literature*. Cham: Palgrave, 2020.

Ové, Horace, dir. *Pressure*. London: British Film Institute, 1975.

Owusu, Akosua Adoma. *Drexciya*. 2010. Accessed October 18, 2022. https://akosuaadoma.com/artwork/2948371-Drexciya.html.

Owusu, Kwesi. "The Struggle for a Radical Black Political Culture: An Interview with A. Sivanandan." In *Black British Culture and Society: A Reader*, edited by Kwesi Owusu, 453–62. London: Routledge, 2000.

Patterson, Orlando. *Slavery and Social Death: A Comparative Study*. Cambridge, MA: Harvard University Press, 1982.

Pestre de Almeida, Lilian. *Aimé Césaire: Cahier d'un retour au pays natal*. Paris: L'Harmattan, 2012.

Pickens, Therí Alyce. *Black Madness :: Mad Blackness*. Durham, NC: Duke University Press, 2019.
Pierre, Jemima. *The Predicament of Blackness: Postcolonial Ghana and the Politics of Race*. Chicago: University of Chicago Press, 2013.
Pietz, William. "The Problem of the Fetish." RES: *Anthropology and Aesthetics* 9 (1985): 5–17.
Pinto, Samantha. *Difficult Diasporas: The Transnational Feminist Aesthetic of the Black Atlantic*. New York: New York University Press, 2013.
Power, Nina. "Counter-media, Migration, Poetry: Interview with John Akomfrah." *Film Quarterly* 65, no. 2 (2011): 59–63.
Primorac, Ranka. "The Place of the Woman Is the Place of the Imagination." In *Emerging Perspectives on Yvonne Vera*, edited by Helen Cousins and Pauline Dodgson-Katiyo, 375–90. Trenton, NJ: Africa World, 2012.
Quashie, Kevin. *Black Aliveness, or a Poetics of Being*. Durham, NC: Duke University Press, 2021.
Quashie, Kevin. *The Sovereignty of Quiet: Beyond Resistance in Black Culture*. New Brunswick, NJ: Rutgers University Press, 2012.
Quayson, Ato. *Aesthetic Nervousness: Disability and the Crisis of Representation*. New York: Columbia University Press, 2007.
Quayson, Ato. *Calibrations: Reading for the Social*. Minneapolis: University of Minnesota Press, 2003.
Quayson, Ato. "Self-Writing and Existential Alienation in African Literature: Achebe's *Arrow of God*." *Research in African Literatures* 42, no. 2 (2011): 30–45.
Quintata, Sergio. "Aimé Césaire y Wifredo Lam: Un diálogo caribeño entre la poesía y la pintura." *Anuario del Colegio de Estudios Latinamericanos* 3, no. 28 (2011): 235–42.
Ra, Sun. *Atlantis*. New York: Evidence Music, 1993.
Ra, Sun. "Berkeley Lecture Part 3." YouTube. Uploaded by Sun Ra Music Channel. Accessed June 23, 2014. www.youtube.com/watch?v=lw51E3_BF9s&t=1495s.
Ra, Sun. *The Heliocentric Worlds of Sun Ra*, vol. 2. New York: ESP-Disk', 2010.
Ra, Sun. "I Don't Give a Hoot. . . . ." In *The Wisdom of Sun Ra: Sun Ra's Polemical Broadsheets and Streetcorner Leaflets*, edited by Anthony Elms and John Corbett, 96. Chicago: WhiteWalls, 2006.
Ra, Sun. "I Have Set before You Life and Death—Choose Life." In *The Wisdom of Sun Ra: Sun Ra's Polemical Broadsheets and Streetcorner Leaflets*, edited by Anthony Elms and John Corbett, 132. Chicago: WhiteWalls, 2006.
Ra, Sun. *The Immeasurable Equation*, edited by James Wolf and Hartmut Geerken. Norderstedt: Waitawhile, 2005.
Ra, Sun. *Jazz by Sun Ra*. Cambridge: Transition Records, 1957.
Ra, Sun. *The Magic City*. New York: Evidence Music, 1993.
Ra, Sun. "My Music Is Words." *Cricket: Black Music in Evolution* 1 (1968): 4–11.
Ra, Sun. *Pathways to Worlds Unknown*. New York: Modern Harmonic, 2019.

Ra, Sun. "The Poor Little Rich One: The Prince of This World. . . . ." In *The Wisdom of Sun Ra: Sun Ra's Polemical Broadsheets and Streetcorner Leaflets*, edited by Anthony Elms and John Corbett, 101–2. Chicago: WhiteWalls, 2006.

Ra, Sun. "Why Don't You Turn Again!" In *The Wisdom of Sun Ra: Sun Ra's Polemical Broadsheets and Streetcorner Leaflets*, edited by Anthony Elms and John Corbett, 108–10. Chicago: WhiteWalls, 2006.

Ra, Sun. *The Wisdom of Sun Ra: Sun Ra's Polemical Broadsheets and Streetcorner Leaflets*, edited by Anthony Elms and John Corbett. Chicago: WhiteWalls, 2006.

Ra, Sun. "Your Only Hope Now Is a Lie." *Hambone*, no. 2 (1982): 98–114.

Reed, Anthony. "After the End of the World: Sun Ra and the Grammar of Utopia." *Black Camera* 5, no. 5 (2013): 118–39.

Reed, Anthony. *Freedom Time: The Poetics and Politics of Black Experimental Writing*. Baltimore: Johns Hopkins University Press, 2014.

Ricoeur, Paul. *Time and Narrative*, vol. 1. Translated by Kathleen McLaughlin and David Pellauer. Chicago: University of Chicago Press, 1984.

Ricoeur, Paul. *Time and Narrative*, vol. 2. Translated by Kathleen McLaughlin and David Pellauer. Chicago: University of Chicago Press, 1985.

Ricoeur, Paul. *Time and Narrative*, vol. 3. Translated by Kathleen Blamey and David Pellauer. Chicago: University of Chicago Press, 1988.

Roberts, Neil. *Freedom as Marronage*. Chicago: University of Chicago Press, 2015.

Robinson, Cedric. *Black Marxism: The Making of the Black Radical Tradition*. Chapel Hill: University of North Carolina Press, 2000.

Rodney, Walter. *How Europe Underdeveloped Africa*. London: Verso, 2018.

Ross, Marlon. "Camping the Dirty Dozens: The Queer Resources of Black Nationalist Invective." *Callaloo* 23, no. 1 (2000): 290–312.

Rotenstein, David S. "Jazz Pianist Sun Ra Attuned to the Music of the Cosmos." *Atlanta Daily News*, April 18, 1992. www.historian4hire.net/ziggy/sunra.htm.

Rowell, Charles. "It Is through Poetry That One Copes with Solitude: An Interview with Aimé Césaire." *Callaloo* 31, no. 4 (2008): 989–97.

Royster, Francesca. *Sounding like a No-No: Queer Sounds and Eccentric Acts in the Post-soul Era*. Ann Arbor: University of Michigan Press, 2012.

Rusert, Britt. *Fugitive Science: Empiricism and Freedom in Early African American Culture*. New York: New York University Press, 2017.

Samatar, Sofia. "An Account of the Land of Witches." In *Tender: Stories*, 147–66. Northampton, MA: Small Beer, 2017.

Samatar, Sofia. "Cities of Emerald, Deserts of Gold." In *Tender: Stories*, 142–46. Northampton, MA: Small Beer, 2017.

Samatar, Sofia. *A Stranger in Olondria*. Northampton, MA: Small Beer, 2013.

Samb, Issa. "The Best Marxist Is Dead." Performance as part of *Black Power! In Tribute to Fred Hampton*, curated by Jean Michel Bruyère and LFKs Collective. Center for the Study of Race, Politics, and Culture, University of Chicago, Chicago, August 13, 2013.

Samb, Issa. "Deconstructing Time." In *Word! Word? Word! Issa Samb and the Undecipherable Form*, edited by Koyo Kuouh, 240–80. London: Sternberg, 2013.

Samb, Issa. "Life Has Long Legs." Unpublished manuscript, 1995.

Samb, Issa. *On the Art of Recording Trivial Ideas, in the Form of a Project of Placing, Displacing, and Replacing the Concept in Its Environment with a View to Precipitating Its Fall*. Kassel: dOCUMENTA (13), 2012.

Samb, Issa. "Poto-Poto Blues." In *Word! Word? Word! Issa Samb and the Undecipherable Form*, edited by Koyo Kuouh, 129–50. London: Sternberg, 2013.

"Un Samedi Après Midi Chez Joe Ouakam." YouTube. Uploaded by Tamsir Ndir. February 21, 2012. www.youtube.com/watch?v=pTAKayrh51Y.

Sarr, Felwine. *Afrotopia*. Translated by Drew Burk and Sarah Jones-Boardman. Minneapolis: University of Minnesota Press, 2019.

Sartre, Jean-Paul. "Orphée Noir." In *Anthologie de la nouvelle poésie nègre et malgache de langue française*, edited by Léopold Sédar Senghor. Paris: Presses Universitaires de France, 1948.

Schmidt-Linsenhoff, Viktoria. "The Court in Dakar: Political Aesthetics in the Post-colony." In *Art History and Fetishism Abroad: Global Shiftings in Media and Methods*, edited by Gabriele Genge and Angela Stercken, 271–88. Bielefeld, Germany: Transcript Verlag, 2014.

Scott, Darieck. *Extravagant Abjection: Blackness, Power, and Sexuality in the African American Literary Imagination*. New York: New York University Press, 2010.

Scott, David. *Omens of Adversity: Tragedy, Time, Memory, Justice*. Durham, NC: Duke University Press, 2014.

Sessolo, Simone. "An Epic of Riots: The Multitude as Hero in *Handsworth Songs*." *Journal of Popular Culture* 47, no. 4 (2014): 742–59.

Sexton, Jared. "'The Curtain of the Sky': An Introduction." *Critical Sociology* 36, no. 1 (2010): 11–24.

Sexton, Jared. "The Social Life of Social Death: On Afro-Pessimism and Black Optimism." *InTensions* 5 (2011): 1–47.

Sexton, Jared. "Unbearable Blackness." *Cultural Critique* 90 (2015): 159–78.

Shabazz, Menelik, dir. *Burning an Illusion*. London: British Film Institute, 1981.

Sharpe, Christina. *In the Wake: On Blackness and Being*. Durham, NC: Duke University Press, 2016.

Shikeith. *The Moment You Doubt Whether You Can Fly, You Cease Forever to Be Able to Do It*. Shikeith.com, 2014. https://shikeith.com/the-moment-you-doubt-whether-you-can-fly.

Sinclair, John. "Collision of the Suns." *Warren-Forest Sun*, April 1, 1967. https://aadl.org/node/192498.

Sivanandan, A. *A Different Hunger: Writings on Black Resistance*. London: Pluto, 1982.

Slaughter, Joseph. "Master Plans: Designing (National) Allegories of Urban Space and Metropolitan Subjections for Postcolonial Kenya." *Research in African Literatures* 35, no. 1 (2004): 30–51.

Smith, Maya Angela. *Senegal Abroad: Linguistic Borders, Racial Formations, and Diasporic Imaginaries.* Madison: University of Wisconsin Press, 2020.

Sojoyner, Damien. "Another Life Is Possible: Black Fugitivity and Enclosed Spaces." *Cultural Anthropology* 32, no. 4 (2017): 514–36.

Soldi, Rafael. "Q&A: Shikeith." Strange Fire. www.strangefirecollective.com/qa-shikeith.

Soyinka, Wole. *Death and the King's Horseman.* Edited by Simon Gikandi. New York: Norton, 2003. First published 1975 by Eyre Methuen (London).

Soyinka, Wole. *Myth, Literature and the African World.* Cambridge: Cambridge University Press, 1976.

Spillers, Hortense. "A Hateful Passion, a Lost Love: Three Women's Fiction." In *Black, White, and in Color: Essays on American Literature and Culture*, 93–118. Chicago: University of Chicago Press, 2003.

Spillers, Hortense. "The Idea of Black Culture." *CR: The New Centennial Review* 6, no. 3 (2006): 7–28.

Spillers, Hortense. "Mama's Baby, Papa's Maybe: An American Grammar Book." In *Black, White, and in Color: Essays on American Literature and Culture*, 203–29. Chicago: University of Chicago Press, 2003.

Spinoza, Baruch. *Ethics.* Translated and edited by G. H. R. Parkinson. Oxford: Oxford University Press, 2000.

Stephens, Michelle, and Sandra Stephens. "Embodied/Disembodied." In *Time: A Vocabulary of the Present*, edited by Joel Burges and Amy Elias, 255–80. New York: New York University Press, 2016.

Stokes Sims, Lowery. *Wifredo Lam and the International Avant-Garde, 1923–1982.* Austin: University of Texas Press, 2002.

"Sun Ra Interview (Helsinki, 1971)." YouTube. Uploaded by Miguel Patrício. August 13, 2013. www.youtube.com/watch?v=AMMWNwVhq5k.

Szeman, Imre. "Who's Afraid of National Allegory? Jameson, Literary Criticism, Globalization." *South Atlantic Quarterly* 100, no. 3 (2001): 803–27.

Szwed, John. *Space Is the Place: The Lives and Times of Sun Ra.* Boston: Da Capo, 1998.

Taylor, Cecil. *Looking Ahead!* Berkeley, CA: Original Jazz Classics, 1990.

Thomas, Douglas. *Sufism, Mahdism and Nationalism: Limamou Laye and the Layennes of Senegal.* London: Bloomsbury, 2013.

Tinsley, Omise'eke Natasha. "Black Atlantic, Queer Atlantic: Queer Imaginings of the Middle Passage." *GLQ* 14, nos. 2/3 (2008): 191–215.

Tinsley, Omise'eke Natasha. *Ezili's Mirrors: Imagining Black Queer Genders.* Durham, NC: Duke University Press, 2018.

Tinsley, Omise'eke Natasha. *Thiefing Sugar: Eroticism between Women in Caribbean Literature.* Durham, NC: Duke University Press, 2010.

Vambe, Maurice. *The Hidden Dimensions of Operation Murambatsvina in Zimbabwe.* Harare, Zimbabwe: Weaver, 2008.

Vera, Yvonne. *Nehanda.* Toronto: TSAR, 2007.

Vera, Yvonne. *Without a Name* and *Under the Tongue*. New York: Farrar, Straus and Giroux, 2002.
Vergès, Françoise. *Monsters and Revolutionaries: Colonial Family Romance and Métissage*. Durham, NC: Duke University Press, 1999.
Wahlberg, Malin. *Documentary Time: Film and Phenomenology*. Minneapolis: University of Minnesota Press, 2008.
Walcott, Rinaldo. *The Long Emancipation: Moving toward Black Freedom*. Durham, NC: Duke University Press, 2021.
Walcott, Rinaldo. "Somewhere out There: The New Black Queer Theory." In *Blackness and Sexualities*, edited by Michelle Wright and Antje Schuhmann, 29–40. Berlin: LIT Verlag, 2007.
Walcott, Rinaldo, Christina Sharpe, Keguro Macharia, and Zakiyyah Jackson. "Diaspora, Humanism and the Global Project of Black Freedom." Inaugural Del & Wanita Smyth Lecture on Peace, Justice and Human Security, York University Virtual Event, February 5, 2021.
Warren, Calvin. *Ontological Terror: Blackness, Nihilism, and Emancipation*. Durham, NC: Duke University Press, 2018.
Weheliye, Alexander. *Habeas Viscus: Racializing Assemblages, Biopolitics, and Feminist Theories of the Human*. Durham, NC: Duke University Press, 2014.
Weheliye, Alexander. *Phonographies: Grooves in Sonic Afro-modernity*. Durham, NC: Duke University Press, 2005.
Wenzel, Jennifer. *Bulletproof: Afterlives of Anticolonial Prophecy in South Africa and Beyond*. Chicago: University of Chicago Press, 2009.
Wilder, Gary. *Freedom Time: Négritude, Decolonization, and the Future of the World*. Durham, NC: Duke University Press, 2015.
Wilderson, Frank. "Grammar & Ghosts: The Performative Limits of African Freedom." *Theatre Survey* 50, no. 1 (2009): 119–25.
Wilderson, Frank. *Red, White & Black: Cinema and the Structure of U.S. Antagonisms*. Durham, NC: Duke University Press, 2010.
Wright, Michelle M. *Physics of Blackness: Beyond the Middle Passage Epistemology*. Minneapolis: University of Minnesota Press, 2015.
Wynter, Sylvia. "Beyond the Word of Man: Glissant and the New Discourse of the Antilles." *World Literature Today* 63, no. 4 (1989): 637–48.
Wynter, Sylvia. "One Love—Rhetoric of Reality?—Aspects of Afro-Jamaicanism." *Caribbean Studies* 12, no. 3 (1972): 64–97.
Wynter, Sylvia. "Unsettling the Coloniality of Being/Power/Truth/Freedom: Towards the Human, after Man, Its Overrepresentation—An Argument." *CR: The New Centennial Review* 3, no. 3 (2003): 257–337.
Young, Kevin. *The Grey Album*. Minneapolis: Graywolf, 2012.
Youngquist, Paul. *A Pure Solar World: Sun Ra and the Birth of Afrofuturism*. Austin: University of Texas Press, 2016.

INDEX

Page numbers in italics indicate figures

abjection, 22, 169, 201, 215n74
absolution, 10, 12, 35, 47, 51, 60, 96, 207
aesthetics, 3, 27, 207; global black, 170; Césaire's, 73, 85, 88, 91, 94–95, 220n35; crisis, 171; Lam's, 64, 85, 88, 91; Ra's, 135, 142, 148, 158, 160–61, 169; Samb's, 135, 139, 142, 148, 158, 169; speculative, 212n54
Africa, 4, 18–19, 27, 32; Black Audio Film Collective and, 110; Césaire and, 66–67, 70, 72, 93; colonial ideologies on, 152; East, 17, 214n61; race in, 144–45; Samb and, 138–39; sub-Saharan, 175–76; West, 20, 131, 213n58, 214n61. *See also* Senegal; South Africa
African diasporic cultures, 8, 13, 27, 159
agency, 103, 210n17, 226n9, 234n50; contingent, 7; narrative, 55; orgasm as site of, 58
Akomfrah, John, 99–100, 105, 107, 112, 115–16, 122, 129, 222n6; *The Nine Muses*, 222n13
alienation, 11, 31, 114, 173–77, 179–84, 186, 191–93, 200, 233n13; Césaire and, 66, 72; Fanon on, 22–23, 176; in *Handsworth Songs*, 103; drapetomania and, 161; natal, 5; release from, 48. *See also* disalienation
Allen, Marshall, 163, 167
anamnesis, 180, 199
anachronism, 46–47; narrative, 28, 37, 57

anachrony, 38, 46, 60; narrative, 38, 45–46, 50
analepsis, 39, 43, 46, 49–50, 55–57, 59; narrative, 28, 37
ancestral belonging, 19, 31, 178
Andrade, Susan, 174, 178
antiblackness, 11–12, 101, 117, 123, 135
anticipation, 3–4, 8–10, 14–16, 72, 115, 151, 179, 206, 215n74; in *Beloved* (Morrison), 53–55, 58–59; Black Audio Film Collective and, 100, 102, 104, 105, 114; of disalienation, 23, 177; ease and, 28, 34, 36–37, 45, 48; in Fani-Kayode's work, 123–24; fugitive, 194–95; in *Notebook of a Return to the Native Land* (Césaire), 68, 79, 83–85, 91–92; prolepsis and, 46; in Ra's work, 159, 161–62, 164–65, 167–68; in Samb's work, 156–58; in *Sula* (Morrison), 47–49, 51, 213n54; of the unknown, 25; utopian desire and, 39. *See also* Bloch, Ernst
Atlantic, 19, 75, 88, 171; black, 15; black queer, 90; postwar, 102
Auguiste, Reece, 15, 100, 107, 115, 222n6
authority, 224n37; black subjection and, 40; colonial, 176; discursive, 118; masculine, 178; monumentality and, 39
autochthony, 19, 181, 189, 196, 203

Bakhtin, Mikhail, 15, 194
Baraka, Amiri, 111, 231n107
Baucom, Ian, 13

Beloved (Morrison), 28, 33–44, 46, 52–56, 174, 213n54, 216–17n13; anachrony in, 60; migration in, 194; orgasm in, 57–59, 84; temporality of subjection in, 217n19; temporality of wounding in, 73; violence in, 200

beyondness, 2–3, 18, 157, 206–8; in Fanon's *Black Skin White Masks*, 23–26; in Morrison's work, 33, 36, 51, 55; in Césaire's work, 94–95, 97; in Black Audio's films, 117, 120, 122, 126, 130; in Samb's work, 154–57; in Ra's work, 158–60; in Vera's work, 173, 177, 187

Black Audio Film Collective, 15, 27, 61, 98–99, 130–31, 223n31; archival images and, 105; *Handsworth Songs*, 29, 100–21, 129, 174, 194, 222n6, 222n13, 224n35, 224n37; *Mysteries of July*, 223n28; *Twilight City*, 15, 29, 100–102, 106–14, 121–29, 150, 183, 200, 222n6. *See also* Akomfrah, John; Auguiste, Reece; Mathison, Trevor

black beyond, the. *See* beyondness

black body, the, 37, 44, 90, 97, 99, 129; Black Audio Film Collective and, 112, 116; historical trauma and, 73; materiality of, 9, 41; subjection time and, 40

black life, 5–6, 10–11, 19, 24, 27, 41–45, 115, 119, 128, 135, 207–8; aesthetic disorder and, 171; in America, 210n17; in Britain, 100–101, 104–5; Césaire and, 88, 95, 97; as commodity, 116; disalienation and, 177; disposability of, 2, 63; Equiano and, 21–22; flesh of, 33; global, 20; modernity and, 211n41; police and, 224n37; precariousness of, 121; Ra and, 142, 161; refusal and, 146; subjection of, 40; transcendence for, 8; violence and, 206

blackness, 6, 10, 13, 42, 61, 63, 90–91, 100, 109–11, 122, 129–30, 202, 207–8, 223n26, 226n9; in Césaire's poetics, 67, 219n19; 1980s British coalitional, 29, 110, 130, 223n30; criminalization of, 113; discourses on, 66; disposability of, 93; *Handsworth Songs* and, 116, 119–20; as menace, 106; nonbeing and, 24, 34, 64; overdetermined, 99; pathologized, 23, 177; potentialities of, 11; queerness and, 88; Ra and, 142–44, 146; racialization of, 108; Samb and, 146–48; subjection of, 45, 118; subjection time and, 40; subjugation of, 101; utopian opacity of, 135; vestibule of, 74, 78; violence and, 3; wounded flesh of, 71–72, 89; woundedness of, 85, 118

Black Panther Party, 146; British, 109

black studies, 6, 8, 12–14, 26–27, 134; American, 19; global, 12, 31, 215n78; melancholic turn in, 44; nonlinear accounts of historical time in, 211n41

black subjection time, 40, 42, 217n19

Bloch, Ernst, 10, 20, 31, 184, 187; on anticipatory consciousness, 9; on hunger, 79–80, 82; messianism of, 97. *See also* self-preservation

body, the, 6, 10, 13, 15, 25, 61, 132–33, 151, 156, 174, 179, 199, 207, 232n5; anticipation and, 9, 32; in the Arkestra's music, 168; Black Audio Film Collective and, 99–100; colonial interpellation and, 177; flesh and, 51, 71, 116, 211n31, 220n35; homoeroticism and, 123; materiality of, 48, 64, 76, 79, 183; Morrison's novels and, 33–39, 52–53, 56; nonbeing and, 22, 99; in *Notebook of a Return to the Native Land* (Césaire), 63–65, 71, 73–74, 76–78, 80–83, 88, 91–92, 94, 97; orgasm and, 58–59; pain and, 3, 24, 45, 171; in Ra's work, 168; subjection and, 173; as threshold surface, 48–49; time and, 16, 31, 182; trauma and, 45, 179; utopian desire and, 29; in *We Need New Names* (Bulawayo), 191–93, 194, 196; *Without a Name* (Vera) and, 184; wounds of, 121

Boykins, Ronnie, 163, 167

Brand, Dionne, 6, 10–11, 25, 157

Breton, André, 65, 69–70

Brooks, Daphne, 9, 55

Brown, Jayna, 11, 13–14, 25, 137, 140, 212n47, 230n86, 232n5

Bruce, La Marr Jurelle, 22, 55, 134, 157, 169, 211n42
Bulawayo, NoViolet, 9, 27, 174–76, 178–79, 204. See also *We Need New Names*
Butler, Octavia, 14, 96, 212n54

Cabrera, Lydia, 63, 70
Campt, Tina, 11, 88
capital, 6, 44, 101, 105, 150–51; finance, 125; French, 137; global, 2, 176; human, 197; white, 40
Cartwright, Samuel, 30, 132–33, 149, 161, 169. See also drapetomania
Caruth, Cathy, 44, 116, 182
catastrophe, 13, 72
Césaire, Aimé, 19, 27, 65, 97–98, 149, 206, 219n1, 219n9, 220n35; *Annonciation*, 96–97, 222n83; *nègre*, 66–68, 76–77, 219–20n19; *A Season in the Congo*, 66, 79; queer poetics of, 86–91. See also *Notebook of a Return to the Native Land*
Césaire, Suzanne, 65, 93
Chandler, Nahum, 135, 220n31
Christian, Barbara, 41, 46
chronotope, 15, 194
colonialism, 11–13, 22, 25, 66, 110, 174, 192, 195, 200; afterlives of, 63; African female body and, 236n90; logics of, 24, 69; Manichaean structure of, 144; in Martinique, 94; mental illness and, 134; phenomenology of violence of, 190; settler, 134–35, 145, 171, 187, 214n61. See also alienation; Fanon, Frantz
Coltrane, Alice, 14, 232n5
Coltrane, John, 187, 230n102
Coly, Ayo, 200, 211n41, 215n78, 236n90
contingency, 7, 23, 69, 193
Crawley, Ashon, 11, 212n47
crisis, 61, 151; aesthetics, 171; avant-garde and, 30, 63; collectivity and, 192; economic, 109, 223n26; of normative thought and belief, 142; postcolonial, 195, 211n41; in Zimbabwe, 174, 233n11
Cuba, 27, 63, 69–70

Dasein, 8, 72, 101
decolonization, 2, 24–25, 63, 176, 215n78
Deleuze, Gilles, 103, 105, 115, 184
democracy, 95; liberal, 2
departmentalism/departmentalization, 94–96
Derrida, Jacques, 97, 199–200, 203. See also specter (Derrida)
desire, 2–3, 9–11, 13, 20, 31, 33, 39–40, 53, 61, 100, 119, 128, 171, 179, 188–89, 199, 225n71; anticipatory, 1, 16, 76, 78–79, 81, 85, 93, 159, 173, 183–84, 187, 192, 205, 232n5; in *Beloved* (Morrison), 46, 57–59; body as site of, 36; for disalienation, 177; embodied, 112, 116; ecstatic, 101; Fani-Kayode and, 122–23; fugitive, 88, 105, 118, 130, 198, 202, 204; fugitive time and, 16, 37, 200; corporeal, 38; in *Notebook of a Return to the Native Land*, 64–65, 72, 76, 78, 81–84, 91; otherwise, 14, 47–48, 65, 212n47; politics of, 26; queer, 6, 125; Samb's, 158; structures of, 178, 196, 200, 235n67; in *Sula* (Morrison), 47, 49–51; temporality of, 29. See also utopian desire
diaspora, 5, 11–12, 18–19, 30, 32, 100, 114, 133, 148, 200, 203–4, 206, 209n14, 223n31; alienation and, 233n13; black, 171; black queer, 111; black queer Atlantic and, 90; black women and, 180; ease and, 60; nation and, 31, 178, 196–97; social life in, 45
diegesis, 46, 114, 121–23, 128, 183. See also nondiegesis
Diome, Fatou, 32; *Le Ventre de l'Atlantique*, 235n67
Diop, Omar Blondin, 138, 153–54, 226n19
disalienation, 23, 29, 65–66, 79, 92, 175, 177; *Without a Name* (Vera) and, 183–84, 186
disposability, 2, 25, 101, 107, 129
divination, 19, 31, 194–95; Zimbabwean, 235n71
drapetomania, 30, 132–33, 161

Drexciya, 21, 214n63
Du Bois, W. E. B., 136, 157

ease, 10, 34, 37–39, 46, 54–56, 200, 216n11; otherwise, 28, 36–37, 49, 51–53, 55; transient, 35–37, 45, 47, 48–50, 52, 57, 59–60, 80; utopian, 36–37, 45, 51–52, 60
easefulness, 28, 34, 37–38, 40, 48–49, 61; otherwise, 57; utopian, 37, 46–47
Edelman, Lee, 89–90
Edwards, Brent Hayes, 5, 68, 142, 148, 196–97, 202, 220n19; *Epistrophies*, 231n107
Elaw, Zilpha, 137, 232n5
emancipation, 24–25, 28, 36, 41–42, 45, 94, 98, 212n47; time of long, 211n41
Equiano, Olaudah, 19–26, 55, 158, 167, 201, 206, 213n58
errantry, 19, 114, 151, 153

Fani-Kayode, Rotimi, 29, 99, 122–26, 128–29, 150
Fanon, Frantz, 12, 25–26, 38, 150, 157–58, 181, 203, 211n41, 215n74; *Black Skin, White Masks*, 7, 22–24, 108, 175, 215n66; disalienation and, 177; *The Wretched of the Earth*, 134. *See also* alienation; nonbeing
Fela Anikulapo-Kuti, 151–52, 162
flesh, 11, 16, 33, 37, 50–51, 67, 76–78, 82, 84, 92, 97, 116, 206, 210–11n31, 220n35; escape from, 206, 232n5; hieroglyphics of, 75–76, 85; rotting, 57, 73, 206; scarred, 56; time and, 15, 194; violence and, 10; wounded, 10, 71–74, 79, 89, 97
Floyd, George, 2, 208
freedom, 3, 5, 8–9, 13, 20–25, 36, 41, 133, 149, 151, 155, 207, 224n37, 235n71; of absolute illegibility, 135; beyond, 25, 157; black, 7, 132; Césaire on, 82, 95; easefulness and, 61; excessive, 22, 51; fugitive time and, 10, 15–16, 35; fugitivity and, 7, 12, 32; gratuitous, 11; *Handsworth Songs* and, 118, 121; Ra on, 142, 159, 161, 168; *Twilight City* and, 121–22, 126, 128–29; *We Need New Names* (Bulawayo) and, 202, 206; *Without a Name* (Vera) and, 182–85, 188–89, 208
Freud, Sigmund, 44, 182, 211n41
fugitive consciousness, 7–8, 20, 214n65
fugitive time consciousness, 4, 134–35, 150, 158, 161, 170, 177; Black Audio Film Collective and, 112; black British, 102; in *We Need New Names* (Bulawayo), 31, 193, 195, 197–99, 203; in *Without a Name* (Vera), 31, 173, 179, 189. *See also* Ra, Sun; Samb, Issa
fugitivity, 6–8, 11–12, 19, 22, 26, 32, 55, 79, 120, 140, 169, 174, 179, 183, 196, 206–7, 214n65; alternative social vision of, 81; analytic of, 18; border, 197; genealogy of, 136; marronage and, 209n14; refugee and, 199; sonic, 187; kinetic, 120
funk, 144, 161, 167–68
futurity, 3; heterosexual reproductive, 89

gender, 83, 85, 224n35; nonconformity, 129
Genette, Gérard, 37, 45–47, 52, 121, 216n9; story time, 46, 49, 55–56, 60. *See also* analepsis; narrative time; prolepsis
Gilroy, Paul, 15, 159, 212n47
Glissant, Édouard, 44–45, 60, 84–85, 114, 133–35, 148, 170–71. *See also* errantry; opacity
global black studies, 12, 31, 215n78
Goyal, Yogita, 236n90, 236n96
Griffin, Farah Jasmine, 58–59

Hall, Stuart, 102, 106, 109, 110, 130, 223n26
Hartman, Saidiya, 5, 7–8, 14, 22, 24–25, 36–37, 40, 43, 105, 149, 154, 202, 212n47, 215n78. *See also* redress; wayward, the
hauntology, 199, 200, 211n41, 215n78
Heidegger, Martin, 8, 101. *See also* thrownness
Henderson, Mae, 54, 56
Hesse, Barnor, 2, 195
homophobia, 123, 135; state-sanctioned, 129
Hopkinson, Nalo, 31, 212n54

262 INDEX

hunger, 29, 62, 196; Bloch on, 79; in *Notebook of a Return to the Native Land* (Césaire), 65, 74, 80–82

Ibrahim, Habiba, 14, 211n41, 217n19
illegibility, 55, 133, 135, 151
Irele, Abiola, 78, 88

Jackson, Zakiyyah, 23, 96, 215n78
Jacobs, Harriet, 20, 208
Jaji, Tsitsi, 5, 100
Jameson, Fredric, 12, 178
Jim Crow, 5, 136
Judy, Ronald, 177, 220n31

Keeling, Kara, 14, 125, 211n41
Kouoh, Koyo, 137, 144, 227n26, 228n61

Laboratoire Agit-Art, 138–40, 228n56
Lam, Wifredo, 27, 65–66, 68–69, 94, 219n1; *Annonciation*, 96, 222n83; influence on Césaire, 86–87; *The Jungle*, 69–70, 85, 87; queer aesthetics of, 86–87, 90; sketches for *Notebook of a Return to the Native Land* (Césaire), 28, 61–64, 66, 69–71, 73–80, 82–88, 91–93, 96–97, 219n1
land, 19, 41, 84, 103, 173–74, 178, 181, 189, 196, 198, 203; ancestral, 31, 174, 185; in *Notebook of a Return to the Native Land*, 73–75, 78, 80; ownership, 42
Lascars, 108–10, 128, 130
liberation, 7, 66, 68, 89, 95, 189; collective, 94; Fanon on, 24
linear time, 12, 38, 86, 89, 211n41; historicism and, 23–24

Macharia, Keguro, 5, 22, 26, 129, 171, 211n41
Mackey, Nathaniel, 14, 22, 167, 187, 208, 214n65
madness, 30, 55, 131, 133–34, 136, 161, 169, 171, 195, 226n9; supposed, 137, 141, 148–49, 151; veneer of, 168. *See also* Bruce, La Marr Jurelle; Ra, Sun; Samb, Issa
marronage, 8, 19, 209n14, 214n65

Martinique, 6, 27, 62–65, 72, 75, 94–95, 98
Marx, Karl, 95–96
masculinity, 181; black queer, 4; normative tropes of, 86
materiality, 83, 143; of affect, 234n50; of the black body, 9, 41; of the body, 9, 48, 64, 76, 79, 97, 183; of sound, 186
Mathison, Trevor, 100, 111, 114, 126, 128–29
Mbembe, Achille, 5, 13, 25, 175–76, 190–91, 196
Mbiti, John, 194–95, 214n61
memory, 4, 8, 11, 13–15, 28–29, 61, 99–100, 188, 203; archival images as reservoirs of, 105; collective, 119, 201; living, 236n96; traumatic, 49–50, 76, 174, 188; unconscious, 45, 120; utopian desire and, 39
Mercer, Kobena, 70, 109, 111, 116, 119, 123–24
messianism, 97
middle passage, 14, 20–21, 44–45, 75, 213n58, 236n96; epistemology, 13
migration, in *We Need New Names*, 174, 189, 194, 200, 202; from West Indies to Britain postwar, 109, 222n13; in *Handsworth Songs*, 102; in contemporary African fiction, 235n67; in *Without a Name*, 183–84
Mlambo, Alois, 176, 233n11
modernity, 15, 159, 211n41; Atlantic, 13; colonial, 14; European, 144, 161
montage, 131, 170, 229n77; Black Audio Film Collective and, 29, 100, 102, 105, 115–16; fugitive time and, 4; in *Handsworth Songs*, 29, 104–5, 112, 115–19, 121, 129; Samb and, 135, 150, 153–55, 158, 161; in *Twilight City*, 108–9, 112, 122; Walter Benjamin and, 150
monumental time, 39–41, 43, 45
Morrison, Toni, 27–28, 34, 39–41, 44–46, 74, 216n9, 216n11, 216n13, 217n19; *The Bluest Eye*, 34, 38, 42; early novels of, 10, 35–36, 80; fugitive time and, 38. *See also Beloved* (Morrison); ease; easefulness; *Sula* (Morrison)

INDEX 263

Moten, Fred, 22, 72, 88, 122, 134, 197; on black fugitivity, 7–8, 146, 149, 183; on black optimism, 11
Mudimbe, V. Y., 24, 226n19
Mugabe, Robert, 187–88, 192
Muñoz, José Esteban, 89–90, 123
Murillo, John, 44, 217n19

narrative time, 38, 43, 60, 175; in *Another Place, Not Here*, 10; in *Beloved* (Morrison), 46, 52, 59; in *Sula* (Morrison), 46, 48–50; of *Without a Name*, 182
nation, the, 102, 173–74, 178, 196, 201, 203
négritude, 28, 30, 65–66, 68, 70, 77, 84, 91; Senghorian, 138, 144. See also Césaire, Aimé
Nehanda, 26, 30–31, 172–73, 177–78, 189, 203, 206–7, 232n5
New London, 29, 100, 107, 114
nonbeing, 11, 24, 34, 37, 45, 54, 57, 60, 64, 99, 207; Equiano and, 20; Fanon on, 22–23, 25, 108, 175, 177
nondiegesis, 112, 114, 121–23, 125, 128, 131
nostalgia, 198–99
Notebook of a Return to the Native Land (Césaire), 15, 29, 57, 66, 68, 72–75, 81, 88–92, 94, 96–97, 100, 116, 204, 219n9, 219n11; Lam's sketches for, 28, 61–64, 69–71, 66, 73–80, 82–88, 91–93, 96–97, 219n1; phenomenological language in, 182; queerness in revisions of, 86, 89, 123; structure of, 220n34
Nyong'o, Tavia, 12, 211n41

Of One Blood (Hopkins), 19, 234n50
Olaniyan, Tejumola, 151–52, 162, 211n41
opacity, 30, 133, 135, 148–52, 154, 163, 169–70, 206; of Dream Science, 17; montage and, 229n77; suggestive, 165. See also Ra, Sun; Samb, Issa
otherwise, the, 9, 12, 14–15, 21, 36, 134, 151, 156, 169, 198, 206, 212n47
Otolith Group, 31, 130

pain, 10–11, 16, 24, 35–36, 38, 40–41, 45–47, 97, 100, 171, 190, 208; embodied, 10, 177; fugitive time and, 3; in *We Need New Names* (Bulawayo), 203; in *Without a Name* (Vera), 177, 179, 181–82, 184
painlessness, 10, 35–36
Passion of Remembrance, The (Blackwood and Julien), 111, 224n35
phenomenological time, 73, 75, 77–78; Edmund Husserl and, 8
phenomenology, 8, 174; of violence, 190–91
Pierre, Jemima, 145, 228n49
poverty, 25, 42–43, 73–74, 110, 174, 176–77, 190, 193–95, 199, 203; anxiety of, 49; in Martinique, 95; in *Notebook of a Return to the Native Land* (Césaire), 77, 81; West Indian, 105
power, 7, 39–40, 85–86, 115, 181; black, 229n7; black discursive, 117–20; colonial, 175, 190; fetish object and, 195; fugitivity and, 179; pseudoscientific racism as mechanism of, 133; state, 176; of symbols, 136; women and, 180
precarity, 2, 106, 109, 199
prolepsis, 16, 23, 32, 43, 46–47, 52, 92, 98, 162, 206; ease and, 59; narrative, 28, 37, 39, 216n9; thrownness and, 101; in *We Need New Names* (Bulawayo), 193

Quayson, Ato, 176–77, 181, 190, 217n13
queer life: black, 125; West Indian, 90
queerness, in the work of Shikeith, 4; in *In Another Place, Not Here*, 6; in the work of Césaire and Lam, 86–91; in 1980s black British identity, 111; in *Twilight City* and the work of Fani-Kayode, 123–29, 225n71

Ra, Sun, 9, 14, 30, 61, 94, 131, 133–36, 139–42, 150, 169–71, 213n54, 227n28; aesthetics of, 158, 161; Afrofuturism and, 212n54; ancient Egypt and, 139, 142–43, 160, 230n93; Arkestra, 140–41, 160, 163–64, 167–68, 230n93; "The Black Man in the Cosmos," 227n42; blackness and, 143, 146; free jazz influences on, 230–31n102; fugitive time and, 158–69; *Jazz by Sun Ra*, 141–42; *A Joyful Noise*, 160; *The Magic City*, 163, 167; myth and, 158–60, 230n93; numerology and, 231n106; "The Outer Darkness," 165, 166; perpetual errancy, 133, 149, 154, 170; philosophy of, 230n86; poetry of, 143, 161–65, 167, 231n104, 231n107; racialized difference and, 144; *The Wisdom of Sun Ra*, 231n106. *See also* Allen, Marshall; Boykins, Ronnie

race, 116, 142, 144–46, 235n71

racialization, 18, 108, 144–46, 175

racism, 106, 109, 116, 123, 226n9; colonial, 145; négritude and, 144; pseudoscientific, 135

radicalism: black, 146; diasporic, 148; Senegalese, 154

redress, 36–37, 51

Reed, Anthony, 14, 67, 165, 212n47

refugee time, 199, 201

reproduction, 88–90, 178; aesthetics of, 85; heteronormative, 86

Ricoeur, Paul, 8, 39, 43–45, 56

Roberts, Neil, 8, 23, 209n14

Robinson, Cedric, 22, 214n65

rootlessness, 19, 174

Samatar, Sofia, 16–18, 212n54

Samb, Issa, 7, 27, 30, 131, 133–40, 142, 148–58, 160–62, 165, 168–71, 213n54, 227n26, 227n28, 229n77; *The Best Marxist is Dead*, 146–48; fugitive time and, 148–58; Marxist Africanism of, 226n19; race and, 144–46; Smithsonian dossier of, 228n56. *See also* Laboratoire Agit-Art

Sankofa Film and Video, 111, 224n35

Sarr, Felwine, 145, 212n47

Scott, Darieck, 7, 211n41

self-preservation, 79–80, 82–83, 88, 92

Senegal, 6, 27, 144–45, 235n67; independence, 136, 138; postcolonial autocracy of, 139; structural adjustment in, 30; United States and, 148

Senghor, Lamine, 68, 220n19

Senghor, Léopold, 30, 66, 137–39, 144–45, 226n19

Sexton, Jared, 7, 11–12, 45, 95

sexuality, 64, 83, 85, 87, 91, 111, 122, 224n35; Martinican, 84

Sharpe, Christina, 2, 11, 21, 25, 42

Shikeith, 1, 3–4, 15, 205, 207

slavery, 22, 25, 28, 110, 171, 217n13; afterlife of, 236n96; agency and, 210n17; poverty and, 42; racialized, 17; sexuality and, 58, 85; violence of, 44, 120

Sojoyner, Damien, 81, 196

solidarity, 66, 78–79, 111, 148, 170, 207, 210n14; black, 90, 100; diasporic, 171; with Movement for Black Lives, 2; pan-African, 5; structure of, 158, 202

South Africa, 180, 191–92, 215n78

South Asians, 110. *See also* Lascars

specter (Derrida), 199, 203; colonial, 216n78; of slavery, 217n13

Spillers, Hortense, 10, 20–21, 40, 51, 76, 85, 89. *See also* body, the; flesh

subjection, 3–5, 11, 24–25, 40, 43–45, 50, 56–57, 59, 76, 84, 95, 101–2, 110, 123, 128, 140–41, 143, 157, 159, 235n67; black British, 29, 100; colonial, 66, 173, 177, 200; Equiano's, 20; escaping, 17; *Handsworth Songs* and, 106–9, 112–13, 119–20; outside of, 3, 33, 54, 71; racialized, 18, 136; refigured, 104; remnants of, 92; structures of, 108, 114, 123, 235n71; time, 40, 43–44, 52, 217n19; *Twilight City* and, 106, 113–14, 121; in *We Need New Names* (Bulawayo), 189–91, 195; in *Without a Name* (Vera), 181, 183–85, 188; wounded flesh as marker of, 72. *See also* black subjection time

Sula (Morrison), 28, 34, 36–40, 42–43, 46–54, 56, 60, 73, 206, 213n54, 217–18n13

surrealism, 63, 66–67, 69

surveillance, 7, 157

teleology, 24, 60
temporality, of queerness, 86, 89, 123; refugee, 199; of trauma, 44, 182; of wounding, 71, 73, 75. *See also* fugitive time consciousness; time consciousness; utopia
Thatcherism, 29, 99, 109, 129–30
Things Fall Apart (Achebe), 177, 192–93
thrownness, 21, 101–2, 104, 106, 112, 117, 119, 120, 122, 128, 130
time consciousness, 4, 8–9, 14–15, 28–29, 174, 201, 204, 213n16, 217n13; drapetomanic, 133, 136, 160; Yoruba, 214n61. *See also* fugitive time consciousness
Tinsley, Omise'eke, 85–86, 90–91
transatlantic slave trade, 14, 21, 68, 138, 171, 214n61
transcendence, 15, 37, 51, 63, 72, 94, 101, 159; bodily, 183; desire for, 3; fugitivity and, 8; imagined, 207; mythic, 169; ontological, 29, 64
trauma, 9, 37, 42, 44–54, 71, 85–86, 94, 118, 174; black, 10, 51, 116; black body and, 41, 73; diegetic, 123; ease and, 52, 60; embodied, 115; of forced relocation, 192; historical, 64, 73, 81; utopia and, 29, 48, 61, 65–67; in *Without a Name* (Vera), 177, 179, 181–83, 185–88
Tropiques, 65–66, 93

unfreedom, 7–8, 12, 41, 159
United States, 2, 6, 20–21, 27, 190; emancipation and, 215n78; migration to, 15, 18, 31, 194, 236n96 (see also *We Need New Names*); Senegal and, 148; sexual hierarchy in, 180
utopia, 12, 25, 29, 36, 61, 193, 199, 212n47; in *Beloved* (Morrison), 54; Césaire and, 65–66, 71, 73, 79, 94, 98; fugitive time and, 3, 15–16; queer, 122; Ra and, 168; *Sula* (Morrison) and, 48; United States as, 201
utopian desire, 9–10, 29, 76, 85; black, 159, 212n47; body and, 64; ceaselessness

of, 207; fugitive time and, 38; Jameson on, 12; Morrison and, 37–39, 51, 53, 59; object of, 15; trauma and, 37; in *Without a Name*, 184–85; Zimbabwe as object of, 199

Vera, Yvonne, 19, 61, 177, 204; *Nehanda*, 172–73, 203, 232n5; *Without a Name*, 15, 31, 173–75, 177–89, 191, 193–94, 233n23, 234n50
vestibularity, 72, 78, 220n35
violence, 17–18, 24, 28, 31, 40–45, 77, 173–74, 181, 193, 198–99; antiblack, 59, 106, 110; in *Beloved* (Morrison), 53, 56, 59, 200; black body and, 90, 123; black life 3, 11, 61, 118, 206; of chain gang, 93; colonial, 175, 195, 200, 214n61; ease and, 60; emancipation and, 215n78; embodied, 13, 120; flesh and, 10, 73; freedom and, 188; fugitive time and, 185; haunting of, 115, 215n74; historical, 29; intimacy of, 179; of Jim Crow, 5; against migrants, 104; *Notebook of a Return to the Native Land* (Césaire) and, 71–73; phenomenology of, 190–91; racism and, 30, 116; sexual, 19, 177; of slavery, 14, 120; of sound, 112; state, 2, 136, 176, 190; temporal, 217n19; time as, 74, 182; traumatic, 37

Walcott, Rinaldo, 7, 111, 121, 144, 161, 167, 211n41, 215n78
wayward, the, 14, 36, 154
Weheliye, Alexander, 72, 170
We Need New Names (Bulawayo), 15, 22, 31, 173–74, 177–78, 189–203, 233n13, 235n61, 235n67; fugitive science and, 235n71; Goyal on, 236n90, 236n96
West Indies, 11, 18, 20, 69, 103, 120; French, 94
whiteness, 44, 89
white supremacy, 2, 18, 22, 136, 145
Wilder, Gary, 94–95
Wilderson, Frank, 4, 11, 112

Woolf, Virginia, 44; *Mrs. Dalloway*, 39, 43, 45, 56
wounding, 10–11, 51, 61, 63, 76, 78, 86, 191, 203, 208; corporeal, 71, 119; discourse of, 71, 80; of the flesh, 65; perpetual, 57; phenomenal, 192; primary narrative of, 117; temporalities of, 29, 64, 71, 73, 75

Wright, Michelle, 13–14
Wynter, Sylvia, 8, 22–23, 214n65

Zimbabwe, 6, 18–19, 22, 174, 187, 193–94, 196–201; Chimurengas, 31, 173; civil war, 183, 188; independent, 176, 190; structural adjustment in, 232n9. *See also* Mugabe, Robert